Publications
of
𝔘𝔥𝔢 𝔒𝔬𝔩𝔬𝔫𝔦𝔞𝔩 𝔖𝔬𝔠𝔦𝔢𝔱𝔶 𝔬𝔣 𝔐𝔞𝔰𝔰𝔞𝔠𝔥𝔲𝔰𝔢𝔱𝔱𝔰

VOLUME LXVII

Committee of Publication

LINDA SMITH RHOADS, CHAIR
FREDERICK D. BALLOU
MALCOLM FREIBERG
HARLEY PEIRCE HOLDEN
CONRAD EDICK WRIGHT

Editor of Publications

JOHN W. TYLER

Aristotelian and Cartesian Logic at Harvard

Charles Morton's *A Logick System*

&

William Brattle's *Compendium of Logick*

EDITED AND INTRODUCED BY
Rick Kennedy

PUBLISHED BY THE COLONIAL SOCIETY OF MASSACHUSETTS
AND DISTRIBUTED BY THE UNIVERSITY PRESS OF VIRGINIA
BOSTON, 1995

Copyright 1995 The Colonial Society of Massachusetts
ISBN 0–9620737–2–5
Printed from the Income of the Sarah Louise Edes Fund

Dedication

*To those who know that thinking is an art
and the study of an art a technology,
that logic is the technology of living well.*

R.K.

Contents

Preface, Notes, and Acknowledgments   ix

Aristotelian and Cartesian Logic at Harvard
by Rick Kennedy

I. Introduction   1

II. Religiously-Oriented, Dogmatically-Inclined Humanistic Logics from the Renaissance to the Seventeenth Century

    A. Melanchthon and Aristotelianism   10
    B. Richardson and Ramism   16
    C. Aristotelianism, Ramism, and Schematic Thinking   25
    D. Puritan Favoritism From Ramus to Descartes   32
    E. Cartesian Logic and Christian Skepticism   37
    F. The Religious and Dogmatic Orientation of *The Port-Royal Logic*   42
    G. Cartesian Logic in British Textbooks   52

III. Charles Morton and *A Logick System*   61

    A. Charles Morton   62
    B. Morton's *A Logick System*   78

IV. William Brattle and the *Compendium of Logick*

    A. Intellectual Reform in the Puritans' Collapsing World   91
    B. The *Compendium of Logick*   93
    C. Brattle: Tutor and Unofficial Professor of Divinity   108

V. Epilogue: Later Constituencies of Religious Logics and The Separation of Logic and Divinity at Harvard   133

A Logick System by Charles Morton
Transcribed by Rick Kennedy and Kathy Nichols

Preface to the Reader   141

I. First Part of Logick
    1. A Logick System   146
    2. Of Predicables   149
    3. Of Antepredicaments   155
    4. Of Predicaments in Generall   160
    5. Of Substance   161
    6. Of Quantity   163
    7. Of Quality   167
    8. Of Relation   173
    9. Of Action and Passion   175
    10. Of Respective Predicaments   177
    11. Of Postpredicaments   181
    12. Of Secondary Simple Terms   186

II. The Second Part of Logick
    1. Of Complex Terms or Propositions   191
    2. Of the Division of Proposition   192
    3. Of the Affections of Propositions   196

III. The Third Part of Logick
    1. Of Syllogism   200
    2. Of Secondary Argumentation   205
    3. Of the Use of Syllogism   209
    4. Of the Division of Demonstration   213
    5. Of Affections of Demonstration   216
    6. Of Topical Syllogism   219
    7. Of Fallacies   231
    8. Of Method   235

IV. Synopsis of Logick   241

V. Memorial Verses of the Logick System   243

Compendium of Logick by William Brattle
Transcribed by Rick Kennedy and Kathy Nichols

The Prolegomenon
    1. Of the Nature and Constitution of Logick   257
    2. Of the Use & Benefit of Logick   258
    3. Of Some General Observables, of, Rules of Truth   260

I. The First Part of Logick
    1. Of Perception, and its Modes   266
    2. Of the Objects of Perception   267
    3. Of Substance & its Divisions   272
    4. Of Affections of Things & their Divisions   273
    5. Of the 5 Universalls [Genus, Species, &c]   275
    6. Of A Totum and Parts, Cause & Effect &c   278
    7. Of a Thing with it's Affections   282

II. The Second Part of Logick
    1. Of Judgment or Proposition   284
    2. Of Proposition it's Division   285
    3. Of the Nature of Incident Propositions   289
    4. Of a Compound Proposition and the Species Thereof   291
    5. Of a Proposition as to it's Quality and Quantity   295
    6. Of the Opposition of Prepositions having the same Subjects and Predicates   297

III. The Third Part of Logick
    1. Of Reasoning, Discourse, or Argumentation   298
    2. Of Simple Syllogisms   300
    3. Of the Figures and Modes of Syllogism   302
    4. Of some Gen: Rules of Syllogism   305
    5. Of Conjunct or Compound Propositions   307
    6. Of Imperfect Argumentations   310
    7. Of Syllog: Apodictical, Topical, & Sophistical   313
    8. Of the Places Whence the Medium if Fetched   318

IV. The Fourth Part of Logick
    1. Of the General Method of Knowing   320
    2. Of Special Method and First of Analysis   322
    3. Of the Method of Composition   324
    4. Of the 8 Principle Rules Relating to Method   326

Index   329

Preface

THE FIRST PART of this book is about an idiosyncratic tradition in logic textbooks that no one has yet described or analyzed. The second and third parts give important examples of textbooks from this tradition, textbooks that have existed only as manuscripts which were passed among students through generations at Harvard College. This tradition in logic and these two textbooks supported dogmatic Christians by asserting that knowledge from God in the mind and divine testimony were absolutely certain forms of knowledge that could be used in logic to demonstrate a wider range of arguments that also attained absolute certainty.

Philipp Melanchthon first popularized this type of religious logic textbook. His logic was basically Aristotelian. In the opening section on Humanism, Religion and Dogmatism, I explore how Melanchthon's innovations helped future logicians transcend the boundaries between Aristotelian, Ramist, and Cartesian logics in the seventeenth century. By the end of the seventeenth century, Ramist logic was declining in popularity and replaced by such logics as the ones reproduced here. The first textbook transcribed here is Aristotelian and the second, Cartesian.

This idiosyncratic tradition in logic and these two examples were not "bad" logics. The logic textbooks developed during and after the Renaissance offered a broader and more slippery kind of logic than the more narrow and formal strains which dominated late Medieval thought, and now dominate Modern logic. Unlike "formal" logic, the humanistic logics of the Renaissance were more subject to the perspectives of authors and communities. The two logics provided here were designed to fit a specific cultural situation: the then provincial college, Harvard, founded by dogmatists, Puritans, who found themselves in the midst of political and cultural transformations that threatened to undermine them. Harvard was an outpost in the history of logic; however, Harvard's position in America as a bastion of Puritans make it an excellent case study in the history of an idiosyncratic tradition of logic textbooks. These textbooks also teach us much about the Puritans, especially about

PREFACE

the epistemology and psychology that supported their particular form of rationalism.

TRANSCRIPTION NOTES:

The following transcriptions of Charles Morton's *A Logick System* and William Brattle's *Compendium of Logick* are from manuscripts written by William Partridge, when he was eighteen or nineteen, while he was a student at Harvard in 1687. The original texts by Morton and Brattle are lost. They were probably destroyed by fire in 1764, when the library burned along with Harvard Hall. Since Partridge's class at Harvard was the first to use Morton's and Brattle's textbooks (the former imported to America in 1686 and the latter's composed in 1686 or 1687), Partridge probably transcribed directly from the original texts. Inconsistencies abound in the manuscript, and much as been standardized here for easier reading, especially margins, titles, and spacing. All spelling, capitalization, and punctuation has been transcribed as accurately as possible from Partridge.

Partridge did not transcribe all of Morton's two-line poems sprinkled throughout every chapter. Another student transcription by Samuel Dunbar from 1721 included all of the poems in their proper places. Kathy Nichols and I have marked all the poems found in Dunbar's version but not Partridge with { }. In the texts, these marks also signal words or phrases that we could not make out in Partridge's version, but were frequently plain in other versions.

Although Partridge's transcription of the texts were for his personal use, they have an important history. Partridge, himself, did not. Born in 1669, he graduated with the class of 1689, but died in 1693, age twenty-three, after assisting in the pulpit in Wethersfield, Connecticut. His notebook survived him to be used by several students and ministers, including Jonathan Edwards, before being housed in the Beinecke Rare Book and Manuscript Library at Yale University, New Haven, Connecticut. I appreciate the Library's permission to publish that manuscript.

PREFACE

OTHER EXTANT TRANSCRIPTIONS:

1. Timothy Lindall (1677–1760), Harvard class of 1695, later a merchant and politician, transcribed in 1693 both *A Compendium of Logick* and what he called *Mr Morton's System of Logick*. The notebook is owned by the Massachusetts Historical Society in Boston, Massachusetts.
2. Daniel Greenleaf (1680–1762), class of 1699, later a parson, physician, and apothecary, transcribed three logic texts: *A Treatise of Logic Extracted from Mr. Morton by Tutor Fitch who taught from 1697–1703*; Brattle's Latin *Compendium Logicae*, and *Compendium of Logick*. His son, Stephen Greenleaf, class of 1723, used the same notebook and added a transcription of Leverett's *Compendium Logicae Vera* in 1720. The notebook is owned by the Massachusetts Historical Society.
3. George Curwin (1683–1717), class of 1701, minister of Salem, transcribed in 1698 Brattle's *Compendium of Logick* into a notebook now owned by the Essex Institute, Salem, Massachusetts. John Barnard's funeral sermon for Curwin (*The Nature and Manner*, Boston, 1717, p. 37) notes that his ability as a logician made him a good preacher.
4. Joseph Sewall (1688–1769), class of 1707, minister of the South (second) Church in Boston, transcribed three of Brattle's textbooks: *Compendium Logicae*, *Compendium of Logick*, and *Enchiridium Metaphysicum*. The notebook is owned by the American Antiquarian Society in Worcester, Massachusetts.
5. David Jeffries (1690–1716), class of 1708, married Brattle's niece in 1713. Very pious, he was the founder of an informal religious club while a student. His transcription of *Compendium of Logick* is owned by the Houghton Library, Harvard University.
6. Obadiah Ayers (1689–1768), class of 1710, later a military chaplain and convert to the Church of England, transcribed *Compendium of Logick* into a commonplace book now housed at the Harvard University Archives.
7. Nathan Prince (1698–1748), class of 1718, was from 1723–1741 a Harvard tutor known for his scholarship and Calvinist orthodoxy, but not good teaching. Thomas Siegel in his dissertation on

PREFACE

Governance and Curriculum at Harvard College in the 18th Century speculates that Prince is the editor of the published version of Brattle's *Compendium Logicae* (1735). This speculation is discussed in chapter four of "Aristotelian and Cartesian Logic at Harvard." Prince's transcription of *Compendium of Logick*, done while a student in 1716, is owned by the Massachusetts Historical Society.

8. Samuel Dunbar (1704–1777), class of 1723, later a minister noted for his devotion to Calvinism, transcribed *A Logick System*, Fitch's *A Treatise of Logick Extracted from Mr. Morton, Compendium of Logick*, and *Compendium Logicae*. This notebook is housed at the Harvard University Archives.

ACKNOWLEDGEMENTS:

During the ten years of my study of Morton, Brattle, and their contemporaries, I have benefitted from kind and helpful librarians while working in very gracious settings. The Harvard University Archives under the friendly leadership of Harvey Holden and the Massachusetts Historical Society with its always pleasant staff made this book possible. Other manuscript and rare book libraries that supported this research include the Beinecke Library at Yale University; the Houghton Library at Harvard University; the John Carter Brown Library at Brown University; the Congregational Library in Boston; the archives of the Congregational Church of Cambridge, Massachusetts; Special Collections in the Mugar Memorial Library at Boston University; the Huntington Library in San Marino, California; the American Antiquarian Society library in Worcester, Massachusetts; the Library of Congress; the British Library; Lambeth Palace archives, London; Dr. Williams' Library, London; and the archives of the Society for the Promotion of Christian Knowledge in a closet in Holy Trinity Church, London, which the archivist kindly made a special trip to open for me.

For the day-to-day research, the libraries at University of California at Santa Barbara and Indiana University Southeast served me well and their librarians were very helpful. John Goodin found for me the important information about the true author of

PREFACE

Coke's logic. The microfilm room in the research library at Bloomington, Indiana, has been enormously useful.

Tim Vivian has been a constant help to me. My ideas about logic have mutated many times. I think Tim has read every draft of every mutation. Jeffrey B. Russell has always been helpful. Thomas J. Siegel and Richard Dickson gave me copies of their dissertations and supplied many hours of enjoyable conversation about our seventeenth-century friends. Harley Holden took me to lunch in the Harvard Faculty club to teach me about Samuel E. Morison and Clifford K. Shipton, two scholars I trail behind. Barbara Shapiro and Peter Schouls gave me good advice. Richard Watson, Steven Nadler, and Martin Klauber graciously sent me books and articles related to my subject. Norman Fiering told me to "do logic" even though I told him that I had never studied logic. Without his writings and support, this project never would have started or reached publication. The works of Lisa Jardine and E.J. Ashworth also got me started. Harold Kirker, my mentor, who is now retired from the University of California at Santa Barbara, embodies for me the ideal humanist tutor.

Indiana University Southeast has supported this research with time, money, and supplies. My colleagues in history—Stephanie Bower, John Findling, Frank Thackeray, and Andrew Trout—were very supportive when I embarked on "doing logic." My colleagues in philosophy—James Barry and William Rumsey—often had to hold my hand. Kathy Nichols, first a student and now a colleague, jumped into the project with enthusiam. Her hard work on the transcriptions while going to graduate school and raising three children in Indianapolis made it impossible for me to complain about my own work schedule. Kathy appreciates the help of Sharon Strange and Robert Marshall. Both of us appreciate the editorial work of Elizabeth M. Burke and John W. Tyler.

Introduction

> Piety, therefore, is only a half of Puritanism. It is the essential part, no doubt; yet unless we consider the machinery of theory and demonstration which accompanied it, we can give no full account of Puritan thought and expression.
>
> Perry Miller
The New England Mind[1]

*P*uritanism was a mixture of tendencies, some of the most important being yearnings for absolutes, certainty, and understanding. Puritans yearned for a rational religion. They believed humans were created in the image of God and thus were rational and spiritual beings, for such was the idea of God then. Rationality and spirituality, rather than being opposite, were seen as intertwined in the intellect which "is a power of the reasonable (or religious) soul, whereby it understands the truth."[2] Puritans, in Augustinian fashion, did not think of the mind and heart as separated; instead, the intellect and religious affections were both faculties of the mind. The mind was considered the same as the soul. Logic was a set of strategies useful to the reasonable religious mind. An educated Puritan's yearnings for rational religion found relief in logic; however, Puritans carefully chose the logic tradition they taught, modifying it according to their needs.

At the beginning of the century, Ramism was the favored logic among Puritans. Toward the end of the century, there were new political and religious developments and Ramism no longer had the cultural clout to support Puritans in their time of need. This book

---

All page citations of Charles Morton's *A Logick System* and William Brattle's *Compendium of Logick* refer to the editions transcribed in this volume.

[1] Perry Miller, *The New England Mind: The Seventeenth Century* (Cambridge: Harvard, 1939), 69.

[2] Charles Morton, *Compendium Physicae*, eds. Samuel Eliot Morison and Theodore Hornberger, *Publications of the Colonial Society of Massachusetts*, vol. 33 (Boston, 1940), 200.

ARISTOTELIAN AND CARTESIAN

prints two influential Puritan manuscript logic textbooks from the late seventeenth and early eighteenth centuries that attempted to meet Puritanism's new intellectual needs. Charles Morton's *A System of Logick* advocated the vigorous Aristotelianism that originated in textbooks by Philipp Melanchthon, Martin Luther's right-hand man in the Reformation. While Morton's textbook was a viable option for the Puritans, Aristotelian logic seemed too limiting to most Puritans. Cartesian logic was more dynamic and William Brattle's *Compendium of Logick* became the most popular and influential logic textbook at Harvard College from the 1690s through the middle of the eighteenth century.

Roman Catholics from Jesuits to Jansenists, Protestants from Anglicans to Puritans, and non-Christians of whatever type in the seventeenth century manipulated logic to support their theologies and serve their constituencies. All three types of logic, Aristotelian, Ramist, and Cartesian, were capable of being oriented more or less in directions to serve Christian education. Puritans relied on religiously-oriented humanistic logics. Of those religiously-oriented logics, there were some which were particularly supportive of their desire for religious certainty. Although humanistic logics, in general, diminished emphasis on absolute knowledge, some dogmatic strains developed. Morton's and Brattle's logics were of this dogmatically-inclined type.

I will be describing in this section of the book the historical context of dogmatically-inclined, religiously-oriented, humanistic logics such as Morton's and Brattle's. Because these logic textbooks were written to serve such a constituency, I devote much of this section to analyzing the motivations and then influence of Morton and Brattle. I will not explain all the parts of each logic. Neither text is important as an example of Aristotelian or Cartesian logic. They are important because they exemplify an idiosyncratic tradition of religiously-oriented and dogmatically-inclined humanistic logic textbooks which were useful in educational settings such as Harvard College.

Textbooks are pedagogical reductions, written to serve as a basis for a tutor's gloss and, hopefully, as a spark to inspire further inquiry. To varying extents, textbooks reflect the values of the society that supports a college. Curriculum and textbook reforms do not march alone according to the whims of one professor. They usually bear witness to the reforms and events that are happening outside of the college. The realms of church and state—the principal patrons of a college—greatly influenced which logic dominated at certain times in certain regions. In the era of humanistic logic, the role of logic in the curriculum and the type taught reflected the society's values and the conclusions that society sought from logic. An amazing number of logic textbooks were written in the seventeenth century by many of the greatest thinkers and many more by unknown tutors.

Walter Ong has called the sixteenth through the eighteenth centuries the Age of Logic, writing: "The study of logic was somehow central to liberal education."[3] Logics competed with each other during this era and educated society was divided over which was the more rational. The late seventeenth century was the high point of this preoccupation in England. Norman Fiering tells us there was an "extraordinary philosophical storm in the Atlantic world of the late seventeenth century in logic, metaphysics, and epistemology."[4] Since metaphysics and epistemology were part of humanist logic, the storm's center was in logic. Dissenting academies in England experimented with new educational ideals and textbooks—Charles Morton's academy leading the way from the late 1670s to 1686. Harvard College experienced radical curricular reforms between 1686 and 1695, and the importance of the discipline of logic in these reforms is shown by the fact that all four of the leaders at Harvard during the period were authors/epitomizers of logic textbooks: President Increase Mather, tutors John Leverett and William Brattle, and Charles Morton, who served first as a fellow then as vice president after 1697. On no other subject did they all write

---

[3] Walter J. Ong, "Introduction" to *A Fuller Course in the Art of Logic Conformed to the Method of Peter Ramus, 1672*, ed. and trans. Walter J. Ong and Charles J. Ermatinger in *The Complete Works of John Milton*, vol. 8 (New Haven: Yale, 1982), 148.

[4] Norman Fiering, "Rationalist Foundations of Jonathan Edwards's *Metaphysics*," *Jonathan Edwards and the American Experience*, eds. Nathan O. Hatch and Harry S. Stout (New York, Oxford, 1988), 76.

textbooks. Morton's and Brattle's were the most innovative, and Brattle's had the longest influence.

Aside from their value as examples of an idiosyncratic tradition, the logic textbooks printed here can also help historians better understand Puritan books, sermons, and correspondence. Late seventeenth-century logic differed on definitions of key terms and levels of certainty accorded to propositions and demonstrations. Some modern historians have erroneously traced a definite influence of Cambridge Platonism and, more generally, latitudinarianism, on New England thought at the end of the seventeenth century, claims based primarily on Puritan appreciation of the writings of Henry More and John Tillotson.[5] Latitudinarian influence is supposed to have contributed to an intellectual transition in the late seventeenth and early eighteenth century from Puritanism to the Age of Reason, from the Age of Lent to the Age of Enlightenment. The outline of this transition seems clear to some: New Englanders appreciated the works of Henry More and John Tillotson and, for a variety of reasons, came to appreciate their less-than-dogmatic view of religion. Daniel Walker Howe writes that "one cannot but be struck by the similarities in style, content, and vocabulary" between some Cambridge Platonists and Jonathan Edwards.[6] But, such a statement seems dangerous to me since shared language does not necessarily mean shared meaning. Context is important. New England Puritans in my understanding interpreted Cambridge Platonism and latitudinarianism in the light of Puritan dogmatic tendencies and applied definitions from their own logics to the writings of More and Tillotson, thereby systematically misunderstanding Cambridge Platonism and latitudinarianism.

For example, though Henry More might himself have accepted a system of probability and certainty that ranked "mathematical cer-

---

[5] The most informed examples of this are Norman Fiering's "The First American Enlightenment: Tillotson, Leverett, and Philosophical Anglicanism," *The New England Quarterly* 54 (1981): 307–344; and Daniel Walker Howe's "The Cambridge Platonists of Old England and the Cambridge Platonists of New England," *Church History* 57 (1988): 470–485. Howe writes "All in all, the Cambridge Platonists seem to have been better received by the American Puritans than they were by their English contemporaries" (pp. 472–73).

[6] See Howe, "The Cambridge Platonists," 472–73.

tainty" or "mathematical demonstration" as less-than-absolute certainty, Puritans reading More's insistence on "mathematical demonstration" would have most likely understood the term as yielding nothing less than absolute dogmatic certainty or divinely communicated certainty. The scales rating the certainty of "mathematical demonstration" in the logics transcribed in this book were not the same as those of the Cambridge Platonists.

If a term such as "mathematical demonstration" could be understood in different ways, the much more loose term "faith" could lead to much confusion. "Faith" is a term in logic signifying the result of testimony. Faith can have many levels of certainty. John Tillotson's most famous book dealing with the logic of Christianity was *The Rule of Faith, or an Answer to the Treatise of Mr. I. S. entitled Sure-footing, etc.* (1666) and was popular among both Puritans and Deists, probably because even his definition of faith could be interpreted in different ways. Tillotson defined "faith" as:

> a term of art used by divines, it signifies that particular kind of assent which is wrought in us by testimony or authority. So that divine faith, which we are now speaking of, is an assent to a thing upon the testimony or authority of God, or, which is all one, an assent to a truth upon divine revelation.[7]

This is a definition of faith that could have been derived from a number of logic textbooks and is very close to the definitions given by both Morton and Brattle. Different interpretations of this definition hinge on the certainty level accorded to divine faith. Tillotson, himself, probably had no dogmatic intent—divine faith would not be the equivalent of science. For Morton and Brattle, however, divine faith is equivalent to absolutely certain knowledge. In Morton's and Brattle's logics, divine faith is equivalent to (or even higher than) science on the scale of certainty.

Harvard students reading *The Rule of Faith* in the light of Morton's and Brattle's logics would think that Tillotson was affirming a much

---

[7] John Tillotson, *The Rule of Faith of an Answer to the Treatise of Mr. I.S. entitled Sure-footing, etc*, 2nd ed. (London: 1676), 5.

stronger certainty than he probably wanted to affirm. Puritans could then appreciate the archbishop's emphasis on morality because Puritans would not consider him lax or lazy about biblical doctrine. However, *The Rule of Faith* could be read at the same time by less dogmatic Christians and unitarians who could interpret it in the light of the blurry definitions of moral certainty that were taught in their own favorite logics. The language of latitudinarians, of which Tillotson was one of the most prominent, was hard to pin down in the seventeenth century and even more vaguely understood in the twentieth. John Bunyan wrote that "as to religion, [latitudinarians] turn and twist like an eel on the angle."[8] Tillotson was one of the most twisting of Bunyan's eels. He hoped to be all things to all people, and he was a master at writing in a way that could be interpreted variously by various readers. To understand the Puritan appreciation of Tillotson, one must understand the logical terms and distinctions that the Puritans brought to the reading of Tillotson rather than simply assuming that Puritans appreciated his latitudinarianism.

We must always remember that logic in the seventeenth century was meant to be used constantly and consciously as the technology of rational living. Logic was not simply a discipline set aside in the corner of one's education. In modern society we tend to rely on an innate natural logic for normal living and apply modern formal logic only in cases of specific need, such as computer software design. For most modern people logic is simply an arcane course taught at college, a type of language manipulation, similar to algebra. Textbooks and manuals of logic in the seventeenth century were not arcane; they were designed to be useful and read even in one's leisure. John Harvard's bequest of his private library to the college included three different logics.[9] Ebenezer Pemberton, a student and friend of William Brattle, owned ten different logic books in his personal library.[10] The largely self-educated Benjamin

---

[8] John Spurr, "'Latitudinarianism' and the Restoration Church," *The Historical Journal* 31 (1988): 66, see also p. 73 for Tillotson.

[9] Thomas Goddard Wright, *Literary Culture in Early New England 1620–1730* (New Haven: Yale, 1920), 265–272.

[10] *A Catalogue of Curious and Valuable Books belonging to the late Reverend and Learned Ebenezer Pemberton* (Boston, 1717).

Franklin read *The Port-Royal Logic* while a boy in Boston. A proponent of right thinking joined with right living, Franklin advocated the importance of using logic to discover, defend, and convince others of the truth. In 1733 he gave his boyhood *Port-Royal Logic* to the Library Company believing that after he had applied its rules he had been led to erroneous conclusions.[11] Franklin, therefore, changed his favored logic when he changed his theology.

The logic manuals that students copied into notebooks were to be kept, reused, and shared with others. The two logics transcribed in this book exist in multiple student transcriptions that were handed down through families. Young Jonathan Edwards, colonial America's greatest philosopher and theologian, carried transcriptions of Morton's and Brattle's logics with him to Yale College. The logics had first been transcribed by William Partridge when a student at Harvard in 1687, then passed on to Warham Mather who passed them on to his half-sister's husband, Timothy Edwards. Timothy passed them on to his son Jonathan. When Jonathan went to college he studied primarily under Elisha Williams, a graduate of Harvard who knew Brattle and Brattle's logic well. Both Williams and Edwards did not think of logic as simply a subject for schools. They both tried to live by the logic they learned at Harvard and Yale. In Williams's later political writings and Edwards's theology and philosophy, logic was the foundation for right living.[12]

As manuals for right living, logic textbooks served in much the same capacity as devotional manuals. Charles E. Hambrick-Stowe's *The Practice of Piety: Puritan Devotional Disciplines in Seventeenth-Century New England* shows how Puritans plagiarized and overtly used Roman Catholic devotional manuals. Morton and Brattle used Roman Catholic and other non-Puritan sources in much the same

---

[11] Benjamin Franklin, *Writings*, ed. J.A. Leo Lemay (New York: Library of America, 1987), 1321 and 337–38; and *Poor Richard's Books: An Exhibition of Books Owned by Benjamin Franklin*, comp. James Green (Philadelphia: Library Company of Philadelphia, 1990), 18.

[12] See Norman Fiering, *Jonathan Edwards's Moral Thought and Its British Context* (Williamsburg: Institute of Early American Culture, and Chapel Hill: University of North Carolina, 1981), 28–48. William Sparkes Morris, *The Young Jonathan Edwards: A Reconstruction* (Brooklyn: Carlson, 1991), 80–82. Edwards was also told to procure and read *The Port-Royal Logic* for his Yale education.

way.[13] Devotional manuals were meant to be useful and so were logic textbooks. Devotional manuals and logic texts were formulaic and part of specific traditions.

A glance at the logic textbooks transcribed in this book will not yield much depth of knowledge about the logic of the era or its relationship to piety and religion. The logic textbooks used at Harvard were deceptively terse. The textbooks were more or less cut-and-paste outlines to be elaborated upon by teachers and compared with other texts, rather than books that stood alone. In order to understand them one has to know what went on in the classroom, the various sources from which cut-and-paste versions were created, and the traditions of logic that gave context to the terms and structure of the textbook and the cultural context. John Morgan in *Godly Knowledge: Puritan Attitudes toward Reason, Learning, and Education, 1550–1640* writes on the dynamics of the classroom that transformed mere curriculum and texts into sources of Puritan living. He writes that "the puritan approach was to accept the basic curriculum, though to modify texts and subjects; to work within existing structures, though to introduce activities which would in practice demonstrate the aphorism that learning was but a handmaid to divinity."[14] Charles Morton wrote his logic textbook for use in his small house-

---

[13] Charles E. Hambrick-Stowe, *The Practice of Piety: Puritan Devotional Disciplines in Seventeenth-Century New England* (Williamsburg: Institute of Early American History and Culture, and Chapel Hill: University of North Carolina, 1982). Related is the possible influence of Ignatius Loyola's *Spiritual Excercises* on Descartes's *Meditations*. Bradley Rubidge reviews the literature on this influence in "Descartes's Meditations and Devotional Meditations," *Journal of the History of Ideas* 51 (1990): 27–49.

[14] John Morgan, *Godly Learning: Puritan Attitudes towards Reason, Learning, and Education, 1550–1640* (Cambridge: Cambridge, 1986), 232. Another similar study of the dynamics of the classroom, and specifically with Ramist logic is Anthony Grafton and Lisa Jardine, *From Humanism to Humanities: Education and the Liberal Arts in Fifteenth and Sixteenth-Century Europe* (Cambridge: Harvard, 1986). Cartesianism in the classroom is discussed in Michael Heyd, *Between Orthodoxy and the Enlightenment: Jean-Robert Chouet and the Introduction of Cartesian Science in the Academy of Geneva* (Boston: M. Nijhoff, 1982); and Martin Klauber, "Reason, Revelation, and Cartesianism: Louis Tronchin and Enlightened Orthodoxy in Late Seventeenth-Century Geneva," *Church History* 59 (1990): 326–339. See also Michael Shank, *Unless You Believe, You Shall Not Understand: Logic, University, and Society in Late Medieval Vienna* (Princeton: Princeton, 1988); and L.W.B. Brockliss, *French Higher Education in the Seventeenth and Eighteenth Centuries: A Cultural History* (Oxford: Clarendon, 1987).

academy in England where he was the only teacher. William Brattle wrote his for the students at Harvard who were being directed by two tutors, himself and John Leverett.

A final note of introduction: the two logics here support the tenets of a new area of philosophical and sociological scholarship in the 1990s, which studies the epistemological foundation that all humans have in trusting each other, weighing testimony, accepting the word of authorities, and having faith. Sociologists have long studied communities of knowledge, but modern epistemology has emphasized self-reliance and the rejection of trust, testimony, authority, and faith. Three important works have recently been published that focus attention on the importance of understanding the role of testimony in human knowledge: C.A.J. Coady's *Testimony: A Philosophical Study*, Steven Shapin's *A Social History of Truth: Civility and Science in Seventeenth-century England*, and John Hardwig's "The Role of Trust in Knowledge."[15] Harvard College supported a community of knowledge built largely on an epistemological foundation of trust, testimony, authority, and faith. That foundation was taught in Morton's and Brattle's logic textbooks. As we today renew an interest in the epistemological importance of these values, terms, and logical techniques, *A Logick System* and *Compendium of Logick* can serve as a part of the past's legacy that will help us in the future.

---

[15] C.A.J Coady, *Testimony: A Philosophical Study* (Oxford: Clarendon, 1992); Steven Shapin, *A Social History of Truth: Civility and Science in Seventeenth-century England* (Chicago: University of Chicago, 1994); and John Hardwig, "The Role of Trust in Knowledge," *Journal of Philosophy* 88 (1991): 693–708.

Religiously-Oriented, Dogmatically-Inclined Humanistic Logics from the Renaissance to the Seventeenth Century

A. Melanchthon and Aristotelianism

Aristotle and subsequent Western logicians through the Middle Ages generally divided logic into two types: scientific and probabilistic. Scientific logic was primarily concerned with securing knowledge in absolute structures such as a syllogism. Probabilistic logic was concerned with judging how strongly one should assent to information and with strategies of communication and persuasion. In the Renaissance many humanists emphasized probabilistic logic over and above scientific logic, especially the complex system of syllogisms emphasized in the High Middle Ages.[16]

Renaissance humanists were generally scholars reacting against the arcane and seemingly monolithic certainties that had been promoted and ascribed to through the Middle Ages. They favored more limited claims in their desire to attain moral reform and they emphasized a strong split between the human and divine, the nat-

---

[16] Historical interpretations of the humanists' transformation of logic fall into three groups: 1) Those who disparage the logic for its degradation of formal syllogistic logic such as William and Martha Kneale, *The Development of Logic* (Oxford: Clarendon, 1962); 2) those who emphasize the continuation of Medieval aspects in the new logic such as E.J. Ashworth in *Language and Logic in the Post-Medieval Period* (Boston: Reidel, 1974), and Charles B. Schmitt, *John Case and Aristotelianism in Renaissance England* (Montreal: McGill-Queen's, 1983); and 3) those who emphasize its sources in Classical rhetoric and new achievements in theories of method such as Wilbur Samuel Howell, *Logic and Rhetoric in England, 1500–1700* (Princeton: Princeton, 1956); Walter Ong, *Ramus, Method, and the Decay of Dialogue* (Cambridge: Harvard, 1958); and Lisa Jardine in "Lorenzo Valla and the Intellectual Origins of Humanistic Dialectic," *Journal of the History of Philosophy* 15 (1977): 143–164, and "Humanism and the Teaching of Logic," *The Cambridge History of Later Medieval Philosophy*, eds. Norman Kretzman, Anthony Kenney, and Jan Pinborg (Cambridge: Cambridge, 1982), 797–807. My introduction fits in the third category. See also E.J. Ashworth, *The Tradition of Medieval Logic and Speculative Grammar from Anselm to the End of the Seventeenth Century: A Bibliography from 1836 Onwards* (Toronto: Pontifical institute of Mediaeval Studies, 1978).

ural and supernatural. Humans, many insisted, were bound to their mundane humanity, an idea which was very appealing to people who wished to avoid the pedantic wranglings of scholastic theologians and focus on human thought and deed. Humanists generally were mildly skeptical instead of dogmatic. Lorenzo Valla (c.1406–1457) was a major proponent of mild skepticism and his work exemplifies the humanist position on dogmatism and his work influenced Rudolphus Agricola (1444–1485), who wrote the first major humanistic logic textbook.[17]

As with almost all clear-cut distinctions between the Middle Ages and the Renaissance, the newness of humanistic logic has been overstated. John of Salisbury's twelfth-century *Metalogicon* has the vitality of pre-Renaissance humanism, rooted as it is in Augustine, Boethius, and others. However, fifteenth and sixteenth-century humanists extensively transformed logic as it was taught across Europe.

Rudolphus Agricola's *De Inventione Dialectica* was the most influential of the first humanistic logic textbooks. Circulating in manuscript after the 1470s and first published in Louvain in 1515, it gained enormous influence in the 1520s and 30s. By 1569 Petrus Ramus, a popularizer of many Agricolan reforms, wrote that "thanks to Agricola the true study of genuine logic had first been established in Germany, and thence, by way of its disciples and emulators, had spread throughout the whole world."[18] The most influential of Agricola's emulators was Philipp Melanchthon (1496–1560), Professor of Greek at the University of Wittenberg and Martin Luther's principal lieutenant.[19] Melanchthon wrote a short biography of Agricola and praised him as

---

[17] See Jardine, "Lorenzo Valla and the Intellectual Origins of Humanistic Dialectic."

[18] Ramus is quoted, in translation, in Lisa Jardine, "Distinctive Discipline: Rudolph Agricola's Influence on Methodical Thinking in the Humanities," *Rudolphus Agricola Phrisius 1444–1485: Proceedings of the International Conference at the University of Groningen, 28–30 October, 1985*, eds. F. Akkerman and A.J. Vanderjagt (Leiden: E.J. Brill, 1988), 39.

[19] See Clyde Leonard Manschreck, *Melanchthon: The Quiet Reformer* (New York: Abingdon Press, 1958); John R. Schneider, *Philip Melanchthon's Rhetorical Construal of Biblical Authority: Oratio Sacra* (Lewiston, N.Y.: The Edwin Mellen Press, 1990); and E.J. Ashworth, *Language and Logic in the Post-Medieval Period*, 13–14.

"the very first to establish needed reform in the discipline of probabilistic logic."[20] But Melanchthon made his own needed reforms on Agricola's reforms. As Wilhelm Maurer has pointed out, Agricola did not shape Melanchthon: rather, he "spurred him on constantly to intellectual reform."[21] Melanchthon's own logic textbooks, *Compendiaria Dialectices Ratio* (1520), *Dialectices* (1528) and culminating with *Erotemata Dialectices* (1547), though rooted in Agricola's new humanist ideals, were fundamentally different in their concern for religious dogmatism and Aristotelian certainty.[22]

Melanchthon was more concerned about protecting the certainty of essential Christian teachings than Agricola. Agricola was "offended" by "the dogmatic strain in high medieval logic" and wanted to avoid the religious controversies of his era; therefore, he greatly diminished the space devoted to Aristotelian syllogisms and categories. By doing so, he diminished emphasis on scientific logic, choosing instead to devote the textbook to probabilistic logic.[23] Melanchthon, being deeply committed to many humanist ideals, supported the new emphasis on probabilistic logic; however, being also committed to Christian reform, he chose to reemphasize those aspects of scientific logic that could best serve Christian reform: Aristotelian syllogistic demonstration and the ten categories. Agricola, a conscientious Roman Catholic, did not attack Christianity; he simply avoided it. Melanchthon, a Protestant reformer, went out of his way to make sure his readers understood the Christian implications of his logic.

The best example of this split between Agricola and

---

[20] Translated in Schneider, *Philip Melanchthon's Rhetorical Construal of Biblical Authority*, 16. See Melanchthon's declamation, *Vita Rodolphi Agricolae*, in *Corpus Reformatorum: Philippi Melanthonis Opera Quae Supersunt Omnia*, vol. 11, ed. Carolus Gottlieb Bretschneider (New York: Johnson Reprint, 1963), 438–446.

[21] Translated in Schneider, *Philip Melanchthon's Rhetorical Construal of Biblical Authority*, 16. See Melanchthon's declamation, *Vita Rodolphi Agricolae*, in *Corpus Reformatorum: Philippi Melanthonis Opera Quae Supersunt Omnia*, vol. 11, ed. Carolus Gottlieb Bretschneider (New York: Johnson Reprint, 1963), 438–446.

[22] Full titles and lists of each textbook's editions are given at the beginning of the *Erotemata Dialectices* in *Corpus Reformatorum*, vol. 13, 508–510.

[23] See Jardine, "Lorenzo Valla and the Intellectual Origins of Humanistic Dialect," 147.

Melanchthon is in their discussions of divine testimony—one of the issues that the new humanistic logics revived from Classical probabilistic logic. Generally, the two logics agree: testimony yields faith rather than science and the degree of certainty of any received testimony depends on the degree of trustworthiness accorded to the testifier. Divine testimony is discussed in both, but in completely different ways. Agricola's *De Inventione* discusses forms of divine testimony in the context of Cicero, so priests and fortune-tellers who interpret signs and read the heavens are discussed.[24] There is no discussion of any particularly Christian form of divine testimony nor of any Christian application. Melanchthon's *Erotemata Dialectices*, on the other hand, emphasizes the Christian certainty in divine testimony as received from the Judeo-Christian God. The infallible authority of God backed the certainty of faith derived from divine testimony handed down through the Bible and church.[25]

The differences between the texts are obvious. Agricola's attitude is not anti-Church, but overall lacks concern for ecclesiastical issues. Melanchthon's attitude is stridently in support of the rational and dogmatic claims of Lutheran reforms, particularly the emphasis on faith and the Bible. Melanchthon's text teaches the certainty of the Bible and ecclesiastical traditions, the faculties of the soul, proper understanding of baptism and justification by faith, the importance of grace, and the Holy Spirit's help in being rational. The book closes with an attack on skeptics for not assenting to the knowledge offered them, thus denying a gift of God. Although later logic textbooks did not follow Melanchthon slavishly, many subsequent textbooks incorporated these religious subjects into logic. Melanchthon can be considered the founder of a tradition of religiously-oriented and dogmatically-inclined humanistic logic textbooks.

Like many of the intellectual developments of the Reformation,

---

[24] Rudolphus Agricola, *De Inventione Dialectica Libri Tres* (Argentinae, 1521), Bk. 1, chap. 24, p. 36. The modern facsimile of a 1539 edition of Agricola's text (Nieuwkoop, 1967) is substantially different from the 1521 edition available on microfilm. The section on testimony and faith in the 1539 text does not include a discussion of divine testimony.

[25] Melanchthon, *Erotemata Dialectices* in *Corpus Reformatorum*, vol. 13, 707–711.

Melanchthon's new logic relied heavily on Augustinianism. As the new tradition in logic developed, Augustinianism, not Aristotelianism, would be the dominant characteristic.

In the sixteenth and seventeenth centuries, Augustine was erroneously believed to have written two logic textbooks: *Categoriae Decem ex Aristotele Decerpta* and *Principia Dialectica*. Bartolomaeus Keckermann (c. 1571–1609), an important textbook author who will be more fully discussed later, wrote a history and justification of Christian logic, emphasizing the example Augustine set as a Christian logician and he cited the above mentioned logics attributed to Augustine.

However, Keckermann, like most of the Augustinian logicians discussed here, placed greater weight on Augustine's polemical and theological writings as examples of good logic put to use for true religion.[26] Keckermann quoted *On Christian Doctrine* on the importance of dialectics (probabilistic logic) for Christians, and it was through that work that Augustine had his greatest influence on the future development of Christian education in the liberal arts. When Augustine dealt with the "use of dialectics" in *On Christian Doctrine*, he explained that the "science of reasoning" was crucial for understanding and that young men should devote themselves to it even though it was developed by pagan philosophers. Augustine advised readers to "take and turn to a Christian use" all that was good in pagan philosophy and institutions.[27]

One of Augustine's most important legacies in logic was his study of the human will, especially the will of those affected by God's grace. His polemical and theological works consistently asserted the role of human will in knowing and reasoning. A long tradition developed in the Middle Ages along Augustinian lines, and, in the Renaissance, Melanchthon developed a specific place in Aristotelian logic for this relationship between will and knowledge.

---

[26] Bartolomaeus Keckermann, *Gymnasium Logicum id est De Usu & Exercitatione Logicae Artis Absolutoiri & pleniori, Liberi Tres* (London, 1606), 27–29.
[27] Augustine, *On Christian Doctrine*, Bk. 2, chap. 11, sect. 60, trans. J.F. Shaw, in *A Select Library of the Nicene and Post-Nicene Fathers of the Christian Church*, ser. 1, vol. 2, ed. Philip Schaff (Grand Rapids: Wm. B. Eerdmans, 1988), 554.

The core of the tradition insisted that only the person blessed by a divine grace is able to reason most rightly and fully on the hardest questions. This aspect of Augustinianism appears clearly in Morton's and Brattle's logics.

Augustine's influence on dogmatically-inclined and religiously-oriented humanistic logics cannot be overestimated. Augustine wrote several books on Christian rationalism such as *Against Academics* and *On the Profit of Believing* that deal with those named specific subjects. However, as Keckermann exemplifies, his work on polemics and theology were more influential. For Melanchthon's logic and other Christian logics that developed after him, Augustine's *On the Trinity* was probably the most influential model of logic at work. *On the Trinity* begins by describing types of misused reason and throughout continually returns to discussions of sources of knowledge, reasoning methods, and his essential theory that the only good reasoner is the good Christian. Being created in the image of God means that men and women have the capability to reason rightly in the finite context of their mortality, but fallen humans can turn aside from the image of God and their reasoning becomes faulty.[28] A selfish soul loving its own power slips "from the whole which is common, to a part."[29] It is by divine grace that humans maintain their likeness in the image of God and thus their reasoning ability. In this manner Augustine weaves his discussion of good and bad logic throughout *On the Trinity*, creating a logic textbook within a theological apology.

Both Agricola's and Melanchthon's logics were published in many editions and greatly influenced English education. Henry VIII in

---

[28] Augustine gives women a lesser position than men in the natural order, but adamantly states "so that the image of God may remain on that side of the mind of man which cleaves to the beholding or the consulting of the eternal reason of things; and this, it is clear, not men only, but also women have" (*On the Trinity*, Bk. 12, chap. vii, trans. Arthur West Haddan in *A Select Library of the Nicene and Post-Nicene Fathers of the Christian Church*, Ser. 1, vol. 3, 158–159). Charles Morton's "Preface to the Reader," in *A Logick System*, justifies his use of English by declaring his compassion for those of either sex who could use logic but have not had the opportunity to learn Latin (p. 141). Brattle's use of the vernacular probably indicates a similar concern.

[29] Augustine, *On the Trinity*, Bk. 12, chap. 11. Trans. Haddan, Ser. 1, vol. 3, 160.

1535 considered Agricola and Melanchthon among the "purest authors" who were to be studied at Oxford and Cambridge and both had long histories of influence there, especially at Oxford.[30] One of Melanchthon's logics (but not Agricola's) was part of Cambridge graduate John Harvard's private library which formed the basis of the first Harvard College library.[31] For three centuries textbook authors were influenced by these two pedagogical reformers, many authors following particularly the religious innovations of Melanchthon. Morton and Brattle followed Malanchthon. Even before these two, the logicians promoted at Harvard were followers of Melanchthon, especially Alexander Richardson.

The beginnings of Puritanism were rooted in a type of Ramist logic which insisted on Melanchthon-style religious dogmatism while revolting against Melanchthon's Aristotelianism.

B. Ramus and Richardson

Petrus Ramus (1515–1572) is a fascinating figure who stole centerstage of the logic textbook trade among most Protestants in the late sixteenth century and again stole the majority of scholarly interest in the mid-twentieth century.[32] His *Dialecticae Libri Duo* (1556) was well within the humanistic tradition. It is most notable for its brevity. Ramus was interested in pedagogical reform and understood the attention span and intellectual capacity of the average teenage student better than most textbook writers. Ramus also wrote polemically, inciting reaction in his young readers, and specifically with the importance of logic.

Ramus was primarily concerned with pedagogically simplifying

[30] Quoted in Lisa Jardine, "Humanism and the Teaching of Logic," 801.

[31] Cited as "Melanchj Logica" in the appendix of Thomas Wright's *Literary Culture in New England 1620–1730* (New Haven: Yale, 1920), 269. Agricola's logic also does not appear in Harvard's 1723 library catalog.

[32] The most recent work on Ramism, covering the life and influence of Ramus on logic and rhetoric from the Renaissance through the nineteenth century in England and America, is Richard E. Dickson's, *Ramism and the Rhetorical Tradition* (Ph.D. dissertation, Duke University, 1992). I benefitted greatly from discussions with Professor Dickson.

the organization of knowledge. Like many humanists he attacked scholastic logic, declaring that he would "abolish all tautologies and vain repetitions."[33] Also like others he emphasized Classical topics or place logic, which fits bits of knowledge into places in a systematic movement from the general to the particular. Ramus gave a simplistic twist to place logic by dichotomizing, which eventually led, in part, to the downfall of his logic's influence. Later humanists considered the dichotomies as unnatural.

More exciting than his textbooks was the romance of Ramus's life and death told to Protestant students for two centuries. Ramus was a convert to Protestantism who was intermittently in trouble most of his life. Nevertheless, he attained high rank in a Roman Catholic university because of his brilliance. The story culminated with Ramus's murder by a disgruntled colleague in the midst of the St. Bartholomew's Day massacre of Protestants in 1572. The story of Ramus was perfect for those who wished to make university life and rationalism heroic. School teachers and college tutors throughout England and Protestant Europe quickly anointed Ramus a martyr for Protestant religion and Protestant rationalism. Two years after his death, the first English translation of the *Dialecticae Libri Duo* appeared with the title *The Logicke of the Moste Excellent Philosopher P. Ramus, Martyr*.[34]

When Roland MacIlmaine translated Ramus's logic into English to encourage the use of the logic developed by a Protestant martyr, he had to face the problem that Ramus did not concern himself with religion in his logic. The religious orientation of Ramus's logic was closer to Agricola's than Melanchthon's. MacIlmaine added a preface that insisted on the text's use to plant the "rule of verity in the hearts of all men, but most chiefly in the breasts of the pastors of the church who have the charge and dispensation of [God's] holy

---

[33] Peter Ramus, *The Logike of the Most Excellent Philosopher, P. Ramus, Martyr*, trans. Roland MacIlmaine, ed. Catherine M. Dunn (Northridge: San Fernando State College, 1969, transcription of 1574 edition), 6.

[34] On Ramus and Ramist reforms, see Walter J. Ong, *Ramus: Method, and the Decay of Dialogue* (Cambridge, Mass.: Harvard University Press, 1958), and Grafton and Jardine, *From Humanism to Humanities*. On English Ramists, see Howell, *Logic and Rhetoric in England, 1500–1700*.

word"; however, the text itself had very little to offer future pastors in their defense of true religion.[35] In the logic's section on testimony Ramus followed Agricola by making no mention of the Bible and referring to divine testimony as "oracles of the gods."[36] Pure Ramists would follow their mentor's avoidance of Christian subject-matter in logic on through the seventeenth century. Christian textbook writers who rewrote Ramist logic, fitting it into a Christianized context, were not, therefore, pure Ramists.

The Puritans were the most prominent less-than-pure Ramists in England and America. During the decade of Ramus's death and MacIlmaine's translation, the Puritans (or more precisely at that time: men with puritan tendencies) were gaining influence in some of the colleges at Cambridge. The connection with Cambridge subsequently became the root of their influence on education throughout England and America in the seventeenth century.[37] Those Puritan educators who appreciated Ramus's pedagogical simplification of logic could also present the life, conversion, and their version of the death of the philosopher-martyr as an inspiring story of integration of piety and intellect. However, they rewrote Ramist logic, just as Melanchthon rewrote humanistic logic. Puritans needed to Christianize Ramus's text. The most useful and famous Christianized Ramist textbooks were written by Cambridge tutors: William Ames and Alexander Richardson. William Ames (1576–1623) was a fellow at Christ's College, Cambridge, from 1601 to 1610, before moving to Holland where he filled several teaching posts. Ten years after his death, four treatises dealing with logic were published under his name in a volume titled *Philosophmata* (Leyden, 1643), the most influential being *Technometria*, which had been written with the help of students after 1631. *Technometria* was

---

[35] *The Logicke of the Moste Excellent Philosopher, P. Ramus, Martyr*, 5.

[36] *The Logicke of the Moste Excellent Philosopher P. Ramus, Martyr*, 37.

[37] Sixteenth-century Ramist logics at Cambridge include William Temple's 1584 Latin edition of Ramus with a commentary, and Friedrich Beurhaus's three Ramist textbooks, one titled *Triumphus Logicae Ramae* (1589). Ramism especially influenced Puritanism at Christ's College in the classes and tutorials of Laurence Chaderton (c. 1536–1604), William Perkins (1558–1602), and George Downame (d. 1634).

very influential among Dutch, English, and American Puritans; however, Ames's primary influence was through his Ramistically organized book of theology: *Medulla Theologicae* (1627).[38] Alexander Richardson's logic textbook has equally vague beginnings in relationships between teacher and students, but even greater influence than Ames's *Technometria*. Perry Miller judged Richardson's *Logicians School-Master* "undoubtedly the most important Ramist work in the background of New England thought."[39] It was the primary logic used at Harvard until replaced by Brattle's *Compendium of Logick*.

Richardson was a tutor and sometime lecturer for a few years after 1587 at the Puritan and Ramist stronghold of Queen's College, Cambridge.[40] The published version of Richardson's logic lectures, *The Logicians School-Master: or, A Comment upon Ramist Logicke* (1629, enlarged 1651), was a collection of manuscript lecture notes that were passed among students for more than a decade before being posthumously published. The subtitle of the book—"a comment on Ramus' Logicke"—indicates that it was not just a text but also a tutor's gloss on Ramist logic. The comments gathered together by students in *The Logicians School-Master* provide a window into a Puritan classroom. Notes later published as textbooks were not a rare phenomena. Books of this type are the product of a number of minds and thus become a type of communal document. *The Logicians School-Master* is most likely based only on what began as Richardson's lectures. When the Puritans dominated the politics of England, *The Logicians School-Master* was republished in a much

---

[38] See Keith L. Sprunger, *The Learned Doctor William Ames: Dutch Backgrounds of English and American Puritanism* (Urbana: University of Pennsylvania, 1979); and the translation of the *Medulla* as *The Marrow of Theology*, trans. John Dykstra Eusden (Durham: Labyrinth, 1983).

[39] Miller, *The New England Mind: The Seventeenth Century*, 500. Miller's appendix, "The Literature of Ramus' Logic in Europe," (pp. 493–501) is excellent.

[40] For the most recent work on Richardson, see John C. Adams, "Alexander Richardson's Puritan Theory of Discourse," *Rhetorica* 4 (1986): 255–274; "Alexander Richardson's Philosophy of Art and the Sources of the Puritan Social Ethic," *Journal of the History of Ideas* 50 (1989): 227–247; "Ramus, Illustrations, and the Puritan Movement," *Journal of Medieval and Renaissance Studies* 17 (1987): 195–210.

larger version in a text probably less tied to its original source than even the first.

Richardson's orientation bore similarities to Melanchthon's. What Melanchthon did to humanistic Aristotelian logic, Richardson did for Ramist logic by integrating into it an Augustinian perception of the relationship between God and humanity. Other Puritan Ramists such as John Milton did not integrate Ramism and Christianity and, maybe because of this, their textbooks were never as popular.

Richardson, in the manner of humanistic logic in general and the religiously-oriented logics in particular, provided an epistemological perspective in logic. For Richardson the rules of art breathed (*spirare*) "a sweet science" into "our glass of understanding." The rules of art were created and governed by God, and it was God who ultimately "breathed" the science into our understanding.[41] Richardson made a point of equating this breathing with the "irradiation" which was taught in divinity classes. In the beginning there was the wisdom of God "which is brought by an irradiation to our understanding." With this irradiation we "see the simples in the things" with our intellects. These simples are received as self-evident axioms and the result is called *scientia*.[42] God is directly involved in this "internal" process of understanding "the simples in the thing" at every level because God not only creates the understanding in us but also created those "simples in the thing" and continues to cause everything that goes on in the world. "Look into the world and every part thereof," Richardson wrote, "and you shall see God's finger in everything."[43] Absolutely certain knowledge is available because God initially and continually radiates knowledge received by the intellect.

There is nothing particularly innovative about Richardson's short discussion of epistemology. It is not fully worked out and relies on vague imagery. Richardson's statements were essentially standard

---

[41] Alexander Richardson, *The Logicans School-Master: or, A Comment Upon Ramus Logicke* (Cambridge: 1629), 18.
[42] Richardson, *The Logicans School-Master*, 19.
[43] Richardson, *The Logicans School-Master*, 78.

Pauline and Augustinian views taught in churches and—as he stated—in divinity course textbooks such as Ames's *Medulla*.

Divine testimony, on the other hand, is not radiated knowledge. When discussing this subject, Richardson stayed within the Pauline, Augustinian, and Melanchthonian tradition, but went further than any previous textbook author in explaining its role in logic.[44] Divine testimony is an "inartificial argument." The terms artificial and inartificial distinguish between sources of knowledge. Artificial arguments are completely within the "art" or technical manipulations of logic. Artificial arguments come from within the mind and are judged by their self-evidence or demonstrability. Inartificial arguments do not begin within the art. Inartifical arguments are "external" rather than "internal." They are accepted from outside of the mind, then brought into the art or process of logic as the equivalent of axioms or at some level of probable knowledge. The distinction between artificial and inartificial arguments is a distinction between axioms that are radiated from God directly into an individual's mind and thus "internal" and "external" testimonies, which are passed among communities of individuals. The most important doctrines of Christianity are testimonies in the Bible or passed through time in the community of the church; therefore, dogmatically-inclined logics had to define and find ways to incorporate thse inartificial, external arguments into logic.

The level of certainty or the level of probability that an external argument is accorded is based upon the credibility and authority of the source of the testimony, not the inherent quality of the testimony itself. To achieve the certainty of an axiom, an inartificial argument must be, in Richardson's words, "backed" by someone else's internal and artificial knowledge.[45] Dogmatically-inclined logics we might say were logics of trust—trust not only in face-to-face relationships but trust in the historical chain of face-to-face relationships.

Richardson did not deal explicitly with cases where inartificial arguments were merely probable, although this would become one

---

[44] Richardson, *The Logicians School-Master*, 60–63 and 222–235.
[45] Richardson, *The Logicians School-Master*, 223.

of the most important subjects in religion, law, and the study of history during the century.[46] Richardson was concerned with giving the Bible a strong position in logic, so his logic would be useful to Puritans. Historians and lawyers had other logics available. For example, a contemporary of Richardson, Abraham Fraunce, published *The Lawiers Logicke, exemplifying the Præcepts of Logicke by the Practise of the Common Lawe* (London: 1588), which dealt with inartificial arguments (what Fraunce called "borrowed arguments") with an emphasis on types of human testimony rather than the certainties of divine testimony.

Richardson emphasized the importance of the truths that passed through communities. Communal knowledge, Richardson believed, is necessary because Adam, before the Fall, was the only individual ever capable of the fullness of human knowledge. For Adam's descendants, Richardson insisted: "All things cannot come under one man's eye of reason." A single individual is too small, too weak. God, therefore, provides an individual and a communal way of knowing—in one a person "sees by himself"; in the other "he may see by another man's eye."[47]

> The Lord hath in wisdom ordained that we should receive some things by reports from others, for as the world was to increase both in men and other creatures, it was impossible that one man should see all things.[48]

Richardson, of course, did not desire humans to be gullible. Scholars must not "take any thing that their authors deliver them without any examination of the things they read."[49] Richardson only tentatively agreed with Keckermann's more optimistic view of testimony:

---

[46] See Coady, *Testimony: A Philosophical Study*; Steven Shapin, *A Social History of Truth*; and Barbara Shapiro, *"Beyond Reasonable Doubt" and "Probable Cause": Historical Perspectives on the Anglo-American Law of Evidence* (Berkeley: University of California, 1991).

[47] Richardson, *The Logicians School-Master*, 61.

[48] Richardson, *The Logicians School-Master*, 222–223.

[49] Richardson, *The Logicians School-Master*, 63.

Keckermann saith, an inartificial argument may be received before an artificial. I do not deny it, but yet you must examine it afterward. God's testimonies only are undenyable, because he cannot lie; but no man's.[50]

Richardson took special care to insist on the importance of making the distinction between inartifical and artificial arguments. Some critics of Ramus had taken the position that there was no such thing as an inartificial argument. For example Thomas Spencer in his *The Art of Logic* (1628) insisted that inartificial arguments were not arguments at all and were "unfitly spoken" by Ramus. Spencer insisted divine testimony had to be viewed as a "moral cause" and not as an argument.[51] Richardson, on the other hand, insisted on Ramus's special place for inartificial argument because relegating testimony merely to moral influence could destroy the foundation in logic for the certainty of Christian orthodoxy.[52]

Without a special category for divine testimony, the Bible's place in logic would be weakened and the traditional tenets of Christian orthodoxy would have to be judged like any other proposition. Richardson's logic clearly offered the Bible and Christianity a stronger position. Although he does not give a precise example, Richardson was insisting that the axiom "the whole is greater than its part" and the testimony "Jesus rose from the dead" have equal certainty. They simply are handled differently. The former is artificial and internal while the latter is inartifical and external. If externally-known testimony was to be judged by the same standards of self-evidence as axioms, then obviously the credibility and authority of the testifier would no longer be of concern. Richardson seems to have realized that such a move in logic would mean the ultimate destruction of the certainty of much of Christian orthodoxy.

The obvious question to follow is: Doesn't the necessity of the

---

[50] Richardson, *The Logicians School-Master*, 63.
[51] Thomas Spencer, *The Art of Logick*, ed. R.C. Alston (Menston: Scolar, 1970), 38.
[52] Richardson, *The Logicians School-Master*, 226–27.

communal transfer of knowledge from human to human mean that the certainty of divine testimony is tainted by human testimony? Richardson answered: No. He insisted there was no element of human testimony in the writings of the Old Testament prophets, New Testament apostles, or other scripture writers, since God circumvents the defect of human testimony by having the Holy Spirit continually guarantee directly to an individual that the scriptures and "that which the Church delivereth" are divine testimony.[53] Richardson reiterated this in an attack on the Roman Catholic Church by insisting that the Holy Spirit, not the church itself, must guarantee the divinity of Christian tradition handed down through the church.

With this continuing role for the Holy Spirit in mind, Richardson implicitly described three roles for God in logic: 1) God internally communicates directly with an individual by breathing the knowledge of axioms into a person. 2) God also internally communicated special knowledge directly into the minds of people such as the Apostles, which then was passed through communities through time as external divine testimony. 3) Lastly, God guarantees to each individual internally the divinity of the divine testimony that is communicated through the community. The epistemology is ultimately based on an individual relationship between God and a human, but retains a crucial role for the Christian community through time.

From the perspective of English Puritans who desired the rules of reason to support Christian orthodoxy, *The Logicians School-Master* was a definite advance over previous humanistic logic textbooks since it explicitly put communal and individual knowledge of orthodoxy under the guardianship of the Holy Spirit.

A textbook, however, is seldom the source of a new idea. Textbooks, rather, support prevailing notions. The epistemology of divine testimony as Richardson explained it was often assumed in the literature of Bible-oriented ministers in the seventeenth century. Richardson, himself, acknowledged that his epistemology was similar to what was taught in divinity classes. Gerhard Reedy in *The*

---

[53] Richardson, *The Logicians School-Master*, 227.

Bible and Reason: Anglicans and Scripture in Late Seventeenth-Century England devotes a chapter to testimony and "external" arguments for scriptural authority. Many of the arguments of non-Puritan divines attempting to prove the authority of scripture used the logical terms and three-fold epistemological role for God that Richardson described. Reedy notes that one minister accorded the Holy Spirit a "special convincing" role in which the "Holy Spirit fills the gap" necessary to confirm divine testimony's divinity.[54]

It was precisely the comprehensiveness of including what so many people only assumed or passed on orally in classes that made *The Logicians School-Master* a favorite logic textbook for Puritans who wanted a logic that explicitly supported Bible-oriented Christianity.

C. Aristotelianism, Ramism, and Schematic Thinking

Ramism may have been favored by most Puritans, but it was not the only kind of logic that dogmatic-minded Christians supported. Many authors wanted to find a middle position between Ramism and Aristotelianism. Charles Morton was directly influenced by one of the Continent's compromise logics: Bartholomaeus Keckermann's *Systema Logicae*.

Keckermann's logic was published in Germany in 1600, and in London in 1606 as the *Gymnasium Logicum*. It attempted a systematic synthesis of Aristotelian and Ramist logic that is sometimes categorized as Philippo-Ramist since it was primarily derived from both Philipp Melanchthon and Petrus Ramus. Sometimes the Philippo-Ramists are called "systematics" because Keckermann popularized a new level of the old systemization and elaborate schematic drawings. Charles Morton's *A Logick System* is a late addition to the Philippo-Ramist or systematic school of logic. Nomenclature can overburden, however, so I will mostly refer to logics such as Keckermann's and Morton's as Aristotelian since that is the dominant format they use.

---

[54] Gerhard Reedy, *The Bible and Reason: Anglicans and Scripture in Late Seventeenth-Century England* (Philadelphia: University of Pennsylvania, 1985), 57–58.

Bartholomaeus Keckermann (1571–1609) taught philosophy at the University of Danzig and wrote many textbooks.[55] Like many humanistic textbook authors, Keckermann was an educational reformer, and he appreciated the pedagogical usefulness of Ramus's logic, especially in that it organized all human knowledge under topical headings that moved from the most general to the most specific. But Keckermann was repelled by Ramus's rebellion against Aristotle.

Like Melanchthon before him, Keckermann wanted to keep what was good in scholastic logic. Keckermann especially appreciated the pedagogical use of diagrams that the schoolmen developed. It was Keckermann who popularized the practice of using elaborate schematic drawings to describe logic, such as those that fill Morton's logic. These diagrams helped students visually outline the relationships between types of knowledge. Examples of Medieval and Renaissance pedagogical helps can be seen throughout Morton's and Brattle's texts, such as Porphyry's genus/species tree, "Barbara Celerant" (a memory device for types of syllogisms), and the AEIO (a memory device for the four kinds of propositions).[56] Richardson, who relied heavily on Keckermann's *Gymnasium Logicum* in *The Logicians School-Master* did not, however, follow Keckermann by including elaborate schematics. Richardson desired to remain more true to Ramus's pedagogy.

Like Melanchthon before him and Richardson after him, Keckermann's logic was oriented toward establishing a rational basis

---

[55] See the entry on Keckermann in the *Dictionary of Scientific Biography*, vol. 7, ed Charles Coulston Gillispie, (New York: Charles Scribner's Sons, 1973), and the section devoted to Keckermann in Neal W. Gilbert, *Renaissance Concepts of Method* (New York: Columbia University, 1960), 214–220. I use the London edition of Keckermann's logic, titled *Gymnasium Logicum id est De Usu & Exercitatione Logicae Artis absolutoiori & pleniori, Liberi Tres* (1606). Keckermann also wrote an influential critique of logic, *Præcognitorum Logicorum Tractatus Tres* (Hanover, 1604). Keckermann's logic is put in its Continental context in Ashworth's introduction to *Language and Logic in the Post-Medieval Period*.

[56] Walter Ong discusses some Medieval devices in *Ramus, Method, and the Decay of Dialogue*, 74–91; and E.J. Ashworth offers technical explanations of "Barbara Celerant" and the AEIO in "Some Notes on Syllogistic in the Sixteenth and Seventeenth Centuries," *Notre Dame Journal of Formal Logic* 11 (1970): 17–33.

for the certainty of Christianity. Keckermann's chapters are seldom without references to the Bible and faith. On the subject of divine testimony, Keckermann wrote, citing Melanchthon, that faith is divided into plain communal faith and true holy faith which is based on the testimony and authority of God.[57] True holy faith, for Keckermann, was caused by the Holy Spirit as an act of grace given to those elected by God.[58] Whole chapters were devoted to invoking God's name and authority, the Christian faith, the sacraments, and theology. The chapter on theology included a large, three-part, fold-out diagram for a whole system of theology.[59]

Although Keckermann attempted to synthesize Ramus with Melanchthon for better use by Protestants, he was criticized by those who believed he had not restored Aristotelian logic to the importance that Melanchthon had accorded it. A reaction against Ramism was spreading throughout the Continent and England led by many humanists who wanted to purify and reinvigorate Aristotelianism.[60] As with other such movements in logic, Christian-oriented texts were written alongside purist logic textbooks. The purists stuck to Classical examples and avoided references to Christianity or contemporary theological debate. Jacobi Zabarella (1533–1589) was one of the purists in the new Aristotelian movement. His various textbooks, especially *Opera Logica*, were justly famous for their adherence to an Aristotelian tradition and avoiding what they considered to be a taint of scholastic Aristotelianism.[61] Zabarella did not even mention the possibility of divine testimony when discussing the role of testimony in logic.[62]

Two Aristotelians in The Netherlands who reacted against Keckermann and had some influence among Puritans were Franco Burgersdijck (1590–1636), Professor of Logic at the University of

---

[57] Keckermann, *Gymnasium Logicum*, 83.
[58] Keckermann, *Gymnasium Logicum*, 84–85.
[59] Keckermann, *Gymnasium Logicum*, 169.
[60] See Schmitt, *John Case and Aristotelianism in Renaissance England*.
[61] Neal Gilbert in *Renaissance Concepts of Method*, 167–170, discusses Zabarella's sources.
[62] Jacobi Zabarella, *Opera Logica* (Hildesheim: Georg Olms Verlagsbuchhandlung, 1966, reprint of 1597 edition), 100–101.

Leiden, and J.H. Alsted (1588–1638), who is most famous for his early attempt at unifying knowledge into an encyclopedia. Alsted followed primarily Burgersdijck. Burgersdijck's logic, *Institutionum Logicarum Libri Duo* (1626 in Leiden and 1637 in Cambridge, England) became a semi-official logic when in 1635 the Estates ordered its use in Dutch schools. Burgersdijck's preface to his logic respectfully criticized Keckermann for bringing too many confusions from Ramism into logic and, significantly, for mixing too much of the certainty of scientific logic into what should be merely probabilistic. Burgersdijck tried to purify some of Keckermann's eclecticisms, and to do so, he followed Zabarella's example by avoiding references to Christian issues.

On the other hand, there were other Aristotelian texts that worked to purify Keckermann of too much Ramism, but still kept an emphasis on Christianity. In The Netherlands, Adrian Heereboord (1614–1659) revised Burgersdijck by reintroducing Christian material into *Ermencia Logica; Seu Synopseos Logicæ Bergersdiciana Explicatio*.[63] In England, several Aristotelians wrote logic textbooks with a moderate religious emphasis, the most influential of these being Robert Sanderson's *Logicae Artis Compendium* (1615).[64]

Sanderson was an Oxford tutor who eventually became Bishop of Lincoln, and his version of Aristotelian logic was especially popular among Oxford tutors with tendencies in keeping with the established Anglican church.[65] Sanderson praised Keckermann's merging of Ramist and Aristotelian logic; however, like

---

[63] My statement is based on an edition published in London in 1662. William Morris in *The Young Jonathan Edwards*, 79–80, notes that Edwards at Yale used a 1660 edition of Heereboord's logic that was bound with a 1651 edition of Burgersdijck's. This would have served to Christianize Burgersdijck. Morris analyzes Heereboord and Burgersdijck pp. 80–102. Heereboord's influence at Harvard was primarily through his *Meletemata Philosophica* (1654); see Samuel E. Morison in *Harvard in the Seventeenth Century*, vol. 1 (Cambridge, MA.: Harvard University, 1936), 233–234.

[64] See Schmitt, *John Case and Aristotelianism in Renaissance England*, and E.J. Ashworth's introduction to Sanderson's *Logicae Artis Compendium*, ed. and intro. E.J. Ashworth (Bologna: Cooperativa Libraria, 1985).

[65] See Ashworth's introduction to Robert Sanderson, *Logicae Artis Compendium*.

Burgersdijck, he believed Keckermann had gone too far toward the Ramists. "I would wish," Sanderson wrote, "that Keckermann be not rubbed often into the hands of youth. Youth ought to be accustomed more to the peripatetic [Aristotelian] boundaries."[66] Sanderson had religious concerns, but less than Keckermann though more so than Burgersdijck.

There is an interesting question at this point. Given the religious orientation of the Puritans, why did they tend to avoid Sanderson's Christianized text and favor Burgersdijck's unchristianized Aristotelianism?

Burgersdijck's logic was long a textbook at Cambridge and at Harvard during times of Puritan control; however, it is very important to note that the text does not appear in writings of the period. I have not found any Puritans quoting from or recommending Burgersdijck's logic or Aristotelianism in general in the way so many referred to Richardson's, Ames's, or Ramism in general. Burgersdijck's logic, it seems, was of special importance in the mid-century Puritan logic curriculum only as a foil to emphasize the virtues of Ramist logic. Later at Harvard, Burgersdijck's logic seems to have become the foil also for Cartesian and Lockean logics. Long into the eighteenth century, Burgersdijck's logic was presented to the students at Harvard as an example of Aristotelian logic—but it seems that it was never seriously taught. By the time Brattle's Cartesian logic overtook Ramist logic as the dominant logic at Harvard, another popular Christianized Aristotelian logic was readily available, Henry Aldrich's *Artis Logicae* (1692)—but it too was avoided in favor of the unchristianized logic of Burgersdijck.

Before we can turn to the question of why Burgersdijck was favored over Sanderson or Aldrich, we need to go even further into available Christianized versions of Aristotelian logic. By at least the 1670s in America, a very good Puritan version of Aristotelianism was available that would have been even better than Sanderson or Aldrich for dissenting academies or Harvard. This Puritan logic textbook was written in English, carefully organized and presented,

---

[66] The translation is by Samuel Howell in *Logic and Rhetoric in England, 1500–1700*, 303.

and filled with explicit support for Calvinistic theology. But it had a strange history and an author that was too religiously radical for even the Puritans.

The title of the text was innocuous, *The Art of Logick*; however, the text was introduced by an extravagant and long "Epistle Dedicatory" to "The Illustrious, His Excellency Oliver Cromwell, Generalissimo of England, Ireland, and Scotland." In the dedication the author proclaimed the book:

> [a] system of logico-theology, as it will medicine the disease, so it will purge out the humor, and serve (with Heaven's concurrence) as the clue of Ariadne, to guide the intricate and perplexed thoughts of the unfixed people...to help them in taking the dimensions and full heights of things, by an infallible rule of certitude.[67]

The "unfixed" skeptics would be fixed by this book. Logic—with grace—"recovers us to our promogenial condition, unclouds the masked mind."[68] Using construction imagery, the author declared to Cromwell that religion is the palisade of a republic and that knowledge was the "cement of religion."[69] Finally the benefits of logic would help "render England the world's utopia, the most felicitous of nations."[70]

The author of these declarations and the person named as the author of the whole work was Zachary Coke, a person unknown to the twentieth century, who was probably searching for a preferment from Cromwell. In the second edition of the text, published in 1657 just before Cromwell's death, a note appeared in the advertisement:

> Though this book go under the name of Mr. Coke, yet most certain it is, that it was made by old Mr. Henry Ainsworth.... When Mr. Coke was in the Low Countries he borrowed the

---

[67] Zachary Coke, *The Art of Logick*, (Menston, Eng: Scholars Press, 1969; reprint of 1654 edition), third page of "Epistle Dedicatory."
[68] Coke, *The Art of Logick*, fifth page of "Epistle Dedicatory."
[69] Coke, *The Art of Logick*, eleventh page of "Epistle Dedicatory."
[70] Coke, *The Art of Logick*, fifteenth page of "Epistle Dedicatory."

manuscript of one nearly related to the said Mr. Ainsworth and (changing a few words, but not the sense) printed it as his own. This is affirmed by the Rev. Allen Gear who was then in Holland and a witness of what is affirmed.[71]

The publisher, John Streater of London, apparently believed there was money to be made from the text but wanted to let readers know that Coke had been found out.

Henry Ainsworth (1571–1622 or 1623), the true author, was a famous and prolific Puritan author and controversialist. Graduating from Caius College, Cambridge, in 1587, Ainsworth continued his residence at the college and gained a reputation as one of Puritanism's up-and-coming thinkers. Roger Williams, founder of the British colony of Rhode Island, heaped extravagant praise on Ainsworth. Williams and Ainsworth were both extremely contentious and uncompromising individuals. Both were thinkers in the most extreme Puritan vein who followed uncompromisingly the ideal of doctrinal purity to such lengths that they eventually had to be shunned as dangerous for the cause even by Puritans. Ainsworth moved to Amsterdam and was the author "wholly or in part" of the Brownists's *Confession of Faith*. Ainsworth published extensively, especially Biblical commentaries, and "left behind him a large quantity of manuscripts which appear to have been dispersed."[72] Coke got hold of a logic textbook manuscript, added his extravagant preface to Cromwell, and had it published as his own. After Cromwell's death and the Restoration in 1660, the book, dedicated as it was to Cromwell and written by a radical exile separatist, would have been avoided by the more moderate Puritans who hoped to avoid offending the new regime.

Due to the book's separatism and radicalism, Puritans at Harvard did not use Ainsworth/Coke's *Art of Logick* as their Aristotelian text-

---

[71] The advertisement is partially quoted in the second edition's Online Computer Library Center (OCLC) citation. The only cited copy of the book is owned by the William Andrews Clark library where a librarian read to me the whole quote over the phone. John Goodin, librarian at Indiana University Southeast, showed me this crucial information.

[72] For Roger Williams on Ainsworth, see Ainsworth's entry in the *Dictionary of National Biography*.

book. But still, why did they use Burgersdijck's logic when Sanderson's or later Aldrich's would have been much better for dogmatically-inclined Puritans? Maybe it was because Sanderson's and Aldrich's were so much more appealing to Christians than Burgersdijck's. Puritan schools seem to have consciously or unconsciously avoided the best competition to Ramist logic and propped up Burgersdijck's as a straw-text which could easily be knocked down. The majority of Puritans in England and America favored first Ramism, then Cartesianism. Aristotelianism was never a dominant logic among Puritans, even though they were obliged to teach it.

D. Puritan Favoritism from Ramus to Descartes

Humanistic educational theory demanded that options be presented to students, and Puritan teachers took pride in the breadth of options offered in their academies in England and on the Continent and at Harvard. Increase Mather in one presidential address at Harvard proclaimed the humanist motto: "Find a friend in Plato, a friend in Socrates, (and I say a friend in Aristotle), but above all find a friend in Truth."[73] Such broad-minded humanism was a goal; but, there was never encouragement of promiscuous intellectual wanderings. Aristotlelianism in the form of Burgersdijck's logic may have been in the curriculum, but there is no evidence it was ever encouraged as a viable option. Another presidential address in 1711 by John Leverett shows more accurately the way students were directed when offered options. He declared that "Harvardians philosophize in a sane and liberal manner, according to the manner of the century." He explained further that students read Ramus "not too scrupulously," and Aristotle, but neither author to the extent that they "cannot grasp the neoterics' rule of truth."[74] This is a fascinating statement! It is a window into the real world of favoritism in Puritan education.

[73] Quoted in Cotton Mather, "An Account of the University," *Magnalia Christi Americana* (London, 1702), Bk. 4, Introduction, pt. 2. sect. 7; translation by Lucius F. Robinson in the 1852 edition, reprinted 1967 by Russell & Russell.
[74] Quoted in Thomas J. Siegel, *Governance and Curriculum at Harvard College in the 18th Century* (Ph.D. dissertation, Harvard University, 1990), 383.

Leverett clearly indicated the favored logic. The neoterics for Leverett in 1711 meant Cartesian and Lockean logicians. Leverett himself had written a Cartesian logic similar to Brattle's. The other two types of logic from the seventeenth century—Ramist and Aristotelian—were presented to the students to provide the breadth required by humanistic education, but they were not taught as viable options to the favored logic.

Leverett's statement also shows how blithely a president could say his students studied Ramus and Aristotle when in fact they studied textbook reductions. Students were not assigned Ramus, Aristotle, Descartes, and Locke, although a few diligent students may have looked into their works proper. If they read whole logics at all, they read Richardson instead of Ramus, Burgersdijck instead of Aristotle, LeGrand or Arnauld instead of Descartes, and LeClerc or magazine versions of Locke instead of Locke's complete *Essay*. More often than not, students did not read whole books. Students at Harvard learned logic primarily from synopses or epitomes first culled from books but afterwards passed around in student notebooks. The diligent tutor helped make sure the students copied the right things, or, in the case of Morton and Brattle, made the short synopsis themselves and passed it among students to copy into their notebooks. There is very little evidence to support the stuffed commencement speeches about reading Aristotle and Plato, let alone a multitude of other great thinkers. The humanistic desire to create brief compendia and epitomes led to a flood of textbooks, many never published in the normal sense of the word. Many were "scribally published" and disseminated through local networks.[75]

One chopped-up Ramist logic published by a tutor for his pupils reveals the extent to which Puritans emphasized logic and favored its Ramist form before the mid 1680s: John Eliot's *A Logick Primer* (1672). Eliot (1604–1690) is famous as "The Apostle to the Indians,"

---

[75] See Harold Love, *Scribal Publications in Seventeenth-century England* (Oxford: Clarendon, 1993). For various assessments of Renaissance textbooks, see Neal Gilbert, *Renaissance Concepts of Method*, 71–73, and Anthony Grafton, "Teacher, Text and Pupil in the Renaissance Classroom: A Case Study from a Parisian College," *History of Universities* 1 (1981): 37–70, and Anthony Grafton and Lisa Jardine, *From Humanism to Humanities*.

one of the few who took seriously the Puritan ideal of bringing Christian/English civilization to those who they perceived to be humans in a state of nature, or uncivilized.[76] American Indians, in their view, had natural reason, but to be civilized needed to have their natural reason augmented by the art of logic. Eliot's *A Logick Primer* was written in English and Natick (in the language of that Indian tribe "syllogistical" was translated as "oggusanukoowae" and "proposition" as "pakodtittumooonk"). The text was a standard short religiously-oriented version of Ramism. In such an educational situation, Eliot desired to give only the briefest epitome of logic—so he taught the essentials of logic that Puritans favored: Ramism. "The use of this iron key," Eliot wrote, would "initiate the Indians in the knowledge of the Rules of Reason" and "open the rich treasury of the holy scriptures."[77] Nothing can exemplify more the intensity of Puritan emphasis on logic than the existence of such a chopped-up text translated for the mission field.

Eliot's logic textbook appeared when Ramism was beginning to lose favor among a younger generation of English Puritans. Even though Ramism remained the favored logic of older authors such as John Milton and Increase Mather, criticism of Ramus was widespread at the colleges. Ramus's dichotomizing was considered unnatural and seldom rigorously applied. His use of topics was said to "go ridiculous lengths to delimit the jurisdiction of the different sciences."[78] And though his criticism of the stagnant quality of syllogisms was accepted, he lacked a subtle understanding of pure Aristotelianism as opposed to its Medieval accretions. Ramus remained an honored martyr, but his place among the great thinkers was declining. A century later, Dugald Stewart, quoting

---

[76] Cotton Mather's sketch of Eliot is reprinted in *The Puritans*, vol. 2, ed. Perry Miller and Thomas H. Johnson (New York: Harper Torchbooks, 1963), 497–511. James Axtell puts Eliot in the context of European work in education among American Indians in *The Invasion Within: The Contest of Cultures in Colonial North America* (New York: Oxford, 1985); see especially the discussion of Eliot's textbooks on pp. 223–25.

[77] Eliot, *A Logick Primer*, (Cambridge, 1672), title page.

[78] Antoine Arnauld, *The Art of Thinking: Port-Royal Logic*, "First Discourse," trans. James Dickoff and Patricia James (Indianapolis: Bobbs-Merrill, 1964), 15. Citations of page numbers in subsequent footnotes are from this translation.

from Thomas Reid, both Scottish logicians, summed up the career of Ramus in the history of "the progress of knowledge":

> It has been justly said of Ramus, that, "although he had genius sufficient to shake the Aristotelian fabrick, he was unable to substitute any thing more solid in its place:" but it ought not be forgotten, that even this praise, scanty as it may now appear, involves a large tribute to his merits as a philosophical reformer.[79]

With Ramism in decline, the last third of the seventeenth century was an exciting era of debate about what should replace the shaken Aristotelian fabric. There were two basic options: a new, invigorated, purer Aristotelian logic, or Cartesian logic. The trouble with Aristotelianism, however, was that it still seemed mired in a bog of technicalities. The humanistic pursuit had always emphasized the "natural" and pedagogically simple. The practice of adding more difficulties to logic than needed had seemed foolish to teachers such as Erasmus, and humanistic educational reforms had been rooted in reaction against the overly-formalized Medieval scholastics.[80] John Milton, thinking of Aristotelians, had condemned logicians as merely "thorn-finches stuffing themselves with thistles and briars."[81] Similar criticism appears in John Locke's attack on logic education.[82] Cotton Mather, following many writers before him, declared to young candidates to the ministry that he could not encourage them "to spend very much time, in that which goes

---

[79] Dugald Stewart, "A General View of the Progress of Metaphysical, Ethical, and Political Philosophy Since the Revival of Letters in Europe," in *Dissertations on the Progress of Knowledge* (NY: Arno Press, 1975), 74.

[80] See "A Declamation on the Subject of Early Liberal Education for Children," trans. Beert C. Verstraete, *Collected Works of Erasmus*, vol. 26, ed. J.K. Sowards (Toronto, University of Toronto, 1985).

[81] John Milton, "Prolusions," *Complete Poems and Major Prose*, ed. Merritt Y. Hughes (Indianapolis: Odyssey, 1957), 627; see also Milton's criticisms of logic in "Of Education," 636.

[82] See *The Educational Writings of John Locke*, ed. James Axtell (Cambridge: Cambridge, 1968), and W. Henry Kenney, *John Locke and the Oxford Training in Logic and Metaphysics* (Ph.D. dissertation, Saint Louis University, 1959).

under the name of logic" since he had "contempt" for "the vulgar logic, learned in our colleges." By vulgar logic, Mather meant what he generically called "any Burgesdicius" which furnishes a "parcel of terms." Instead of leading to Truth, Aristotelian logics only enabled "one to carry on altercations, and logomachies, by which the force of truth may be a pleasure, and by some little trick, evaded."[83]

Good logic, for most humanistic educators in the late seventeenth century, had to be natural. Cartesianism seemed more natural than Aristotelianism. For Cotton Mather the good logics were "treatises, that clear up the maxims of reason, and may strengthen you and sharpen you in the use of it." This was not the job of "any Burgesdicius" and Milton and Locke would have agreed. Cotton Mather recommended instead the most natural and useful logic textbook of the era: *Ars Cogitandi*, also called *The Port-Royal Logic*.[84]

The Port-Royal Logic (1662) was a Cartesian-based textbook that was amazingly popular after the 1660s and on through the eighteenth century. Its popularity was due to its deemphasis of terms and mechanisms in logic and to its forthright support of the "universal church" against the wiles of skepticism and lazy thinking.[85] The textbook was designed to teach Cartesian logic and was written specifically for use in the Little Schools of the Jansenists. It was rooted in the Augustinian epistemology and psychology which had become the hallmark of logic textbooks following Melanchthon's *Erotemata Dialectices*. *The Port-Royal Logic* was the high-point of the tradition of dogmatically-inclined and religiously-oriented humanistic logics. The decline of Ramus's influence and the rise of *The Port-Royal Logic*'s influence seem directly related.

By 1711 when President Leverett assured his listeners that Harvard students were not studying so much Ramist and Aristotelian logic that it hindered their learning of Cartesian logic, the old favorite in logic had been overthrown for a new one, *The Port-Royal Logic*. As was typical, however, students worked with

---

[83] Cotton Mather, *Manductio ad Minsterium: Directions for A Young Candidate of the Ministry* (Boston, 1726), 35–36.

[84] Cotton Mather, *Manductio ad Minsterium*, 35–36.

[85] In the 1683 and subsequent editions, Arnauld even expanded the religious direction of the text because of "theological disputes." See "Preface to Fifth Edition."

synopses prepared by their tutors and learned from *The Port-Royal Logic* by reading Brattle's *Compendium of Logick*.

E. Cartesian Logic and Christian Skepticism

Historians of Puritanism and Christianity tend to misunderstand the role of Cartesianism among dogmatically-inclined Christians. They tend to see Cartesianism only as a predecessor to modern secularism when in many ways it was the opposite. Cartesianism was born in the midst of a war waged between skeptics and dogmatists. It was not a war of Christians versus atheists, rather, between Christian groups as to the relationship between human minds and God's mind. The most extreme skeptics insisted that human minds acted alone. Here again the role of testimony and faith in logics exemplifies the antagonism between skeptics and dogmatists. Dogmatists demanded that divine testimony was available to humans and based on the absolute authority of the testifier; "divine faith" was the result. Divine faith is a logical term, not theological, for it was absolute knowledge learned from the absolute knower. Skeptics demanded that divine testimony, if it existed, was always filtered through humans and was, therefore, merely human testimony resulting in "human faith." For dogmatists, "divine faith" ranked as high or higher than "science" on the scale of certainty. For skeptics "divine faith" was really "human faith" which always ranked lower than "science" on the scale of certainty. This skepticism was fomented largely by despair over the terrible heretic-chasing of the church in the late Middle Ages and Reformation. Richard Popkin in *The History of Scepticism: From Erasmus to Spinoza* treats Erasmus as one of the most influential popularizers of the new Renaissance skepticism because he pled ignorance in debates about Christian dogma. For Erasmus and later Christian skeptics, the opinion was that the church must be peaceful and tolerant of intellectual diversity since human minds did not have access to the truth in God's mind.[86]

Christian dogmatists, whether Protestant or Roman Catholic,

---

[86] Richard H. Popkin, *The History of Scepticism from Erasmus to Spinoza* (Berkeley: University of California, 1979).

disdained the perspective of such peacemakers. Dogmatists might disagree with each other about the route of God's communication to humanity—direct revelation, scriptures, creeds, Church Fathers, pre or post-Constantinian church traditions, apostolic succession, and others—however, the dogmatists all agreed that the skeptics committed the sin of denying what God offered. God gives knowledge and leads people—at least some—to secure truths. To be a skeptic like Erasmus was a subtle way of turning one's back on God.

Of course, in a general sense this was an old battle in Christianity. Many in the history of Christianity have to some extent maintained pietistic or fideist principles which insist that rationalism hinders Christian faith. The majority of church leaders, however, have insisted that the fullness of Christianity requires rationalism. The church supported the birth of universities and the revival of Classical logic. "To appeal to dialectic [logic]," wrote an eleventh-century theologian, "is to appeal to reason; and not to do so is to deny the image of God in man."[87] This has been the dominant tradition in Christianity, and dogmatic theology has been based on the integration of divine revelation and human reason.

Yet, in the sixteenth and seventeenth centuries, skeptics within the church increasingly attacked the integration of divine revelation and human reason and thereby attacked the foundations of dogmatic theology. The greatest minds of the age were involved in these debates, and the direction of science, religion, philosophy, and politics were thereby transformed. Blaise Pascal described the situation:

> There is open war among men, in which each must take a part, and side either with dogmatism or skepticism. For he who thinks to remain neutral is above all a skeptic.[88]

Logic textbooks were written to support both sides in the war. Those following the tradition of Agricola and Ramus tended to

---

[87] Quoted in Richard Southern, *Saint Anselm: A Portrait in a Landscape* (Cambridge: Cambridge, 1990), 51.

[88] Blaise Pascal, *Pensées*, # 131, trans. A. J. Krailsheimer (New York: Penguin Books, 1966), 63–64.

avoid giving any emphasis to information given by God and tended to emphasize human reason working alone. They implied what Montaigne baldly stated in *An Apology for Raymond Sebond*: that their intellectual foundation was "man in isolation—man with no outside help."[89] "Man in his highest state," Montaigne believed, can find "nothing solid, nothing firm, only vanity."[90]

For dogmatists, there was no reason to consider humanity as alone. For dogmatically-inclined and religiously-oriented rationalists, intellectual certainty was a joint venture between God and humanity. To fervent dogmatists who persevered after the knowledge God offered, Montaigne was an egocentric and lazy thinker who masked his mental indolence as humility. His ideas were seductive but represented the easy and wide road to Hell. Pascal condemned Montaigne for a lack of the rigorous thinking necessary for the pursuit of Godly knowledge. He condemned him for seeking only to be fashionable, for talking nonsense deliberately, and inspiring "indifference regarding salvation."[91] Pascal's Cartesian associate, Antoine Arnauld, in *The Port-Royal Logic*'s section on "faulty reasoning," described Montaigne as a shallow pedant, contradicting everything, contemptibly motivated by egotism.[92]

René Descartes (1596–1650) first responded to the skeptics using the autobiographical approach of Montaigne. In his *Discourse on Method* (1637), Descartes told the story of his early education and personal struggle with skepticism, how he found himself "beset by so many doubts and errors that I came to think I had gained nothing from my attempts to become educated but increasing recognition of my ignorance."[93] His search for sure foundations of knowledge eventually led inward. In 1619, on a day of solitary reflection in a German inn, Descartes recalled to his readers: "I found myself as it

---

[89] Michel de Montaigne, *An Apology for Raymond Sebond*, trans. M.A. Screech (London: Penguin, 1987), 13.

[90] Montaigne, *An Apology for Raymond Sebond*, trans. M.A. Screech (New York: Penguin, 1987), 67–68.

[91] Pascal, *Pensées*, #680, #780: 243, 263.

[92] Arnauld, *The Art of Thinking: Port-Royal Logic*, Bk. 3, chap. 20, sect. 6, 271–273.

[93] René Descartes, *The Philosophical Writings of Descartes*, vol. 1, trans. John Cottingham, Robert Stoothoff, Dugald Murdoch (Cambridge: Cambridge, 1985), 113.

were forced to become my own guide." He was fearful at first, and "like a man who walks alone in the dark, I resolved to proceed slowly." The goal was a "true method of attaining the knowledge of everything within my mental capabilities."[94] His method began with doubt. In order to clear his mind, he wrote, "I kept uprooting from my mind any errors that might previously have slipped into it." Though he indulged in skepticism at this point, he assured his readers that "in doing this I was not copying the sceptics, who doubt only for the sake of doubting and pretend to be always undecided; on the contrary, my whole aim was to reach certainty—to cast aside the loose earth and sand so as to come upon rock or clay."[95]

Descartes began his great counter-attack on the skeptics by beating the skeptics at their own game, by taking up the strategy of individualism and doubt. Descartes, however, took individualism and doubt further and deeper into a realm where it yielded certainty. Descartes believed "that all whom God has given the use of...reason are obligated to use it principally to try to know him and to know themselves."[96] He believed that skeptics had given up the obligation.

Descartes was a man of great faith, not doubt. His famous "I think, therefore, I am" has become a symbolic assertion of modern philosophy's reliance on the individual self; however, Descartes's philosophical system relied on his belief in God, not the autonomous self. Knowledge of God was innate in humanity, Descartes wrote in his *Meditations on First Philosophy* (1641). "And indeed it is no surprise," he asserted, "that God, in creating me should have placed this idea in me to be, as it were, the mark of the craftsman stamped on his work."[97] In order to prove the existence of anything outside himself, Descartes proceeded after his proof of his own existence to prove the existence of God who communicated and verified true knowledge to human beings. In this, Richard Popkin has noted, Descartes followed the same path as John Calvin

---

[94] Descartes, *Philosophical Writings*, vol. 1, 119.
[95] Descartes, *Philosophical Writings*, vol. 1, 125.
[96] Letter to Mersenne, 15 April 1630, quoted in E.M. Curley, *Descartes Against the Skeptics* (Cambridge: Harvard, 1978), 13n.
[97] Descartes, *Philosophical Writings*, vol. 2, 35.

and other Reformers in their "attempt to objectify subjective certitude by attaching it to God."[98]

Descartes adopted the autobiographical style of Montaigne in the *Discourse*; but, whereas the urbanity of Montaigne still makes pleasant reading, Descartes's story is embarrassing to the modern reader. Even in the seventeenth century, the story of Descartes's discovery of a metaphysical foundation to knowledge was lampooned and attacked as a drunken episode in the life of a religious fanatic. The story deals with three dreams he had in that lonely German inn in which the Spirit of Truth convinced the young Descartes that he had a divine destiny "to create a *scientia mirabilis*," to build a fortress of knowledge. Descartes's epiphany was then sealed by a vow to make a pilgrimage to the shrine of Our Lady of Loreto, which he subsequently accomplished.[99]

The circularity of Cartesian epistemology's reliance on God's validating authority did not go unnoticed and was criticized by contemporaries. Later in the century, Leibniz criticized the method as "Take what you need, and do what you should, and you will get what you want."[100] One of the first to note this circularity was Antoine Arnauld (1612–1694), a young theologian who later became the most influential popularizer of Cartesian logic. Just after finishing his doctorate, Arnauld wrote the "Fourth Set of Objections," which were published along with Descartes's *Meditations*, in which he respectfully raised the question of "how the author avoids reasoning in a circle" when the veracity of clear and distinct ideas was made contingent upon a God whose own existence depended on the assumption that clear and distinct ideas

---

[98] Popkin, *The History of Scepticism from Erasmus to Spinoza*, 191. See also, Edward Downey, *The Knowledge of God in Calvin's Theology* (New York, 1952), and Dewey Hoitenga, "Faith and Reason in Calvin's Doctrine of Knowledge," in *Rationality in the Calvinian Tradition*, eds. Hendrik Hart, Johan Van der Hoeven, Nicholas Wolterstorff (Lanham: University Press of America, 1983), 17–42.

[99] Bernard Williams, *Descartes: The Project of Pure Enquiry* (Atlantic Highlands: Humanitities, 1978), 16. For an intriquing interpretation of the role of these dreams in Descartes's work, see Gregor Sebba, *The Dream of Descartes*, ed. Richard A. Watson (Carbondale: Southern Illinois University, 1987).

[100] Quoted in Williams, *Descartes: The Project of Pure Enquiry*, 32.

were true.[101] Descartes's response was a bit slippery and many were not convinced, but Arnauld wanted to be convinced and never raised the objection again. Descartes recognized in the young theologian a kindred mind and noted Arnauld's "goodwill towards myself and the cause I defend."[102] This goodwill was evident at the very beginning of Arnauld's "Objections" where he compared Descartes favorably to St. Augustine and wrote that the new philosophy was based in Augustinianism.[103] Though many were not convinced by Descartes's defence of himself, Arnauld was won over and became a staunch defender of the new philosophy.[104]

In spite of his critics, Descartes was extraordinarily successful and quickly moved to the forefront of the intellectual world of Western Europe. He must have believed he was accomplishing his divine mission. From the 1630s to the early eighteenth century there was a small school of "brilliant Cartesians" who "flashed like meteors upon the intellectual world."[105] Although the complete structure of Cartesianism broke down in the eighteenth century, brilliant Cartesians such as Arnauld and Malebranche had lasting influence upon the thinking of dogmatically-inclined Christians, who in turn influenced the logic curricula of their schools and colleges.

F. The Religious and Dogmatic Orientation of *The Port-Royal Logic*

Descartes vainly hoped that his *Principles of Philosophy* (1644) would be used in "Christian teaching" and become a popular textbook;

---

[101] Descartes, *Philosophical Writings*, vol. 2, 150.

[102] Descartes, *Philosophical Writings*, vol. 2, 154.

[103] See Stephen R.L. Clark, "Descartes' Debt to Augustine," *Philosophy, Religion, and the Spiritual Life*, ed. Michael McGhee, (Cambridge: Cambridge, 1992), 73–88.

[104] Arnauld wrote two letters to Descartes in 1648 expressing his satisfaction with Descartes's responses. These letters and his minor objections are analyzed in Steven Nadler, *Arnauld and the Cartesian Philosophy of Ideas* (Manchester: Manchester University, 1989), 24.

[105] Richard Watson, *The Breakdown of Cartesian Metaphysics* (Atlantic Highlands: Humanities, 1987), 21.

however, it was Arnauld's logic textbook, commonly called *The Port-Royal Logic*, that spread Cartesian logic throughout Europe, England, and America.[106] Of Arnauld's logic text, William and Martha Kneale wrote that it "was widely accepted and continued to dominate the treatment of logic by most philosophers for the next 200 years."[107] Wilbur Howell in his *Eighteenth-Century British Logic and Rhetoric* notes the direct influence of this text on all of the popular logic texts of that century in Britain.[108]

The Port-Royal Logic was written in the context of Cartesianism and Jansenism, an Augustinian movement within the French Roman Catholic Church. Of these two, Jansenism invigorated the text and encouraged its popularity. Whereas Descartes's writings avoided direct discussion of Christianity, Arnauld's textbook was full of Jansenist piety and declared in its preface "that reason and faith are in perfect harmony, as two streams originating in a common source, and that we cannot go far from the one without departing from the other."[109]

Cornelius Otto Jansen (1585–1638), a Dutch Roman Catholic theologian, had watched Dutch Calvinists and English Puritans debate predestination and free will at the Synod of Dort

---

[106] On Descartes's hopes for his *Principles*, see Williams, *Descartes: The Project of Pure Enquiry*, 21–22.

[107] Kneale, *The Development of Logic*, 321.

[108] Wilbur Samuel Howell, *Eighteenth-Century British Logic and Rhetoric* (Princeton: Princeton, 1971), 299–371.

[109] Arnauld, *The Art of Thinking: Port-Royal Logic*, "Preface to fifth edition," 5. Dickoff's and James's translation is rather loose and has been criticized by those concerned that it might lead to misunderstandings about terms and their context that a more literal translation would avoid. (See Richard Watson, "The *Port-Royal Logic* in the Twentieth Century," *Journal of the History of Philosophy* 5 (1967): 55–60; and Roland Hall's review of *The Art of Thinking* in *The Philosophical Quarterly* 16 (1966): 75–76.) For the purposes of my book, which avoids precise discussion of terms, the translation is the most easily accessible and serves to express the vigor of Arnauld's thought without confusing the essential structure of the book. I confess that my own language skills do not include the ability to work from the originial French text, but I have endeavored to check my quotes with both seventeenth-century Latin editions and *L'Art de Penser: La Logique de Port-Royal*, 3 vols. eds. Bruno Baron von Freytag Loringhoff and Hervert E. Brekle (Stuttgart-Bad Cannstatt, Friedrich Frommann Verlag, 1967).

(1618–1619). Even though a Roman Catholic, Jansen agreed with the synod's affirmation of the Augustinian/Calvinist doctrines of unconditional election, limited atonement, total depravity of humans, irresistibility of grace, and final perseverance of the saints.[110] Eventually, Jansen became the Bishop of Ypres. Hating the influence of the Jesuits, he wrote an enormous work that was published posthumously in 1640 as *Augustinius*. In it he advocated a thorough return to Augustinian doctrines as the necessary antidote to both Protestant schism and Jesuit emphasis on humanity's role in divine grace. Due primarily to the power of the Jesuits, *Augustinius* was condemned by the Inquisition a year after publication and again in a Papal Bull of 1643. The "Augustinian strain of piety," however, has never been without adherents.[111] Jansenism spread among many of the pious in France and the Low Countries without official sanction.

Although one rooted in Roman Catholicism and the other in Protestantism, Jansenism and Puritanism have obvious similarities that did not escape the notice of Jansenism's opponents. They both tended toward rigorous thinking and modest living, while spurning the dominant culture around them.[112] The standard characterization of Jansenism in the polemic literature of the era was that it was Calvinist. However, Jansenism was not Calvinist. It appeared so because Jansenism and Calvinism were rooted in Augustine's severe understanding of predestination and grace.

Although the *Augustinius* was their tangible beginning, most Jansenists were not adherents to a book of theology. Jansenists ranged from controversialists such as Pascal and Arnauld, to quiet nuns, monkish *solitaires*, and pious women of the nobility. What

---

[110] For the synod's influence on Jansen, see Alexander Sedgwick, *Jansenism in Seventeenth-Century France* (Charlottesville: Virginia, 1979), 48.

[111] The term "Augustinian strain of piety" comes from Perry Miller's analysis of Puritanism in *The New England Mind: The Seventeenth Century*, 3–34.

[112] For an overview of the whole Jansenist movement, see Sedgwick, *Jansenism in Seventeenth-Century France*. For a more spirited Roman Catholic perspective which puts Jansenism in the context of other French reform movements, see H. Daniel-Rops, *The Church in the Seventeenth Century*, trans. J.J. Buckingham (New York: E.P. Dutton, 1963), 327–425.

drew them together was primarily their hatred of the religious laxity that seemed to be prevailing in the church. They were intense believers, wary of concessions to human weakness, and adamant against any perceived dilution of God's sovereignty. "What is essential," wrote one Jansenist, "is to relate everything to God and to salvation and to mistrust oneself in every way, not by wiser vanity or more enlightened pride, but by an awareness of one's own injustice and misery."[113] Jansenism, therefore, was a rigorous mentality rather than an intricate system of point-by-point theology. A visiting archbishop among the Port-Royalists described the nuns: "As pure as angels and as proud as demons."[114] Most Jansenists did not want to debate fine points of theology, but they were dogmatic about the essentials of piety—the depravity of humanity, the awesomeness of God's sovereignty, and humanity's dependence upon grace alone for salvation.

Intense, rigorous, and dogmatic, the Jansenists posed a threat to the Jesuits and the royalist forces who were unsure of Jansenists' political and ecclesiastical loyalty. To the chagrin of these antagonists, Jansenism had no formal organization or leadership that could be disbanded. However, there was one very visible bastion of Jansenists upon which they could focus their attack: the Cistercian abbey near Versailles named Port-Royal des Champs and, later, the daughter house of Port-Royal in Paris.

Jansenists were persecuted for half a century with varying intensity. Antoine Arnauld, the most prominent theologian of the group, was removed from the faculty of the Sorbonne in 1656; he subsequently engaged in more Jansenist and Cartesian polemics, and was exiled to The Netherlands in 1679.[115] With him in exile

---

[113] Sedgwick, *Jansenism in Seventeenth-Century France*, 34.

[114] H. Daniel-Rops, *The Church in the Seventeenth Century*, 362.

[115] On the life and thought of Arnauld, see Steven M. Nadler, *Arnauld and the Cartesian Philosophy of Ideas*; "Arnauld, Descartes, and Transubstantiation: Reconciling Cartesian Metaphysics and Real Presence," *Journal of the History of Ideas* 49 (1988): 229–246; R.C. Sleigh, *Leibniz and Arnauld: A Commentary on Their Correspondence* (New Haven, Yale University, 1990); and John Kilcullen, *Arnauld, Bayle, and Toleration* (Oxford: Clarendon, 1988).

was Pierre Nicole who is often considered a co-author of *The Port-Royal Logic*.

The Port-Royal Logic was first written for the education of the son of the Duc de Chevreuse, one of the important patrons of the Port-Royalists. Arnauld was undoubtedly the principal author, but the work began, at least, as a collaboration with Pierre Nicole.[116] As explained in the "Forward," the book was initially written in four or five days after a dinner conversation with the duke. Subsequently the work assumed larger proportions as the authors began to conceive its possible importance as a general textbook to be circulated in manuscript among the students of the loosely organized Little Schools of Port-Royal.

The term Little School actually meant a school that did not teach children past the age of nine; for the Jansenists, it was a conscious misnomer for the Port-Royal schools which taught a complete curriculum that could include the equivalent of college courses. H.C. Barnard in his *The Port-Royalists on Education* explained that the Jansenists used the diminutive term in order not to appear as competition for Jesuit academies and colleges and the central university.[117] The schools were not institutionalized. Many of the Port-Royal *solitaires*—men who were loosely gathered into a semi-monastic life at the Port Royals—tutored small circles of students. These tutorial groups developed a reputation for quality and

---

[116] *The Port-Royal Logic* was initially published anonymously. Pierre Nicole is usually cited as the co-author, and he certainly had something to do with its authorship; however, the text closely follows Arnauld's thought, and I follow James Dickoff and Patricia James in citing only Arnauld as the author. Alexander Sedgwick believes that Pascal was "very likely" one of the authors (p. 97) since it was written during the period that the *Pensées* was being written. Arnauld and Pascal shared much in common; however, it seems unlikely that Pascal was an author any more than others in the Port-Royal circle who might have offered suggestions as the manuscript circulated. See Rick Kennedy, "The Application of Mathematics to Christian Apologetics in Pascal's *Pensées* and Arnauld's *The Port-Royal Logic*," *Fides et Historia* 23 (1991): 37–52.

[117] Howard C. Barnard, *The Port-Royalists on Education: Extracts from the Educational Writings of the Port-Royalists* (Cambridge: Cambridge, 1918), 22. See also H.C. Barnard, *The Little Schools of Port-Royal* (Cambridge: Cambridge, 1913).

innovative methods.[118] Publicly, the Little Schools existed for only fourteen years; however, they quietly continued for years providing tutorials. Three times they were suppressed, the last time in 1656, and were officially disbanded in 1660, two years before the publication of *The Port-Royal Logic*.

Arnauld never taught in a Little School, but he was concerned with education. He wrote several textbooks including one on grammar, which offered spelling reforms and "A new method of teaching how to read easily in all kinds of languages."[119] The fact that *The Port-Royal Logic* was written while the Little Schools were suppressed and published after they were officially disbanded indicates that the education program of Port-Royal was continuing unofficially among the dispersed *solitaires*. Initially, Arnauld explained, his logic text circulated in manuscript before publication was "forced" upon its authors.[120] *The Port-Royal Logic* uses the plural when it discusses its authors, indicating that the logic grew to its published form with material added by *solitaires*. The precise authorship of textbooks was not of concern in the seventeenth century as we have seen with Richardson and will see with Brattle. Originally *The Port-Royal Logic* was published anonymously, but it was well known to be a Jansenist text and tied to Arnauld.

---

[118] As an example of their innovative methods, a card game was invented for the students in which "imperial and papal lines took the place of the usual suits. Each card bore the name and history of a particular emperor or pope. A game of two-handed whist was concocted whereby the longer reign took the trick and the loser repeated from memory the details on the card" (L.W.B. Brockliss, *French Higher Education in the Seventeenth and Eighteenth Centuries*, 90). The importance they placed on education is shown by one of their dictums: "Nothing is more detestable" than people who treat a tutor like a "hireling." (Barnard, *The Port-Royalists on Education*, 99). See also Robert Lang, "Rhetoric *Les Petites-Ecoles* of Port-Royal," *Communication Monographs* 25 (1958): 208–214; Jan Meil, "Pascal, Port-Royal, and Cartesian Linguistics," *Journal of the History of Ideas* 30 (1969): 261–271; and Steven Nadler, "Cartesianism and Port-Royal," *Monist* 71 (1988): 573–584. Nadler shows that few of the solitaires were committed to Cartesian philosophy as a whole. The schools cannot be considered disseminators of an integrated Cartesian philosophy.

[119] Antoine Arnauld and Claude Lancelot, *Grammaire Generale et Raisonnee* (1660). The quote in the text is from an excerpt in Barnard, *The Port-Royalists on Education*, 142.

[120] Arnauld, *The Art of Thinking: Port-Royal Logic*, "Foreword," 4.

The Port-Royal Logic is not a polemic against other logic systems; rather, it is an essay in common-sense logic. When describing the sources for his logic, Arnauld first cited Descartes "who is distinguished as much for clarity of mind as others are for confusion."[121] He then noted that some remarks and one small section were derived from Pascal's *The Geometrical Mind*. As for other popular textbooks of the era, Arnauld wrote that he incorporated "all that was really useful" from them, "including, for example, the rules for the figures of the syllogism, the classification of expressions and ideas, and certain reflections on propositions." Traditional aspects of logic such as categories and topics emphasized by Aristotelians and Ramists he deemed "quite useless," but included them anyway since they were "short, easy, and common."[122]

Even though Arnauld included the topics, he used the opportunity to comment against cluttered discourse and thinking. "Nothing smothers good seed," he wrote, "as much as an abundance of noxious weeds." The extent to which Arnauld avoided polemics is exemplified by his response to the possibility that he was anti-Aristotelian: "Our whole treatment of the rules of logic," Arnauld wrote, "is taken from [Aristotle's] *Analytics*." He further declared *The Port-Royal Logic* "contains more from Aristotle than from any other author, for all the precepts of logic belong to Aristotle."[123] Although Arnauld was not being completely honest with this statement, it shows his earnest desire not to alienate readers. "Whatever contributes to the book's being read," he pragmatically noted, "contributes to its usefulness."[124]

Logic textbooks in the Age of Logic were always amalgamations; there is no such thing as a pure Aristotelian or Ramist or Cartesian logic text. Walter Ong characterizes for example the Ramean "recipe" as including

---

[121] Aside from the *Discourse* and *Principles*, Arnauld relied heavily on Descartes's *Rules for the Direction of the Mind* (Descartes, *Philosophical Writings*, vol 1: 7–78) which was unpublished at the time but passed through Arnauld's hands in manuscript during the 1650s.

[122] Arnauld, *The Art of Thinking: Port-Royal Logic*, "First Discourse," 12–13.

[123] Arnaud, *The Art of Thinking: Port-Royal Logic*, "Second Discourse [1664]," 25–26.

[124] Arnauld, *The Art of Thinking: Port-Royal Logic*, "Second Discourse [1664]," 21.

[the] Platonic doctrine of ideas, considerably attenuated, Aristotle's logic in snippets, some Ciceronian dialectic and rhetoric, scraps of medieval syllogistic, the medieval drive toward greater quantification of models for thought—all this put together with humanist impatience over elaborated scientific formalism and a real concern for the realities of the human life world.[125]

What *The Port-Royal Logic* had beyond these elements in its recipe was an all-encompassing dynamism. Descartes is considered the father of modern philosophy largely because he broke down artificial categories, raised the universal importance of mathematics, and optimistically emphasized discovering new knowledge. Aristotelian and Ramist logical strategies tended to confirm and systematize static knowledge, while Cartesianism emphasized the method of geometry which was open-ended and expansive. Knowledge in Aristotelian and Ramist logics tended to be categorized or boxed in ways that kept one type of knowledge from infiltrating another. Keith Sprunger has described Puritan-Ramists as encouraging a "six-sided view of life" in which logic, grammar, rhetoric, mathematics, physics, and theology were categorized separately.[126] Cartesian logic was more comprehensive and unifying, purporting that knowledge was an upside-down pyramid rising from a storehouse of a few axioms expanding to who-knew-where.

Within the context of the dynamic characteristics of Cartesian logic, *The Port-Royal Logic* was especially good at incorporating the role of external knowledge (testimony) into its discussion of axioms, thus enhancing Cartesian logic's ability to satisfy the requirements of those who wished to support the rationality of dogmatic Christianity. Like Richardson, Arnauld knew that for logic to support dogmatic Christianity, it was necessary to fashion a special role for external knowledge that was equivalent to the role of self-evident internal knowledge.

---

[125] Ong, "Introduction," *Complete Works of John Milton*, 165–66.
[126] Sprunger, *The Learned Doctor William Ames*, 117.

The Port-Royal Logic gives a role for external knowledge in Cartesian logic most clearly in a practical chapter on "Some important axioms which can serve as the basis for great truths."[127] In that short chapter, Arnauld lists eleven "axioms" which he considered the most useful as the starting points for expanding knowledge. The first seven affirm normal Cartesian types of internal knowledge, such as "clear and distinct" ideas of existence, cause, perfection, and motion. Axioms eight and nine state that mysteries will always exist because of the insurmountable mathematical proportion of a finite mind's relation to the infinite mind of God. Axiom ten touches on a external knowledge, that which has been revealed to the finite mind by divine testimony. Divine testimony is absolutely certain.

> The testimony of one who is infinitely powerful, infinitely wise, infinitely good, and infinitely truthful must persuade our minds more powerfully than the most convincing reasons. We can be more certain that the infinitely intelligent is not deceived and that the infinitely good does not deceive us than we are that we are not deceived in the most clear things.[128]

Axioms eight through ten deal with "the ground of faith" and the eleventh with human testimony. The first seven axioms deal with "internal" and the last four with "external" testimony. In Ramist terms: the former are "artificial" and the latter "inartificial."

Following the idiosyncratic tradition as it had already developed in logic textbooks, Arnauld made it clear that the product of testimony is faith not science; however, he goes so far as to insist that faith based on divine testimony is actually more certain than science. This does not make sense and can be dismissed as a rhetorical flourish—if science is absolute knowledge, how can there be more-than-absolute knowledge? Brattle would use the same rhetoric.

---

[127] Arnauld, *The Art of Thinking: Port-Royal Logic*, Bk. 4, chap. 7, 323–325.
[128] Arnauld, *The Art of Thinking: Port-Royal Logic*, Bk. 4, chap. 7, 324–325.

Arnauld had been more careful in an earlier section that pointed out that the distinction between science and faith is a distinction in method, not in the level of certainty attained. The first method is demonstrative from internal axioms known within each human. The second method is external, using knowledge gained through the complex means of testimony, tradition, and divine confirmation.

The essential epistemology undergirding *The Port-Royal Logic* is Christian. God is actively communicating with individual minds and has communicated collectively throughout history. Why was it important to have God communicate both internally and externally? It would have been less complicated epistemologically to have God implant Christian doctrine internally. Arnauld offers an answer that is similar to Richardson's but Arnauld's is from a Roman Catholic perspective. Arnauld's answer places more emphasis on God's desire to keep each individual humble and submissive to the church. Arnauld further explained that the internal and external means of knowing shows God's love for the simple-minded in that "God, willing that a knowledge of the mysteries of faith be accessible to the simplest of the faithful, had the goodness to accommodate himself to this weakness of the human mind." God "did not make this knowledge depend upon the individual examination of each point proposed for belief, but instead he gave as a certain sign of the truth the authority of the universal Church."[129] Like God, "The universal Church cannot err."[130]

As with Richardson, God has three epistemological roles, but the role of the Holy Spirit is tied more closely to an authoritative church. God's first role is implanting axioms in the mind. The second is giving specific testimony to certain individuals who pass it on through various means such as Scripture and ecclesiastical tradition. The third is guaranteeing the divinity of the divine testimony being passed through human communities. The "universal Church" that cannot err

---

[129] Arnauld, *The Art of Thinking: Port-Royal Logic*, Bk. 3, chap. 20, sect. 6, 286. "Faulty Arguments Arising from the Objects Themselves," Bk. 3, chap. 20, sect. 6, 286; see also Bk. 4, chap. 12, 338–339.
[130] Arnauld, *The Art of Thinking: The Port-Royal Logic*, "Faulty Arguments Arising from the Objects Themselves," Bk. 3, chap. 20, sect. 6, 286–287.

in its role as guarantor of a testimony's divinity was, in the mind of seventeenth-century thinkers such as Arnauld and Bishop Bossuet, an earthly extension of the Holy Spirit. God in the person of the Holy Spirit directs the "universal Church"—not necessarily any one geographic or historical bureaucracy—which validates divine testimony.

G. Cartesian Logic in British Textbooks

The Port-Royal Logic was amazingly popular and influential considering its roots in a dissident and suppressed group of Roman Catholics, and its author forced to live in exile.[131] Forty-four French editions of *The Port-Royal Logic* were published on the Continent in the two hundred years after it was first published in 1662. Eighteen of those were in the eighteenth century and ten in the nineteenth. There were twelve translations into Latin and, in the eighteenth century, translations into Spanish and Italian. Twelve editions were published in England: eight in English and four in Latin.[132]

Important for Morton's logic and especially Brattle's was another popular Cartesian logic that drew from *The Port-Royal Logic* by another suppressed Roman Catholic: the *Institutio Philosophiae secundum Principia D. Renati DesCartes, Nova Methodo adornata et explicata, In usum juventatis Academicae* by Anthony LeGrand. First published in 1672, the logic portion of the text was only the first sixty-eight pages of a four-hundred and sixty-page octavo volume. In 1680, LeGrand greatly expanded the text by publishing a more sumptuous

---

[131] There is no comprehensive study of *The Port-Royal Logic*'s influence; however, preliminary information is available in Brockliss, *French Higher Education*, 197–204; Howell, *Logic and Rhetoric in England, 1500–1700*, 342–363, Charles W. Hendel, "Foreword" in Dickoff's and James's edition of *The Art of Thinking*, xvii-xxv, and Richard Watson, "The Port-Royal Logic in the Twentieth Century," *Journal of the History of Philosophy* 5 (1967): 55–60.

[132] These numbers come from the list of editons and translations in *L'Art de Penser*, vol. 2, ed. Loringhoff and Brekle, 19–23. As for the editions in England, there is a distinctive break between the eight published before 1717 and the four published after 1818. This break might indicate a general abandonment of Cartesian logic, but we must keep in mind the influence of *The Port-Royal Logic* on logics that were popular in the eighteenth century.

quarto edition. In the latter form this large textbook went through four editions in England between 1680 and 1694, and another four on the Continent. The final 1694 edition was an English translation titled *An Entire Body of Philosophy*.[133] In the 1680 edition, LeGrand rewrote the logic section to more closely follow *The Port-Royal Logic*. As stated in the Latin title, the *Institutio* was written for young scholars. The book was a missionary venture written by a Roman Catholic in England who hoped to stem the tide of skepticism in that country.

Very little is known about Anthony (Antoine) LeGrand (1629–99).[134] He was born and educated in Douai, France, where he joined the Recollects, a strict branch of the Franciscan Order. He was apparently motivated by a spiritual zeal common in seventeenth-century France. Francis de Sales, Vincent de Paul, and Blaise Pascal were only three of the more famous individuals caught up in the fervor. The Trappists, Carmelites, and Sulpicians flourished as more rigorous and more spiritually-minded branches of old orders. The Jansenists flourished even though officially suppressed. The Recollect branch of the Franciscans along with the Jesuits devoted themselves to missionary work abroad.

In accord with the missionary zeal of his order, LeGrand accepted a post in the heart of enemy territory: Oxfordshire, England. From 1656 until his death forty-three years later, LeGrand worked among the Roman Catholics around Oxfordshire and London where he probably served as a tutor to many young Roman Catholics. Christian missionary activity often emphasizes education; however, LeGrand could not establish a formal school like missionaries in other countries

---

[133] Anthony LeGrand, *An Entire Body of Philosophy*, trans. R. Blome (London, 1694). All English quotations of the *Institutio* will be from Blome's translation; however, I will also cite the book, chapter, and subheadings of the 1680 Latin edition. Blome states in his subtitle that his edition included "large additions of the author, never yet published." At least in the logic section, there were no "large additions" although there are a few minor changes.

[134] For LeGrand, see John K. Ryan "Anthony Legrand 1629–99: Franciscan and Cartesian," *New Scholasticism* 9 (1935), 226–250; 10 (1936), 39–55, and the *Dictionary of National Biography*. For the most extensive study of LeGrand in the context of Cartesianism see Richard Watson's "Introduction," to Antoine LeGrand, *An Entire Body of Philosophy* (New York, Johnson Reprint Corporation, 1972), v–xi, and *The Breakdown of Cartesian Metaphysics*, 93–96.

because the Roman Catholics were politically suppressed in England. He could, though, publish the textbook *In usum juventatis Academicae* for the use of students in the Protestant schools of England.

There is a missionary quality to LeGrand's logic textbook. It was written without reference to specifically Roman Catholic doctrines such as eucharistic transubstantiation; yet it demanded that those seeking knowledge must follow the example of the Roman Catholic "Renatus Descartes...who by a method, before his time but imperfectly known, restored philosophy from the very foundations, opening a sure and solid way to mankind into the inmost recesses of nature."[135] While advocating Descartes, the *Institutio* also lifted whole sections from *The Port-Royal Logic*, leaving out those examples that would offend a Protestant reader. LeGrand probably desired to accomplish two goals: first, to diminish the influence of skepticism in England and, second, to surrepticiously build a Roman Catholic foundation under the intellects of English students. The latter goal rested on a premise similar to one held by Arnauld—set people on the course of right thinking and it will lead them eventually to the "universal Church," which was Roman Catholic, not Protestant.

Cartesianism does not seem to have converted many English Protestants to Catholicism; however, it did make its way into the English universities and later dissenting academies. Cartesianism reached England soon after Descartes published the *Discourse*, and translations and editions of the *Discourse* were soon "adopted as texts in the English Universities."[136] Cambridge University was especially open to the new philosophy. A former student of St. Johns College published a poem in 1649 attacking the "harsh abstract logical notions" of scholastic philosophy and praised the Cartesian for its "use in the affairs of life."[137] In 1659, Cambridge's

---

[135] LeGrand, *Entire Body of Philosophy*, trans. Blome, "The Preface" sect. 2.
[136] Sterling Lamprecht, "The Role of Descartes in Seventeenth-century England," *Studies in the History of Ideas* 3 (1935): 187.
[137] John Hall, *An Humble Motion to the Parliament of England concerning the Advancement of Learning and the Reformation of the Universities* (London, 1649), 26; see also Marjorie Nicholson, "Early Stages of Cartesianism in England," *Studies in Philology* 26 (1929): 361, and Lamprecht, "The Role of Descartes in Seventeenth-century England," 195.

Henry More wrote in his book-length proof for *The Immortality of the Soul* that he wished "to encourage the reading of Descartes in all public schools or universities."[138] Sterling Lamprecht believes that the popularity of Cartesianism grew in stages, with an eager, youthful embrace of the "new philosophy" in the 1640s and 50s, then criticism of Cartesianism rising in the 1660s and 70s. Even during the period of criticism, however, Cartesianism was still popular at Cambridge.[139] The truth of this is evident from the letters of Roger North who, when he entered Jesus College in 1667, reported:

> I found such a stir, about Descartes, some railing at him, and forbidding the reading of him, as if he had impugned the very Gospel, and yet there was a general inclination, especially in the brisk part of the university, to use him, which made me conclude, there was somewhat extraordinary in him, which I resolved to find out, and at length did so....Nothing gained on my judgment, as to his Piece de Methode, but the rule of not building upon doubts, but first to find out what is most clear, and then as from a foundation, proceed to other matters, as far as you can walk, with like clearness.[140]

It was just a few years after North wrote this that LeGrand's *Institutio* became available, and by 1692, it was reported by Anthony Wood that LeGrand was "a Cartesian philosopher of great note" and that his text was "much read in Cambridge."[141]

Cartesian logic in the form of the *Insitutio* and *The Port-Royal Logic* seems to have also been much studied in the dissenting acade-

---

[138] Henry More, *Immortality of the Soul*, ed. A. Jacob (Boston: Matinus Nijhoff, 1987), "Preface," sect. 15, p. 20. Henry More's relationship with Cartesianism has been often studied, especially for his vehement rejection of it after an initial embrace. More rejected only aspects of Cartesianism and never abandoned those aspects of Cartesian logic that followed Platonic lines, such as Descartes's proof of the existence of God from an idea in the human mind.
[139] Lamprecht, "The Role of Descartes in Seventeenth-century England," 199, 195.
[140] Quoted in Mark Curtis, *Oxford and Cambridge in Transition, 1558–1642* (Oxford: Clarendon, 1959), 257–58.
[141] Anthony Wood, *Athenæ Oxonienses*, vol. 2 (London, 1692), 620.

mies, semi-secret schools for dissenters from the Anglican church. Because of their precarious existence, we have very little record of their textbooks; however, Charles Morton's leading dissenting academy had both of these logic texts available and Morton, himself, knew them well. J.W. Ashley Smith transcribes available lists of known textbooks used at different academies in his *The Birth of Modern Education: The Contribution of the Dissenting Academies 1660–1800*.[142] The earliest list Smith found was one used sometime before 1698 and shows the typical humanist layering of Ramist, Aristotelian, and Cartesian logic in a curriculum much like that at Harvard. The textbooks were by Heereboord, Burgersdicius, Milton, and Ramus along with what Smith transcribed as *Ars Cogitanda*. Smith cited Jean LeClerc as the author of the *Ars Cogitanda*; however, the text was most likely Arnauld's *Ars Cogitandi*. Jean LeClerc wrote *Logica, sive Ars Ratiocinandi*, which was published in London in 1692. (Another list from around 1700 includes what Smith again calls the *Ars Cogitanda*.[143]) Available evidence points to extensive dissemination and use of *The Port-Royal Logic* in dissenting academies, with at least Morton's using the *Institutio*.

The "stir" about Descartes and the "railing at him" that North saw at Cambridge in 1667 came primarily from neo-Aristotelians whose rantings continued throughout the rest of the century. There were two famous critics of Cartesian logic in the 1690s, both of whom illustrate the sort of Aristotelian criticism in vogue at the end of the century. Their point of attack was on the dogmatic and religious character of *The Port-Royal Logic*, the *Institutio*, and Cartesianism in general. John Sergeant (1622–1707) in his *The Method of Science* (1696) and *Solid Philosophy Asserted, Against the Fancies of the Ideists* (1697), and Henry Aldrich (1648–1710) in his *Artis Logicae Compendium* (1692) both named *The Port-Royal Logic* as a principal source of the popularity of wrong-headed Cartesian

---

[142] J.W. Ashley Smith, "Appendix A," *The Birth of Modern Education: The Contribution of the Dissenting Academies 1660–1800* (London: Independent Press, 1954), 269–286.
[143] Ashley Smith, *The Birth of Modern Education*, 274.

logic; Sergeant went after LeGrand's logic too.[144] Both men feared that Cartesianism would encourage fanatical religion in England.

Sergeant's texts were meant to reform the curricula at the two English universities by attacking *The Port-Royal Logic* and the *Institutio*. Sergeant allowed that Arnauld's text had retained much from scholastic logic, but "it has many unproved suppositions, and bare sayings without offering any proof." Sergeant wrote of the *Institutio*: "Mr. LeGrand's method says much, but proves little; and I believe both [Descartes] and himself, did first consider and survey the whole scheme of their doctrine, and then fitted their logic to it, which is preposterous and praeternatural." Sergeant also criticized *The Port-Royal Logic* for having a pre-set agenda: that Arnauld and whoever else contributed to the text "calculated it for that particular sort of philosophy they had espoused which could bear no evidence."[145]

Sergeant declared that Aristotelian logic was more rigorous, careful, and productive because it emphasized syllogisms and did not get caught up in dreamy subjectivity. Descartes's logic was especially dreamy he thought. In the preface to both *The Method of Science* and *Solid Philosophy Asserted*, Sergeant called Descartes and his followers fanatics and enthusiasts and wrote that their Cartesianism would cause and support other fanatics and enthusiasts. With histrionic language, Sergeant warned that Cartesianism had "dilated itself into diverse nations; and his scholars and followers are of such eminent rank and name" that the philosophy must be stopped. Although correctly noting that Cartesianism relied on "inward means" to knowledge, he found this the "method of fanatics." Like Leibniz's characterization of Cartesianism as "Take what you need, and do as you should, and you will get what you want," Sergeant characterized Cartesianism as "spiritual alchemy" based on "whimsical fancies" ultimately bringing "a kind of enthusiasm to

---

[144] See Sergeant and Aldrich in the *Dictionary of National Biography*. Wilbur S. Howell's *Eighteenth Century British Logic and Rhetoric* discusses both men's logics. For Aldrich there is also a privately printed biography by W.G. Hiscock, *Aldrich of Christ Church 1648–1710* (Oxford, 1960).

[145] John Sergeant, *The Method of Science*, (London, 1696), "Preface Dedicatory," n.p.

philosophy." And for the most cutting critique: "Was ever such Quakerism heard among philosophers?"[146] Sergeant reminded his readers in several works that Descartes discovered "I think, therefore, I am" in a manner not befitting an English gentleman. Descartes "fell for some few days, into a spice of enthusiasm; nay, was brimfull of it; and fancied he had visions and revelations so much that he seemed crack-brained, or to have drunk a cup too much."[147]

Like Sergeant, Aldrich warned against *The Port-Royal Logic*. Aldrich reported its Jansenist roots and described the dogmatic mind of its author. *The Port-Royal Logic* abounds in declamations, Aldrich wrote, "a great many of them superfluous, and all of them arrogant." He continued: "Everything which [Arnauld] puts forth on his own behalf, he pronounces haughtily, as if ex cathedra;" and "he perspires in explaining them as if he were giving assistance to a collapsing world."[148]

Sergeant and Aldrich were right—by the standards of moderate skepticism in England. Aldrich's characterization of Arnauld's logic begins to offer an description of the people who appreciated *The Port-Royal Logic* and an explanation for that appreciation. Sergeant and Aldrich feared that Cartesianism could too easily be put to use by those they considered fanatics—Quakers, Puritans, and Jansenists. But Sergeant and Aldrich are unfair to condemn only Cartesian logic. Ramist logic, as we have seen, could be designed to serve the cause of Puritan "fanatics." And so too could Aristotelian logic.

Sergeant was himself sometimes considered a fanatic, and he was a member of a group of Roman Catholic thinkers, the Blackloists, who promoted Aristotelian logic for the cause of their true religion.

---

[146] Leibniz quoted in Barnard Williams's *Descartes: The Project of Pure Enquiry*, 32; Sergeant, *The Method of Science*, "Preface Dedicatory," n.p.

[147] Lamprecht, "The Role of Descartes in Seventeenth-century England," 213–14; see these characterizations in a more drawn out form in John Sergeant, *Solid Philosophy Asserted*, (London, 1697), "Preface," n.p.

[148] This paragraph is translated by Howell in *Eighteenth Century Logic and Rhetoric*, 55.

Sergeant had converted to Roman Catholicism after college and become a priest. As a Blackloist, he was allied with Kenhelm Digby (1603–1665), who is cited and quoted by both Morton and Brattle. The name Blackloists came from their leader, Thomas White, who sometimes used the alias Blacklo.[149] White's own logic, *Controversy-Logicke, or the Method to Come to Truth in Debates of Religion* (Paris, 1659, enlarged second edition Roan: 1674), was more a Roman Catholic polemic than a logic textbook.

Digby introduced Thomas White to Descartes around 1644, and both men initially had high hopes for Cartesianism as a foundation for rational Christianity against the mitigated skepticism of the Anglicans. Digby and White, however, eventualy withdrew their support from Cartesianism and devoted themselves to Aristotelianism.[150] The essential reasons that such thinkers first embraced Descartes and then pulled back into Aristotelianism involved the implications of Cartesianism on the corporeality of angels, resurrected bodies, and Roman Catholic understanding of the Eucharist. Cartesianism's separation of spirit and matter seemed to destroy the concept of spiritual substance necessary for an orthodox Christian understanding of bodily resurrection and the Eucharist. Also, the role of the senses in gaining knowledge seemed lacking in Cartesianism. Aristotelianism, on the other hand, did not threaten these Christian doctrines and offered a solid foundation against skepticism in the ten Aristotelian categories. The categories delineated characteristics which separated subjects: a number cannot be a substance, an apple cannot be the opposite of a stone, a color cannot be an action.[151] Categories were sources of absolute

---

[149] See Beverley C. Southgate, "'Cauterising Tumour of Pyrrhonism': Blackloism Versus Skepticism," *Journal of the History of Ideas* 53, (1992): 631–645. Southgate, whose *"Covetous of Truth": The Life and Work of Thomas White, 1593–1676*, will be published in 1996, wrote to me that she knows of no connection between LeGrand and the Blackloists.

[150] For Digby and White, see their entries in the *Dictionary of National Biography*; for their interest in Descartes, see Lamprecht, "The Role of Déscartes in Seventeenth-century England," 189–195.

[151] John of Salisbury offers an excellent history and analysis of the importance of categories in *The Metalogicon*, trans. Daniel D. McGarry (Gloucester, MA.: Peter Smith, 1971), 155–165.

certainty useful, among other things, in counteracting assertions of skeptics who doubted the capability of attaining knowledge. Thomas White and the Blackloists relied on the categories as the basis of human certainty to oppose rising skepticism in England.[152] Sergeant and Morton followed.

The neo-Aristotelianism of the late seventeenth century could be turned to "fanatical" use just as could Ramism and Cartesianism. Puritans and Blackloists were dissenters in England and shared the same desire to undermine the rising skepticism of the era with dogmatically-inclined logic.

To sum up, a special branch of humanistic logics was created by Melanchthon which was religiously-oriented, and the logics that followed after him can be divided according to the extent that they emphasize the foundations of dogmatic certainty in both internal and external knowledge, knowledge implanted in the mind by God, and knowledge from testimony which has its certainty confirmed by the Holy Spirit. This idiosyncratic tradition comprises logics from each of the era's dominant types: Aristotelian, Ramist, and Cartesian. The more dogmatic of these logics were for the most part founded by those of strict Augustinian tendencies such as Melanchthon, Richardson, and Arnauld, who emphasized predestination and the necessity of grace in order to use logic rightly and to its fullest potential.

The Puritans were a community of rational Christians using logic. They chose the logics to be taught in their schools with an eye towards supporting their community. In the late seventeenth century, they moved away from Ramist logic and experimented with Aristotelian and Cartesian logics in an effort to find a logic better able to support them in troubled times. Morton and Brattle offered the two most viable options which drew from different parts of the Melanchthon-Richardson-Keckermann-Arnauld tradition of logic.

---

[152] See Southgate, "Blackloism Versus Scepticism," 637.

Charles Morton and *A Logic System*

Norman Fiering names Charles Morton as "America's first professional philosopher."[153] But in the view of New Englanders at the time, Morton was transatlantic Puritanism's most famous educator, a hero who upheld the standards of Puritan education in a time of oppression. Though a hero, Morton did not rest on his laurels in exile; instead, he vigorously continued his work and in the process inspired the young William Brattle and the rising generation of New England's intellectual elite before his death in 1698. His last recorded words were "Excellent things! If I could receive them and live up to them!"[154] Charles Morton was more than a generation older than William Brattle. Brattle met Morton in 1686 when, as a twenty-four-year-old tutor at Harvard, he was awed by the sixty-year-old exile from England who had just arrived on the provincial frontier of America. At Morton's funeral, the scholars of the college walked before the hearse, Brattle and President Mather walked behind. The funeral sermon contrasted the life of the persecuted Puritan educator-hero with "the life of persecutors [which] was as a vapor."[155]

Brattle himself died nineteen years later in 1717, beloved, it seems, by everyone even during the contentious times between the late 1680s and early 1720s. He had been tutor, chaplain, unofficial professor of divinity, and either leader or co-leader of the college for decades. Increase Mather had hoped Brattle might fill Morton's position as vice president of the college, but Brattle, in his humility, turned down the post just as he later turned down election as a fellow of the Royal Society.

Morton and Brattle exemplify Puritanism at its best. They

---

[153] Fiering, *Moral Philosophy at Seventeenth-Century Harvard*, 207.
[154] Samuel Sewall, *The Diary of Samuel Sewall*, vol. 1, ed. M. Halsey Thomas (New York: Farrar, Straus and Giroux, 1973), 391.
[155] Sewall, *The Diary of Samuel Sewall*, vol. 1, 391.

integrated piety and intellect in a way that inspired the generation that led Puritanism into the eighteenth century. Their logic textbooks exemplify the best of late seventeenth-century experiments with humanistic logic and filled Puritanism's need for post-Ramist logics. The influence of their textbooks cannot be separated from the two men's roles as models of rational living. Readers of their textbooks usually knew the authors personally or by reputation. Former students of Morton's praised their teacher and reported that the manuscript textbooks he wrote were for their use and that he "explained" them in his lectures.[156] Notes of his lectures are not extant, but we can surmise how he explained his logic textbook.

A. Charles Morton

Charles Morton was born in Cornwall on February 15, 1626/27, and at age twenty, in 1646, entered Queen's College, Cambridge—Alexander Richardson's old college—when it was fully under Puritan control.[157] In 1649, Morton transferred to Oxford where the Puritans had recently ejected Anglican academics and begun installing teachers of their own persuasion. Morton joined Wadham College. At that time, a scientific circle was being formed around John Wilkins, Wadham's newly appointed warden. Wilkins later became Bishop of Chester after the Restoration and exemplifies the type of moderate Puritan which Morton's conscience could not

---

[156] Edward Calamy, *A Continuation of the Account of the Ministers, Lecturers, Masters, and Fellows of Colleges, and School-masters who were Ejected and Silenced after the Restoration in 1660* (London, 1627), 197.

[157] The best biography of Morton is Samuel Eliot Morison's introduction to volume 33 of the *Publications of the Colonial Society of Massachusetts*, which transcribed the *Compendium Physicae* (hereinafter cited as Morison, "Charles Morton"). Morison's first footnote gives a bibliography of sources, to which should be added J.W. Ashley Smith's discussion of Morton and his curriculum in *The Birth of Modern Education: The Contribution of the Dissenting Academies 1660–1800*, 56–61, and Norman Fiering's chapter on Morton in *Moral Philosophy at Seventeenth-Century Harvard*, 207–238.

emulate.[158] Later, in a vindication of dissenting academies, Morton pointed out the error of pinning morality and piety "to the university's sleeve" since "evil examples" abound at them and "learned men, even philosophers, may be delivered over to a reprobate mind."[159]

It is not clear when Morton left Oxford. He received his MA in 1652, and was a minister to Presbyterians back in Cornwall in 1655. He lost that job in 1660 with the restoration of the crown. He then began preaching privately. Beginning in 1661, Parliament passed a series of repressive acts called the Clarendon Code, and then in 1673 passed the Test Acts which denied non-Anglicans many political rights, especially the right to be a student or teacher at the legally chartered universities. Students and teachers were required to swear an oath of allegiance to the state church and its Thirty-nine Articles. Many moderate Puritans swore the oaths; however, others, such as Morton, were unable to compromise their beliefs and went into a semi-underground culture of dubious legality. Those in the underground were loosely considered Protestant dissenters or Roman Catholic recusants. "Dissenters" describes a variety of nonconformists, but was especially applied to the Calvinistic Puritans who began creating quasi-legal institutions to support their needs—especially the need to educate clergy of their own.[160]

After the Test Acts were passed, private "academies" began to form to take the place of an Oxford or Cambridge education. Students went to live in the home of someone with a reputation for

---

[158] See Barbara Shapiro, *John Wilkins, 1614–1672: An Intellectual Biography* (Berkeley: University of California, 1969). See also the discussion of the intellectual life at Cambridge and Oxford during the late 1640s to 1660 in Mordechai Feingold's "Isaac Barrow: Divine, Scholar, Mathematician," and John Gascoigne "Isaac Barrow's Academic Milieu: Interregnum and Restoration Cambridge" in *Before Newton: The Life and Times of Isaac Barrow*, ed. Mordechai Feingold (Cambridge: Cambridge University, 1990), 22–37, 250–290. Peter Lake's *Moderate Puritans and the Elizabethan Church* (Cambridge: Cambridge, 1982) deals with an earlier period but is a standard introduction to various types of mentalities within Puritanism.

[159] Calamy, *A Continuation of the Account*, 19–93.

[160] See Michael R. Watts, *The Dissenters* (Oxford: Clarendon, 1978), and Herbert McLachlan, *English Education Under the Test Acts: Being the History of the Non-Conformist Academies 1662–1820*, (Manchester: Manchester University, 1931).

ARISTOTELIAN AND CARTESIAN

education who was willing to teach them in exchange for a reasonable amount of money. No charters, licenses, oaths, or institutional traditions hedged in the growth of new house-schools. They offered as good or better a liberal arts education as was available at the universities. The term "academy" was a Platonic reference, but was also associated with the Genevan Academy established by Calvin in 1559, as a Protestant alternative to legally chartered universities. In England, the title "university" and the right to award degrees required a Royal Charter. English dissenters, wanting no legal hassles, chose their terms carefully and made no pretense to offering a degree. (Harvard College in America was far enough away to not worry about the letter of the law and it did offer degrees.)

Most dissenting academies quietly began in the tradition of ministers supplementing their income by tutoring live-in students. Morton probably began tutoring while a minister (he later got in trouble for this in New England) and there was probably a period in the early 1670s when his part-time teaching became full-time. At that point he was living on Newington Green in Stoke Newington on the south edge of London, which was populated by many well-off dissenting families. By the late 1670s, Morton's school was one of the best and most well-known of the quasi-underground academies.[161]

When Morton moved to Newington, another prominent academy already existed on the green, one run by Theophilus Gale (1628–77/78). Gale had been a fellow at Magdalene College, Oxford; he was expelled in 1660, whereupon he started an academy in 1666. Samuel Lee (1625–1691), a minister and college friend of Morton's, was also nearby. Morton, Gale, and Lee made for a sort of intellectual troika for dissenters in Newington—an easy walk from Lambeth Palace, the Bishop of London's residence. The two academies led dissenting education in the late 70s and 80s and continued to be a force even after Morton and Gale were gone. Gale

---

[161] J.L. Tayler's *A Little Corner of London (Newington Green) with its History and Tradition of a Non-Conformist Meeting House* (London, 1925), has a chapter on "The Morton Period and Its Struggle for Personal Freedom," in which pp. 20–29 deal with Morton.

became Lee's colleague in the pulpit just before Lee emigrated to New England in 1678. Gale then turned his academy over to Thomas Rowe (1657–1705). After Morton's academy was shut down, the Gale–Rowe academy carried on. In the early 1690s, Rowe tutored Isaac Watts, who was arguably the most influential educational reformer in the eighteenth and early nineteenth-century Anglo-American world.[162]

Very little is known of the exchange of ideas among the dissenters in Newington, and the relationship between Gale and Morton can only be surmised. Morton was revered for his wide-ranging intellectual activity. Gale was considered one of the brilliant men of that era of intellectual vitality in London. Gale is little remembered today however, probably because though he wrote many books, he devoted his life to writing *The Court of the Gentiles* (1669–77), a very long book. The book was widely read by contemporaries, but historians now tend to dismiss it as a jumble of bad history and philology with an unhappy merging of Cambridge Platonism with Calvinism. Cotton Mather referred to Gale as a "well-known writer." Increase Mather noted in 1681 that Gale had not yet "received his full meed of praise as a theologian."[163] Recently Norman Fiering has published a study on Gale's moral philosophy and its value in the intellectual context of the era.[164] Morton's relationship with Gale is unknown, but we know his attitude about big books: "A great book," he often stated to his students, repeating the old motto, "is a great evil."[165]

Morton wrote short books addressing distinct subjects. Gale synthesized a wide range of ideas into a grand vision. Morton was more conservative. He accepted parts of the newer philosophies but merged them more carefully with older intellectual traditions. This

---

[162] For these men and schools see McLachlan, *English Education under the Test Acts;* Smith, *Birth of Modern Education;* the *Dictionary of National Biography;* and Theodore Hornberger, "Samuel Lee (1625–1691), A Clerical Channel for the Flow of Ideas to Seventeenth-Century New England," *Osiris* 1 (1936): 341–355.

[163] Cotton Mather, "An Account of the University," *Magnalia Christi Americana*, Bk. 4, Introduction, pt. 3, sect. 3.

[164] Fiering, *Moral Philosophy at Seventeenth-Century Harvard*, 279–294.

[165] Calamy, *A Continuation of the Account*, 211.

is what made Morton a better textbook writer—and possibly more influential in the long run.

It is very likely that Gale encouraged Morton to study Roman Catholic thinkers such as the Blackloists, LeGrand, and Arnauld. Gale, who had lived two years in France, appreciated some of the Roman Catholic thinkers. Gale became a proponent of Jansen and Jansenism among English dissenters. Norman Fiering writes that as much as John Norris is called the English Malebranche, Gale should be called the English Jansen.[166] Jansenism, to Gale, was a vigorous and modern Augustinianism that offered an alternative to the intellectual and spiritual laxity spreading in both Protestantism and Catholicism. Gale published this view in *A True Idea of Jansenisme* (1669).

Newington Green, then, was an exciting common on which to live with Gale and Morton teaching in their house-schools. Between the two men, Newington Green offered excellent libraries. Morton's was large and Gale's was enormous by contemporary standards. Gale willed a large portion of his books to Harvard College which by one account doubled the size of the American library.[167] The reputation of the green attracted some of the dissenters' most promising students, and through them comes most of the personal information we have about the academies in Newington. Ironically, one of the best sources for information about Morton is a student who turned antagonist. Samuel Wesley who converted to the established church of England and fathered John and Charles, wrote two famous attacks on dissenting academies. Almost the whole purpose of dissenting academies, Wesley wrote, was to teach "King-killing doctrines" and aversion to the episcopal order.[168] Wesley, however, could not help but appreciate Morton, whom he described as a "good, though mistaken man who was I think, the most consider-

---

[166] Fiering, *Moral Philosophy at Seventeenth-Century Harvard*, 281.
[167] Tutor Henry Flint makes this count; see Morison, *Harvard in the Seventeenth Century*, vol. 1, 290–91.
[168] Samuel Wesley, *A Letter from a Country Divine to His Friend in London Concerning the Education of Dissenters in their Private Academies*, 2nd ed. (London, 1704), 6.

able in England in that way, for the number of his pupils, and politeness of his learning."[169] By Wesley's description, Morton's academy had more to commend it than the one led by Gale/Rowe. Wesley described Morton's academy as

> the most considerable [in England], having annexed a fine garden, bowling-green, fish-pond, and within a laboratory, and some not inconsiderable rarities, with air-pumps, thermometers, and all sorts of mathematical instruments.[170]

Daniel Defoe, Morton's most famous student, also found the academy and its master exemplary of the best dissenting education. Defoe especially praised Morton's innovation of teaching and writing textbooks in English rather than Latin. Students, Defoe declared, learned their languages; "yet it is observed of them, they were by this made masters of the English tongue, and more of them excelled in that particular, than of any school at the time."[171]

Teaching in the vernacular was not formally accepted in the curriculum or classes at established universities on the Continent or in England. The academies, however, sanctioned the use of the vernacular. The book publishing market and broadening visions of education merged to make teaching and writing in the vernacular increasingly common-sensical. The Little Schools of the Jansenists were leaders in educational reforms such as using vernacular texts. *The Port-Royal Logic*, for example, was originally written in French.[172] In England the dissenters picked up on the new trend. Morton was an early proponent, and his justification was innovative and broad-minded. He had students copy his justification into their notebooks when they took down his logic, also presented in English. A student's transcription of that justification is printed in this volume. It shows Morton at his best: wittily poking fun at pedants, extolling the nobility of the English language, hopeful of

---

[169] Wesley, *A Letter*, 5.
[170] Wesley, *A Letter*, 6.
[171] Quoted in Smith, *Birth of Modern Education*, 58.
[172] See Barnard, *The Port-Royalists on Education*.

spreading reasonableness, even to educating women, and supporting the cause of teaching a useful education.

Morton wrote several vernacular textbooks—"manuscripts...for the use of his private academy."[173] Though there is no complete bibliography of these manuscript textbooks, his students later said "there were certain systems of the several arts and sciences, which he drew up for their use."[174] The most famous of these manuscripts is the *Compendium Physicae*, published by the Colonial Society of Massachusetts in 1940 (Vol. 33). Norman Fiering found two other manuscript textbooks in the Harvard Archives: *A System of Ethics* and *Pneumaticks or a treatise...about the Nature of the Spirit*, the latter being the study of spirit (or mind) in theology, angelography, and psychology. Appended to the *Pneumaticks* is *The Souls of Brutes*.[175] Morton's *A Logick System* is published here. These four texts are only known to exist in Harvard student notebooks; however, they were most likely originally written between 1675 and 1685 for students at the Newington academy. For Morton, each was part of a whole, forming—to a large extent—a body of interrelated knowledge. To understand one, all should be studied. Morton was influenced by the seventeenth-century spirit of encyclopedic systemization of knowledge.[176] We "have need of some methodicall frame," Morton wrote in his logic, "to hold things together."[177]

One-volume encyclopedic textbooks were not rare. LeGrand's

---

[173] Arthur O. Norton, "Harvard Text-Books and Reference Books of the Seventeenth Century," *Transactions, Colonial Society of Massachusetts* 28 (1935), 421. Norton only cites Morton's logic and physics textbooks.

[174] Calamy, *A Continuation of the Account*, 197. Samuel Wesley in *A Letter* cited mathematics as Morton's "chiefest excellence" (p. 5), but there is no mathematics in any of the extant textbooks.

[175] Fiering, *Moral Philosophy at Seventeenth-Century Harvard*, 211–227, analyzes these three works and shows their context. The texts appear in the student notebook of Ebenezer Williams, the transcriptions done in February 1708.

[176] Fiering, *Moral Philosophy at Seventeenth-Century Harvard*, 17, and "President Samuel Johnson and the Circle of Knowledge," *William and Mary Quarterly*, 3rd series, 28 (1971): 199–236.

[177] Morton, *A Logick System*, 238 of typescript.

Institutio fits this description. The Dutch published several.[178] In 1704, the English published their first alphabetically organized encyclopedia. Keckermann's schematic drawings were designed in part as a tool to facilitate integrating all parts of the curriculum into one huge schematic system. But, as mentioned previously, Morton did not like big books. Morton liked writing multiple volumes that supported each other.

Aside from Morton's manuscript textbooks, an eighteenth-century account of Morton's life by Edward Calamy cited published works which included social pieces drawn from scripture on peacemaking, pride, and gambling (not cited is an essay purportedly by Morton called *The Great Evil of Health Drinking* (1684)). Calamy also cited speculative pieces by Morton on the Ark of the Covenant and Morton's belief that some migrating birds might literally nest in heaven for a while.[179] On economics, Calamy cited a letter of Morton's written "to prove there is no such absolute need of money as men generally think." In science, Morton's practical suggestions for fertilizing the sandy soil of Cornwall was printed in the *Philosophical Transactions* (April 1675). Calamy, himself, printed complete transcriptions of Morton's twenty-one-page "Vindication" of dissenting academies and thirteen-page "Advice to Candidates for the Ministry, under the present discouraging Circumstances."[180]

The most significant publication of his lifetime was the essay *The Spirit of Man*, published in Boston in 1692. The one-hundred-page essay on the active person whose soul and body are joined was not part of his textbook system but can be juxtaposed with his earlier *Pneumaticks*, which dealt with the soul separated from the body. The spirit of a man which has been sanctified by grace, Morton

---

[178] The most popular Dutch encyclopedist among seventeenth-century Puritans was Johann Heinrich Alsted (1588–1638); see Morison, *Harvard in the Seventeenth Century*, vol. 1, 157–159.

[179] See Cotton Mather's speculation on this that cites a conversation with Morton in *Selected Letters of Cotton Mather*, ed. Kenneth Silverman (Baton Rouge, Louisiana State, 1971), 113–114.

[180] Calamy, *A Continuation of the Account*, 177–211.

claimed, is active and "it disposes him diligently to teach...and diligently to learn; to make diligent search." The "unsanctified" man has a "pitiful, base, and useless spirit; inclining only to sottish sloth and idleness."[181]

While a teacher, his work was his students. His students later declared him "renowned," and even Samuel Wesley, when attacking his school, refused to say anything bad about his teacher. Morton one time pounced on a foolishness as "A sorry sort of arguing!" but such outbursts were meant to be part of "a fatherly way of teaching."[182] In accord with his humanism, Morton wanted to be a father to his students. A father or a tutor, he recommended, should "not make orations, or speeches to his children or scholars," but should speak to them in a "familiar way."[183] In Morton's "Advice to Candidates for the Ministry," Morton merged the role of a minister with those of a father and a tutor. Family, church, and school were entwined in his mind just as they were in his house-school on Newington Green.

The closest Morton comes to explaining a philosophy of education is in *A Logick System* when describing action and passion: Morton likened education to heat passing from a fire to water "so the teachers learning doth not pass into the learner but exciteth a new learning like it self."[184] This shows an educational philosophy probably derived from Augustine's *Concerning the Teacher*. The most important role of a teacher is to awaken an understanding of what God has already communicated into a student's mind. That fundamental knowledge can then be put to use by the student. Morton's logic textbook must be understood in the context of this philosophy.

The role of teacher, then, was not different from that of a Puritan minister—to turn listeners' minds inward to discover what

---

[181] Charles Morton, *Spirit of Man*, (Boston, 1692), 63–64; see also the discussion of divine grace on pp. 23–24. See also Norman Fiering, *Moral Philosophy at Seventeenth-Century Harvard*, 211–227.
[182] Calamy, *A Continuation of the Account*, 191, 200.
[183] Calamy, *A Continuation of the Account*, 200.
[184] Morton, *A Logick System*, 175 of typescript.

is known by the soul and to look for the signs of divine grace. The minister is not an intermediary of knowledge or grace, nor is the teacher. The minister and teacher "exciteth" the "active spirits" in the congregation or classroom. It is not surprising that teaching and ministry were often interchangeable careers. The minister and the teacher hoped to excite all listeners, although they believed the divine grace that creates "active spirits" exists only in the few.

In this light, we can see why Augustinian/Puritan educational philosophy cannot be separated from the doctrine of predestination. In *The Spirit of Man* and in *A Logick System*, Morton speaks of what he calls hot spirits, active spirits, or spirits whose wills are the recipients of divine grace. Morton's educational philosophy and his textbooks primarily served those who believed they were recipients of grace, walking the narrow path rather than the wide path which diverged toward Hell. Morton disdained laxity, laziness, and any easy slide into skepticism. Morton advised young ministers and tutors to flee from "the mongrel worship" of those "who are scarce half friends to the Reformation."[185]

Some of those who have written on Morton in the past have tried to make him more cosmopolitan than he was. Morton, like Brattle, was a moderate and tolerant man, but this should not blind us to the essential Puritan core of both men. Take for example one of Morton's distichs from his logic text:

> Change not in things divine keep what is old
> In Phylosophicals you may be bold—[186]

Like a man propelling a rowboat forward while keeping an eye on a point on the shore to ensure a straight movement, Morton advised students to keep their eyes focused on the past in religious matters so as not to lose their direction.[187]

---

[185] Calamy, *A Continuation of the Account*, 206.
[186] Morton, *A Logick System*, 236 of typescript.
[187] Morton, *A Logick System*, 236 of typescript.

Morton published a long poem in England that is even more revealing of the mentality of dissent that fired his mind. In *Some Meditations on the History recorded in the first fourteen Chapters of Exodus, in Meeter* [date unknown], the Jews are people of conscience in the land of Egypt who are asked to compromise for political reasons:

> Moses, O Moses help me (Pharo'h cryes)
> Go worship now your God, go sacrifice;
> Only let it be in the Land, I pray,
> To going out, reason of state saies nay.
> ...
> You may your own God keep and conscience too
> Though amongst us, like us you seem to do.[188]

No such compromise can be made and the conclusion of the story is that the dissenters win their right to leave. The poem foretells, in a way, Morton's own destiny.

Morton's academy was closed as a result of nit-picking legal persecution used against some of the dissenting academies whose teachers had graduated with an MA from Oxford or Cambridge. The move was cynical and superficial on the part of the prosecutors, cynical since it relied on selective enforcement of a meaningless traditional oath taken at the universities and superficial since there were many academies, such as the other on Newington Green, led by men who had not received an MA from Oxford or Cambridge. Morton got caught in a half-baked purge of dissenting academies and was arrested for perjury—operating so near the bishop's palace probably did not help.

Morton defended himself in his "Vindication," which begins in lawyerly fashion by focusing on definitions and the cynical application of the oath; however, it gains vitriolic momentum throughout. It culminates in exclaiming that the conscience of dissenters prohibits them from attending or sending their children to universities

---

[188] Charles Morton, *Some Meditations on the History Recorded in the First Fourteen Chapters of Exodus, in Meeter* (London, date unknown), 10.

in dire need of reformation. The universities are full of "manifest danger," of "evil examples" and "general looseness" that are "contagious." If "the plague or other contagious disease should fall into the universities," parents would of course remove their children and have them safely taught in private situations. "Now if men may or would do so for securing their bodily lives, they should do so much more with respect to their souls." Thus having declared the universities full of moral diseases that any loving parent would recoil from, Morton further rises in his lost cause to warn about the "learned men" who "have gotten the university preferments into their hands." They "may be delivered over to a reprobate mind, or mind void of judgment." They may nickname "Truth" with their own little ideas, baptizing "their own conceits with the name of orthodoxy." The dissenters are not against universities, he writes, they "desire and pray for [the university's] continuance and reformation, that those fountains may be clear, and then 'tis hoped that the streams which flow from them will be clear also."[189]

The fountains would not be cleared during Morton's lifetime. His defense of dissenting education and criticism of the universities fell on deaf ears. Morton was forced out of business, but found himself sought by Harvard College. Returning home he was "so infested with processes from the bishop's court" that Samuel Eliot Morison surmised he eagerly embraced the opportunity held out to him in New England.[190]

Harvard College was where many dissenters placed their hopes of keeping the fountain clear. Theophilus Gale gave most of his library to Harvard, and later another English dissenter, Thomas Hollis, showered the college with money and its first professorships. Many English dissenters who never saw Harvard were willing to support the college. Puritanism was a transatlantic culture, and Morton was as well known to Harvard as Harvard was to Morton.

New Englanders were especially proud of their college. Cotton Mather in the 1690s devoted book four in his magisterial history of New England to the history of the college and to ten biographies of

---

[189] Calamy, *A Continuation of the Account*, 192–95.
[190] Morison, "Charles Morton," xviii–xix.

ARISTOTELIAN AND CARTESIAN

illustrious graduates. In 1674, the colony, with the generous support of twenty English patrons, erected a new college building, the largest and finest building in all the English colonies. A president's house was erected in 1680.[191] A proud history and two fine buildings graced Harvard when Increase Mather, the acting president, extended the possibility of the presidency to Charles Morton, the dissenters' most illustrious educator in England.

Despite the grandeur of the provincial college, its position was precarious in 1686, and it was that precariousness that prevented Morton the opportunity of being its president. Harvard College as an institution was just as dubiously legal as any dissenting academy in England, actually more so. Unlike the dissenting academies, which carefully tried to avoid any encroachment on the prerogatives of royally charted universities, Harvard claimed a valid charter as a college, not through the king, but the Massachusetts Bay Company charter. Usurping the right of a "university", the college granted degrees, even Doctorate in Divinity or Theology. The only sign of Harvard's wariness about such an action was that it awarded only one doctorate in the seventeenth century—to Increase Mather.[192]

Politically, England began in the late 1680s experimenting with ways to rule New England, and Puritan control of institutions such as Harvard was threatened. The dissenting academies, like the Little Schools of Port-Royal, existed at the displeasure of the state and acted cautiously. Harvard flaunted its freedom until the Puritans' Massachusetts Bay Company charter was revoked, thus revoking Harvard's charter. Harvard's leaders became more politically cautious between 1684 and 1692, when the charter was in question—although it was a period of Harvard's most radical curriculum reforms. In that tenuous time, Morton was tentatively offered the presidency of Harvard if he came to America. Although Morton was more qualified for the presidency than anyone else in New England, to place Morton at the head of the college at that moment would have been tempting the wrath of those who had

---

[191] Bainbridge Bunting, *Harvard: An Architectural History*, comp. Margaret Henderson Floyd (Cambridge: Harvard, 1985), 15–16.
[192] See Morison, *Harvard College in the Seventeenth Century*, vol. 2, 490–491.

shut down his school in England. So, after his arrival in June 1686, the offer was withdrawn and he amicably took another job offered him, that of minister in the neighboring village to Cambridge.

Increase Mather continued to head the college through several administrative reorganizations and was amazingly successful not only in holding things together during more than a decade of political turmoil, but also in encouraging growth and reform. Mather did this by hiring good men and letting them do their work. Mather, himself, was often absent from the college, juggling the whole colony's political and religious problems. At Harvard his great success was to encourage those actually running the college to experiment with the curriculum and to think about the role of Harvard in the British Empire.

Four men ran Harvard for Mather. Charles Morton offered his wisdom regularly as a fellow and later as vice president of the college. William Brattle and John Leverett were two trustworthy tutors Mather hired and who after 1696 filled other roles at the college. William's brother Thomas Brattle eventually came in as treasurer. Mather was not just a figurehead president, but his many activities required that he delegate much authority to these four.

Morton, Brattle, and Leverett were initially charged by Mather with invigorating the college which for some time had been in a "low, sinking state," said Mather.[193] Over the next decade enrollments increased, a long-range building program began, and the curriculum was modernized. The curriculum reforms began with works imported from Morton's academy and were supplemented by textbooks by Brattle and Leverett.[194]

---

[193] "Diary of Increase Mather," *Proceedings of the Massachusetts Historical Society (1855–58)*, 317.

[194] There is no warrant for Samuel E. Morison's statement, "it is difficult to find any positive achievement of Mr. Mather's on behalf of his alma mater," (*Harvard College in the Seventeenth Century*, vol. 2, 504). Mather was in charge; he was a patron for both Morton and Brattle, and his own speeches indicate that he was at the forefront of an invigorated humanist atmosphere at Harvard. See Michael Hall's *The Last Puritan: The Life of Increase Mather* (Middletown: Wesleyan, 1988), 198–201. For the building program which accompanied the curriculum reform, in part instigated by Morton, see Rick Kennedy, "Thomas Brattle, Mathematician-Architect in the Transition of the New England Mind, 1690–1700," *Winterthur Portfolio* 24 (1989): 231–45.

Morton's role as an advisor to Mather, Brattle, and Leverett is evident from the use of his textbooks, his appointment to the first vice presidency, and the college's prominence at his funeral; however, there is very little information about the particulars of Morton's influence. At age sixty and beginning a new pastorate, his direct involvement was probably minimal. Cotton Mather, when writing a history of Harvard in the 1690s, mentioned only the "prudent government" of Brattle and Leverett from 1688 to 1692, when Increase Mather was in England.[195]

Morton certainly did not slide quietly into old age. He was arrested the year after his arrival for preaching that God would replace the new royal government of New England with a revived Puritan government. His trial for sedition ended in acquittal because of a jury made up of the "factious rabble."[196] Morton spent his life on the edge of the law, a member of an outgroup, bent on purity of conscience. Morton was a hot-spirited man full of grace. In 1692, he wrote about spirits like himself in his most important philosophical work. He remained a lively grandfather figure to the college and he thrilled many of the students even in the late 1680s and 1690s, teaching them about modeling the life of reason and responsibility to one's conscience.

Responsibility to one's conscience was an especially dominant idea in that era. Puritans and other dissenters politically relied on the defense that they were merely following their consciences. Morton had proclaimed the dissenters' obligation to their consciences when refusing to send their sons to universities. President Mather, while away from the college in 1691 and pleading the Puritan cause before Queen Mary, told her:

> In New England they are generally those that are called Non-Conformists, but they carry it with all due respect to others....It is not in the power of men to believe what they please, and therefore I think they should not be forced in

---

[195] Cotton Mather, "An Account of the University," *Magnalia Christi Americana*, Bk. 4, Introduction, pt. 2, sect. 6.
[196] Samuel E. Morison, "Charles Morton," xxii.

matters of Religion, contrary to their persuasion and consciences.[197]

In response to their realization that Puritanism in England and America would remain only a minority religion in a larger culture, Mather, Morton, Brattle, and others increasingly emphasized the rights of communities in matters of conscience (their churches, the fellowship of believers). In fact, Morton and Brattle worked the issue of conscience into their logic texts—Morton in his section on "quality" and Brattle in his overall Cartesianism, which was founded on introspection.

Morton's *The Spirit of Man* also discusses the role of conscience. "The Spirit of man," Morton wrote, "is the Candle of the Lord, Searching all Inward Parts of the Belly; not in an Anatomical, but moral sense; The Understanding is set up by God in man (as a Candle) to search and find out by its Exercise, all those Inward Acts and Inclinations which would otherwise lie hidden and undiscovered."[198]

In *The Spirit of Man* he writes that there is a "diversity of spirits" in humans: "the hot, the cold, and the moderate." The moderate and cold made up the majority of people. Puritan ideals were manifested in hot spirits. Morton described himself when he wrote of hot spirits:

> Their firmness is farther fortified by might in the inner-man (Eph. 3.16) whereby they are stedfast, unmoveable, always abounding in the work of the Lord. (I Cor. 15.18) for, if their well considered reasons do fix their purposes; Much more will their well grounded faith establish them. In a work; its own nature is lovely; but grace super-induced renders it most exemplary, amiable, and useful in the world.[199]

Morton recognized the variety of spirits in people, and he believed Christ's threat in the book of Revelations to spit out the

---

[197] Increase Mather, "The Autobiography of Increase Mather," *American Antiquarian Society Proceedings*, New Ser. 71 (1961): 334–335.
[198] Morton, *Spirit of Man*, 12.
[199] Morton, *Spirit of Man*, 87.

luke-warm with the cold. Morton's *A Logick System* was designed as a foundation for "well considered reasons" for hot-spirited minds.

Perry Miller theorized in his massive study, *The New England Mind*, that unrelenting pursuit of rationalism in Puritanism caused a tension between those defending orthodoxy and those pursuing reason that led eventually to a decline in orthodox Puritanism. Morton's logic textbook was designed to have the opposite effect. He offered a foundation for orthodox Puritanism by writing an eclectic Aristotelian logic. Miller's theory may be correct in some cases; however, those who studied Morton's logic, for example Jonathan Edwards, found no tension between defenders of orthodoxy and pursuers of reason.

B. Morton's *A Logick System*

When as a younger man Charles Morton abandoned Cambridge in favor of Oxford, he moved into a stronghold of Aristotelian logic. A list of textbooks recommended to students includes "Aristotle, Porphyry, Boethius, Ammonius, Gilbertus Porretanus, Agricola, Mathesius, Melanchthon, Sturm, his commentator Erythraeus, and Keckermann." The most influential logic textbooks at Oxford were John Case's *Summa Veterum Interpretum in Universam Dialecticam Aristotelis* (1584) and Robert Sanderson's *Logicae Artis Compendium* (1615).[200] Oxford was a bastion of humanistic Aristotelian logic and does not seem to have been too influenced by either Ramist or

---

[200] Ivo Thomas, "Medieval Aftermath: Oxford Logic and Logicians of the Seventeenth Century," *Oxford Studies Presented to Daniel Callus* (Oxford: Clarendon, 1964), 297–311. See also Schmitt, *John Case and Aristotelianism in Renaissance England*, and E.J. Ashworth's introduction to Robert Sanderson, *Logicae Artis Compendium, Language and Logic in the Post-Medieval Period*, and Ashworth, "The Eclipse of Medieval Logic," in *The Cambridge History of Later Medieval Philosophy*, eds. Norman Kretzman, Anthony Kenney, and Jan Pinborg (Cambridge, England: Cambridge, 1982), 787–796.

Cartesian logic.[201] Charles Morton transmitted that Oxford training to his students on Newington Green and brought the tradition with him to Harvard.

A glance at *A Logick System*'s table of contents exposes the text's Aristotelian form. The predicables, antepredicaments, and predicaments which begin the text had begun standard Aristotelian texts for centuries. Morton's blunt statement "A man is not a stone," is the type of self-evident knowledge founded on classifications that Aristotelian logic emphasized. Skepticism was foolishness when it denied the certainty of such a truth, according to Morton. The prominent place of the predicaments (or categories) and the emphasis on substance, quantity, quality, and relation, were also standard in humanistic Aristotelian textbooks. Ramist and Cartesian logics did not begin this way or emphasize these categories. The forced march from predicables through terms and syllogisms to the inevitable "fallacies" had bored centuries of students and inspired outrage in humanistic educators such as Milton and Locke.

A glance at the table of contents, however, does not expose the difference between Morton's use of Aristotelianism and other Aristotelian textbooks such as Thomas White's or Henry Aldrich's. I will guide you to the most interesting parts of Morton's text— those derived from the idiosyncratic tradition developed by Melanchthon that were most useful to the Puritans. Those interested in the history of the standard parts of Morton's Aristotelian logic should turn to the many other studies which are available on the subject.[202]

Before analyzing the non-standard aspects of Morton's text, we must begin by understanding his sources. Morton cited three prin-

---

[201] See W. Henry Kenney, *John Locke and the Oxford Training in Logic and Metaphysics* (Ph.D. dissertation, Saint Louis University, 1959). John Yolton gives no role to Cartesian or Ramist logic at Oxford in the early eighteenth century; see his "Schoolmen, Logic, and Philosophy," *The History of the University of Oxford*, vol. 5, ed. T.H. Aston (Oxford: Clarendon, 1986), 565–593.

[202] The two best sources on the eclectic forms of humanistic Aritotelianism are Charles Schmitt's *John Case and Aristotelianism in Renaissance England* and books and articles by E.J. Ashworth.

cipal sources: Smith, Burgersdijck, and Sanderson.[203] Burgersdijck and Sanderson had both written popular texts in the standard Aristotelian format, with Sanderson's being more religiously inclined than Burgersdijck's. Morton probably used both as basic models for organization and content. Samuel Smith's *Aditus ad Logicam* (Oxford: 1613, with many subsequent editions) was a similar model, but offered a pedagogical extra: it is filled with diagrams like those used by Morton. Morton would have known the *Aditus ad Logicam* from his student years at Oxford. Samuel Smith (1587–1620) was an otherwise obscure fellow at Oxford whose textbook continued to be used at Oxford long after his death.[204] Morton's *A Logic System* was more visionary than the three texts he cited as sources. For starters, Morton wrote in English and all three of the above were written in Latin, and Morton employed an encyclopedic system for his textbooks, which none of his sources used.

Another source Morton probably used was John Prideaux's *Hypomnemata: Logica, Rhetorica, Physica, Metaphysica, Pneumatica, Ethica, Politica, Oeconomica* (Oxford: 1650?), a collection of textbooks gathered in one, which Morton probably read when at Oxford. Prideaux (1578–1650) was Rector of Exeter College, Oxford, then Regis Professor of Divinity, and finally Bishop of Worcester. It is likely he wrote the textbooks when at Oxford for students and later had all the books published together. Prideaux's logic section is Aristotelian and firmly in the religious tradition of Melanchthon. Stylistically, Prideaux's use of bracketted rhymes interspersed in the prose text may have been Morton's model for his own text.

Prideaux and Smith used diagrams. Ainsworth's *Art of Logick* vigorously used diagrams. Keckermann's *Gymnasium* and Jacobi Zabarellae's *Opera Logica* (1582) both used large summary diagrams. Morton's use of diagrams is excessive for the era, but not uncommon.

Morton's use of English was not entirely uncommon. Morton

---

[203] Morton, *A Logick System*, 146 of typescript.
[204] For Smith see the *Dictionary of National Biography*.

probably knew of John Newton's collection of vernacular textbooks which were published in the 1650s–70s.[205] Like Morton's logic, Newton's Aristotelian *An Introduction to the Art of Logick* (1671) began with a preface justifying education in the vernacular.

There were many sources for Morton to draw from and in no case is *A Logick System* wholly innovative. Even Morton's most interesting eccentricity—its three-part chapters of prose, poem, and diagram—was loosely based on a recommendation by a German educational reformer. There are no specific models behind *A Logick System*; rather, there is a general familiarity with the traditional Aristotelian form, the pedagogical experiments of his age, and a viewpoint similar to many late seventeenth-century dogmatists that Aristotelianism was better than Cartesianism as an epistemological foundation to counter the increasing skepticism of the era.

Morton's rejection of Ramist and Cartesian logics is not clearly stated in the textbook, but is quite evident. Morton knew well both *The Port-Royal Logic* and LeGrand's *Institutio*, yet his text shows little influence from either. Given Morton's knowledge of Jansenism from his friend Gale and his reliance on many Cartesian scientific ideas directly lifted from LeGrand's *Institutio* in his science textbook, *Compendium Physicae*, it is surprising that Morton rejected the Cartesian logic of Arnauld and LeGrand.[206]

Morton referred to the "The Jansenist Logick" only to disagree with it.[207] A revealing example of Morton's rejection of *The Port-Royal Logic* is Morton's reference to risibility as a specifically human characteristic. Arnauld had attacked this traditional use of risibility; Morton was unconvinced.[208] Also, Morton's section on method includes no discussion of the importance of geometry as a model for analysis and synthesis and sticks to the pre-Cartesian treatment. *The Port-Royal Logic* also criticized Ramists for too much

---

[205] A bibliography of his textbooks is included in the entry on him in the *Dictionary of National Biography*.
[206] The footnotes to Morton's *Compendium Physicae* by Theodore Hornberger indicate the great extent to which Morton relied on LeGrand in that textbook.
[207] Morton, *A Logick System*, 195 of typescript.
[208] Arnauld, *The Art of Thinking: Port-Royal Logic*, "Second Discourse," 24.

dichotomizing; Morton conceded to the Ramists that dichotomizing was "best for acuracy."[209]

Morton, like other Aristotelians, was unwilling to deny the senses an important role in knowledge. Cartesian logic emphasized perception in the mind and warned of the deceitfulness of the senses, whereas Aristotelianism balanced mental perception with knowledge gained through the senses. At one point in the text Morton tips the balance in favor of the senses: "Individuals are more knowable than species, bec: they are perceived by the senses, species only by reason and speculation."[210] Morton was unwilling to accept the essential Cartesian dichotomy of spirit and matter that turned Cartesians away from considering the senses as capable of providing clear knowledge of something.

Aristotelian categories, definitions of substance, and emphasis on the senses were the key features in Morton's choice of Aristotelianism over Cartesianism or Ramism as the best logic to teach young Puritans. Most importantly, the category of quality offered a place in logic to apply predestinarian theology to the problem of certainty.

The predicament of quality always included "habits or dispositions" which were either "infused or acquired." Aristotle, in his *Categoriae,* calls an "infused habit" an "inborn capacity." Aristotle used the example of a boxer or wrestler who *acquires* the skills of their sport but has *infused* or inborn capacities to be a boxer or wrestler.[211] Logic was not a "habit," but the knowledge that logic worked with was. The quality of being human meant having an *infused* ability to be rational, but logic was *acquired*. Logic textbook authors throughout history could easily make such a distinction without reference to Christianity; however, authors such as Morton considered it an opportunity to stretch the Aristotelian discussion of quality and habit into a particular Christian perspective.

---

[209] Morton, *A Logick System,* 189 of typescript.
[210] Morton, *A Logick System,* 183 of typescript.
[211] See Aristotle, *Categoria,* 8b. 25–30, 10b. 1–5, trans. E.M. Edghill in *The Works of Aristotle,* vol. 1, ed. U.D. Ross (Oxford: Clarendon, 1928).

To see what Morton did, we can compare his section on quality with the sources he recommends. Burgersdijck and Sanderson perfunctorily wrote a standard Christian example: God could infuse people with such things as faith, hope, charity, and the gift of tongues.[212] Samuel Smith stretched it in *Aditus ad Logicam*. Smith included in the discussion of habit the interpretation that Melanchthon/Augustianian infusion is by the grace of the Holy Spirit—extraordinarily—as doctrine into the minds of the Apostles—or ordinarily—as faith into the elect.[213] Morton followed Smith.

Even though Smith and Morton stretched the definition of habit into something more useful to Christians, we can see from Ainsworth/Coke's *The Art of Logick* that Smith and Morton were actually more moderate than some extremists. Ainsworth, the separatist Puritan in Amsterdam, stretched his section on quality to support his concern for "church polity." Like Smith, Ainsworth had "infused" mean a "singular grace of the Holy Ghost into men's minds."[214] However, Ainsworth carried distinctions in habits to such lengths as to distinguish operative practical habits which were "more perfect by the special help of the holy Ghost"; this eventually culminated in distinctions between theology and church polity—a very important point for a separatist Puritan.

Morton's scheme has the predicament of quality relate to the Augustinian understanding of will and assent—similar to Melanchthon's position in *Erotemata Dialectices*. Morton has infused grace incline the human will toward intellectual assent to the certainty of God's Word. Puritans realized that they must accept their minor position in an empire dominated by a church infected with skepticism. Morton's logic supported the Puritan perspective that they were the recipients of a grace that made them the chosen few in a wrong-headed world.

The category of quality as these various authors saw it is best

---

[212] Franco Burgersdijck, *Institutionum Logicarum*, Bk. 1, chap. 6, sect. 4; Robert Sanderson, *Logicae Artis Compendium*, Bk. 1, chap. 11, sect. 3.
[213] Samuel Smith, *Aditus ad Logicam*, 9th ed. (Oxford, 1684), Bk. 1, chap. 10, 34–36.
[214] Coke, *The Art of Logick*, 33.

seen in schematic form (See Figures 1–4). It is the final branches of each diagram which usually indicate the special interest of the author. Just as Ainsworth's final branches deal with what interested him—church polity—Melanchthon's final branches indicate what most interested this most gentle dogmatist—toleration. (Toleration and dogmatism are compatible for Melanchthon and many humanistic logicians.) Morton's final branches also deal with church polity, but from the more ominous perspective of schism and heresy—of which he probably would have accused Ainsworth.

Figure 1: Religion in Melanchthon's Predicament of Quality

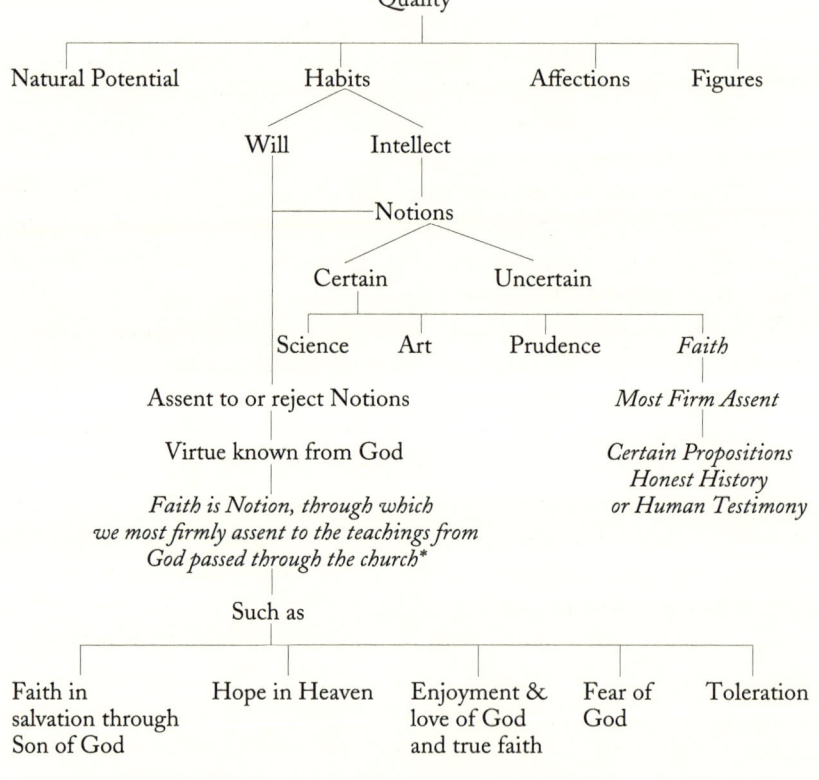

*Italics added for emphasis.

Figure 2: Religion in Burgersdijck's Predicament of Quality

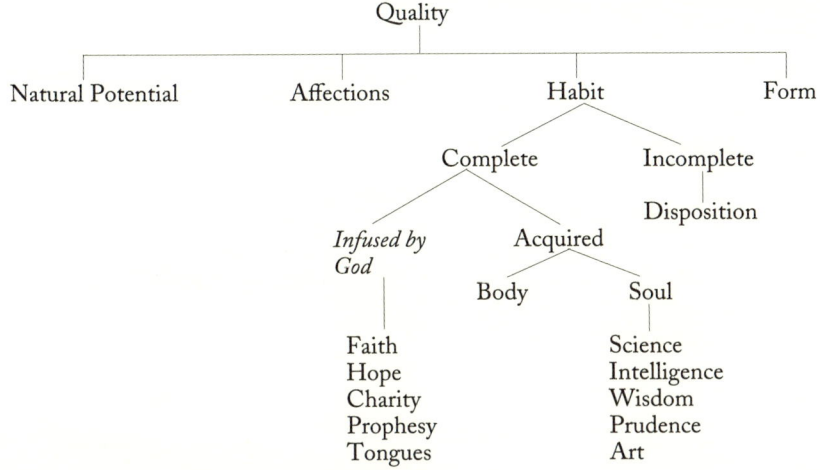

All four schemes are pictures of the way religion was given a role in Aristotelian logic. In three of the diagrams, the role of the Holy Spirit and grace is prominently positioned between the final branches and the genus. It is clear in these logics that Melanchthon, Ainsworth, and Morton considered anyone denying the doctrine of grace or the active help of the Holy Spirit would not be expected to reason completely well.

That vision is not clear cut in Burgersdijck. Burgersdijck gave a standard, serviceable, Christianized version of habit: the infused qualities were the biblical gifts discussed by St. Paul. But Burgersdijck gave only a minimal description. His vision was hardly even religiously-oriented let alone dogmatically-inclined. The possibilities of habit were not elaborated on in his work. In viewing the tables of contents of these various textbooks, there is little to distinguish the various Aristotelian logics of the era; however, the category of quality evidences important differences. The chapters on quality provide windows into the inclinations of the authors and the degree of Christian skepticism or dogmatism that a teacher wanted to convey to his students.

ARISTOTELIAN AND CARTESIAN

Figure 3: Religion in Morton's Predicament of Quality

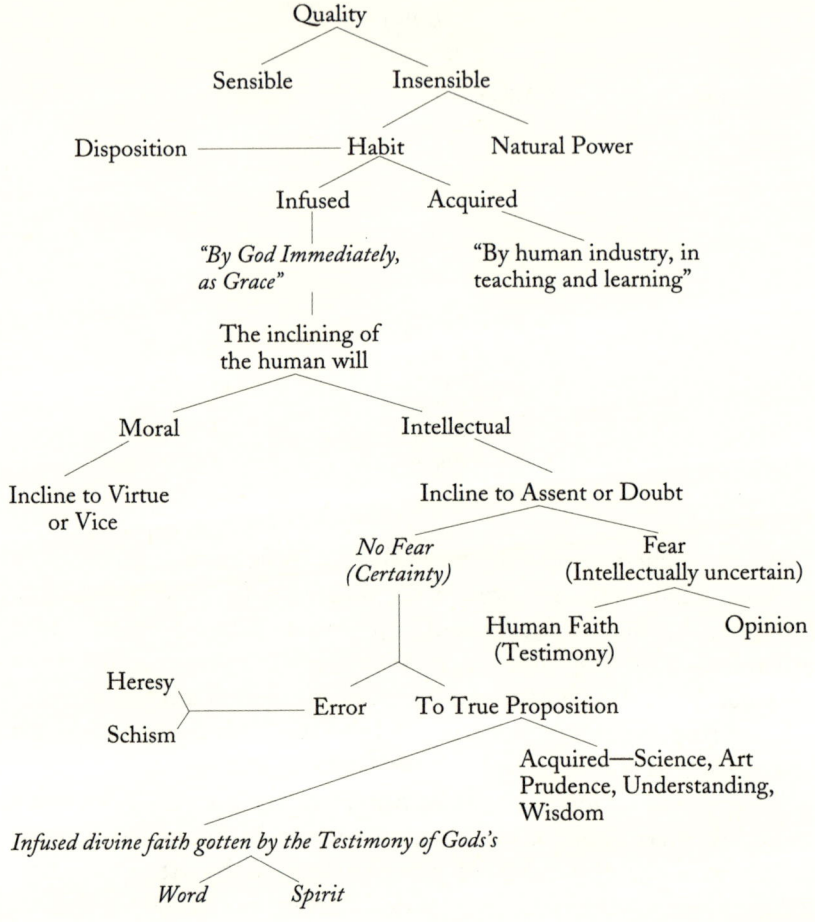

Another idiosyncratic Christianization in Morton's logic lies beneath the seemingly innocuous title "Of Topical Syllogism."[215] This was a common chapter in Aristotelian logics which dealt with syllogisms that require only probabilistic assent. Because of humanist

---

[215] Morton, *A Logick System*, 219 of typescript.

Figure 4: Religion in Ainsworth's Predicament of Quality

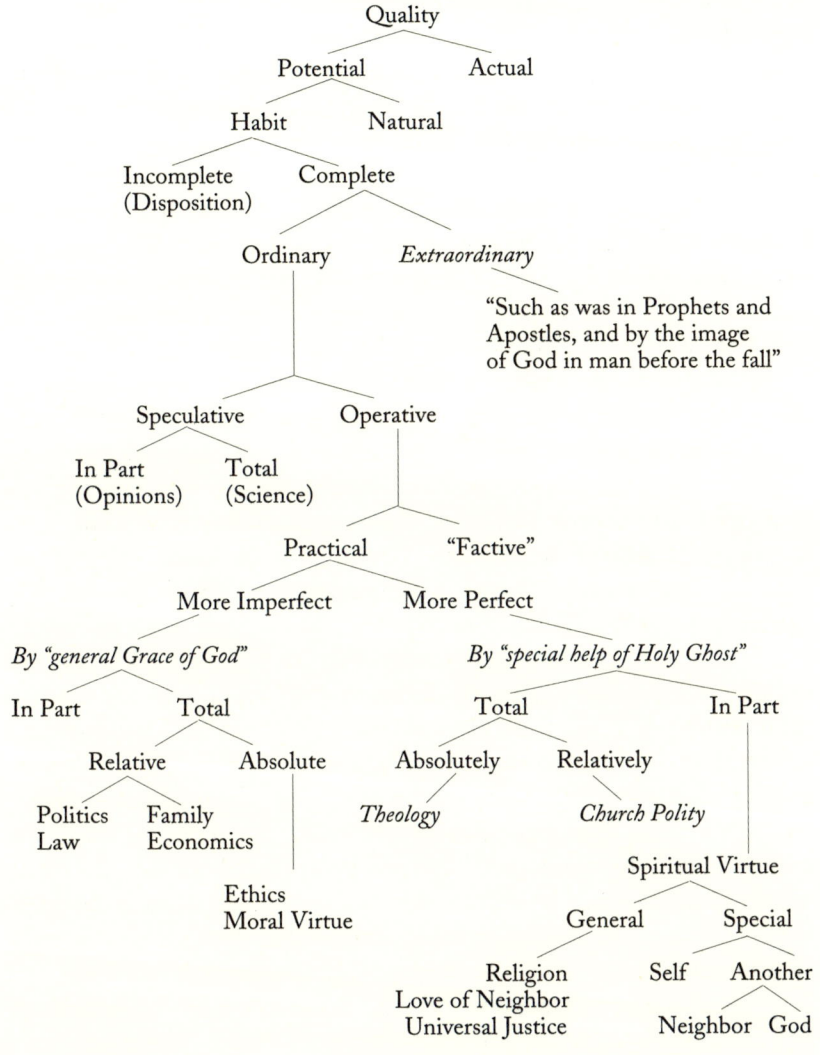

influence, Aristotelian logics diminished emphasis on syllogisms; however, no humanist logic denied the importance of learning basic syllogism types. Among the types, the topical syllogism increased in importance because it fit best with the skeptical tendencies of humanists. Topical syllogisms recognized the weakness of the premise, the weakness of the structure of demonstration, and the weakness of the conclusion. They were the syllogisms of humility and moderate skepticism.

Charles Morton made his chapter on topical syllogisms the biggest chapter in the whole section on syllogisms. Why should a dogmatist emphasize such a chapter? Because a conscientious dogmatist, more than anyone else, is required to draw a clear line between what is probabilistic and what is absolute.

All of the dogmatically-oriented logicians I have been discussing shared the humanist belief that most of what humans do with logic is probabilistic. Humanistic logic emphasized rational decision-making based on non-absolute knowledge. However, the dogmatists needed to clearly delineate the existence of *some* absolute certainty. For dogmatically-oriented Aristotelian logicians, chapters on topical syllogisms, like chapters on quality, were good places to distinguish the probabilistic from the absolute.

Morton's religious intensity obviously rises in this chapter. He quotes 2 Thessalonians 3:2 to imply that unreasonable and wicked men don't use topical syllogisms well. He attacks Quakers as a group that do not use topical syllogisms property—in an obvious effort to distinguish the subjectivity of fanatics from rational subjectivity. He offers terse examples about separation of church and state and that it is better a hand cut off or eye plucked out than the whole man perish. He reiterates the distinction between artificial (internal) and inartificial (external) knowledge showing the certainty attainable from both. He closes with a comparatively long and very idiosyncratic discussion of the certainty of divine testimony and the certainty and uncertainty of types of human testimony.

The chapter on topical syllogisms is the most original and idiosyncratic part of Morton's textbook. Sanderson and Smith, for example, gave the normal cursory overview of topical syllogisms in the *Logicæ Artis Compendium* and *Aditus ad Logicam*, and neither has any of the religious materials or discussion of testimony. Coke/Ainsworth's *The Art of Logick* has a large section on testimony in syllogisms—as should be expected—but did not handle the subject in the way Morton did. As with the category of quality, Morton, however, did have sources to draw from. Melanchthon's *Erotemata Dialectices* is the obvious foundation for the tradition Morton was working in. Melanchthon offered a long discussion of topics under the heading "De Locis Argumentorum," which carefully distinguished probabilistic knowledge from the certainty offered by God both internally in axioms and externally in testimony.[216]

Based on the tradition developed by Melanchthon, Morton's discussion of quality and topical syllogisms turned banal parts of traditional logic into vital discussions. It is easy to imagine Morton, the hot-spirited tutor who saw his job as similar to a minister, using the opportunity of teaching these parts of logic as a means to confirm the dogmatic resolve of Puritan students that they stand on firm knowledge while the rest of the British were falling into a morass of skepticism.

But Morton, himself, did not teach from his logic once he got to Harvard. He offered it to Brattle and Leverett, but Brattle and Leverett were more excited by something else Morton brought: *The Port-Royal Logic* and the *Institutio*. No one opposed Morton's *A Logick System*; however, it apparently fell among other logics, such as Burgersdijck's, that were recommended to students, but were not favored. A tutor might easily point out the parts of Morton that agreed with Cartesian logic, but Morton's *A Logick System* seems to have sunk into a batch of logics mentioned to students in the way described at one dissenting academy:

> Twas our custom to have lectures appointed to certain times, and we began in the morning with logic; the system we read was Hereboord, which is the same generally read at Cambridge. But our tutor always gave us memoriter the harmony or opposition made to him by other logicians.[217]

---

[216] Melanchthon, *Erotemata Dialectices*, Bk. 4, especially 642–652.
[217] *A Defense of the Dissenters Education in their Private Academies* (London, 1703), 4.

ARISTOTELIAN AND CARTESIAN

Three transcriptions of *A Logick System* exist: Partridge's, Timothy Lindall's, written in one month in 1693, and Samuel Dunbar's, composed three weeks in May of 1721—thirty years span the first and last. Interestingly enough, in 1723, Tutor Flynt produced a list of textbooks used at Harvard; it included Brattle's and Burgersdijck's logics, but did not include Morton's.

The greatest interest in Morton's logic appears to have been between late 1697 and 1703 when Jabez Fitch was a tutor. He edited his own very short version of Morton's logic which he used with his students.[218] Dunbar's transcription in 1721 includes both Morton's *A Logick System* and Fitch's *A Treatise of Logick Extracted from Mr. Morton*. In Dunbar's hand, Morton's book is sixty-five pages whereas Fitch's is only sixteen. Fitch became a minister in 1703. The fact that Fitch's trimmed-down version of Morton's text had Morton's full discussion of habit under the category of quality and the essential religious arguments in "Of Topical Syllogisms," sheds light on Fitch's own commitment to Puritan dogmatism.

After Fitch resigned there does not appear to have been much interest in Morton's logic even though Morton's *Compendium Physicae* remained popular at Harvard. Morton's logic had its greatest influence in England where Morton, himself, taught from it. In New England, aside from Tutor Fitch's classes, *A Logick System* remained a viable but seldom-read option.

Cartesian logic was the "new" logic of the era, and its system was more exciting and less technical than an Aristotelianism that had an established reputation for stuffiness and unnecessary complexity. Cartesian logic also had an important advocate: William Brattle. Morton might be the beloved old man in the next town, but Brattle was actually at Harvard, first as tutor and then as the confidant and guide to the tutors. Brattle, whose influence at Harvard was enormous, established Cartesian logic as the dominant logic in the curriculum.

---

[218] See Clifford K. Shipton, *Sibley's Harvard Graduates*, vol. 4 (Cambridge: Harvard, 1933), 201–206.

William Brattle and *A Compendium of Logick*

A. Intellectual Reform in New England's Collapsing World

William Brattle, four years before he met Charles Morton, wrote:

> Reading without understanding is one way to introduce the tongue of a parrot into the head of a rational creature: This heedless reading is that, that hath caused many men parrot-like to talk of things so by rote, and so absurdly, that one would be ready to think, that man might properly suffer the distribution of Animal in genere, into rational and irrational beings.[219]

Brattle, who studied under Morton, never became Morton's parrot. He certainly learned much from Morton, who introduced him to LeGrand's and Arnauld's new logics; but Brattle went his own way—towards Cartesianism—and wrote his own logic textbook.

Brattle went a different direction than Morton possibly because, being one of a new generation of leaders in New England, he understood the intellectual needs of the rising generation better than Morton. Brattle knew the troubles facing Harvard students and young ministers better than Morton, and felt Cartesianism offered better strategies. Brattle and Morton could have been described the way Aldrich had described Arnauld: "perspiring...as if he were giving assistance to a collapsing world."[220] New England *was* a collapsing world in the minds of strict Puritans.

Puritan New England had been in deep trouble since the late 1670s. The threat of Indian wars, French imperialism, rising com-

---

[219] William Brattle, "An Explanation of the Preceding Ephemeris," *An Ephemeris of Cælestial Motions* (Cambridge, 1682), first page of essay.
[220] Translated by Wilbur S. Howell in *Eighteenth-Century British Logic and Rhetoric*, 55.

mercialism, and rapid growth causing an increasingly pluralistic society combined to eat at Puritan assurance in their divinely ordained role as "New English Israel." Their charter was revoked in 1684. In 1686, the year Charles Morton immigrated, New England's first royal governor arrived with an Anglican priest, took control of the colony, and forced the members of South Church to allow Anglican services in their meeting house. Although the governor was exceedingly moderate considering the changes he legally could have forced upon Massachusetts, Puritans interpreted his every act as a blow against their New English Israel.

During the same period, the college seemed to be collapsing. When William Brattle's older brother was a student, Harvard was at the lowest point in its history. Bad leadership had incited its few students to boycott the college in the winter of 1674–75, and with an Indian war in the summer of 1675 draining the economy, few students returned. The president was removed from office, but the new president could not bring the college out of its dismal state. The average size of the graduating class during the years William Brattle was a student declined to about four.[221]

Puritans feared collapse and inquired of God and each other what could be done to shore up the walls of their Jerusalem. The Salem witch trials in 1692 may be seen as a misguided response to the collapse of the Puritan commonwealth and town culture. Divisive debates between friends and colleagues on church membership, baptism, and minor ecclesiastical procedures were also misguided responses to the economic, political, and spiritual problems of the times.

Many people, however, productively faced the needs of the era. The 1680s and 1690s was a period of great creative response—Congregationalists adjusted themselves to an imposed cosmopolitan situation which included religious toleration, increased secularization of politics, and acceptance of a dissenting position in an empire with a state church. Much of the most creative thinking came from young men graduating from Harvard from the late eighties to the

---

[221] Morison, *Harvard in the Seventeenth Century*, vol. 2, 423.

turn of the century—young men who were taught by Brattle and Leverett. Significant reforms were accomplished such as strengthening ministerial power, broadening church membership, and downplaying the distinctive ecclesiastical procedures developed earlier in the century. This last reform served to help New England Puritans feel greater unity with dissenters in England, Presbyterians in Scotland, and various Calvinists in Europe—their natural allies. The foundation of all these reforms was in logic. Logic offered the rational strategies to guide reform. At some point in the late seventeenth century, Harvard increased the amount of time devoted to teaching logic. After graduation, the young clergy emphasized more strongly the importance of rationalism working hand-in-hand with piety to guide the reform movement. William Brattle's logic textbooks were at the foundation of this reform movement.

B. The *Compendium of Logick*

From 1687 until at least 1743, probably until 1767, Brattle's *Compendium of Logick* or the textbooks based on it made Cartesian logic dominant at Harvard. The logic served New England in the manner generalized by Norman Fiering: "the long term impetus in America was toward philosophical structures that would reinforce and protect the essential elements of the inherited religious tradition."[222]

This is not to say that Cartesianism was introduced to Harvard in Brattle's logic. Cartesianism as a philosophy and science had been gaining a foothold at Harvard already in the middle 1680s. The year before Brattle wrote his version of LeGrand's *Institutio*, Nathaniel Mather, reviewing the masters' theses of the last few years, wrote from Dublin to his brother Increase, "I perceive the Cartesian philosophy begins to obteyn in New England."[223] Descartes's works had been published for half a century and copies

[222] Fiering, *Moral Philosophy at Seventeenth-Century Harvard*, 241.
[223] Nathaniel Mather to Increase Mather, *Massachusetts Historical Society Collections*, ser. 4, vol. 8, 63.

were owned in New England. A Harvard student named Benjamin Lynde bought a copy of Descartes's *Opera Philosophica* (Amsterdam, 1656) in January 1686.[224]

Cartesianism had already entered the Harvard curriculum in bits and pieces through English mechanical philosophy and mathematics. It also entered through books and textbooks coming from Holland, a country with a close theological relationship with New England and where Descartes lived and published from 1628 to 1649.[225] By 1692, Cartesianism had gained so much attention in New England that the term was used imprecisely by the judges in the Salem witch trials as an explanation for how the "evil eye" works.[226]

In the 1680s, the term Cartesianism gained the cachet of intellectual glamour which Newtonianism would gain a few decades later. Many New England Puritans found in Cartesianism—just as Henry More had in his own early works—a philosophical fortress which emphasized the spiritual over the physical and focused attention on the activity of God in the human mind/soul.

Cartesian logic is recognized by its overall form. Rather than

---

[224] Besides Lynde's book, Norton's "Harvard Text-Books and Reference Books of the Seventeenth Century" (p. 402), lists a copy of the *Meditations* (Amsterdam, 1654) passed between three Harvard students beginning in 1658.

[225] Thomas McGahagan, in his *Cartesianism in the Netherlands, 1639–1676; The New Science and the Calvinist Counter-Reformation* (Ph.D. diss, University of Pennsylvania, 1976), discusses the Cartesian influence on authors popular at Harvard such as Franco Burgersdijck and Adrien Heereboord; however, he writes that "the leading opponents of Cartesianism in the Netherlands were those influenced by English Puritanism" and that "the assumption that Cartesianism was religiously neutral, if not conservative, must be tested against the failure of the anti-Cartesians to see matters so" (2). Brattle's logic shows that—at least in logic— a very different situation existed in New England. See the comparable reactions to Cartesianism at the universities of Utrecht and Leiden in Theo Verbeek, *Descartes and the Dutch: Early Reactions to Cartesian Philosophy 1637–1650* (Carbondale, Il.: Southern Illinois University, 1992), and the Academy in Geneva in Heyd, *Between Orthodoxy and The Enlightenment*, and Klauber, "Reason, Revelation, and Cartesianism," 326–339.

[226] "Letter of Thomas Brattle," *Narratives of the Witchcraft Cases 1648–1706*, ed. George Lincoln Burr (New York: Charles Scribner's Sons, 1914), 171–172. See also Rick Kennedy, "Thomas Brattle and the Scientific Provincialism of New England, 1680–1713," *The New England Quarterly* 63 (1990): 592–594.

beginning with separating genus and species and further categorization, then concluding with a long discussion of types of syllogisms, as was the usual form of Aristotelian logic, Cartesian logic progresses from an emphasis on what is known in the mind to an emphasis on a method of analysis and synthesis modeled after the rules of geometry. Rather than being mired in technical definitions and matching types of arguments to types of syllogisms, Cartesian logic deemphasizes such technical matters and calls for an easier and more "natural" method of constructing new knowledge based on simple introspection. Descartes's *Rules for the Direction of the Mind* and *Principles of Philosophy* were models, but authors such as Arnauld more fully developed the form into a usable textbook format. Brattle's four-part text—Perception, Judgment, Reasoning, and Method—was the standard format of most Cartesian logics. The first and last parts were usually the most distinctive because the first part dealt with Cartesian epistemology and the last summarized the whole by emphasizing the model of geometry. Many Cartesian textbooks gave more space to syllogisms, topics, and other more traditional components of logic, but the core was always on analysis and synthesis.

At Harvard there were several Cartesian logic textbooks written, each with variations on the basic format. Brattle's *Compendium of Logick* was the first and most fully developed. Then, after Increase Mather returned from England in 1692, Brattle and Leverett wrote two more Cartesian logic textbooks in Latin, rather than English, and condensed into the form of catechisms. (Mather apparently encouraged the tutors to return to Latin and write short catechisms. Mather's own Latin catechism in Ramist logic was resurrected the year of his return and appears in a student notebook.)[227] John Leverett produced a condensation of Brattle and LeGrand titled *Compendium Logicae Vera, Renati Descartes Collectae in usum Pupillorum* (1692). Brattle composed *Compendium Logicae secundum Principia D: Renati Des-Cartes propositum in usum Pupillorum* (c. 1692).

[227] Mather's textbook is included in the 1692–1693 notebook of Walter Prince at the American Antiquarian Society; Leverett's was transcribed in 1720 by Stephen Greenleaf into the notebook of Daniel Greenleaf at the Massachusetts Historical Society.

ARISTOTELIAN AND CARTESIAN

Although most students were exposed to somewhere between three to eight logic textbooks, Brattle's *Compendium of Logick* became the favored or standard text. By 1723, Brattle had died, but a textbook list submitted to the Overseers at Harvard still named Brattle's work as mandatory. The list comprised: Ramus, Burgersdijk, and "a manuscript called the new logic extracted from LeGrand and Ars Cogitandi."[228] This last was Brattle's *Compendium of Logick*.

The various sizes and number of manuscript logic textbooks available is most visible in Stephen Greenleaf's transcriptions into his notebook, all done in one hand in a short period of time. Four logics were transcribed: Fitch's extract from Morton (twelve pages), Brattle's catechism (thirty-three pages), Brattle's *Compendium of Logick* (fifty-two pages) and Leverett's *Compendium Logicae Vera* (thirty-nine pages). Given the question and response format of Leverett's and Brattle's catechisms, the *Compendium of Logick* has around three times more information in it than the others. Non-manuscript textbooks such as Richardson's *Logicians School-Master* continued to be discussed in class; however, Richardson's role in the curriculum had clearly declined by 1753, when a student wrote in his copy:

The Author's knowledge sure was great,
But it is grown now out of date.[229]

The 1723 textbook list called Cartesian logic the "new logic." In 1718, a 1709 graduate of Harvard wrote that his father was "well acquainted with the Philosophy & Logick in reputation in his day"—taking it for granted that a new logic ruled his own time.[230] Many have thought that the "new logic" was Lockean. Benjamin

---

[228] Henry Flynt, "A Particular Account of the Present Stated Excercises Enjoyned the Students," is printed in Morison's *Harvard College in the Seventeenth Century*, vol. 1, 146–147.

[229] Quoted in Norton, "Harvard Text-Books and Reference Books of the Seventeenth Century," 426.

[230] John Barnard, "An Autobiographical Fragment," *Congregational Quarterly* 4, (1862): 381.

Rand, in his history of philosophical instruction at Harvard, considered it "doubtless" that the tutors "moulded their instruction" on Locke's *Essay Concerning Human Understanding* soon after 1690, but he offered no evidence of its regular use in the curriculum until 1743, when in fact the *Essay* joined Brattle's logic in the curriculum.[231]

First Cartesian logic then later both Cartesian and Lockean logic were called the "new logic." Harvard tutors do not seem to have pitted Lockean logic against Cartesian during the first half of the eighteenth century. One reason for this may be that Locke's *Essay* was so long that teachers and students relied on edited versions which often diminished the distinctions between Locke and Descartes, for example Jean LeClerc's "short preview" of Locke's *Essay*, which appeared in periodicals and eventually in a single-volume collection called *The Young Students Library, containing Extracts and Abridgments of the Most Valuable Books Printed in England and in the Foreign Journals* (1692). This magazine version of Locke was probably what most Harvard students read since it was in Harvard's library by 1723.[232] Another popular example is John Wynne's *An Abridgement of Mr Locke's Essay Concerning Human Understanding* (1731), which excised Locke's most inflammatory statements against Cartesianism, including the whole of book one.[233]

Harvard taught Lockean and Cartesian thought jointly and did not present the differences between the two. Brattle's logic was not officially removed from the curriculum until 1767, when the tutorial system of instruction was reformed and the first of a series of specific Instructors in Logic was named. These tutors preferred to

---

[231] Benjamin Rand, "Philosophical Instruction in Harvard University from 1636 to 1900," *Harvard Graduates Magazine* 37 (1928–29): 36; see also Thomas Siegel, *Governance and Curriculum at Harvard College in the 18th Century*, 329, 378–388, for evidence of the use of Locke's *Essay* before 1743.

[232] See Norman Fiering, "The Transatlantic Republic of Letters: A Note on the Circulation of Learned Periodicals to Early Eighteenth-Century America," *William and Mary Quarterly*, ser. 3, 33 (1976): 648–650.

[233] See the introduction by J.G.A. Rogers to John Wynne, *An Abridgement of Mr. Locke's Essay Concerning Human Understanding* (Bristol: Thoemmes, 1990).

teach from Isaac Watts's logic—which merged Lockean logic with ideas rooted in *The Port-Royal Logic*.

By the second quarter of the eighteenth century, Brattle's *Compendium of Logick* diminished in use probably because textbook publishing began to develop. *The Young Students Library* was one among many new published sources which supplanted the use of manuscript notebooks passed through generations. The textbook trade was a growing industry in the seventeenth and eighteenth century and reflected teaching trends in the expanding education market. In New England the market for texts surpassed the cost of production finally in 1735, at which time a textbook based on Brattle's Latin catechism was published as the *Compendium Logicae Secundum Principia D. Renati Cartesii*. This was New England's first published logic textbook, and the venture was profitable enough that a new edition was released in 1758.[234] This text is listed in all modern indexes and histories under Brattle's authorship, but this is a mistake. An editor exhibited great freedom in putting it together and the published work is so different from the original source that it was published without naming Brattle as the author. The most interesting parts of the published *Compendium* are the footnotes in the "Prolegomenon" which cite Locke, More, and others. These footnotes show how the editor and a tutor freely merged ideas from thinkers who are often categorized as antagonists to Cartesianism.

The title page of Brattle's original *Compendium of Logick* proclaims its derivation from LeGrand's *Institutio* and the systems of others. Brattle was a creative compiler in the juxtapositions, order, and eclectic use of his sources. Brattle began with a prolegomenon so students could get a quick overview of the whole text. The style of Brattle's preface sets it firmly in the lineage of LeGrand's *Institutio* and other straightforward textbooks which eschewed the more literary model of *The Port-Royal Logic*'s introduction. The

---

[234] The 1758 edition was published by Johanne Draper. Thomas Siegel in *Governance and Curriculum at Harvard College in the 18th Century*, 277–279, discusses developments in the type and use of textbooks. Siegel in footnotes, 387–388, speculates on the reasons for publication and the possible editors/authors, proposing "Nathan Prince, perhaps with the help of Henry Flynt."

prolegomenon also establishes Brattle's use of LeGrand's expanded 1680 edition of the *Institutio* instead of the shorter 1672 edition: the first statement, that the mind is "obnoxious to much error" in the search for truth and good, is taken directly from the 1680 edition.

Brattle appreciated LeGrand's succinct language, but added Arnauld's ideas where he thought appropriate. In a few places, Brattle turned to other sources, but mostly he relied on LeGrand and Arnauld, the dynamics of which merging are evident in the definition of logic. Sometimes Brattle freely changed the organization such as the placement of a summary of Cartesian Rules of Truth in the prolegomenon. LeGrand used the stock humanistic phrase that logic is "the art of *right* thinking," whereas Brattle used the phrase advocated by Arnauld that logic is just the "art of thinking." Brattle explained that although the adjective *right* "makes a better sound, and at first sight may seem needful, yet on due search is found to be needless, yea inaccurate," since Aristotle shows that the term art implies doing something right.[235] Brattle's criticism was lifted directly from Arnauld's "second discourse" which was added to *The Port-Royal Logic* in 1664 and appeared in subsequent editions.

The process of drawing from LeGrand and Arnauld while contributing his own twist to the book is best seen in Brattle's discussion of the ten categories or predicaments which the Aristotelians emphasized—remember the crucial importance of the category of quality to religiously-oriented Aristotelians. Brattle's description of the ten predicaments comes from *The Port-Royal Logic* and it is the most explicit difference between Morton's and Brattle's texts. Morton explicitly encouraged the use of the ten predicaments. Brattle stated that the ten predicaments "are altogether unprofitable." Arnauld had only stated that the ten "are in themselves of little use."[236] Brattle made his adamant declaration based on the two criticisms he found

---

[235] Brattle, *Compendium of Logick*, 257 of typescript.
[236] Brattle, *Compendium of Logick*, 269 of typescript; and Arnauld, *The Art of Thinking: Port-Royal Logic*, Bk. 1, chap. 3.

in LeGrand: 1) that Aristotelians irrationally divide *ens* into substance and accidents, and 2) that the predicaments do not all make sense.[237] Having justified his strong statement, Brattle then went back to *The Port-Royal Logic* to show that the ten predicaments can be rearranged into seven, proving his point with a distich from *The Port-Royal Logic*.[238] Brattle ended the section by leaving both the *Institutio* and *The Port-Royal Logic* behind by offering a long quote from Kenhelm Digby—one of the Blackloists who influenced Morton—declaring that "the doctrine of the predicaments as it is now taught by the Aristotelians...never was taught or thought of by Aristotle."[239]

It would be tedious to go through the whole of Brattle's editing; however, the example of the ten predicaments indicates Brattle was more than simply a compiler or editor. He at times inserted strong personal statements into the text and promoted his own position by avoiding, deleting, or juxtaposing passages from the *Institutio* and *The Port-Royal Logic*. The creativity is limited, as is true of most textbooks, which are frequently formulaic. However, we can see the core position of the book—its Cartesianism.

The core formula begins with natural introspection, from which it builds. "Reason innate with us is the foundation," Brattle wrote. Then, logic, the techniques of reasoning, is "framed and superstructed" on what was innate in order better to attain certainty, to detect errors, and better understand the workings of the mind.[240] Cartesian logic was a simplified structure, which emphasized a method of beginning with doubting and yielding certainty—an alliance of analysis and synthesis. Arnauld introduced one of the most persistent images of this essential method: the descent into a

---

[237] Brattle, *Compendium of Logick*, 269 of typescript, and Blome, 19.
[238] Distich in Arnauld, *The Art of Thinking: Port-Royal Logic*, Bk. 1, chap. 3, 44, and Brattle *Compendium of Logick*, 270 of typescript.
[239] Brattle, *Compendium of Logick*, 272 of typescript.
[240] Brattle, *Compendium of Logick*, 259 of typescript.

LOGIC AT HARVARD

valley and ascent up the mountain of knowledge. LeGrand and Brattle were firmly Cartesian in this regard and repeated Arnauld's image of traveling down into the valley and on up the mountain.[241]

"If we would philosophize in earnest," Brattle wrote using the standard Cartesian phrase, "we must lay aside all the prejudices of infancy and youth."[242] Doubt, however, must be understood only as a means to truth, not an end. Whereas "a skeptick," Brattle wrote, was full of "folly and unreasonableness," "to doubt of things and to suppose them to be all false only for the obtaining of more full and direct knowledge is a laudable method."[243] Having doubted with common sense and for the right purpose, "we infallibly prove a truth and demonstrate the same to others."[244] The journey is triumphant.

Typical of Cartesian logics, the fourth part of the book emphasizes logic's dynamic ability to expand intellectual certainty in a way analogous to the method of geometry. Euclidian geometry starts with a few axioms and builds on those. Compare the short discussions of method and demonstration in non-Cartesian logics with the long final section on analysis and synthesis, geometrical method, and rules of truth in the *Compendium of Logick*. Lists of rules are common in Cartesian logics, and Brattle begins and ends his text with such lists.

The emphasis on "Rules of truth" come from Descartes's own *Rules for the Direction of the Mind* which was written in 1628, although not published until 1684 in Dutch, and 1701 in Latin.[245]

---

[241] Brattle, *Compendium of Logick*, Bk. 4, chap 2; LeGrand *Institutio* Bk. 4, chap. 21, sect. 13 (p. 98 of Latin); derived from Arnauld, *The Art of Thinking: Port-Royal Logic*, Bk. 4, chap. 9, 328. For the best discussion of the method and especially its influence on Locke, see Peter Schouls *The Imposition of Method: A Study of Descartes and Locke* (Oxford: Clarendon, 1980), 9–21, in which Schouls uses the terms resolution and composition instead of analysis and synthesis.

[242] Brattle, *Compendium of Logick*, "Prolegomenon," chap. 3, 16; for equivalent, LeGrand, *Institutio*, Pt. 1, chap. 2, sect. 3.

[243] Brattle, *Compendium of Logick*, "Prolegomenon," chap. 3, 18; adapted from LeGrand, *Institutio* Pt. 1, chap. 2, sect. 3–4.

[244] Brattle, *Compendium of Logick*, "Prolegomenon," chap. 1, 8; for equivalent, LeGrand, *Institutio* "Prolegomenon," chap. 1, sect. 13.

[245] Descartes, *Rules for the Direction of the Mind in Philosophical Writings*, vol. 1, 7–78.

ARISTOTELIAN AND CARTESIAN

Arnauld, when writing *The Port-Royal Logic*, had a manuscript copy.[246] LeGrand probably did not have a copy of Descartes's *Rules* and relied on Arnauld; however, LeGrand organized his whole logic around explaining ten "rules of truth" which dealt primarily with analysis rather than synthesis. Arnauld offered sets of rules different from those offered by LeGrand, which dealt primarily with analysis, before giving eight over-arching rules as "the method of science." Brattle, when writing his *Compendium of Logick*, chose to summarize LeGrand's ten rules in his "Prolegomenon" and copied almost exactly Arnauld's eight rules at the end of book four. Brattle's first list of rules focuses on perception of ideas and axioms; his final set are clustered in twos and address definitions, axioms, demonstration, and method (ordering).

Although rule oriented, Cartesian logic insists that the rules must be natural, honest, and not overemphasized. Rule six calls for no "abuse" of ambiguity of which overzealous Aristotelians were guilty. Rule seven calls for "handling things, as much as we can, according to natural order." Brattle explains the "as far as we can" as that logicians can be too rigorous in their application of rules, which leads them astray of common sense.

Brattle wrote in the same spirit as Arnauld, who wrote often of "common sense" and believed logic was best used by "fair people" using their "native wit."[247] The spirit of fairness and understanding the limits of human minds softens and balances the dynamic dogmatism of Cartesian logic. Fair people using natural wit, in rule eight, can dissect a genus into its species just as Aristotelian logic advises without falling into the reductive and stifling mentality associated with scholasticism.

The *Compendium of Logick* is dynamic and yet moderate. Unwarranted skepticism is destroyed. The Anglicans' intellectual laxity is implicitly condemned, and Puritan assurance is affirmed—all this while recommending introspection, natural reason, common

---

[246] See the footnote by Dickoff and James in Arnauld, *The Art of Thinking: Port-Royal Logic*, 302.
[247] See especially Arnauld *The Art of Thinking: Port-Royal Logic*, "Second Discourse [1664], 28, and Bk. 3, chap. 9, 204.

sense, and an understanding of the limits of the human mind. Humility and dogmatic firmness characterized Brattle's logic textbook. Having given an overall introduction to the text's Cartesianism and closing with the type of humility advocated, we can now look at its specific support of scientific certainty of divine testimony. The dogmatic quality of Brattle's logic can best be seen if we compare the section where he delineates levels of certainty for modes of knowledge with the "normal" Anglican and latitudinarian delineations that Barbara Shapiro in *Probability and Certainty in Seventeenth-Century England* culled from books by the intellectual elite of England (Figure 5).

Figure 5: Shapiro's Degrees of Assent

KNOWLEDGE	METHOD	CERTAINTY
God's Knowledge	None	Absolute, infallible certainty
Science A: mathematics, metaphysics (in part)	Logic, mathematical demonstration	Compelled assent
Science B: direct or intuitive knowledge	Immediate sense experience, introspection	More than moral certainty
Belief: Religious belief, history, & conclusions about everyday life	Observation, analysis of reports of others of their observations	Moral certainty at best
Opinion	Gathering evidence including second-hand reports of sense observation & reports of other opinions	Probability, "mere" probability, plausibility

ARISTOTELIAN AND CARTESIAN

In Shapiro's delineation, note that "Belief" encompasses most of religion; yet, "Science B" contained the moral precepts of Christianity. Religion on Shapiro's scale had no absolute certainty, not even the compelled assent of mathematical demonstration. Of this era in epistemology, Shapiro writes that the "quest for certitude was not abandoned, but it soon became evident that only mathematics and a few logical metaphysical principles were capable of demonstration in the strict sense."[248]

Although true as a broad generalization of the leading intellects of the age, Shapiro's diagram ignores the epistemological categories used by Christian dogmatists throughout the empire. Many dogmatists, such as the Puritans in New England, were willing to categorize many aspects of religion into "Belief" and "Opinion" (and/or "Mystery"); however, the central core of their theology was categorized as absolutely certain. The following diagram reflects the epistemological categories used by Arnauld, LeGrand, and Brattle: (Figure 6).

Brattle derived his section on levels of certainty from the *Institutio* and *The Port-Royal Logic*. In the *Institutio* and *The Port-Royal Logic*, divine testimony is listed among a set of axioms from which to build mathematical demonstrations. Both LeGrand and Arnauld indicated that divine testimony actually yields a higher level of certainty than any axiom. LeGrand wrote it this way: "the testimony of a being sovereignly intelligent, wise, and true is of greater efficacy to persuade, than any other of the most strong and evident reasons that may be." Then as an example, LeGrand used a biblical quote: "Thus since God tells us that they are blessed who are persecuted for righteousness sake, we are to hold it for an undoubted truth." It was an apt example for Jansenists, Puritans, and English Roman Catholics—each a group persecuted for righteousness sake.

Brattle, following his sources, also distinguished between science, opinion, error, and faith. These categories were derived from

---

[248] Shapiro, *Probability and Certainty in Seventeenth-century England: A Study of the Relationships between Natural Science, Religion, History, Law, and Literature* (Princeton: Princeton University, 1983), 4–5, 29.

Figure 6: Brattle's Degrees of Assent

KNOWLEDGE	METHOD	CERTAINTY
Science or Faith A: Knowledge Revealed by God	Science derived from mathematical/geometrical demonstration based on clear & distinct axioms; Faith A derived from clear divine testimony which can stand alone as a conclusion or serve as an axiom for Science	Absolute certainty
Opinion	Unable to demonstrate with mathematical certainty nor derived from divine authority	Attended with fear or wavering of understanding
Faith B	Based on human testimony (history, hearsay knowledge)	True or doubtful according to the differences of authority upon which it relies

Augustine's *On the Profit of Believing* and could be found increasingly in humanistic logics of all types since they were important concerns of the era.[249]

---

[249] Arnauld cites Augustine on "understanding, belief, and opinion" in his "Fourth Set of Objections" (Descartes, *Philosophical Writings*, vol. 2, 152); in *The Art of Thinking: Port-Royal Logic*, Bk. 4, chap. 1, 293–94.

"Science," Brattle wrote, "is that certain and evident knowledge which we have of anything." Opinion "is not plainly certain knowledge but is attended with a certain fear or wavering of the understanding." Faith "is a proposition grounded on the testimony of another, which may be true or doubtful according to the difference of the authority on which it relies. Thus the faith which we have in God is most firm because we know that he is true and cannot lie. But human faith has always something of uncertainty in it."[250]

Note the two levels of "faith". One is human and one is divine (Faith A and B in the diagram). As with Arnauld, LeGrand, Morton, Richardson, and all the way back to Melanchthon, the faith based on divine testimony (or authority) has a certainty level equivalent to science. Faith and science were kept distinct; however, the distinction broke down when it came to practical application. Faith A is absolutely certain in and of itself but also can be accorded the rank of an axiom (or first principle) for use in mathematical/geometrical demonstration. When a clear statement in holy scripture can be used as an axiom, the distinction between faith and science becomes blurred. This is crucial for understanding the logic in the rational religion of Puritans. Brattle further blurs the distinctions between divine testimony and axioms, and divine revelation and first principles, in an interesting statement which he never fully developed: "There is a power innate with us whereby we do assent to first principles," which are "true and immediate" and "*cause faith*" (my emphasis).[251] The power Brattle was writing about was divine grace, it seems to me. In the tradition of religiously-oriented logics, God actively participated in confirming the certainty of axioms/first principles and, through the Holy Spirit, confirmed the divinity of divine testimony. Thus absolute certainty through demonstration or faith needs the active participation of God.

Having two types of faith also helped to delineate the boundary between theological doctrines that were absolutely certain and theological doctrines that were mysteries or opinion. Brattle, in comparison to other religiously-oriented logicians, seldom used overt

---

[250] Brattle, *Compendium of Logick*, Pt. 3, chap. 3, 166–68; for equivalent, LeGrand, *Institutio*, Pt. 3, chap. 19, sect. 1–4.
[251] Brattle, *Compendium of Logick*, Pt. 3, chap. 3, 168.

theological examples in the textbook; however, his manuscript sermons leave a wealth of examples of logic applied to theology. These sermons presented to students by the author of their principal logic textbook can be used to help us understand the glosses that Brattle no doubt applied to his text when he taught logic. Brattle often preached on the distinctions between theological certainties and mysteries of the faith. For example, the Trinity, he often preached, was a mystery beyond the reach of certainty; however, "belief of this mystery is the duty" of a Christian.[252] In one sermon of 1711 directed to the tutors and students, Brattle more carefully delineated what was certain and what was a mystery in the Trinity. The key to the delineation was finding what in the Trinity was of Faith A and what was of opinion.[253] In this Brattle echoed *The Port-Royal Logic* which made a similar distinction between mystery and certainty:

> There are some things which are certain in their existence, yet incomprehensible in the manner of their existence: Though unable to conceive how they can be, we are certain that they are. What is more incomprehensible than eternity? And yet what is more certain?[254]

For Brattle the nature of the Trinity was a mystery of the faith, but since its existence could be demonstrated clearly from biblical references, its existence was certain (Faith A). For him, there was clear and distinct divine testimony of the Trinity in 1 John 5:7–8 which mentions three witnesses: the Father, the Son, and the Holy Spirit.[255]

It should be noted that the validity of this particular verse was hotly debated in the sixteenth and seventeenth centuries since Erasmus had shown that it was an addition to the text in the

---

[252] Brattle sermon on baptism, date obscured, but probably December 1696, 1. Unless otherwise noted, all Brattle sermons are from the Houghton Library at Harvard University.
[253] Brattle sermon, August 26, 1711 PM, 3.
[254] Arnauld, *The Art of Thinking: Port-Royal Logic*, Bk. 4, chap. 1, 298.
[255] The doctrine of the Trinity was also taken for granted as divine testimony by LeGrand, *Institutio*, Pt. 4, chap. 22, sect. 14. Arnauld discusses the Trinity in *The Art of Thinking: Port-Royal Logic*, Bk. 4, chap. 12, 339.

Middle Ages. However, many dogmatists on both the Catholic and the Protestant side argued for its biblical veracity, and, although almost all Bibles no longer include this statement, the King James version and the Geneva version had it. Brattle was not unaware of the debate, but believed that Erasmus had not given enough evidence to warrant the deletion of that crucial proof-text for the doctrine of the Trinity.[256] The important point is that concerning the Trinity, Brattle, in complete consistency with the epistemology and logic taught at Harvard, could show the certainty of its existence while still maintaining the mystery of its workings. Brattle applied a similar treatment to the doctrine of predestination.[257]

Such use of logic to support divinity had been assumed by Alexander Richardson and most Puritans. Brattle, however, plays a very special role in the merging of logic and divinity at Harvard because he was the unofficial professor of divinity who taught a crucial generation of New England's early eighteenth-century clergy. To understand the full effect of his logic in New England, we need to turn to a discussion of Brattle and his influence. Brattle's synthesis played an important role throughout the eighteenth. Divinity and logic in the Harvard curriculum were not separated until the nineteenth century.

C. Brattle: Tutor and Unofficial Professor of Divinity

William Brattle was the second son in a wealthy merchant family of Boston.[258] In the relatively new social structure of New England, William's birth was "of the first order," while, in the context of the empire, he was only "of the better sort": the urban merchants and professionals on whom rested most of the political dynamism and

---

[256] Brattle never offered arguments for the validity of 1 John 5: 7–8; however, he probably agreed with Cotton Mather's arguments in *A Christian Conversation... The Mystery of Trinity* (Boston, 1709), 4–6.

[257] See Brattle sermon, May 5, 1700.

[258] See Edward-Doubleday Harris, *An Account of Some of the Descendants of Capt. Thomas Brattle* (Boston, 1867), and Rick Kennedy, *Thomas and William Brattle in Puritan Massachusetts* (Ph.D. diss., University of California, Santa Barbara, 1987).

intellectual vitality of Stuart Britain.[259] The early wealth of the Brattle family had been established in America by William's maternal grandfather, William Tyng. Tyng emigrated to New England sometime between 1636 and 1638. He must have been fairly wealthy when he emigrated because he quickly established himself as a merchant and land speculator. He purchased a prominent and large part of Boston which would eventually become Brattle Close (an area now covered by the Government Center). Tyng died in 1653, after an active life of public service, and left an estate valued at £2,774, one of the largest in the young colony. Included in the estate was a substantial library of over a hundred books on a wide variety of subjects.

Tyng left no sons to inherit his property, and much of it eventually passed to his daughter Elizabeth who married Thomas Brattle a few years after Tyng's death. Thomas was the first of his family to come to America. He was born around 1624, in England, and in 1656 shows up in Massachusetts records as a merchant. Brattle, just like his father-in-law, led the active political life that was expected of the "best" men. He served as a captain in the militia, a deputy on the General Court, and selectman and treasurer of Boston. He and Elizabeth raised seven children, born two years apart, starting with another Thomas in 1658 and ending with the third brother, Edward, in 1670. Edward was the only son to follow his father into the militia and active commerce. The Brattle sisters all married advantageously: Elizabeth (b. 1660) to the merchant Nathaniel Oliver; Katherine (b. 1664) to another merchant, John Eyre, who died in 1700, then to Wait-Still Winthrop who died in 1717; Bethiah (b. 1666) to the merchant Joseph Parsons, and finally Mary (b. 1668) to another wealthy merchant, John Mico. The network of in-laws formed a powerful family alliance, and, combined with their cousins the Dudleys, the extended Brattle family was involved in all of Boston's major political and social activities during their generation.[260]

---

[259] "Diary of John Leverett," Harvard University Archives, vol. 1, 15.866 vt, 76.
[260] See Bernard Bailyn's *The New England Merchants in the Seventeenth Century* (Cambridge: Harvard University, 1955) for the classic study of the class to which William Brattle's family belonged. Bailyn in my opinion applies a paradigm of declining piety among this class too rigidly, especially when dealing with individuals such as Thomas and William Brattle and Samuel Sewall.

ARISTOTELIAN AND CARTESIAN

Thomas and William were peculiar in that they were the only children in their family to pursue the intellectual life and both were happiest in isolation from political and social Boston. When they went off to Harvard as teenagers they turned their backs on the commercial Boston that was the source of their family's wealth and power; and yet, it was that wealth that supported them throughout their lives, and it was their family's network of power that backed them in crucial educational and religious controversies.

There was, however, more than just wealth and power in the family background of William Brattle; there was also firm piety joined with an insistent reformer mentality. Beginning around the time of William's birth, father Thomas Brattle was a leader in one of Boston's biggest religious controversies which led to a broader conception of church membership and the creation of a new church in Boston.[261] William Brattle was seven years old, his brother eleven, when the controversy was finally resolved. At impressionable ages, the two brothers saw the inner workings of reform in New England and their own reformist mentalities were surely engendered then.

William Brattle entered Harvard when the student population was perhaps not much more than ten, and tutors were hard to find and could not be induced to stay long. Students themselves would often leave for months before returning. Cotton Mather, a schoolmate, was about the same age as William but had entered Harvard when he was eleven-and-one-half years old, two years before Brattle. Cotton was temperamentally unsuited for dealing with the stress of collegiate living. He formed no close friendships with his classmates and took every opportunity to go home to Boston for long spells to be taught by his father. This Mather later wrote the history of the college and harbored hopes of becoming its president; yet in truth, he loved only the idea of the school. He never loved the actual life of Harvard as did Brattle.

The gregarious Brattle formed his lifelong friendships in

---

[261] See Hamilton Andrews Hill, *History of Old South Church*, 2 vols. (Cambridge: Riverside Press, 1890); and R.G. Pope, *The Half Way Covenant: Church Membership in Puritan New England* (Princeton, N.J.: Princeton University, 1969).

LOGIC AT HARVARD

Cambridge and loved the liveliness of the college. William even got along with Cotton and, throughout later struggles, retained Cotton's respect if not his friendship. Brattle's closest bonds were with his classmates John Leverett and James Oliver. They arrived at college together and only death separated them. William's tie with Leverett was so close that their names were inevitably coupled in the college records and in the letters and diaries of their students. They were born the same year, went to grammar school together, entered Harvard together, took their Master's degrees together, were college tutors together, and married within a month of each other. The third in the Cambridge troika, James Oliver was a chemist and doctor, reportedly "beloved, pious, and useful."[262] One of Leverett's former students described these three around the turn of the century: "all settled in Cambridge and as it were in the same street; one a professor of the Law, the other of divinity, the third of physick; and all eminent in their kind."[263]

The founders of the college had specifically desired to foster "a collegiate way of living" rather than model the school after the Continental universities that boarded their students "here and there at private houses."[264] Brattle moved in among his peers and as tutor lived among his students. When in 1697 he became the minister of the meeting house a block away from the college, he married and moved into a house nearby where students were always welcome.

During his student years, Brattle wrote small articles and poems for an almanac. His first was *An Ephemeris of Cælestial Motions* (1682). Almanacs fulfilled the requirements of an MA thesis and their usefulness and popularity insured their publication. Most

---

[262] John L. Sibley, *Biographical Sketches of Harvard Graduates*, vol. 3 (Cambridge, Mass.: Charles W. Sever, Univeristy Bookstore, 1885), 198. Brattle's manuscript funeral sermon for Oliver is dated April 11, 1703.
[263] "Diary of Josiah Cotton," *Publications of the Colonial Society of Massachusetts* 26 (1925): 280.
[264] Mather, "An Account of the University," *Magnalia Christi Americana*, Bk 4, Introduction, pt. 1, sect. 2. See Melanchthon's declamation, *Vita Rodolphi Agricolae*, in *Corpus Reformatorum: Philippi Melanthonis Opera Quae Supersunt Omnia*, ed. Carolus Gottlieb Bretschneider (New York: Johnson Reprint, 1963), 11, 438–446..

interesting was a forceful essay, "An Explanation of the Preceding Ephemeris...," where Brattle began by encouraging his readers to ask why eclipses happen and not be satisfied with knowing just when they happened, like most almanac readers. This is when he declared that "reading without understanding is one way to introduce the tongue of a parrot into the head of a rational creature."[265] After his death, he was praised as one who "searched everything to the bottom"; at twenty years old, he was already trying to encourage others to do the same.[266]

The most interesting clues concerning Brattle's mind are in his argument that England and her colonies should revise their calendar—a bold assertion worthy of a fledgling intellectual reformer. During Brattle's life, England and the other Protestant countries of Europe refused to switch from their Julian calendar, which started the year in March and inefficiently handled leap years. In his essay, Brattle explained the history and deficiencies of the English calendar and praised the reform of Pope Gregory XIII who decreed in 1582 the use of a better system which took his name. Protestant countries refused to follow the pope, thus making them ten days out of sync with the Catholic countries. William showed the central tenet of his mind when he organized his own almanac from January to December in the manner of a Catholic calendar and and argued that the better calendar should be accepted on its obvious merits, rather than refused for its popish source. It was not until 1699–1700 that Denmark and the Dutch and German Protestant countries relented to Roman Catholic efficiency; still other Protestants held back. Brattle was even more sensible than the great English mathematician, John Wallis, who in 1699 was adamantly opposed to the calendar of "our popish neighbors."[267] It would not be until 1752 that England would bow to the Gregorian calendar.

---

[265] William Brattle, "An explanation of the preceding ephemeris," *Ephemeris of Cælestial Motions*, first page of essay.
[266] Benjamin Colman, *A Sermon...After the Funerals of...Mr. William Brattle...and...Mr. Ebenezer Pemberton* (Boston, 1717), 27.
[267] John Wallis to the Bishop of Worcester, June 30, 1699, Royal Society of London, LBC 12.129.

LOGIC AT HARVARD

Given Brattle's commitment to rational thinking and desire to educate others so as not to be mere parrots, it is not surprising that he was invited to be a tutor at Harvard in 1686. Increase Mather had already recruited John Leverett to help him rebuild the college and needed two tutors he could trust to run the day-to-day affairs of the college since he was going to continue to live in Boston. Mather, therefore, did not recruit—as was the usual practice—fresh graduates who could only be expected to stay at the college until a ministerial position opened up; he chose two relatively older and more stable alumni.

Brattle and Leverett were not alone in Cambridge with the responsibility of teaching. During the seventeenth century, collegiate education, without the systemization we are accustomed to, was very flexible. Around Cambridge, a circle of men of different expertise opened their homes to students for an afternoon or even a year or two, training them in what today would be called professions. This was especially true for the few graduate students who remained in Cambridge. This is the meaning behind the student quote given earlier that referred to Brattle, Leverett, and Oliver, after 1696 and before 1707, as "professors" of divinity, law, and medicine. There were no professorships, not officially. Unofficially, these men served in the informal educational network just as many did before and after—until official professorships and graduate schools were created. Thomas Brattle, officially the college treasurer, was unofficially active as professor of astronomy and mathematics from 1689 to 1713.[268] Charles Morton served as an informal professor to the college and, at one point, overstepped unstated boundaries and had to be asked to scale down what was beginning to look like a competing college.[269] The unofficial professors were probably not paid but were provided young assistants to help them in their work.

Aside from Morton, Thomas Graves, who also like Morton lived in Charlestown, apparently supported and advised young Brattle

---

[268] See Rick Kennedy, "Thomas Brattle and the Scientific Provincialism of New England, 1680–1713," 584–600, and "Thomas Brattle, Mathematician-Architect in the Transition of the New England Mind," 231–245.
[269] Morison, "Charles Morton," xxiv.

and Leverett and probably helped with other students. Thomas Graves had been hired as a Harvard tutor in 1666 when a comparably venerable twenty-eight years old. Graves had been fired by the president who, himself, was fired after the student boycott of 1674–1675. Graves "would not renounce the Church of England" and was probably siding with the students against the president. During the boycott of the college, Graves tutored in his home and thereafter never lost his connection to the college even while working as a physician and judge. When Mather, Leverett, Morton, and Brattle were actively running the college, Graves seems to have been brought closer in the orbit of the college. When Graves died in 1697, Leverett and Oliver, the "professors" of law and medicine, bore his coffin to the grave. Graves was a "professor" to them, unofficially teaching law and medicine during the late 1670s, 80s and 90s. William Brattle and Charles Morton were also at the funeral. The unofficial network of men serving as teachers was understood at the time although it can only be partially pieced together today.

Brattle moved from being an official to unofficial teacher when he married and became minister at the church next to the college. However, more than Mather, Leverett, and Morton, Brattle constantly participated in college affairs from 1686 to his death in 1717. He became the "professor" of divinity, but just as importantly, he became the "chaplain" in a college that did not believe in formal chaplaincies.[270] It was probably Brattle's continued influence at the college that made it seem obvious to Increase Mather that Brattle should be either vice president or president. After Leverett resigned his tutorship and President Mather continued to live in Boston, Brattle was the only one around to advise the young tutors when a decision had to be made. In fact, if one wished to create a longer list

---

[270] Puritans discouraged the idea of having chapels with worship services separate from the community church, especially at colleges. Throughout the seventeenth and eighteenth century, Harvard students were to worship at the town meeting house on Sundays, with intermittent sermons given in various places. Holden Chapel was donated to the college and finished in 1742, but served mainly as a lecture hall. There was no official chaplain at Harvard; however, the town minister along with the Hollis Divinity Professor served in the capacity of chaplain.

of Brattle's informal positions, one would have to add that he was the unofficial president of the college between Increase Mather who left in 1701 and John Leverett who came back in 1707. During those years, the elderly Samuel Willard was officially the acting president, but Willard continued to serve his Boston church. Understanding that the trip from Boston across the Charlestown ferry (and later bridge) to Cambridge was about two hours one way in those years, and that there is very little evidence that Willard did much besides preside at commencements, it seems obvious that Brattle was the *de facto* leader of the college from 1701 to 1707.[271] This inference is supported indirectly by such minor facts as that in 1705 a committee from Charlestown inquired of "Mr. Brattle and the fellows" whether a recent graduate was qualified to keep their grammar school; and that when Willard was too sick to attend the 1707 commencement, Brattle and Tutor Flynt ran it. Whatever his unofficial duties, almost every remembrance after his death cites his importance to the college and the Cambridge church. Tutor Flynt's personal diary, for example, gave several eulogies, including: "God has made him an instrument of much good to this land, the college, the churches here, and to his own church in particular. As he lived to God and the benefit of men, so he died leaving many legacies amongst his friends."[272]

Much of Brattle's influence at the college has long been known, but the direction it took has been misunderstood. In most histories, Brattle appears as an opponent of Increase Mather, and as having unpuritan tendencies. These misunderstandings must be addressed before the influence of his textbook can be understood.

Brattle's relationship with Increase Mather has been extrapolated from Cotton Mather's diary statements in 1699, where Cotton declared that the colony had divided into two ecclesiastical "parties," one made up of those who followed the leadership of the Mathers and the other being "a company of head-strong men...full

---

[271] Thomas Siegel and I differ on this point; see his *Governance and Curriculum at Harvard College in the Eighteenth Century*, 221.
[272] Henry Flynt, *Diary of Henry Flynt, 1675–1760*. Transcribed by Edward Dunn, Harvard University Archives (February 15, 1717), 188.

of malignity to the holy ways of our churches" who "invite an ill party through all the country."[273] The event that sparked this statement was the founding of what would become known as the Brattle Street Church by Thomas Brattle and a group consisting largely of members of the extended Brattle family. The new minister was Benjamin Colman, a former student of William Brattle and John Leverett. Historians have overemphasized Cotton Mather's belief that there were two "parties" with Increase Mather and William Brattle on opposite sides. Even Samuel E. Morison interprets Brattle's and Leverett's work at Harvard in a way calculated to denigrate Increase and Cotton Mather. Morison furthered the tradition of historians whose hatred of the narrow-mindedness of the Mathers and Calvinism encouraged them to raise the Brattles into champions of enlightened liberalism.[274]

Contrary to this interpretation, evidence indicates that Increase Mather loved and trusted William Brattle. It was Mather who called Brattle to be tutor in 1686. It was Mather who put Brattle and Leverett in charge of Harvard while he was away in England. And it was Mather who recommended Brattle to the church in Cambridge in 1697. Twenty years later Mather expressed his pleasure that he had been the one to convince the church to hire Brattle.

---

[273] Cotton Mather, *Diary of Cotton Mather*, vol. 1 (New York: Ungar, American Classics Series, 1957?), 325–26.

[274] The nineteenth-century roots of the Brattles-as-liberals tradition are found primarily in two influential books: Josiah Quincy's *The History of Harvard University*, vol. 1 (Cambridge: John Owen, 1840), 127, which stated that the Brattles and Leverett "were not adherents to the rigid doctrines" of the early established Congregational Church of New England, and Samuel Kirkland Lathrop's *A History of the Church in Brattle Street, Boston* (Boston: W.M. Crosby and H.P. Nichols, 1851), 16, 18, which contrasted the "free air of the wilderness" breathed by the Brattles with the "ignorance and prejudice" of the Mathers. These interpretations influenced John L. Sibley, see his *Biographical Sketches of Graduates of Harvard University*, which became the standard reference work on the Brattles, Leverett, and people associated with Harvard in the seventeenth century. Many recent historians, no longer harboring antagonism to the Mathers, still tend to rely on traditional viewpoints drawn from Quincy and Lathrop. John Corrigan's *The Prism of Piety: Catholick Congregational Clergy at the Beginning of the Enlightenment* (New York: Oxford, 1991), 17–27, is the most recent work on the subject from the traditional perspective.

This does not mean that Mather and Brattle were confirmed allies in all things. During one of Mather's experiments with designing a new Harvard charter around the time the Brattle Street Church was founded, Mather removed both the Brattle brothers from leadership. Governor Bellomont wrote to Samuel Sewall, a friend of both the Mathers and the Brattles, stating that William Brattle had been removed out of "personal prejudice" and asked whether he should "humor Mr. Mather's selfishness and pedantic pride, or do right to the virtue, learning, and merit of Mr. Brattle."[275] The Mathers were a defensive father and son, but the father soon recognized that he had wronged someone whom he wished to support. In 1702 after he was removed from the presidency, Mather recommended Brattle to be the on-site vice president of Harvard while a new president be appointed as an absentee figurehead. At forty years old, Brattle was considered too young by Mather for the presidency; however, Mather did note in this recommendation that "I take [Brattle] to be sincerely pious, and fully as orthodox as [the Rev. Samuel Willard, then vice president]."[276] Five years later, Mather appears to have pushed for Brattle's election to the presidency of Harvard.[277] At Brattle's death, Increase Mather remorsefully noted that he had found "much comfort in [Brattle's] conversation." Brattle's will specified that Increase Mather "whether present or absent" at the burial should receive a traditional gift of a scarf and gloves.[278]

These facts make it clear that Brattle and Mather were not opponents mired in factional parties. Much has been made of the

---

[275] Letter from Lord Bellomont to Samuel Sewall, 17 August 1700, *Records Commission of Boston* (Boston, 1917), ser. 2, vol. 2, 139–40.

[276] "Draft of a Letter from Increase Mather to the Speaker of the House," October, 1702, *Publications of the Colonial Society of Massachusetts* 49 (1975), 195–96.

[277] Mather's support for Brattle's presidency is the context of Brattle's letter to Mather, as found in *Publications of the Colonial Society of Massachusetts* 49 (1975): 218.

[278] Mather's eulogy for Brattle is in the preface to Joseph Sewall's sermon *Precious Treasure in Earthen Vessels* (Boston, 1717). William Brattle's will is published in Edward-Doubleday Harris, *An Account of the Descendants of Capt. Thomas Brattle*, 17–25.

one break in their friendship when Mather removed him from the corporation of the college; however, Mather was at the most volatile point in his life during that time and alienated several of his fast friends—as did Cotton Mather at the same time. Around the same time as he removed Brattle, he so insulted the mild-mannered and revered Samuel Willard of South Church that Willard announced he would never visit Mather's house again. He announced this to Samuel Sewall who had also earned the ire of his long-time friend by recommending that Mather's resignation from the presidency might be the best thing for the college. But, the events of late 1699 to late 1700 should not be the standard by which we judge the intellectual alliances of New England. The calmer years of the decade before and after are a better measure. The decade of the 90s was especially crucial, and it was during that era that Cotton Mather praised the "prudent government" of the college by tutors Brattle and Leverett.[279]

The second distortion of Brattle's thought which is built on the first distortion is the belief that he had unpuritan tendencies. As I have shown, Brattle's orthodoxy was attested to by Increase Mather. The large collection of Brattle's manuscript sermons that have rarely been mined also clearly preach Calvinistic orthodoxy and fear of backsliding into lax Anglicism. The influence of "anglicanization" that Harry S. Stout perceives in the "Brattle group" centered at Harvard is subtle but in no way unorthodox.[280] Many historians have labeled Brattle with various levels of liberalism based on his ecclesiology, not his theology. A principal goal of the ecclesiastical reforms he instituted in his own church and encouraged in his students' churches was to increase the proportion of church members to the town, thus bringing the town and church membership ratio closer. Benjamin Colman spoke of Brattle's success in this at the close of his funeral sermon:

---

[279] Cotton Mather, "An Account of the University," *Magnalia Christi Americana*, Bk 4, pt. 1, sect. 6.
[280] Harry S. Stout, *The New Engand Soul: Preaching and Religious Culture in Colonial New England* (New York: Oxford, 1989), 131–160.

I shall only further observe how the blessing of Heaven has attended Mr. Brattle's ministry; which he confined it may be too much to his own flock, but the church has increased so under his watch and care that in a manner the whole town is come into the church-state.[281]

Brattle also believed strongly in the role of minister as watchman and shepherd over the congregation/town. This role for the minister was in part founded on the fact that the ministers were the most likely to be trained in logic and could therefore best bind rationalism to piety. Brattle was a leader in the movement to increase the power of the minister over the congregation in the hope of regaining some of the unity of first generation churches and towns in New England. He and many former students were accused of demanding "Romish" power for the minister; however, they desired this power principally for the purpose of increasing the church membership which was often dwindling under the stern hold of laity who were not extending the "rational charity" that earlier generations had advocated when judging the fitness of townspeople to become church members. They also believed the ministerial office could be used as a bastion against declining piety.[282] John Corrigan points out that in the struggle to increase ministerial power, "rationality" played a key role. He quotes Charles Chauncy's *The Only Compulsion* (Boston, 1739) that ministers, to fill their proper role, should "inform their understanding; convince their judgments; make use of those persuasions" and generally strengthen themselves in logic. "The duty of ministers," Corrigan writes, "was to impress upon their congregations the truth of certain doctrines. It was assumed that the minister could detect the truth, and in this rested his authority."[283] Brattle no doubt

---

[281] Colman, *A Sermon...After the Funerals of...Mr. William Brattle...and...Mr. Ebenezer Pemberton*, 36.
[282] See Stout, *The New England Soul*, 106–111. See also David D. Hall, *The Faithful Shepherd: A History of the New England Ministry in the Seventeenth Century* (Chapel Hill: University of North Carolina for the Institute of Early American History and Culture, 1972).
[283] John Corrigan, *The Hidden Balance: Religion and Social Theories of Charles Chauncy and Jonathan Mayhew* (Cambridge: Cambridge, 1987), 38.

would have agreed, since teaching rationality in the ministry was his life's work. Brattle's leadership in strengthening the power of the ministerial office among former students was so important that it was the theme of the funeral sermon preached for Brattle in Cambridge.[284]

Like many ministers, Brattle fought against the diluting of New England's church-town relations by forced toleration of multiple churches in each town. The new political situation made it so towns could no longer limit the type and number of churches. No longer would the whole town be identified with one church. Religious toleration was imposed after 1686, but that did not mean the Congregationalist easily embraced religious diversity. Brattle could be extremely partisan toward Congregationalism. In 1704 he tried to stop a Quaker from calling a meeting in Cambridge, and in 1709 he tried to thwart the establishment of an Anglican church in Braintree because the Anglicans there, in their missionary zeal, were attacking the local Congregational church.[285] Brattle's actions earned the ire of Francis Nicholson, a powerful colonial official, sometime governor of Virginia and Maryland, and a zealous proponent of Anglicanization in New England. Nicholson either met Brattle or heard of him while fulfilling his duties to the crown and later declared that Brattle was "a rigid Independent [Congregationalist]" trying to thwart the missionary goals of the Church of England.[286] This characterization does not fit with the usual historical interpretation that Brattle was soft on Anglicanism and overly tolerant or lax.

That historians have disagreed with Nicholson and declared Brattle a moderate or lax Congregationalist is tied to an overre-

---

[284] Joseph Stevens, *Another and Better Country... To which is added a discourse, had by him at Cambridge after the Death of the late Reverend Mr. Brattle* (Boston, 1723).

[285] Morison, *Harvard College in the Seventeenth Century*, vol. 2, 470–71; Letter to the Bishop of London, Fulham Palace Mss, Archives of the Bishop of London, Lambeth Palace Library, London (transcipts are in the Library of Congress), box 4, 35–36.

[286] Henry Newman to Dr. Smallridge, 9 March 1713/14, Society Letters, CS2/4, p. 18 in the archives of the Society for the Promotion of Christian Knowledge (SPCK), London.

liance on a bit of dubious evidence. Just as the evidence of Cotton Mather's diary has been blown out of proportion, so too the letters of a Brattle student, Henry Newman, have been taken out of context to create and justify a wrong interpretation of Brattle.

Henry Newman (1670–1743) graduated from Harvard in 1687, and stayed at the college until 1693, earning his MA and serving as librarian. In 1703 he moved to England, where, unmarried, quiet, and meticulous, he was able to live off a small stipend as secretary to the Society for the Promotion of Christian Knowledge (SPCK).[287] Francis Nicholson was a powerful man in the Anglican missionary organizations that employed Newman. Nicholson, hating Congregationalism, at one point accused Newman, a former Congregationalist, of working against the missionary goals of both the SPCK and the closely allied Society for the Propagation of the Gospel (SPG); Newman had retained his old friendships and continued to correspond with people such as Brattle and Colman in New England. Newman's employment was in jeopardy—Nicholson was right that Newman was not always precisely loyal to his patrons. In good conscience, the young secretary tried to straddle non-conformity and conformity. As Nicholson's serious charges had to be met, Newman felt compelled to defend himself by convincing his judges that William Brattle was a crypto-Anglican.

Newman's first letter stated that Brattle desired to become an Anglican priest but remained a Congregationalist because he feared crossing the Atlantic. Newman further stated that Brattle and Leverett were better missionaries than the members of the SPG since they "made more proselytes to the Church of England than any 2 men in all America." The absurdity of these statements indicates the desperation Newman felt since he was normally much more even-handed. He ended this extravagant letter explaining his motive for writing: "by acquiting" Brattle and others of anti-Anglicanism, "I shall acquit myself of the crime of corresponding with them."[288]

---

[287] See Leonard W. Cowie, *Henry Newman: An American in London 1708–1743* (London: SPCK, 1956).
[288] Newman to Smallridge, 18. See also Newman to Mr. Taylor, March 29, 1714, SPCK, Society's Letters, CS2/4, 31–32.

Newman saved his job, but Brattle has ever since been painted with what Brattle would have considered a libel. Quotes from Newman's letters about Brattle and Leverett appear in almost all the important studies of the men and Newman's motives have never been examined.

The truth is that Newman was, in fact, guilty of not being fully loyal to his patrons in the Church of England. For example, Benjamin Colman, then a member of the Harvard Corporation, wrote to Newman about ten years after the above event asking his advice about solving Harvard's recurring problem of a dubious legal status. Colman recommended that the king should be asked for a charter. Newman's reply was not in the interest of his patrons; rather, he wrote saying that Harvard should not apply for a charter because when it was granted, the Church of England would have too much influence on the college—it "would interfere with your present condition in religious matters and cramp all that liberty you now happily enjoy."[289] Newman's employers would not have been pleased with a secretary who gave such advice. Newman knew it and asked that the letter be kept confidential.

Brattle's work at Harvard has too long been interpreted in the light of Newman's libel rather than Nicholson's knowledge. Nicholson was right. Brattle was a "rigid independent." In ecclesiastical matters forced on the Congregationalists by the new political situation, Brattle appreciated some Anglican examples. For example, Brattle did want to broaden his church's influence in the town in a manner similar to an English village-parish and then increase the power of the minister in the church. As for bishops, he never was antagonistic to their existence. He apparently agreed with John Leverett (and John Calvin) that the office of bishop could serve a prudential purpose.

Brattle was a "rigid independent" in the way John Winthrop and Increase Mather were. Brattle seems to have believed along with Leverett that Anglicans and Congregationalists were merely "con-

---

[289] Henry Newman to Benjamin Colman, October 20, 1722, SPCK, New England Letter Book, CN3/1, vol. 1.

tending parties" within the same "English church."²⁹⁰ This was not Congregational liberalism. It had been a long-held position in New England dating back to John Winthrop. During Brattle's lifetime it was being encouraged by English ecumenical movements supported by Increase Mather.

Rather than weaken Puritanism's intellectual dominance in New England, Brattle's principal goal was to strengthen it. This is important for the context of Brattle's logic textbook. Brattle was not motivated by Anglican tendencies or a blind willingness to adopt new intellectual trends simply because they were new. He was a thoughtful Puritan charged by his colony with training its future leaders, and he took this job seriously. By the end of his life, the pulpits and governments of New England were filled with his former students. The respect his students paid him throughout their lives resulted from his intellectual and religious character, which exemplified a piety married to intellect. The success of his logic book is rooted in the example of the author.

Brattle had a vision for Congregationalism's cultural role in New England. As a boy he had watched his father help found Boston's third Congregational church—a church designed to meet new needs in the actual congregation. Thomas and William faced a similar strife when they helped found a fourth Congregational church. But William, a peace-loving soul, tried to stay in Cambridge, at his own church, and out of the fray. He offered his counsel but would not be drawn into the political battle. In 1700, Brattle wrote to a former student, "I hopefully shall for ever be cautious how I let my religion spend itself in those trifling controversies." He trusted in God's plan and found "weightier things to exercise my thoughts."²⁹¹ In his pulpit that year, he devoted many sermons to encouraging peacemaking and toleration, such as one in March or 1700, which declared "the name of God is dishonored,"

---

[290] Quoted in Arthur Kaledin, *The Mind of John Leverett* (Ph.D. dissertation, Harvard University, 1965), 248.
[291] William Brattle to Mr. Dudley, 18 November 1700, Massachusetts Historical Society, C.E. French manuscripts.

the spirit of God is grieved, and "religion suffers" when we forget that "true wisdom is peaceable."[292]

True wisdom meant for Brattle the logical certainty of Christian dogma. Peaceable did not mean undogmatic. Puritanism's break with Anglicanism and its continuing fear of being subsumed into the Church of England was rooted in antagonism to what the Puritan's perceived as skeptical tendencies and lax theological commitments. Brattle was peaceable; however, he taught his students Puritan firmness. One student reported that Brattle

> countenanced virtue and proficiency in us and every good disposition he discerned with the most fatherly goodness;...he searched out vice and browbeat and punished it with the authority and just anger of a master.... He did his utmost to form us to virtue and the fear of God and to do well in the world; and with...tears he dismissed his pupils when he took leave of them, with pious charges to them.[293]

When Brattle died, Samuel Sewall, who had years before advised his son to carefully listen to Brattle while at Harvard, noted in his diary: "He was a father to the students of Harvard College,... my fast friend."[294] One former student and friend remembered Brattle as a "very humble, excellent scholar, meek though naturally of quick and strong passions."[295] Another wrote that Brattle led an "austere and mortified life," not allowing himself the conceit of a periwig, demanding simple dedication to Puritan values from his students.[296]

William Brattle was a conscious educator; he did not fall into teaching. The teaching role of father, tutor, and minister encompassed his life. In one of his sermons he preached that "there are two ways in and by which religious and godly persons do instruct

---

[292] Brattle sermon, March 16, 1700.
[293] Sibley, *Biographical Sketches of Harvard Graduates*, vol. 3, 201.
[294] Sewall, *Diary of Samuel Sewall*, vol. 2, 846.
[295] Sibley, *Biographical Sketches of Harvard Graduates*, vol. 3, 203–204.
[296] Colman, *A Sermon...after the Funerals*, 35; and Sewall, *Diary of Samuel Sewall*, vol. 1, 449.

the children of men": by counsel and good example. The latter he believed was the more effective of the two since godly examples "ordinarily do make deeper impressions upon the hearts of men, and win upon men more than precepts do."[297]

Brattle believed people needed a trusted counselor, "some spiritual guide, to lay open their distressed case before some man of God, to make confession of their sin before him."[298] As a Protestant, he claimed no power of absolution; yet, as with Tutor Flynt who felt the need to "unbosom" himself, there was "comfort and relief" in "confessing our sins before man."[299] Brattle became the "spiritual father" to many who passed through Harvard, hearing their confessions, helping them with their theological and career struggles. He was "exceeding prudent," John Barnard remembered, "to whom all addressed themselves for advice."[300]

Henry Flynt (1675–1760) was educated by Brattle and Leverett, hired as a tutor two years after Brattle moved from the lectern to the pulpit, and remained a tutor until his death. His principal importance was his endurance in an unremunerative position. He links the era of Brattle with the era of those who carried New England into the nineteenth century.[301] Like many of his contemporaries, Flynt struggled with belief in the doctrine of predestination, and historians have considered him representative of the transition out of Puritanism's intellectual hegemony in New England. Flynt's form of rational religion, however, was rooted in Brattle's logic—the logic he studied as a student and later taught to his own students.

Flynt's biographer, Edward Dunn, explains that the tutor's "sallies into new ideas were always qualified by traditional thought patterns," especially when dealing with crucial doctrines such as the Trinity, the divinity of Christ, and the Bible's status as divine testi-

---

[297] Brattle sermon, 10 March 1705–6, p. 6, Houghton Library, Harvard University, MS Am 1100.
[298] Brattle sermon on James 5:16, c. April, 1712, p. 4.
[299] Brattle sermon on James 5:16.
[300] Sibley, *Biographical Sketches of Harvard Graduates*, vol. 3, 204.
[301] See Edward Dunn's *Henry Flynt*, and Shipton, *Sibley's Harvard Graduates*, vol. 4, 162–167.

mony. Flynt was no theologian and was not a penetrating thinker; like most people in similar jobs in provincial situations, he dealt with disputes on doctrine by referring to other's thoughts. Brattle's private counsel to Flynt in theological matters was probably similar to the counsel he gave his congregation, which comprised the faculty and students of the college, to whom he sometimes directed his sermons specifically. In a series of sermons on "contending for the faith," Brattle advised an "inward intenseness" in the "holy contest" of that era when their New English Israel seemed to be collapsing. He warned that the mind could be led astray and that there was danger in engaging in doctrinal disputations without "constancy and perseverance" in orthodoxy.[302] Flynt would have been sitting in the congregation when Brattle warned against despising "common and plain truths" while becoming fond of "mysterious and dark truths."[303]

Flynt was joined on the Harvard faculty by Edward Wigglesworth who knew Brattle well and can be considered Brattle's successor as professor of divinity. After Brattle—the unofficial professor of divinity—died, agents for Harvard began lobbying in England for funds to establish an official divinity program. Once funds were secured, Benjamin Colman recommended Wigglesworth for the first professor's chair as a man whose preaching showed "solid judgement" and "clear method"—both primarily logical terms which were applied to preaching.[304] Wigglesworth had learned from Brattle, and Colman believed Wigglesworth would be a pious, rational, and orthodox successor.

Colman was right. Like Brattle, Wigglesworth taught students that stability and certainty could be found in logical foundations—as can be seen when he led the fight against an old threat to logical religion: "enthusiasm," a term used throughout the seventeenth and eighteenth centuries to describe overly pietistic or fideistic Christianity. Brattle had tried to keep enthusiastic Quakers out of

---

[302] Brattle sermon, February 18, 1704 on Jude:3, p. 1.
[303] Brattle sermon, May 5, 1700, on James 4: 17, p. 5.
[304] Ebenezer Turell, *The Life and Character of the Reverend Benjamin Colman* (Boston, 1749), 55.

LOGIC AT HARVARD

Cambridge. Wigglesworth had to defend Harvard from another enthusiast: George Whitefield, the traveling evangelist.

Whitefield had almost no direct knowledge of Harvard or its curriculum, but chose to attack the college publicly for unorthodoxy. The Harvard faculty were justly upset by the charges Whitefield tossed out against them, and jointly, Harvard's president, professors, tutors, and lone Hebrew instructor issued *The Testimony...Against the Reverend Mr. George Whitefield* (Boston, 1744). *The Testimony* was written by Wigglesworth, the new divinity professor, with the help of the rest of the faculty.[305]

The Testimony's argument was that Whitefield was an "enthusiast" and had thus crossed into an area of Christianity that dangerously abandoned the sure-footing of divine testimony in the Bible and self-evident truths in the mind. Like good academics, they quoted directly from Whitefield's published journal and sermons where Whitefield reported that he acted on instruction from dreams and "sudden impulses and impressions upon his mind." Whitefield, they wrote, "imagines" these impulses to be "from the Spirit of God," but does not test them. He does not use doubting properly. The academics then affirmed the standard epistemology of religiously-oriented and dogmatically-inclined logics:

> For our strong faith and belief, that such a motion on the mind comes from God, can never be any proof of it; and if such impulses and impressions be not agreeable to our reason, or to the revelation of the mind of God to us, in his Word, nothing can be more dangerous than conducting ourselves according to them; for otherwise, if we judge not of them by these rules, they may well be the suggestions of the evil spirit.[306]

---

[305] That Wigglesworth was probably the main author of *The Testimony*, I assume, since he wrote *A Letter to the Reverend Mr. Whitefield by way of Reply to his Answer to the College Testimony Against him and his Conduct* (Boston, 1745), which reiterated the Lockean condemnation of his "enthusiasm."

[306] *The Testimony of the President, Professor, Tutors and Hebrew Instructor of Harvard College* (Boston, 1744), 4. In New England's Great Awakening, such testing of the strong affections was also a theme of Jonathan Edwards' *A Treatise Concerning Religious Affections,* preached in 1741–1742 and published in 1746.

ARISTOTELIAN AND CARTESIAN

Those historians who have believed Whitefield that Harvard was falling into unorthodoxy have not taken into account how the logical foundations of the orthodoxy of Puritan faith continued to be taught at the college. The role of the Bible as divine testimony which acts in concert with the knowledge God communicates directly into human minds was considered the foundation of orthodoxy by both Brattle and Wigglesworth. Wigglesworth more fully developed his position in lectures he published. In *The Sovereignty of God in the Exercises of his Mercy...Two Published Lectures at Harvard College* (Boston, 1741), Wigglesworth condemned the "pernicious tendency" he found in English pamphlets advocating universal salvation.[307] Wigglesworth began his logical analysis of the universalists by insisting that one must begin a proof from clear divine testimony in Scripture, not humanitarian ideas of divine mercy. In *A Seasonable Caveat Against Believing Every Spirit: With Some Direction Trying the Spirits, Whether They are of God* (Boston, 1735), Wigglesworth also insisted that any immediate revelation in the mind must be tested against the Bible. The Bible, he "proved," was "given by inspiration of God, and since the God of truth cannot deny or contradict himself," no immediate revelation could contradict biblical teachings.[308]

Such statements were found in fourth-year divinity lectures and built on the foundation of the first two years' logic curriculum. As you will recall, Brattle's *Compendium of Logick* delineates two types of faith—human and divine—of which the divine is from God as revealed in the Bible, and has the certainty of science because "we know that he is true and cannot lie." Harvard offered a diverse curriculum, however; its favored logic supported divinity courses with a unified perspective of rationality. This is especially clear in Wigglesworth's emphasis on right thinking as a gift of divine grace—a tenet clear in both Morton's and Brattle's textbooks. In *A Seasonable Caveat* Wigglesworth declared that:

> the understanding of man in his natural state is so much blinded, that without the gracious influences of God's Holy

---

[307] Wigglesworth, *The Sovereignty of God*, (Boston, 1741), 6.
[308] Wigglesworth, *A Seasonable Caveat*, (Boston, 1735), 5.

LOGIC AT HARVARD

Spirit, it will never apprehend divine truths, in such a manner as that the heart shall be suitably affected and the life governed by them; yet that immediate operation of God upon man, which is now necessary to remove the natural blindness of his understanding, and make him of discerning divine truth aright, is not an immediate revelation of divine truth to his understanding, but only a gracious removal of those impediments which would not have suffered his understanding to perceive those truths in a spiritual manner, whatever way they might be revealed to him in, whether immediately by the written word of God, or immediately by inward revelation.[309]

In another published set of lectures on the imputation of Adam's sin on his posterity, Wigglesworth closed his preface with a statement as heart-felt as any by Brattle about the crucial importance of teaching at Harvard the right thinking necessary to strengthening New England in the midst of its perceived decline. He "earnestly" requested the prayers of his readers,

that God would graciously lead me from time to time into a clear apprehension of divine truths; that he would enable me to represent them to the satisfaction and establishment of those, who will probably hereafter be the dispensers of them, to his people through the land; and that he would strengthen me to bear the great application, which my own insufficiency, and the importance of the duties of the trust reposed in me, call for.[310]

Flynt and Wigglesworth were the two most prominent long-term fixtures at Harvard who carried on the use of Brattle's logic in the classroom and were themselves greatly influenced by the man.

---

[309] Wigglesworth, *A Seasonable Caveat*, 9–10.
[310] Edward Wigglesworth, *An Enquiry into the Truths of the Imputation of the Guilt of Adam's First Sin to his Posterity* (Boston, 1738), "preface," n.p.

ARISTOTELIAN AND CARTESIAN

Their emphasis on apprehension of divine truths in the mind, divine testimony, and the need of grace for right thinking clearly helped support their insistence on old Puritan orthodoxies. Wigglesworth, especially, is an example of the kind of new Puritan Brattle had hoped to encourage who could vigorously uphold great Puritan truths in a religious culture that was in danger of following the lax and skeptical tendencies of the Church of England.

Brattle's intellectual influence spread in many directions. John Barnard (1681–1770), one of New England's eighteenth-century intellectual leaders, was personally and intellectually influenced by Brattle. Barnard called both Brattle and Leverett his college tutors, with Leverett his special tutor—this indicating how the tutoring overlapped in those years even though there was a system of assigning one tutor to a whole class for all four years of the curriculum.[311] Barnard called Leverett and Brattle "those two great men," and he described Brattle as "cherished by candidates for the ministry, exceeding prudent, to whom all addressed themselves for advice."[312]

For Barnard, it was a "liberal education" because he was not taught to parrot the thinking of his tutors. Though Barnard reported he did not take full advantage of his undergraduate years, after graduation when he began to study divinity he put the tools of free thinking he had gained to work—first on the question of true theology:

> I read all sorts of authors, and as I read, compared their sentiments with the sacred writings, and formed my judgement of the doctrines of Christianity by that only and infallible standard of truth; which led me insensibly into what is called the Calvinistical scheme (though I never to this day have read Calvin's works and cannot call him master), which sentiments, by the most plausible arguments to the contrary,

---

[311] John Barnard, "Autobiography of John Barnard," *Collections of the Massachusetts Historical Society*, ser. 3, 5 (1836): 182.
[312] Sibley, *Biographical Sketches of Harvard Graduates*, vol. 3, 204.

that have fallen in my way (and I have read the most of them), I have never yet seen cause to depart from.[313]

This is a wonderful passage for a view into Brattle's informal divinity classes and the way Cartesian logic was applied to theology. Barnard starts with no preconceptions, gathers wide and diverse information, uses "judgement"—a logical term— comparing ideas to the Bible—the "infallible standard of truth"—and arrives at the truth which happens to be Calvinism.

Most modern readers of this passage will not be surprised by the outcome: Of course! Raise a person a Calvinist, give him Calvinist teachers, inundate his life in Calvinism, and of course he will think he is disinterestedly using logical method when he comes up with Calvinism as the most rational religion. Most modern readers will believe that Barnard engaged in circular reasoning and took a logically unacceptable leap in proclaiming the infallibility of the Bible. However, in terms of the Cartesian logic of his era, Barnard's method was accepted and was consistent with the religiously-oriented logic taught at Harvard. In the eyes of his contemporaries, Barnard was one of New England's best intellects. President Ezra Stiles of Yale College—a man who placed great pride in his own logical abilities—praised Barnard's logic as "equaled by few in regard either of readiness of invention, liveliness of imagination, or strength and clearness in reasoning."[314]

Jonathan Edwards did not graduate from Harvard, but he was the student of one of Brattle's students. Elisha Williams, one of Edwards's early teachers, was a Harvard graduate who taught from Brattle's logic and *The Port-Royal Logic*. Williams was spiritually awakened in Brattle's church while a student and became close to his minister. He became rector of Yale from 1725 to 1739 and was remembered by a later Yale president, Ezra Stiles, as "well versed in

---

[313] Barnard, "Autobiography of John Barnard," 186.
[314] Shipton, *Sibley's Harvard Graduates*, vol. 4, 501–514.

logic."[315] No one logic textbook or person can be credited as the source for the rational certainty of Flynt, Wigglesworth, Barnard, Williams, and Edwards. But in each we see, at least, Brattle's logic as a brick in the foundation of their dogmatic certainty in crucial Puritan doctrines.

I do not want to give the impression that New England's intellectual elite was monolithic in its view of rational religion. Some students influenced by Brattle moved away from the doctrine of predestination and others from even the Trinity, employing Cartesian logic in a way that Brattle did not sanction to bolster their position. They found scriptural material to support their own positions. By insisting on a more limited set of axioms than Brattle, in effect they moved quite far from Brattle's position. John Corrigan's *The Hidden Balance: Religion and the Social Theories of Charles Chauncy and Jonathan Mayhew* (1987) is an excellent study on two clergymen who experimented with a less dogmatic application of Cartesian idealism to the Puritan tradition. Mayhew wrote thoughtful notes on Pascal's *Pensées* in his commonplace book that indicate a tentative distrust of Cartesian optimism similar to Pascal's. On one page Mayhew commented that God was more interested in the will than understanding, and that God is not just a God of "geometrical truths."[316] Brattle and many of the students who learned from his logic textbooks embraced Cartesian dogmatic confidence; however, there were others more tentative and wary. They were, however, only a minority in the first half of the eighteenth century.

---

[315] See Norman Fiering, *Jonathan Edwards's Moral Thought*, 33–34, where he discusses Williams's use of *The Port-Royal Logic* and notes that Yale's use of a logic in the senior year was odd but indicates the possibility that Arnauld's text might have been used in moral philosophy or even as a capstone book in that it encompassed much of what had gone before it in the curriculum. See the biographical sketch of Williams in Shipton, *Sibley's Harvard Graduates*, vol. 5, 588–98.

[316] Jonathan Mayhew, "Notes on Pascal" (Mayhew Papers, Special Collections, Mugar Memorial Libary, Boston University), 3.

Epilogue: Later Constituencies of Religious Logics and the Separation of Logic and Divinity at Harvard

One Sunday, Brattle declared to his congregation:

> Indeed, the times are corrupt, and God is angry, and what judgments we may live to see, God only knows. However, this we may be assured of, that let floods of wrath come down upon this land, yet as for those few that walk in the integrity of their hearts, they are in the hands of God. He will protect them....[317]

Brattle's *A Compendium of Logick* was a textbook for corrupt times. So was Morton's *A Logick System*. Thomas Brattle, brother and friend of the two logicians, saw the Salem witch trials as a result of a breakdown of right thinking and evidence of corrupt times. "That the Justices have thus far given ear to the Devil," Thomas Brattle wrote, "I think may be mathematically demonstrated to any man of common sense."[318] Carefully stating his argument in logical terms, Brattle insisted that instead of divine testimony being the foundation of certainty, the judges were turning the colony's law over to diabolical testimony: "I think it will appear evident to any one, that the Devil's information is the fundamental testimony that is gone upon the apprehending of the aforesaid people."[319] The Devil, he went on, is a liar; whereas, "God is a God of truth; and the good Spirits will not lie." Thomas Brattle then pleaded that this and other arguments should convince people to pray with "earnest supplication" that God direct the judges to stop the proceedings and aright their wrongs; otherwise, he concluded, if "God does not gra-

---

[317] Brattle sermon, Prov. 10: 9, c. March 1705/6.
[318] "Letter of Thomas Brattle," 182.
[319] "Letter of Thomas Brattle," 182–83.

ciously appear for us, I think we may conclude that New England is undone and undone."[320]

Underlying Brattle's rhetoric is the premise that right thinking will help save New England, that logic will save New Englanders from listening to the Devil. In this Thomas Brattle essentially affirmed the perspective of the logic textbooks by Morton and his brother. Without the certainty of divine testimony that cannot deceive, then New England is "undone and undone."

William Brattle's Cartesian logic—drawing from a tradition of religious and dogmatic logics going back to Melanchthon—was taught to students as the most natural and rational method of discovering, maintaining, and expanding dogmatic certainty in Christianity. In the eighteenth century, many Lockean and Scottish Common Sense logic textbooks carried on the religiously-oriented tradition with their emphasis on God's role in the mind and in delivering and confirming divine testimony. Isaac Watts's *Logic, or the Art of Reason*, which was first published in 1725, and popular for the next hundred years, was the most influential Lockean version of a religiously-oriented and dogmatically-inclined textbook used in the British Empire. Scottish textbooks derived from the work of Thomas Reid, Professor of Moral Philosophy at the University of Glasgow, increasingly became influential and continued to emphasize God's communication in the mind and through divine testimony.

When Brattle's textbooks disappear from the curriculum in 1767 when the Overseers at Harvard reformed the structure of teaching, so that tutors would be assigned to subjects rather than students, the president and faculty ruled that Watts's *Logick* and Locke's *Essay* were to be the textbooks taught by the logic tutor. Thomas Siegel's analysis of the textbooks sold out of Jeremiah Condy's bookshop in Boston from 1759 to 1770, shows that Watts's *Logick* and *Philosophical Essays* were among the most popular books bought by Harvard students during that era. After the turn of the century, Watts's importance in the Harvard curriculum diminished.[321] Ten

---

[320] "Letter of Thomas Brattle," 183, 186.
[321] The 1766–1767 curriculum reform is discussed in Siegel, *Governance and Curriculum at Harvard College in the* 18th *Century*, 123, and Condy's bookshop analysis is 312–314, especially 314n.

logic tutors of various levels of religious dogmatism passed through the college before 1795, when Levi Hedge (1766–1844) was appointed tutor. Hedge moved the college away from Watts more toward the Scottish logicians.

Hedge was a dependable addition to the faculty, and in 1810 he was promoted to the first College Professorship of Logic and Metaphysics.[322] After Brattle, Hedge is the second Harvard teacher to write an influential logic textbook which served students for more than half a century. The first edition of *Elements of Logic: A Summary of the General Principles and Different Modes of Reasoning* was published in 1816. The third edition of 1821 was revised slightly and printed with smaller type to make it more affordable. In 1843, the third edition was again reprinted. An anonymous book reviewer in 1816 criticized Hedge's text for being short and devoid of rhetoric; however, it was useful.[323]

Choosing not to follow the tradition of Brattle and Watts, Hedge avoided the religious aspects of logic. Even when dealing with testimony, Hedge offered no category of divine testimony. As for "transmitted or traditional," knowledge, he wrote:

> The general principle with regard to this sort of testimony is, that the further it travels from its original source, that is, from the immediate witness of the fact, the weaker it becomes.[324]

This is straight Lockeanism and Scottish Common Sense without any of Locke's or Reid's digressions to explain how divine testimony or holy scriptures did not fit the general principle of testimony. The most telling statement follows when Hedge deals with testimony of supernatural events or miracles:

> These, contradicting our invariable experience, and opposing the well known laws of corporeal nature, are in themselves

---

[322] See Rand, "Philosophical Instruction in Harvard University From 1636 to 1900," 40–43.
[323] *The Centinel*, March 20, 1816. Harvard University Archives (HUG 300).
[324] Levi Hedge, *Elements of Logick* (Cooperstown, 1843), 92.

the highest degree improbable; and require for their belief a testimony so ample, and attended by such circumstances, as would render its falsehood no less miraculous than the fact attested.[325]

This statement offers little solace to religious students. Hedge's logic, replacing the influence of Watts's logic, is the first de-Christianized logic textbook to have significant influence in the Harvard curriculum. Up until the end of the eighteenth century, logic at Harvard was taught with a religious orientation. With the new century and Hedge's text, logic and religion were separated.

By 1795, when Hedge was hired, the undergraduate curriculum served an increasingly diverse constituency. The logic course was no longer expected to service a particular religious orthodoxy and the logic curriculum no longer was designed to serve the divinity curriculum. Between 1803 and 1808, the door was thrown open for basic changes in the relationship of Calvinistic Christianity to Harvard's curriculum when a controversy developed over what type of religious man would become the third Hollis Professor of Divinity. David Tappan, the second chair holder, had been a Calvinist like his predecessor Wigglesworth. A Unitarian was appointed Tappan's successor and a Unitarian became president of the college.

The Unitarian triumph at the college caused the Trinitarians to create their own seminary at Andover in 1808. Within the next two decades, a rapid succession of specialized graduate schools for ministers were established throughout the country which separated the undergraduate curriculum from divinity.[326] The new separation of divinity from the undergraduate curriculum freed logic from serving any specific religious constituency. Hedge was elevated to a new

---

[325] Hedge, *Elements of Logick*, 100.
[326] See Morison, *Three Centuries at Harvard*, 187–191; Conrad Wright, "Early Years of the Divinity School," *Harvard Alumni Bulletin* (March 20, 1954), n.p; and William Warren Sweet, "The Rise of Theological Schools in America," *Church History* 6 (1937): 260–273; and Mark A. Noll, *Princeton and the Republic, 1768–1822* (Princeton, N.J.: Princeton, 1989).

professorship of logic in 1810, and Harvard created its own graduate divinity school in 1815. It is no coincidence that the logic professor felt free to publish a new, non-religious, logic textbook the year after his logic classes became free from subservience to divinity classes.

The demise of religiously-oriented and dogmatically-inclined logic textbooks closely follows the development of the modern university in the nineteenth century. Without the need to teach divinity, undergraduate curricula throughout the country could freely be secularized. Also the religious diversity of the student body and faculty in most nineteenth-century colleges encouraged expectations that classes would support a limited, generic, and largely moral Christian sensibility rather than a specific dogmatic theology. Instead of teaching the foundations of rational Christianity in freshman and sophomore logic classes, a newer form of Christian sensibility was increasingly taught in obligatory moral philosophy classes during the senior year.

Modern logic avoids the epistemology, psychology, and emphasis on decision-making that made humanistic logic so important in colleges; however, the old humanistic logic is being revived, in part, in the late twentieth century, often under the general title of "critical thinking." The new courses and textbooks often renew the humanistic concern for practical merging of thought and life. They avoid the narrowness of modern logic in an attempt to embrace rational decision-making in general. In the context of such breadth, religious-based critical thinking textbooks can flourish in colleges which serve specific religious constituencies. At Calvin College in Michigan, a philosophy professor has published a textbook titled *Return to Reason*, which is a type of critical thinking manual that could be described as religiously-oriented and dogmatically-inclined.[327] This short textbook, which is used in philosophy courses at several Christian colleges, is split into two parts: "The Way of Argument" and "The Way of Reason" and simplifies the teachings of a new Calvinistic movement called Reformed Epistemology.

---

[327] Kelly James Clark, *Return to Reason: A Critique of Enlightenment Evidentialism and a Defense of Reason and Belief in God* (Grand Rapids: Wm. B. Eerdmans, 1990).

ARISTOTELIAN AND CARTESIAN

Although this movement relies heavily on the philosophy of Thomas Reid and John Calvin, its essential Augustinianism makes it similar to Morton's and Brattle's logics. In this context, *Return to Reason* shows that the humanistic tradition of religiously-oriented and dogmatically inclined logic has not died.[328]

---

[328] I confess not to know much about logic in American Roman Catholic colleges; however, Christopher Derrick in *Escape From Scepticism: Liberal Education as if Truth Mattered* (Peru: Sherwood Sugden, 1977), using the example of Thomas Aquinas College in California, advocates an Augustinian-based Thomism as the best epistemology for liberal education. As in the seventeenth-century, dogmatically-oriented Protestants and Roman Catholics can still share fundamental epistemological views.

Charles Morton

A Logic System

The preface to the Reader.

When I consider the Singular parts and Industry of some persons, and that of either Sex, who have not the Command of Learned Languages, nor have had the opportunity to attain them; methinks I find a compassion stirring in my good nature, and inclineing me to do what I can for them, To Cherish their noble desire of knowledge, and in some measure to give it satisfaction. What pity it is that Reasonable Souls should not be Improved to the utmost; that Ingenious minds should Languish for want of matter to work uppon. Tis true Indeed, they are at present busied but it is for the most part in things below their Souls, and their extensive capacities; and unless Religion or Conscience raise the mind to matters of the highest nature: the witt and Industry of most men is wholly Imployed in purveying for the body, and progging to satisfie its sensuall appetites. mean while there is little or no provision for the noble & high born soul it self: no knowledge for the Intellect to feast upon; no contemplations to be well digested as a nourishment for a solid and growing wisdom!

My purpose is therefore to translate or compose (as the matter will bear) short systems or breviaries of various kinds of learning in our mother tongue, that so all sorts of the Ingenious may be something more worthy the looking after than what they are generally Imployed about.

The knowledge and fear of God is indeed the Topp of wisdom; but next under it, and in subordination to it, is good Literature; for hereby men Arrive nearer the Top of Jacob's Ladder, whose bottom is sett upon the earth, where the Beasts may graze about it; and the upper and in the highest heaven; but the middle hights are for the Angells, and Angelicall souls to Traverse.

Some that have drudged in books may think that i have prophaned the mysteries of Ceres, and done phylosophy wrong by exposing it to vulgar eyes: others also may Laugh at the undertaking, as a fruitless and Impertinent Labour, Because our Tongue will not express many things without a Tedious circumlocution, or some cramp words that will be as hard to understand as Greek and Latin [if they be not the very same] such as, Genus, Species, prædicable, prædicament, subject, adjunct, homogeneall, heterogeneal, & such like, especially in the art of Logick.

To all Which I answer. That some of these Gentlemen have so much affected to use such terms in their popular discourses as hath taken of a great deale of their horrour; So that a vulgar eye will not soe terribly be started at them, because their ears have been somewhat acquainted with them. A part of the present designe is to explain the harder phrases whereby such adorn'd discourses may be better understood; and so not yeild an Uncertain sound and become altogether useless. And although the vulgar Tongue cannot so fully express all things, as might be wished; yet it may do it sufficiently to let men see, that there is something considerable in humane Learning; and that Scholars who more fully comprehend those matters, are no such pittifull and contemptible things as now the world does make them.

Now by the most of men one profitable is valued beyond all the Liberall arts; but hereafter Tis hoped they will account those Liberall, to be of a more noble allay. And if by this means Phylosophy shall obtain a better esteem; then I hope no wrong is done thereto, by showing in some sort what it is to the view of the common people.

Again it is Well Known that many of the best Learned [such as, Bacon, Digby, Raynolds, Wilkins, Beylo, More, &c] have soe enobled our Language with Phylosophicall discourses, that forreigners are said to have Addicted themselves to our Tongue, for those works sake written therein; being not content with Translations which they Judge (with good Reason) must needs fall short of the originalls.[1]

Now supposing that those worthies did this for high & prudent ends, Their examples (in some Measure) may become our warrant. Besides those excellent mens Writings may be better Apprehended by our country men, & so become a more generall, as well esteem, as usefulness. Add to this A profession of any Ignorance, why any man should be secluded from the Investigation of any Truth; Seeing God has made his great works to be sought out of all those that have pleasure therein. [Psalms: III:2.].

Nor do I know but that this Little Light hung up in the entry thereof, may Invite some active spirits to trye a farther passage, Into the more secret chambers of Phylosophy: yea may not some be excited to an unwearied and Irrefragable Industry; In getting the more usefull tongues when they perceive their subserviency in those matters: and at Length Arrive unto a per-

---

[1] Francis Bacon (1561–1626) published in English his *The Great Instauration and The Advancement of Learning*. Kenelm Digby (1603–1665), Henry More (1614–1687), and John Wilkins (1614–1672) wrote many works in English. "Raynolds" might be Richard Rainolde (d. 1606) who wrote a rhetoric textbook in English, but the book does not seem to have been popular after its publication in 1563. I have not been able to find "Beylo," or some name like it, but suspect it might be one of the pseudonymns attached to Thomas White (1593–1676) who wrote several philosophical works in English, including *Controversy-Logicke, or the Method to come to Truth in Debates of Religion* (1659). White's most common alias was Blacklo.

fection [at least] capable of making discreetly some natural experiments, whereby they may light on happy Inventions to the Augmentation of science.

Not to mention the Noble Emulation that may be stirred hereby to A greater Industry in those, that have had the benefit of a better education: As also the handsomer converse among men, when things rather than persons shall be the subject of their discourse. what is said may I hope suffice to make Apology for this present undertaking, which is professed to have no other ends, then Gods glory and the Generall good of Men.

The End of the preface.

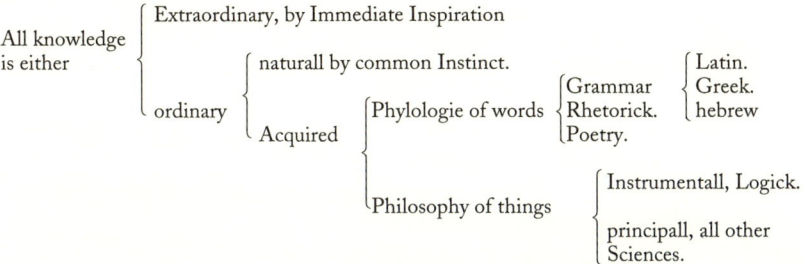

Principall Philosophy is the comprehension of all Arts & Sciences so far as by naturall light they can be acquired (i.e.) by teaching, Learning, and Study can be gotten.

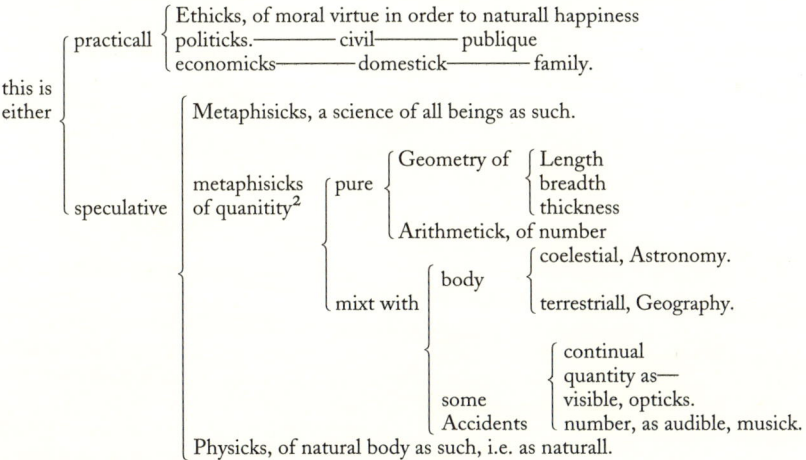

[2] Dunbar's version calls this simply "mathematicks."

A Logick System

Beings are
- notional, as terms of Art which have no being or existence but in the thoughts of men.
- Real
  - Creator, God.
  - creature
    - Substance
      - Spirit or thinking substance
        - Angells
          - Good.
          - Bad.
        - souls of men
      - body or extended substance
        - Simple
          - heavens (say the Aintients)
          - Elements, fire, water, earth, air.
        - mixt
          - Imperfectly as meteors
            - Airy; winds.
            - watery
              - clouds, mist, same.
              - Rain Snow &c.
            - fiery
              - thunder &c.
              - comets (vulgarly said)
          - perfectly
            - Inanimate
              - stone, not fusil nor ductile.
              - metal, both—&c—
              - mineral,—none—
            - Animate
              - Insensible plant
                - herb.
                - shrub.
                - Tree
              - sensible animal
                - Irrational brute
                  - Airy, birds
                  - watery, fishes
                  - earthy, beasts
                - Rational man
                  - John
                  - Thomas
                  - William
                  - &c.
    - Accidents
      - Quantity
      - Quality
      - Relation
      - Action
      - Passion
      - Whereness
      - Whenness
      - Situation
      - Habit

CHARLES MORTON

Porphyries Tree[3]
Diagram. A. To Chap[t]. 2.

Highest Genus Absolute | Being / Real / Creature | Transcendentalls above all the Predicaments.

Highest Genus Predicamentall—Substance

Subalternates { Body / mixt / Perfect / Living / Animal } Predicamentalls which are in some Predicament.

Lowest Species—man[4]

John
Thomas
William

Individualls under A Predicament

Diagram. B. To Chap[t]. 3.

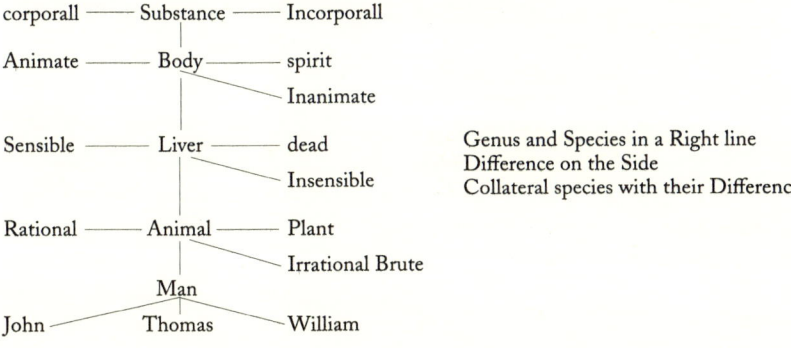

Genus and Species in a Right line
Difference on the Side
Collateral species with their Differences

---

[3] Porphyry (b. 232/233 AD) was a pro-Aristotelian and anti-Christian logician who was influential in neo-Platonic education. St. Augustine praised Porphyry for improving "upon both Plato and Plotinus." The "tree" seems to have been a later development by those teaching from Porphyry's *Isagoge* and his two commentaries on Aristotle's *Categories*. See Christos Evangeliou, *Aristotle's Categories and Porphyry* (Leiden: E.J. Brill, 1988) and Porphyry: *On Aristotle's Categories*, trans. Steven K. Strange (Ithaca: Cornell, 1992).

[4] Partridge makes a mistake here by extending the Predicamentalls bracket to include "man." He does not do it in chapter 2, nor does Dunbar in his version.

A Logick System

1. Its Distinction. into
Natural. Men's common Reason.

Artificial
- **Systematicall** A summary of Logical precepts or a book of it. {as} Smiths Logick. &c.[5]
- Habitual a quality in the mind
  - Grounded on Reason.
  - Gotten by Study & use of præcepts.

2. Its Definition
Habitual Logick is An Art of thinking. or an Art directing the mind in the knowledge of things.
Note, 'Tis the Instrumentall Phylosophy, and Therefore first Learn'd because a man must be first furnished with Instruments [or books] before he can doe any works.
3. Its Object [or matter which it treats of] are terms of Art (i.e) Artificiall new names given to things.—besides the proper & grammaticall words. See.*

*Animal. cald genus.—
Man.—species.
Socrates.—Individuals—[6]

¶ Because terms are not so much the outward words as the Inward conceptions therefore they are called **Notions**. and because formed in the mind after the proper or first **Notions** therefore cald Second Notions.

---

[5] Dunbar's transcription has "Smith's, Sanderson's, Bergersdicius his logick." The Smith mentioned is probably Samuel Smith's *Aditus ad Logicam* (London, 1613) which was popular at Oxford for most of the seventeenth century. See Wilbur S. Howell, *Logic and Rhetoric in England 1500–1700*, 292–299 for a discussion of Smith's logic. The other neo-Aristotelian sources are Robert Sanderson's *Logicae Artis Compendium* (Oxford, 1615) and Franco Burgersdijck's *Institutionum Logicarum* (Cambridge, 1647).

[6] Lines such as this indicate copying a portion of the sentence above.

CHARLES MORTON

¶ Those terms have no being but (objective only) in the understanding; therefore are no longer then they are thought of. Any real Being that I think of is (objective) in my understanding; but not (objective only) for it may have a being when I think not of it.

¶ Every Art hath its proper terms which A man utterly unacquainted with that art, understandeth not. Such A man being asked What is this? would Answer in the First notions, as what the Artist would call [A Hammer] he would call [a peice of Iron fastened to a stick][7] [A mallet] (a small longer stick fastened to a short thicker one) [A Cheezel] an (Iron broad and thin at one end, with a thicker peice of wood fastened to the other) &c.

¶ This is enlarged on to show why Logick gives new names to things that they may be more distinctly & easily understood, that as the Artist calls for his tools by the Artificial name: so the mind may Recall her notions, & order them easily by the help of those terms, & therefore these new hard words are not useless & Impertinent.

> Terms are as handles fixed to a thing:
> usefull; as bonds that flesh to market bring

4. Its end, is to direct the understanding [as moral habits regulate the will) Note understanding (or Intellect) & will are two cheif faculties in man wherby he is distinquished from a brute.

5. Its parts, are 2 answerable by the 3 acts of the Intellect
{ apprehension
  composition
  discourse

   1. Apprehension is of simple terms, that is such as represent one thing to the mind. & they are 1mary or 2dary.

      1. Primary Simple term, is when one word or notion express one thing. As Animal, Man, Learned (in the first notions) or Genus, Species, Accident (in the 2d notions).

      2. Secondary, or raised from the former, is when more words or notions signifie. But one thing, (as a Reasonable Animal) signifies (a man) or (in 2d notions) a (Genus with its difference) signifies the (species) and this is done in Definition. or (an Animal Rational or Irrational) Represents a Distributive notion of an Animal to my thoughts in division.

---

[7] Partridge's use of brackets and parentheses is erratic.

A Logick System

2. Composition. is the joyning more simple terms together in a sentence by the verb substantive (is) either { Expressed / Implyed } as a Man is a Rational Animal or Species is a genus with its difference. As Socrates walks. that is, Socrates is walking.

¶ the 2d part of Log. directs this act by Proposition.

3. Discourse or Ratiocination. (not External in words, but Internal in thoughts).

    1. Illative (or Inferentiall) which draws (or Inferrs) one proposition (as a conclusion) from one or more (as promises) in Syllogism.

    2. Ordinative (or methodicall) which Rightly disposes the parts of a Discipline, In Method.

        Logic by its 3 parts dos the Intellect.
        to (Apprehend, compound, discourse) direct.

Synopsis Cap. 1 of Logick

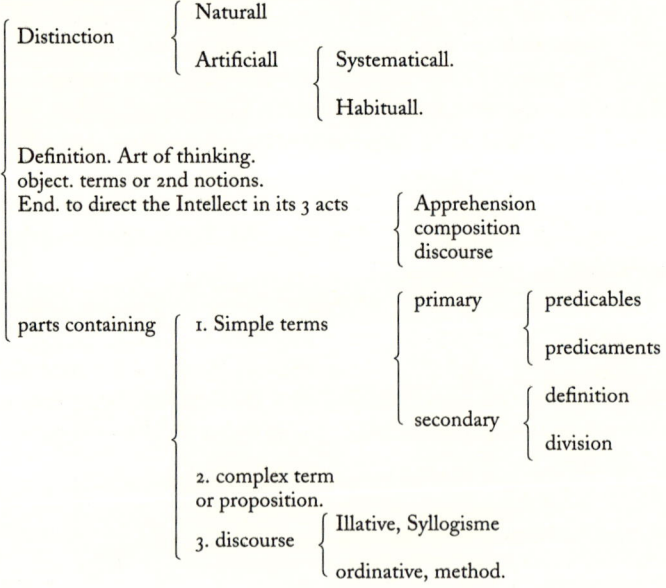

The First Part of Logick of { predicables | Definition.
Predicaments | Division. }

Cap. 2.   of Predicables.[8]

Predicables are such as are apt to be spoken (that is affirmed or denyd) of things and that either
of { one. Individuall.
more. Universall. }

1. Individuall (or singular) is that which is under the lowest Species, and can be no further divided into compleck things thô it may into parts of a thing.
¶ Animal [the Genus] can be divided into man and brute. [the five species thereof] man the species may be divided into all singular men as Socrates, Plato, Arist. &c. But one of those being Individuall can be no farther splitt unless into parts & peices (as body, soul, head, hands, &c.) Indeed the same name as (John) may be attributed to divers singular men (as John Rogers, John Roberts &c.) but neither of those Johns (the thing or person) can be divided or Attributed to any other person in the world.
¶ All things existent in the world are Individualls. Genus and Species may have essence and being, and may have somewhat affirmed or denyed of them, as an Animal is sensible. A man is not a stone But nothing hath existence or actuation of being out of its causes but a singular. for man were not to be found were it not for John, Tom, William, or some other person or Individuall:

---

[8] Although rooted in Aristotle's *Categoriae*, chapter. 2, this discussion of predicables is highly influenced by early Medieval developments which William and Martha Kneale in *The Development of Logic*, 187, think might be rooted in Porphyry's *Isagoge*, principally the *quinque voces* of species, genus, differentia, property, and accident. Morton's use of "Porphyry's Tree" and neo-Aristotelianism's general use of predicables as discussed here indicates an acceptance of post-Aristotelian developments by humanistic logicians even though their rhetoric emphasized purifying Aristotelianism of its Medieval accumulations. Such reliance on post-Aristotelian developments is evident throughout *A Logick System*.

A Logick System

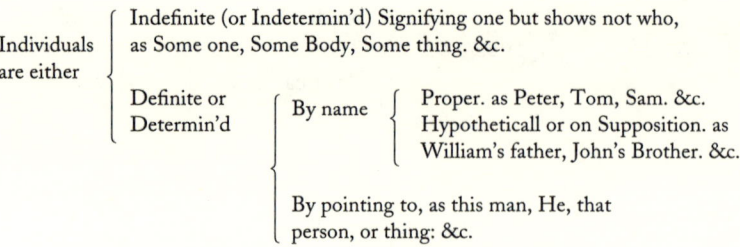

Individuals are either
- Indefinite (or Indetermin'd) Signifying one but shows not who, as Some one, Some Body, Some thing. &c.
- Definite or Determin'd
  - By name
    - Proper. as Peter, Tom, Sam. &c.
    - Hypotheticall or on Supposition. as William's father, John's Brother. &c.
  - By pointing to, as this man, He, that person, or thing: &c.

A Single one or Individuall! What,
Indefin'd Proper, Suppos'd pointed at

2. Universalls are apt to be predicated of more than one, that is may Answer to Questions

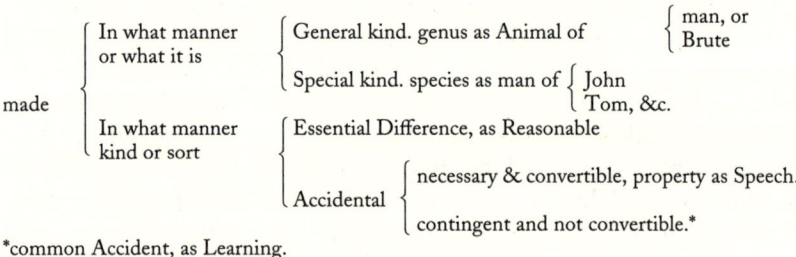

made
- In what manner or what it is
  - General kind. genus as Animal of { man, or Brute
  - Special kind. species as man of { John, Tom, &c.
- In what manner kind or sort
  - Essential Difference, as Reasonable
  - Accidental
    - necessary & convertible, property as Speech.
    - contingent and not convertible.*

*common Accident, as Learning.

As what is man? An Animal (genus) What is Socrates? A man (species) what kind of Animal is man? A Rational (difference) or speaking Animal (property) or what kind of man is Socrates? Learned (Accident)

¶ properties do primarily belong to the Genus or species because they are Inseparable from the whole kind, but Accidents are variable and therefore cheifly are predicated of and ascribed to Individualls.

¶ that speech is said to be a property of man because by outward articulate sounds it signifies the inward Thoughts. therefore A parrot which knows not what he says doth not speak but only Imitate words and sounds.

¶ some will have properties to be essentiall not Accidentall and then they thus distribute the universalls as Predicables

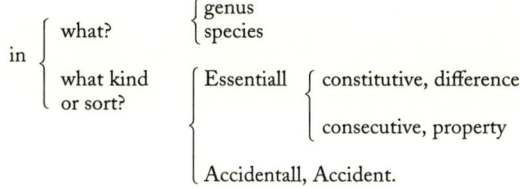

1. Genus or Generall kind is that which is predicated of more species. As Animal of Man or Brute. for if I ask what is man? you may Rightly answer an Animal. And so what is a brute an Animal,

Genus is
- highest
  - absolute, as being
  - predicamentall, as Substance
- Subalternate, as body, mixt. &c.

¶ Highest Genus is above all and can never be a species. Lowest species is below all (next the Individuall) and can never be a Genus. { genus / species } +

Subalternates are between both and are both
¶ Genus hath two or more species under it.

{ In respect to what { Below / above } so Animal is { Genus of man. / Species of living. }
Genus is also { next. So Animal to man. / Remote. So body or substance to man. } }

[151]

A Logick System

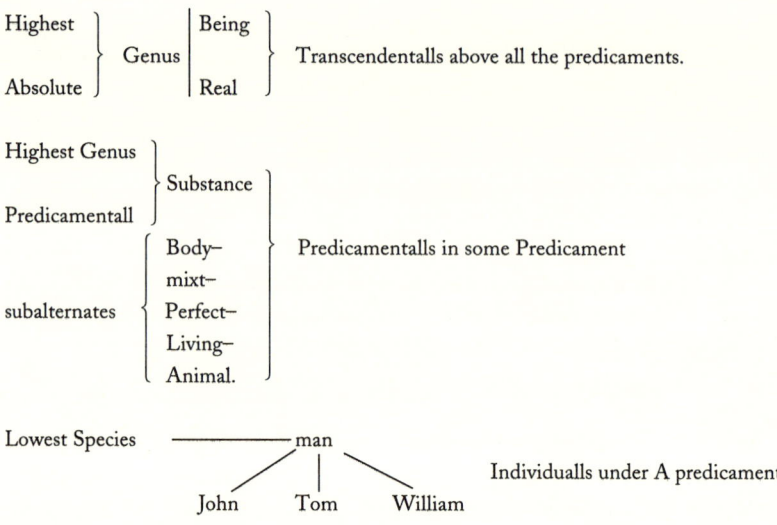

2. Species or speciall kind is that which is under a Genus, or rather that which is predicable of more Individualls, as man of John, Tom, William &c.
¶ Predicable, that is apt to be predicated though actually it be not, for the nature of a species may be conserved in one Individuall. So man was a species when only Adam was created. So the sun or moon &c. are species thô there be but one Individuall of their kind. for if there were many more they might be all called Sun and Moon.

> Genus above, Species below are seen.—
> and Subalternates take their place between

3. Difference is that which answers essentially to the question (what sort kind or manner) as what sort of Animal is man? Rational (that is the difference)

> The offices of Difference are.

1. To divide the genus into species: so Rational splitts Animal into man and brute; for the animal that is Rational that is man; not Rational is brute: in this respect difference is called divisive.

2. To constitute the species [together with the Genus] so animality & Rationality do essentially constitute a Man, and so it is call'd constitutive.
¶ That as Diff. is cald constitutive, because 'tis an essentiall part, so property (thô some will have it to be essentiall too) yet is said to be consecutive or following not makeing the nature of the thing. So Risibility (or power of Laughing) or the power of Speech, do follow upon Reason, but Reason which is the difference makes the man.

> Genus and difference do the species make
> Properties after difference place do take

4. Property is predicated as the Diff. of the Species, but consecutive and in a secondary order to Diff. (as was said) they are of 4 sorts.
  1. only not all, as to be a Physitian, only of the species of man not of every Individuall man.
  2. All not only, as to have two leggs. of man all naturally, but not only, for birds have so, this is the meanest property, for property naturally Imports only, it may therefore be called a community Rather than a Property.
  3. All and only, not always, as the venerable hoary head of man, but not in youth.
  4. All, only, and always, as the power of Laughing & Speaking of man. This is the cheif property and 'tis here especially meant, for the other 3 may be Accounted common accidents.

> Not only, not all, not always possest
> I mean; not only, always is the best

¶ That the power of speaking belongs to all men (Thô Infants and dumb persons can't actually speak)
Because 'tis a Perfection due to the humane nature. & therfore such persons are said to have the power of speaking in the first act thô not in the second. and so seeing is ascribed to a blind Animal, because sight is the perfection of the Animal nature.

Property
- Genericall what follows the Genus and is converted with it as going to an Animal.
- Specificall what follows the species & is converted with it as speaking to a man.

¶ Convertible is when the predication will turn with an all, as all men speak, & all that speaks is a man.

¶ They are also said to be necessary to the subject because they are due to the naturall perfections of that thing whereof they are properties.

5. Accident is predicated as property, but contingently, not necessary, or convertible, so Learning of a man. Whiteness of a wall. &c. they are of 2 sorts.

   1. Inseparable (by mans hand or art) as blackness from A crow

   2. Separable (by mans hand or art) as whiteness from A wall. All Accidents are separable by our thought.

¶ Separation by thoughts (or mental) is called Abstraction. Which is twofold:

   1. Precisive is when we can think of one thing without thinking of the other: Thus I can abstract cheife properties, as I can think of A man without thinking of the power of his speech, but that I cannot do what the Diff. Rationality: for that is Implied and Included in the formall conception of man.

   2. Negative when I can deny the thing In my mind or suppose the contrary without any contradiction or Absurdity (thô perhaps it cannot be without falshood) See common Accidents (thô Inseparable actually or manually) yet may mentally be Abstracted; Thus I can think or say (the Crow is white) and yet not think or speak a contradiction (Thô a falshood) for blackness thô it be truly in a Crow is not essentiall to it: for it might be a crow thô it were not black. Soe I can think away thô not wash away the redness of a brick for it might be a brick thô it were not red. But now I cannot say of a property [man is not Risible] without A contradiction and absurdity because this is an essentiall and necessary property of man. Essentiall consecutive [as property] thô not essentiall constitutive [as Diff] as is before noted.

$$\left\{ \begin{array}{l} \text{Precisive is of what laid aside} \\ \text{Negative is of what may be denied} \end{array} \right\}$$

¶ Therefore Diff. can no ways be separated & abstracted. properties can be abstracted precisively not negatively. Inseparable Accidents may be abstracted negatively. Separable Accidents may not only mentally but actually or manually be taken quite away.

CHARLES MORTON

Abstraction precisive takes property
All common Accidents I can deny.—

Synopsis. Cap. 2.

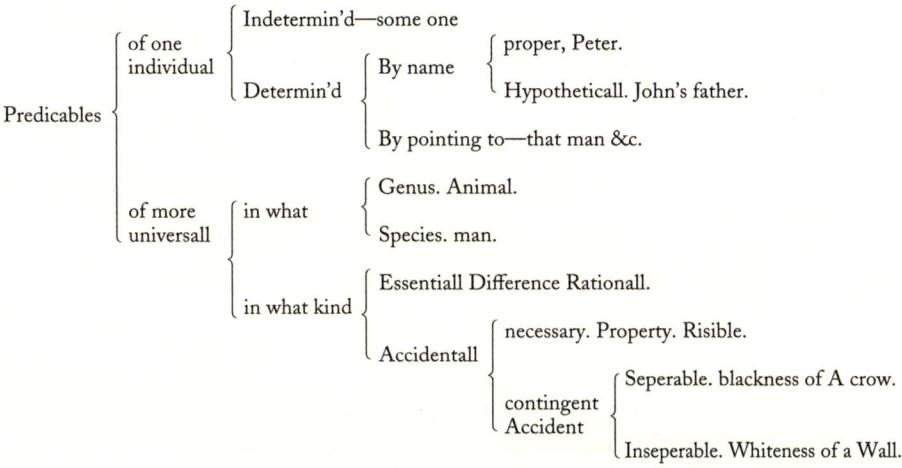

Cap. 3.   Of Antepredicaments.

Antepredicaments are somethings needfull to be foreknown (by way of preface) for the better understanding the predicaments. There are Definitions, Divisions, and Rules.
1. Definitions 3. Æquivocalls, univocalls, & Denominatives.
2. Divisions. 2. of words, and things.
3. Rules. 2. of things under the same common Genus, & things not seen.

1. Definitions 3.
  1. Æquivocalls are where the name is the same but the Reason of that name is different; so dog is an Æquivocall name; of the barking Animal 'tis the natural name, of the dog fish, and of the dog starr a borrowed name: for 'tis not cald dog. Because tis a barker but because 'tis a constellation so painted on the globe, of the fish (not as barker neither, but) because it hunts fishes as dogs do beasts.

A Logick System

¶ All figurative speeches are Æquivocalls So christ is a door, way, vine &c.

¶ you cannot understand the truth or falshood of a sentence before you know in what sense the words are taken, therfore the Logicall Rule is first distinguish of words, before you define or determine of things.

2. Univocalls are where is the same name & reason of the name or common nature. So Animal is the common name of man and beast, for the same Reason Bec: both are sensible Living creatures (which is the nature of an Animal)

Univocalls are either
- perfect such as are before mention'd
- Imperfect cald Analogicall words, which are Referred to univocalls.

Analogicalls have the same name & nature (as univocalls) but not Equally & depending one of the other. So being it is a Common name for Substance & Accident, but substance hath more of being then Accidents. & Accident would have no being but as depending on substance. so God and Creature are both said to be beings.

3. Denominatives are when words are of a like signification and are derived one of the other. as Justice, Just, Justly. Three things belong to

Denomination
- the subject denominated, as Aristides.
- the form or Accident denominating, as Justice.
- the denominative or aggregate comprehending both, as Just.

¶ By form is meant any predicable (in what sort soever) Whether it be difference, property, or Accident. for a man may be denominated Rational from Rationality (the Diff.) risible from risibility (the property) White from whiteness (the common Accident).

¶ Just is said to be an Aggregate both of subject & form, because it is an Adjective, now adjectives in Grammar are never said to stand alone, and therefore they always suppose some substantive thô not expressed, such as man, thing, &c. So when one saith Just, he is understood to mean a Just man, a good, a good thing.

CHARLES MORTON

$\left\{\begin{array}{l}\text{Equiv: Univocalls, with their Analogates}\\\text{Subject and form do make Denominates.}\end{array}\right\}$

2. Divisions 2. of things and of words.
    1. of things into }   Substance | Everything in the world is
                        Accident | one of those

    Great Aristotle all created things
    under 2 common heads (sub, Acci) brings

1. Substance is that wherein Accident inheres, as man in whom is Learning, virtue, honesty, &c.
2. Accident is that which Inheres in a Substance, as Learning, honesty, &c.
¶ To Inhere is to be in, not as part (as the branch abides in the vine) nor locally (as wine in the Glass) but so as it cannot be unless it be in, as Learning cannot have a being unless it be in some man: whereas the branch or the wine might be the same, thô they are removed from the vine or glass.
Accident's being is in being.

    In not as part nor place nor can absent
    that does inhere and is an Accident.

¶ Thô Accidents can be absent from substances without their destruction, yet they cannot be without their own; therefore take an Accident Individuall (as this blackness) from its Individuall subject (this paper) one without it cease to be.
¶ And from this it follows that no Individuall Accident can shift subjects, or pass from one subject to another. therfore when whiteness comes of from the wall on my cloathe; 'tis not the whiteness separated from its subject, but part of the lime which is its subject doth come of with it. and when a blackness seems to be taken of, and put on again upon a Liquor, it is not the same numericall or Individuall blackness that was before but a new produced. This rule is of great use in the controversie of **Transubstantiation**. For the Papist say that the same Accidents of bread (Colour, tast, smell, figure &c) do pass from the bread to the flesh when the substance is

A Logick System

chang'd; but Protestants say 'tis Impossible. Bec. 'tis contrary to the very nature of an Accident.

2. of words into
{ Abstract & concrete, as Learning & Learned.
Simple & complex as Learned, & Socrates is Learned. }

Abstract is the substantive of an Accident, & consider'd without the consideration of the subject. for I may think of the nature of Wisdom and folly, virtue & vice, &c. without Applying them to any man.
Concrete is the adjective of an Accident and therefore does always Imply a substantive or subject to be joyned with it. as Wise Implies a man as well as Wisdom, or whereas Wisdom signifies it selfe without any consideration of man.
Simple is any word or words (how many soever) that have no verb joyned to make it a sentence, as horse, man, Loved, hated, &c. or a good honest Just man, &c.
Complex is a sentence made by a verb joyn'd to other words. This sentence is cald A proposition which is allways form'd by the verb substantive (is) as is before shown, Cap. 1. Socrates walks, or is walking.

Abstract—as Justice. concrete is as Just
Simple—as man, & complex, man is dust.

3. Rules Antepredicamentall are 2.
   1. ℞ [9]. whatsoever is predicated (essentially) of the predicate is also predicated of the subject. as in this Proposition [Socrates is a man] Socrates is the subject, man is the essentiall predicate, (or thing affirmed) now whatsoever may be essentially said of the predicate man, may be truly also said of the subject Socrates, as man is an Animal Rational, Risible, &c. and therefore so is Socrates.

{ What predicate essentially they do,
of predicate, may of the Subject too— }

---

[9] ℞ is a symbol for the Latin *recipere* which means to receive. Used mostly by physicians since the Middle Ages, the use here to delineate rules is an idiosyncrasy.

[158]

2. Rx. Genus, as that are put subordinately or one under another have the same species and Difference, but not so put have Divers; as substance, body, Liver, Animal, are put one under another, (se Diagram B) all these have the same species: as man which is the next species to Animal is Remote to Substance, body,: &c. these have also the same Diff. for corporeall is the divisive Diff. of substance, & the constitutive Diff. of body, and so of the rest. but if they are so disposed in subordination then have they Divers species & Differences, as subj.

¶ the Diagram B of substance (& so it might be of other predicaments) is cald Porphyries tree. To which we shall again have Recourse when we come to the Definition of a Predicament.

Synopsis. Cap. 3.

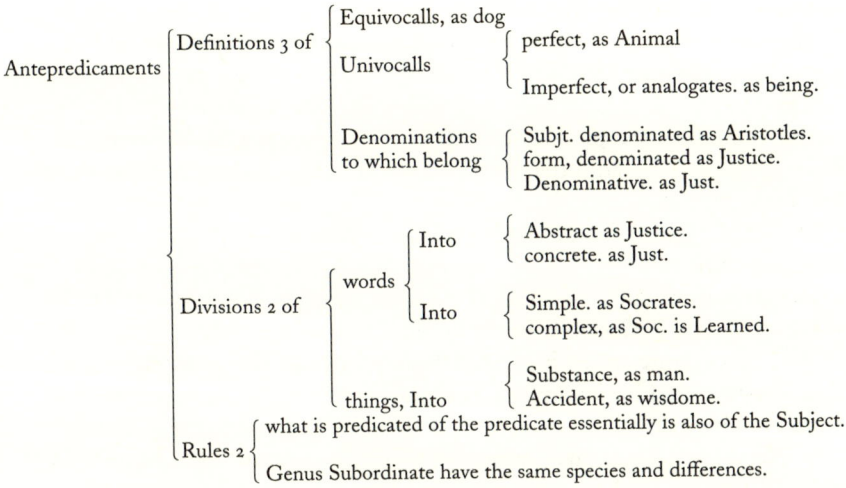

[159]

A Logick System

Cap. 4th   Of Predicaments in Generall[10]

A Predicament is a Troop, or Series, or order of things in their Genus & species Rightly disposed, over and under another, & the Differences on the side: see Porphyries Tree Diagram B.

| They are in | Substance | Quality | Action | whereness | site | all things in the world are |
| number so | Quantity | Relation | position | whenness | habit | Referred to one of these. |

All which are comprehended in these two verses

> A man, tall, wise, that once his friend, did Greet
> Buried, In Greece, new, lies, in winding Sheet

But that it may be directly there are 5 Requisites. namely that it may be
1. Real being (& not notion) for thô the Predicament, or order be but a notion, yet the matter therein handled & disposed are things & Real beings.
2. Univocall, bec. the predications of the Genus^s & Species are univocall, Equivocals can't be admitted before they be distinquished & their right sense assertayn'd.
3. Universalls that is Genus^s or Species; for Individuals are under and not in a Predicament.
4. Whole and compleat, as Man, not a part as head, hand &c. which are not directly, but Reductively in the predicament of their whole.
5. finite. for infinite are excluded whither they be positive or negative.
    1. Positive, as God, who can have no Genus or common nature with any of his creatures.
    2. Negative, (which may rather be called) Indefinite, than Infinite) as not a man, not a horse &c. now those words signifie nothing certain, & therfore can be referred to no certain order of things.

> To Predicaments five things are Requisite,
> Real, Univ: Univers: Whole, Finite

---

[10] Predicament is another name for category.

CHARLES MORTON

Synopsis Cap. 4th.

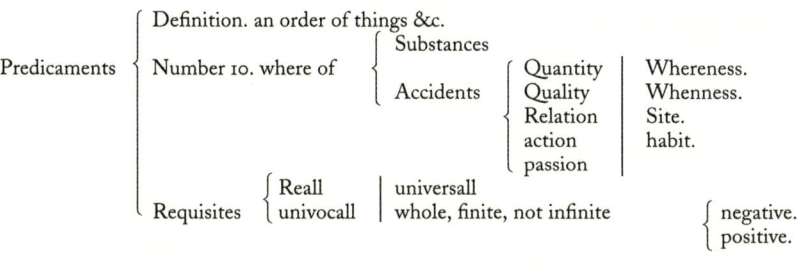

Cap: 5th   Of Substance

Substance is a being subsisting of it Self and subject to Accidents. Subsisting, with its Diff. of it self not to exclude depending of God, but on other things as Accident dos on Substance. Subject to Accidents is its property, & that of the 4th kind, & of the best with a distinction of Immediate and mediate.

1 Immediate subject of Accidents may be an Accident, and this sustained by a farther subject.

2 Mediate and Ultimate which lastly sustains all, and this is only Substance [as the sweetness of honey is delightfull] where delightfulness (an Accident) is Immediately said of and subjected in sweetness (an Accid, too) but mediately of honey (the substance) which doth lastly sustain both the sweetness and delightfulness: much like a chain of divers links that hangs at by one and by a nail fastened to a wall; one link indeed sustains another, but all are held up by the nail. Sub, is divided 2 ways, as subsisting, & as Subject to Accident.

1. as Subsisting into   { Spirit of those pneumantic or Doctrine of Spirits.^{II}
its proper Species   { Body-Physics or natural Phylosophy.

---

^{II} Morton's understanding of spiritual substance has far reaching consequences on his understanding of human procreation. In the *Compendium Physicae*, 143, Morton wrote against "the Antients" who believed the male seed "active" and female "passive." Morton insisted on "spirituous matter" in both male and female that is "conjoyn'd" along with "grosser matter" to produce a child.

A Logick System

2. Subjt. to Accident Into first & second.

1. First substances are Singular or Individuall cald first Bec: primarily Accidents are inherent in them.
2. Second substances are universalls (genus & species) Bec: they are but 2dary subjects to adjuncts or accidents: for man (the species) is said to be learned Bec: this or that particular man is so; and were there no Individual man learned, Learning could not be ascribed to mankind.

$$\left\{ \begin{array}{l} \text{Spirit \& Body, Substance \& Species} \\ \text{But first and Second its Subjecting ways} \end{array} \right\}$$

Canons, Rules, Propositions, or properties of Substance are chiefly 4.

1. Substance hath no contraries; for contraiety is peculiar to quality. therefore fire and water are said to be contraries, not in respect of the substance but of their contrary qualities, heat and cold.
2. it hath no degrees (of being) this also belongs to qualities. It may indeed be greater or less, more or less, extension it has, but not Intention. as a tree is not more (that is rather) a substance than a hair, thô it be a greater substance. a hair has as truly and as many Accidents, as a tree.
3 It admits contraries into it, Remaining still numerically (or Individually) the same. So the same numericall water is hot & cold

$$\left\{ \begin{array}{l} \text{successively in intense} \\ \text{together in remiss} \end{array} \right| \text{degrees.}$$

¶ degrees in qualities are accounted 8 in number; one (as of cold) will consist in the same substance with 7 (as of heat) 2 with 6. 2 with 5. &c. but 8. will not admit one of the contrary: therefore 8 are intense degrees and all the rest Remiss.
4 Second substances and their Differences are univocally predicated of the first substances, as Socrates or Plato (the first substance) is a man (the second substance) is Rationall (its difference).

[162]

Synopsis Cap. 5th

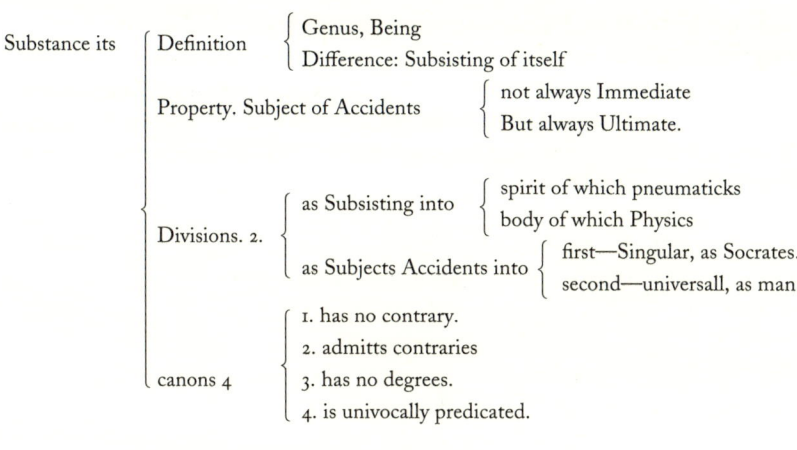

Cap. 6th   Of Quantity

Quantity is an Acci: (as all the rest that follow are) whereby a subject is said to be extended; that is having one part out of another. extension is either ⎰ penetrable.
⎱ Impenetrable

1. penetrable is the having parts so out of parts as that it can have them all together in a point of space, or at pleasure can expatiate them to a larger space by this also more things can be in the same space together. therefore this penetration is not such a peircing, as a Gimlet, Borrier or nail pierceth wood; for these only remove the wood out of the way by cutting it of or thrusting it asides. This extension is proper to spirits which may be in the same space wherein bodies or other spirits are without mutual Impediment (Legion for we are many)[12] This may be illustrated by Gods

---

[12] The penetrability of spiritual substance is extensively discussed by Henry More in several works, especially *The Immortality of the Soul*. The parenthetical remark comes from Mark 5: 1–20 where Jesus asks a demon-possessed man his name and the evil spirits reply "My name is Legion for we are many."

universall prescense, whom if body could exclude from any where he were not Infinite (which is contrary to the name of the Deity)
2. Impenetrable in having parts so out of place as that they can't be together, nor can any body be in the same space with another be it never so small, therefore as one comes in the other goes out, so as beer comes in the cup the air goes out. &c. This extension is open to bodies & materiall things, & is the extension of Quantity. What dimensions cannot penetrate

$$\left\{ \begin{array}{l} \text{Spirits Extension, doth possess no Space} \\ \text{But things that are notional fill a place} \end{array} \right\}$$

The Species of Quantity are $\left\{ \begin{array}{l} \text{continual.} \\ \text{discrete.} \end{array} \right.$

1. continuall whose parts are connected by a common term that is by some Indivisible connecting the divisible parts of Quantity. the species of continuall quantity are 3
Length, having one dimension
Breadth— 2—s   These are more fully handles in Geometry,
thickness —3—s   as number in Arithmetick.

1. Length (cald line) is only long and hath no breadth or depth; such as are an Inch, span, cubit, yard, mile, &c. its common term is indivisible point, so the middle an{d} end of a line is the common point or term of the 2 halves.
¶ Line is a very equivocall word and is used many ways: as for a line printed or written in a book: a small line drawn by a pen; a cord streched out: a boundary. &c. but here 'tis only taken for the bare length of any thing, which therefore is cald its line.
2. breadth (surface or outer face of a thing) has 2 dimensions, viz, long & broad, (or outward & sidewise) but no depth. Such are board measure, glass measure, land measure: as a feet square, a perch square, An Acre, A hide of land (that is 30 acres) &c.—Its common term is line. which thô divisible according to length, yet not to breadth; for it has no breadth; for it has no breadth and so it is a term.
3. thickness (called solid, & body-Mathematicall, distinct from body physicall which is in substance) has 3 dimensions, Length (onwards)

breadth (sideways) & depth (downwards or upwards). Such are timber measure (cald solid or cubicall) as a foot square of wood which is formed like a die; so a foot square of water &c. Its common term is surface (as it has no thickness) for if I conceive a body to be divided into 2 parts, I must conceive abroad surface passing thrô it, where that division is made: this conceived surface is the one common term which renders the body continuous before the actual division; but after that division two surfaces do emerge instead of that one; and then the two parts clapped, together will be but continuous (or touching) but not continuous (or whole).

$$\left\{\begin{array}{l}\text{Continual Quantity is Long Broad Thick}\\\text{Discreet in Number for Arithmetick.}\\\text{Lines common in point \& Surface line}\\\text{Surface the Parts of Body doth combine.}\end{array}\right\}$$

2. Discrete quantity is number whose parts are not connected, but consist of a multitude of severall unites. the smallest number is 2.

Number is divided

1. into $\left\{\begin{array}{l}\text{number numbering, as 1. 2. 3. \&c. abstracted from all things.}\\\text{number numbered, as 1. 2. 3. \&c when applied to any thing.}\end{array}\right.$

So when I number my eggs I say 1. 2. 3. which if they were number numbering they would make 6. but in numbers numbered it is but 3 and is no more than 1. 1. & 1.

2. Into numbers $\left\{\begin{array}{l}\text{cardinal. as 1. 2. 3. \&c. so called because cheif}\\\text{ordinal as } 1^{st}. 2^{d}. 3^{d}. \&c.\end{array}\right.$

$$\left\{\begin{array}{l}\text{As number under these Distinctions fall}\\\text{Numbring Numbred, Cardinal, Ordinal}\end{array}\right\}$$

Canons of Quantity are 4.

1. Quantity has no contrary. a straight and crooked line are contrary not as lines, but in respect of their qualities straightness and crookedness.

A Logick System

2. Quantity has no degrees, is not more and less, thô greater & less.

3. From Quantity things are said to be equal & unequal; for Equality is when divers things have the same quantity or measure.

4. Quantity may always be divided or augmented; at least in our thoughts thô not actually. there may be a least **Physical** (cald Atom) but no least **mathematicall**, and so may be said of a greatest, for there is nothing so great but; can still think it greatest here that pretty Riddle and seeming contradiction (yet true) **you cannot do what you can as** for you cannot in your thoughts add to number as much as you can add; for you can still add more. or ask as much money as you can and; I will give it you. The solution is you can't do **Actually** what you can **Potentially**.

¶ Thô most men incline to allow this last canon, yet some think that there are on both sides difficulties insoluable about it. one Instance I Remember is this. if a man go a mile by steps, as say, he at first going passes half way and there stays; and then he begins again and goes half of what was left, and there stops; and so again & again. now the question is if he still proceeds in this order when he shall come to the end & the answer is, never. for he will still have a half before him. but we see men do go to the end of a mile; therfore they do not always go over a half before they go over a whole; and therefore the last half is as big as the last whole (which is absurd) or the last half hath no half nor is further divisible. And yet on the contrary there are many demonstrations, that there is never so little part but it may be still be divided. I shall mention 2 undeniable proofs. Suppose 2 concentricall circles, and a thred fastened at the center (C) the other end streched out to (A) and movable upwards towards (B) now if there be a least point, let the line at (A) be moved towards (B) so much as that conceived least, and it will appear that the line will move less in the inner circle towards (D) and so there is a less than the least (which is absurd) or else there is no least. again suppose 3 of these least indivisibles standing in a row and touching one the other 'tis manifest the 2 outermost must touch that in the middle either in whole or part. if in whole then there is a penetration of dimensions (which is contrary to the nature of Quantity and is absurd), but if it touch in part then it has pii, and so the least has a less (which is absurd) and therefore there is no least.

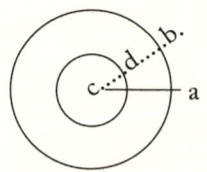

$$\left\{\begin{array}{l}\text{Contraries or degrees 'twill not admit,}\\ \text{It equals, is potential Infinite—}\end{array}\right\}$$

Synopsis. cap. 6th

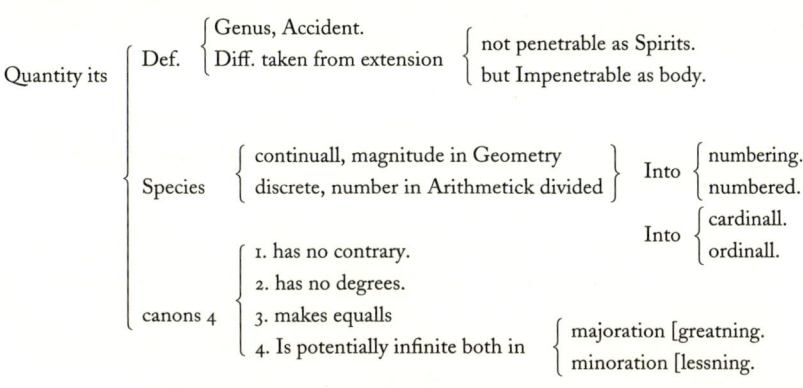

Cap 7th   Of Quality

Quality is an Acci. whereby the subject is said to operate; as heat whereby the subjective is said to heat, warm, melt, or burn &c. 'tis known also by answering the question (Accidentally) what manner, kind, or sort of? as what kind of man is Socrates? Ans. Honest, wise, learned, &c.

Species of quality are
- Insensible
  - natural power & its lower degree Impotens.
  - Habit — — — Disposition.
- Sensible
  - proper to one sence patible quality—passion
  - common to more senses form and figure.

1. Natural power & Impotens is a quality Implanted by nature to be the next principle of some act. as the power of seeing is the next principle whereby we see [the remote principle is the Animal nature] its Impotens is where the eye is weak and sees badly.

A Logick System

naturall power is 2 fold
- 1. active. whereby the Subject can do Something, as the power to melt.
- 2. passive.————Suffer or be as metal to be melted.

2. Habit & disposition is a quality superadded to the power whereby it is enabled more easily to act Thus
- infused
- acquired

1. Infused by God Immediately, as Grace: the art of Bezaliel and aholiab to embroider: the knowledge of the tongues in the Apostles; prophesy &c.[13]

2. Acquired by humane Industry, in Teaching and Learning, as Phylosophy, and manuall acts. Acquired are gotten either in
- habit
- disposition

1. Habit is gotten by many acts (or few valid & Intense) and is not easily removed from its subject.

2. Disposition is by few acts (or weak and remiss) and is easily Removed. Thus a man having a natural power of Reasoning (which a dog has not) by instruction, study, and exercise getts an habit of Logick; or an Art superadded to the nature of Reasoning. now he that is a beginner & hath made small progress, or he that slightly & superficially minds it, attains but to a Disposition which by disuse he will soon forgett. so in manufactures. &c—habits are either.

1. moral, subjected in the will enclining to do some moral action, as virtues, vices.

2. Intellectuall, subjecting in the understanding enclining to assent to some proposition.—the privative of Assent is doubt; 'tis when one hath no Reason to encline to either part: or when in

---

[13] The extent of infusion in Bezaliel and Aholiab is clear in Exodus 35: 30–35: God filled Bezaliel "with an excellent spirit of wisdom, of understanding, and of knowledge in all manner of work, to find out curious works, to work in gold, and in silver, and in brass, and...to make any manner of fine work. And [God] hath put in his heart that he may teach others, both he and Aholiab....Them hath he filled with wisdom of heart to work all manner of cunning embroidered and needlework...." Prof. Morris Wilhelm helped me read these names and directed me to the book of Exodus.

our thought there is equal Reason on both sides. illustrated by a ballance in equilibration, when both scales are empty & both equally filled. hence that rule in doubtfulls tis safest to deny Assent, or, (in practicalls) best not to meddle.

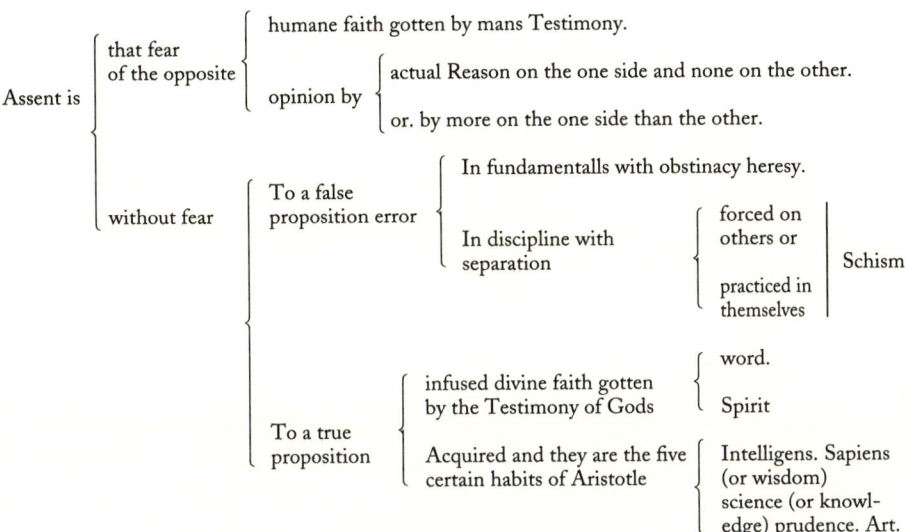

{
The Privative of all assent is Doubt—
Assents are some with & some without—
Opinion, Humane Faith give weak assent,
False Error Heresie Scism are evident—,
Assur'd in Truth is Faith Divine Assent,
Intelligence Sapience, Science Prudence Art
}

1. Intelligens is a habit enclining the understanding to assent to principles, that is such generall propositions, that no one with the least pretence of Reason can deny.
Of such some are
    1. Speculative. as every whole is greater than its part.
    2. Practicall. as God is to be worshipped. do to another as thou wouldest &c.

3. operative. as believe an Artist in his Trade if sense or Reason contradict not.

¶ The Difference between
- practicall. as doing a moral action. as to do justice
- practical. or making an artificial work. as making shots &c.

The word, doe, is equivocally Applied to both, soe a shoemaker that is dilligent in his calling; but is no good workman: does or lives well; but does or makes ill: whereas a cut purse that is Artificall in his trade, does (as to Moralls) ill; but does (as to art) his work very well:

¶ A man is said to be an Intelligent man who is well stored with such principles or maxims or at least readily assent to them when he hears them, but if any be so foolish or perverse to deny them, he is to be turned of as a Brute. The Rule is, Against principles one who denys principles there is no disputing.[14]

2. Sapience or wisdom enclines to assent to more Generall conclusions from most general principles; as nothing can be and not be at the sometime: Bec: contradictories cannot be both true or every thing is either perfect or Imperfect. bec. contradictories cannot be both false.

¶ The difference between Intelligens that assents to principles, and Sapience which draws conclusions from these principles. Such a Sapiens is metaphysicks.

3. Science or Knowledge enclines to assent unto necessary conclusions by the evidence they have from their next and peculiar causes—As a Table is a wooden materiall therfore it is combustible.

¶ The Diff. between Sapiens, whose conclusions are from most generall principles that concern all things, And science which is from more particular principles, and such as Respect the matter in hand.

4. Prudence assents to practicall or morall conclusions; which concern manners and govern morall actions; as this is just I must do it.

---

[14] Although awkwardly stated here, this Aristotelian adage (An obstinate skeptic cannot be argued with) was commonly used against skeptics by all forms of dogmatically-inclined humanistic logics.

5. Art assents to conclusions effective or operative. As great materialls can better bear then be born. therefore such must lie low in a building.
Art is either
- mentall, as Grammar, Rhetorick, poetry, Logick.
- manuall, a Smith, carpenter, Taylor. &c.

¶ of these 5 Intellectuall habits Sapiens and Science are speculative; prudence, is practicall: Art, is operative: but Intelligence is all three: (viz) speculative, practicall, operative.

{ Sapience Science, Speculates, Prudence Practical
Art operates, Intelligence is all }

3. Patible quality and passion is equality that is the object of one only sense. as colour to seeing: sound to hearing. &c.
¶ Passion is not a Passion of the mind—As love, hatred, Anger, &c. nor predicamentall passion as opposed to action; as to be Loved, hated, beaten, &c. but it is a patible suddenly passing away. as as the appearance of a flash of Lightning, the bounce of a gunn, paleness by fear, Redness by Anger &c.

{ Patible Quality affects one Sense
Its passion is of little permanence. }

4 form and figure, those 2 seem rather kindes then degrees (as all the rest are). Their Generall name may be shape and these two the species then of shape is a common object of more senses. Is defined a quality arising from the termination of the parts of Quantity.

The Species of Shape are
- form of animates—as of man, horse, tree. &c.
- figure of inanimates—as stone. or artificial shape of a house, Table, &c.

figure is either
- Round
- Angular

As is more fully handled In Geometry

{ Form is of Animates, Shape Natural,
Figure of things Shaped artificial—. }

A Logick System

Canons of Quality.

1. only qualities are contraries, as hot and cold, hard and soft.
2. only qualities have degrees; Intension, Remission, more or less.
3. from qualities things are said to be like or dislike. likeness or similitude is where divers things have the same quality; Dissimilitude where diverse, so one egg is like another in colour, figure, &c. but an oyster is unlike an apple.

{ Qualities have their Con: & Degrees
  From the thing are alike as Egg to Egg. }

Syn: cap. 7.

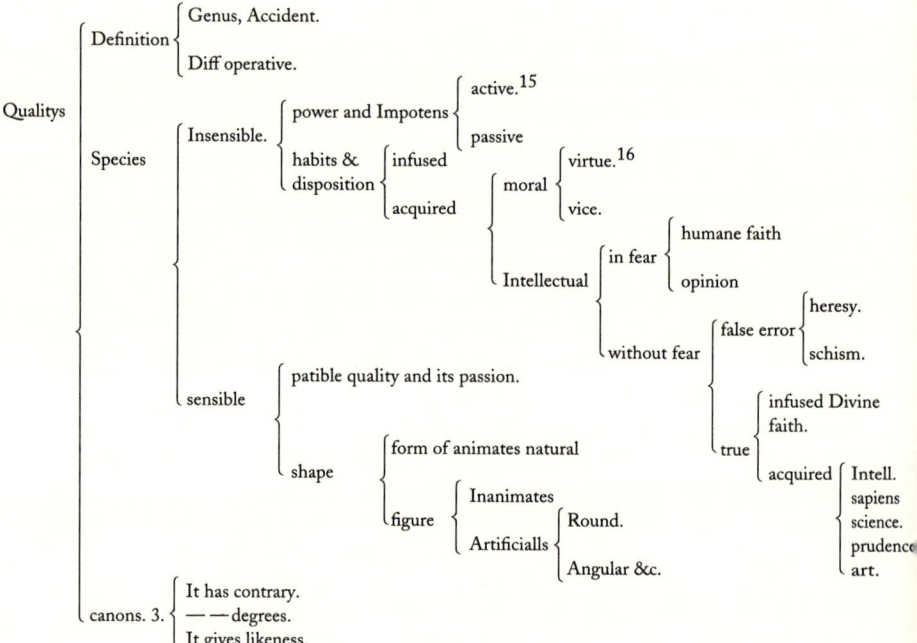

[15] Dunbar mistakenly positions the "active" and "passive" under the operative definition.

[16] Dunbar mistakenly positions "virtue" and "vice" under infused habits.

CHARLES MORTON

Cap: 8th.   of Relation

Relation is an Accident whereby one thing Respects (or is Referred to) another, as fatherhood, sonship, Dominion, Servitude, &c. to every Relation are 3 Requisites

1. The Subject   ⎧ these mutually Respect each other & may be one or
                              ⎨ the other by turn. if the father be subject the son is cor
2. The corrolate   ⎩ relate (et è contra)

3. The ground or reason is either
⎧ Quantity in which is founded equality & inequality
⎪ Quality — — — similitude & dissimilitude.
⎨ Action— are — founded most others. as conjugal, herile,[17] possession
⎩ &c.

                ⎧ To 3 in each Relation have an Eye,
                ⎨ The Subject Correlate & Reason why
                ⎪ Three grounds Relation are built upon
                ⎩ Quantity, Quality, and Action—

Species of Rational as between knowledge and the thing knowable.
Relation are
                           ⎧ of like name, as friend, brother, Sister. &c.
                Real ⎨
                           ⎩ of divers name, as father & son, husband & wife. &c.

there is a   ⎧ Transcendentall which belongs to diverse predicaments
Distinction   ⎪   especially to the 4 last, which are cald Respective.
of Relations   ⎨   Involved in the essence.
belong   ⎪ Predicamentall which is peculiar to this one; & this we
                ⎪   have only now to do with; the other to metaphysick.
                ⎩   accidentally Superadded to the essence.

                        ⎧ Transcendent, Predicamental, Rational   ⎫
                        ⎩ Real of like or Diverse names (that is all)— ⎭

---

[17] "Of or pertaining to a master," OED.

A Logick System

Canons of Relation.

1. Relates are Reciprocable or converted with an (of) as the father is the father of the son; & the son is the son of the father.
2. Relates are together in nature, that is when 2 things inferr or deny each other, and neither is the cause of the other, so father and son inferr each other, for if there be a father he has a son; and if there be a son he has a father; and so do deny each other and neither is the cause. the father indeed is the cause of the son as a man begetting but not formally as the father; for paternity, or fatherhood is no more the cause of filiation, or sonship, than sonship is of paternity; the man is the cause of the man, but not the Relation of the Relation.
3. Relates are together in knowledge, for when I know him to be a father I know he has a sonne.
4. correlates put and Remove each other, that is a correlates are in being, one, more, or none, so are Relations as one man that has 10 sons has to paternity: if 5 dye he has 5 paternities left, if all die he has none; and it may be said he was a father but is not. and so of the son he was a son but is not when his father is dead.

$$\left\{\begin{array}{l}\text{Reciprocal by (est) \& are together,}\\ \text{In nature knowledge made or mark if either.}\end{array}\right\}$$

Syn: cap. 8th

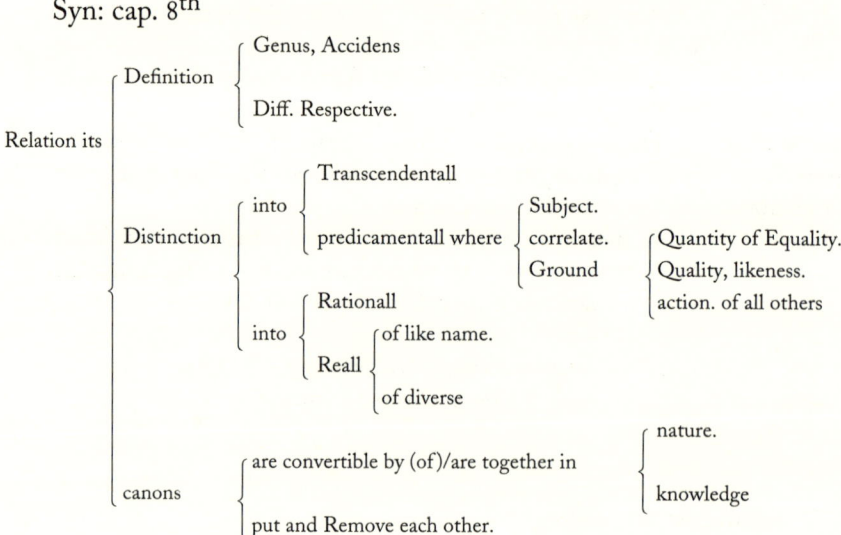

Cap. 9th   Of Action, and Passion

These two have always their actuall being & existence together, & therefore are so handled.

1. Action is an Accident whereby the subject is said formally to act or do any thing, or that which dos constitute the subject in the actuall being of an Agent, and therefore denominateth him so.—

this Agency is
- fundamentally from quality as John is a seer (in species) from the natural power of seeing.
- formally from Action, So John is said to be a seer (individually) from the very act of seeing.

Species of action are
- Immanent, whose effect is in the agent, as when one thinks, wills, proposes, &c.
- Transient, as when one speaks, works, executeth Intentions. &c.

¶ of Immanent is that famous Question debated with Arminians, viz: whether there be any new Immanent act in God? i.e. whether he changeth his purposes or occasions as we do? Denied, bec. he is unchangable and cannot see better Reasons.

¶ When an action is said to be transient, 'tis not as if the action it self went over to another subject, for accidents never pass from subject to subject nor if the effect be an Accident, as the heating of water by a fire: dos that pass over for the same Reason? For if heat did pass from the fire it would loose heat by heating. but it is thus; the heat of the fire continually begetts a heat in the water, which therefore serves to pass but dos not; for the heat in the water is not of the same numericall heat, with that in the fire but is another begotten by it; so the teachers Learning doth not pass into the learner but exciteth a new Learning like it self, & so in the motion of bodies.

> Qualities power, action formality
> Immanent in Transient without doth lie

Canons 9.

1. Actions are contrary as heating and cooking.
2. Actions are intended and Remitted as this fire hath more than that both by Quantity, heat, cold.

3. Actions always inferr passion, if there be heating Something is heated.

2. Passion is an Accident, whereby the subject is said formally to suffer, or be any thing, or rather whereby it Receiveth the term produced by the agent, so the agent, so that which is said to be heated receiveth the heat produced by the fire.

Species
- Intentionall that makes no Sensible change in the subject as to be thought of, Loved, &c.
- Transmutative makes sensible as in water when it is heated.

Intentional, to action term doth give
Sensible change is by Transmutative.

Canons are 3 like unto action.
1. Passions are contrary 2. have degrees. 3. Inferreth action.

Syn. cap. 9.

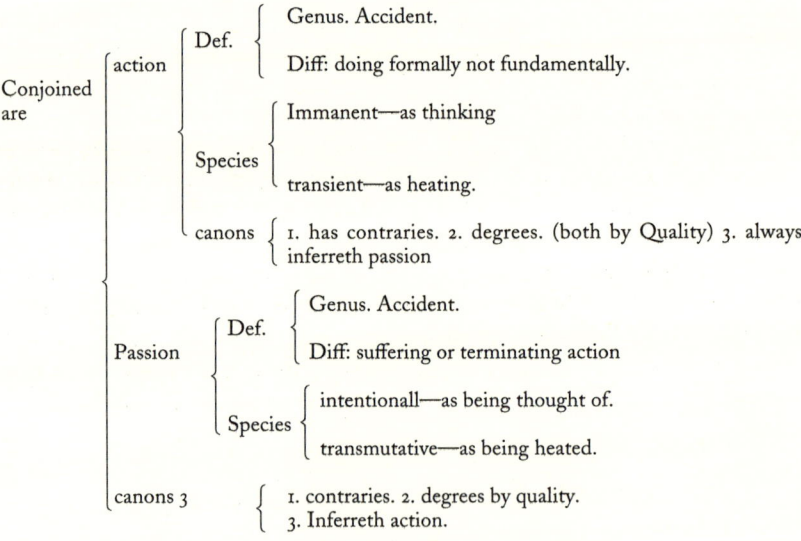

Cap. 10.   of Respective Predicaments   { where | site
                                          { when | habit

1. Whereness is an Accident answering the question Where? and denominates the subject to be some where, as in the house, field, London &c. or tis the transcendentall Relation between the subject & place.
¶ tis said to be an Accident by the aintients, but the neoterics or latter Phylosophers will account this (and the 3 that follow) but modes of being, & not compleat beings, and therefore not Accidents.

Distinctions of whereness are 3. Repletive, definitive, circumscriptive.
   1. Repletive of that which fills all places, so God only who is neither Included in, nor excluded of any place, is called omniprescence.
   2. Definitive, is prescence in a place after the manner of a spirit, that is, when the whole thing is so in the whole space that it may be in any part of the space. So an Angell may be in the whole room, and so again next moment may be in any part or point of the room: but a spirit thô it dos extend it self to a certain space, yet dos not posess that space so as to expell any other body or spirit but may be together with it. tis called penetrability, as it is before noted. cap. 6. of quantity.
   3. Circumscriptive, is the prescence of anything in a certain space after the manner of a body. this is here intended and is Impenetrability. see cap. 6.
   Species of whereness circumscriptive are as various as places, all which are comprehended in the 2 globes, and are discoursed of in   { Astronomy.
                                                                                                                                        { Geography.

Canons of Whereness circumscriptive are.

   1. Every body hath its where, places being concreated with bodies.
   2. no two bodies can have the same (be they never so minute) bec: bodies are Impenetrable, (as is said before).
¶ hence we say (against the Lutherians consubstantiation) the reall body of christ, and reall body of bread cant consist in the same space. therefore the Papist make it transubstantiation. changing the body of bread into the body of christ yet keeping the Accident of bread; but this is contrary to the other Logicall Rule [Accidents can't change subject.] the truth is, Jesus Christ hath a Reall prescence in his Sacraments [not only fancied] but it is a Reall Spiritual not a Reall corporall: a Presence to faith and not to sence.

A Logick System

  Replete, Defin'd, and Circumscription
  Each body hath its where, no 2 have one

2. Whenness is an Accident answering to the question When; or it is the transcendentall Relation between a thing and time. it denominates the subject to be at some time, yesterday, tomorrow, now, 7 years hence or since &c. this is in some duration, which is 3 fold.
  1. Eternity, the duration of a thing without beginning or end; 'tis only proper to God.
  2. Everlastingness, which hath beginning but no end, as Angells and mens souls.
  3. Time, which has beginning and end, as all naturall bodies and forms of beasts.
  species of whenness are according to the parts of time—
{ Past, of this history and chronologie.
Present, now Physical, the best part of time, not methodical which is but a term or point is to a line.
Future, of this prophesy, & future care.

¶ the nature of time consists in succession or flux, like a river made up of continual passing water between whose parts Instant or now is [as was said] a common term, as point in Quality to line, this mode the Aintients count time a species of Quantity

  Eternity, everlastingness sublime—
  of God and Spirits are, of bodies time

Canons of Whenness.

1. Time has before and after [but not Eternity which is said to be a continuall now expressed in Hyeroglyphicks by a circle whose line has no form but ends in it self.
2. Time is created with body and therefore said by some to be but a mode of body, and no distinct being or Accident
¶ A mode is an Inseparable Appurtenance to a thing.
3. there is a time for every thing which is fit and seasonable, 'tis called opportunity the best of time.

  { Time hath Succession (none Eternity) }
  { Concreate best is opportunity— }

CHARLES MORTON

3. Situation. is an Acci: whereby the subject is said to have an order of parts in space.

¶ Site Respects the parts, **as where**, the whole, A thing may change site, when it doth not place, it answers to the Question [in what posture] as standing, lying, sitting, Leaning &c.

the species are
- upside, downside—belonging to all things.
- foreside, backside ⎫
- Rightside, leftside ⎭ to Animals Directly, to others only in respect of Animal.

Inside, outside, may be referred to the other

> Above, below, are common unto all
> before, behind, Right, left, to Animal

4. Habit is an Acci: whereby the subject is said to be formally habited. 'tis materially habited by some substance, as gown, coat, cloak, &c. 'tis the trancendentall Relation of a body to the moral habit. therefore 'tis not the gown but the having on the gown (or gownation as you may call it] that is the Accident and this we say is inherent, thô that gown but adherent or adjacent. this Answers the Question [how clad]

species [of] habit are
- naturall—as hairs, feathers, skin, scale, &c.
- Artificial
  - necessity, as the feathers keep warm, and cover nakedness
  - ornament as bands, cuffs, jewels, &c.

All may be
- partiall, of a part only, as hat, show, glove. &c.
- totall, of the whole together without distinction of
  - handsome
  - vain
  - costly
  - mean
  } habit

{ Habits by nature, provided are, Art,
  For need or ornament to whole, or part. }

{ The Canons of Habit are
  1. Habits must be suitable to the Quality or Imployements of the Person.
  2. Habits show the mind for they are
      ultimate { after what manner
                 and
                 with what Person } we associate ourselves.

  Habits unsuitable Become a Sin,
  Are outward signs of what is lodged within. }

Syn. cap. 10.

Respective Predicaments
{
  In general { Genus. Acci:
               Diff: Answer to Question { when { in what posture—
                                                 how clad—
                                         where }
  In particular
  { Whereness
    { Distinction { Repletive of God.
                    Definitive, of created Spirits { Angels
                                                     souls of man.
                    circumscriptive, of bodies }
      Species, According to all places handled by { Astronomy.
                                                    Geography.
      canons { every body has its where.
               no 2 have the same. }
    }
    Whenness
    { Distinct: { Eternity of God, having no beginning nor end.
                  Everlastingness. of Spirits having beginning, no end.
                  time. of bodies. having no beginning, and end. }
      Species according to time { past, yesterday.
                                  present, now.
                                  future, tomarrow. }
      canons { time has Succession
               was created with bodies
               is fitted for all purposes, the best is opportunity. }
    }
    Site
    { Species { upside, downside —to all things.
                foreside, backside
                Rightside, leftside } to Animals
      canons { site respects parts
               site may be altered in the same place }
    }
  }
}

[180]

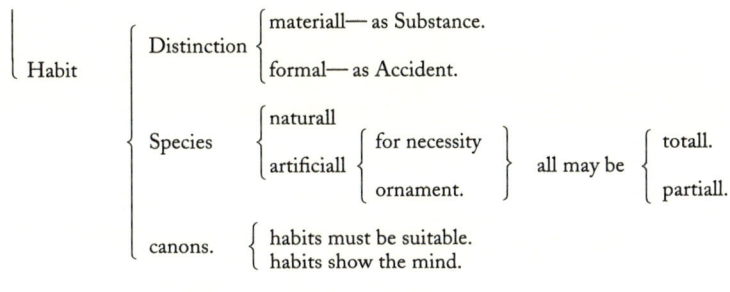

Cap. II.   Of Postpredicaments

Postpredicaments, a Doctrine explaining the Predicaments as Appendix or Postscript to them. opposition, priority, motion, & modes of having

1. Opposition, is a diversity of 2 simple terms, which cannot agree either between themselves, or in a 3^d, at the same time, & in some respect of part.
¶ 1. of 2 terms [as virtue, vice] but if one be opposed equally to two, [as liberality to prodigality and covetousness] they are called disparate not opposite.
2. Simple terms, [as white, black] to distinguish from the opposition of Propositions which are complex terms, and belong to the second part of Logick as he is white, he is black.
3. not between themselves; for white cant be black.
4. nor is a 3^d term, namely a 3^d Individual, as John is white, therefore it cant be said of John, he is black. but in a 3^d generation or species they may agree, as white is a quality or colour so it is black too.
5. at the same time; so water cant be at the same time hot and cold, though it may successively.
6. in the same Respect as a sword may be rendered to a madman as his proper goods, but not as a madman; so that it is first to render the man his sword and it is not fit; may be both true but not in the same Respect.
7. In the same part: so an Ethiopian is black and white, namely in the skin and tooth.

{ Two Simple terms that do each other thwart }
{ In third, in the same time, respect, and Part— }

A Logick System

Species of opposition { Relative — contrary.
privative — contradictory.

1. Relative, between relative terms, as if he be a father to John he cant be Johns son.
2. contrary, between contrary terms, contraries are such as most differ under the same species;—as black and white whereas black and yellow are said to be diverse, but not opposites. So hard and soft, smooth and rough, hot and cold, are contraries.

¶ these do mutually expell each other out of the same subject and are only qualities

3. Privative, is between privative terms; that is any Positive Acci: & is absence, from a capable subject as sight and blindness.

¶ if the subject be uncapable the absence is not privation, but bare negation, as we say not [a stone is blind] but [a stone does not see or is not seeing] but a horse may be properly said to be blind. the absence of sight in a horse is blindness [a privation] in a stone is not seeing [negative]

4. contradictory, between contradictory terms; that is express affirmative and negative. a man and not a man &c.

{ Opposed, Relation, Contrariety, Privative terms, & Contradictory. }

¶ contradiction is the greatest opposition, admitting no mean either of participation or of abnegation. A mean of Participation is a third thing of which both may be affirmed in one Respect or other. A mean of abnegation is a third thing of which both may be denied in one respect or other.[18] Relatives and contraries may have a mean of participation; so the same man may be a father and a son in Respect of divers persons; and the same water may be hot and cold in divers times, or at the same time in remiss degrees. Privatives may admit a mean of abnegation; as a stone is neither seeing nor blind, but not seeing nor void of sight. but contradictories admit neither. not participation; for nothing is both man and not man. nor abnegation; for their is nothing that is not either man or not man.

---

[18] This sentence is not completely transcribed by Partridge.

CHARLES MORTON

$$\left\{ \begin{array}{l} \text{Relates Contraries affirm'd, Privaties deny'd} \\ \text{But Contradictories no mean abide.—} \end{array} \right\}$$

2. Priorty. posteriority and simulty are modes whereby one thing with respect to another are said to be before, after, and together with. there are 6 of these; I shall speak of priority, which will show the rest. priority is either in

    1. Time, when one is ended before another begins, as Abraham: &c. Moses, that either—not ended— — —as Abraham and Isaac.

    2. nature, that from which another is derived, and is not converted as to a necessity of existence so Genus is before species; Animal before man, which are not converted, for thô it be necessaryly true [if there be a man there is an Animal] yet on the other hand it follows not convertible [if there be an Animal there must be a man] for it may be a beast, yea beasts were made when yet man was not.

    3. Knowledge, that which is first known or knowable, and that is either

        1. in respect of the nature of things, and in themselves. So a species is more knowable than an Individuall; because species cant be defin'd by an essentiall Definition [as man is a Rational Animal] Whereas Individualls can only be Described by a number of Accidents. as [Socrates is a Learned man, born at athens &c.]

        2. In Repect of us, that is more easily perceived by us. So Individualls are more knowable then species; bec: they are perceived by the senses, species only by reason & speculation.

    4. Order, that which is accounted, placed, named, or numbred first, as the preface to a book.

    5. Cause, that which is the cause of another.

either $\left\{ \begin{array}{l} \text{natural, as wood of a table} \\ \text{formal, as the soul of a man} \end{array} \right\}$ Efficient, as God of the world.

End, as Gods Glory, means Good.

6. Dignity or worth, as the prince is before the subject; thou art worth 10000 of us. 2 Samuell 18.3[19]

---

[19] The followers of King David in exile expressed their need for their leader with this formula.

A Logick System

3. Motion. Its terms and species

1. Terms { from which, left.
          { to which, acquired.

2. Species 6.

{ 1. **Generation.** from not being to being, as generation of man
  2. **Corruption,**—being to not being,— the death— — } both Instantaneous.

{ 3. **augmentation,** less quantity to greater, as from a quart to Gallon.—
  4. **dimunition,** as greater quantity to a less, as gallon—quart—

5. Alteration quality to quality { Essentiall. as from hot to cold, divers.
                                   gradual. as from hot to hotter, the same. } all Successive.

6. location or locomotion; from place to place, as from London to Dover.

{ Generate & Corupt, Augment & Diminish }
{ Altering & Placing Motions kinds of finish. }

4. Modes of having [because of the equivocall sense of the word habit derived from having] are usually accounted. 8. but I think 3 will serve, for habit is put[20] either.

    1. in generall, for every positive Acci: So habit is opposed to privation, whence that

---

[20] "Put" should be "But."

[184]

R { from privation to habit is not Regress, that is an Accident once totally out of a subject can never

Return to it again the same in number.

2. particulary

for { habit, the species of agility, which is the higher degree of dispositon.

habit, in the Last Predicament, as cloak, coat, &c.

{ Habit for all Positive Accident
One kind of Quality last Predicament. }

Syn. Cap. II.

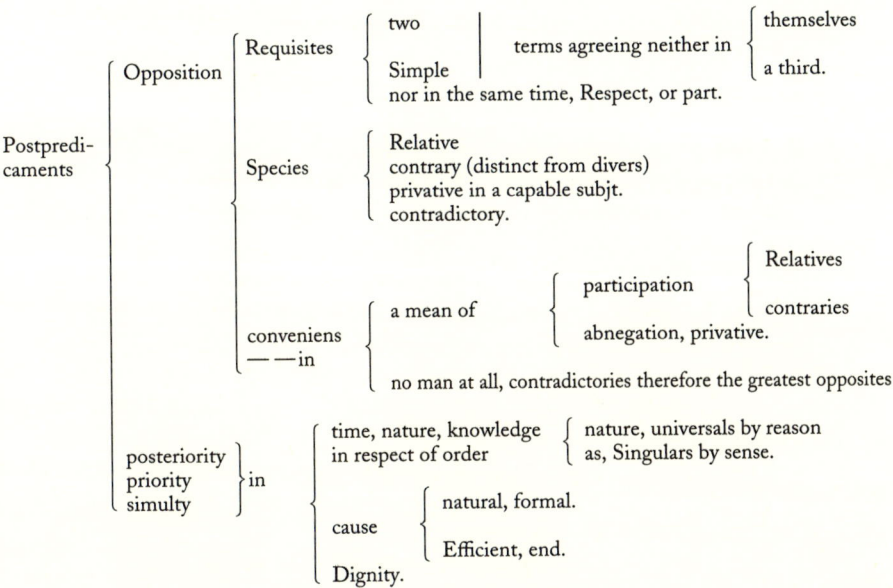

A Logick System

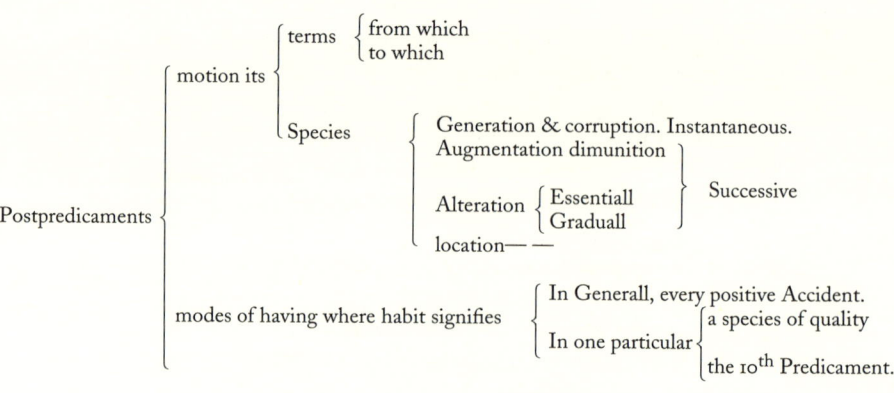

Cap. 12.   of Secondary simple terms { Definition. Division.

The primary simple terms	predicables	Antepre-dicaments	being finished now	Definition
	predicaments with their	Postpre-dicaments	follow the secondary	Division

1. **Definition** is the explication of a name or thing.
   1. **of a name** (nominal) explains the signif: a word that either by
      1 **more common words**, as sacrament [a sacred seal of the covenant] trinity [.3. in. 1.]
      2. Etymologie [that is the Reason of the name] as prophesie [a speaking before] Apostle [one that is sent] evangelist [A bringer of glad tidings]
   2. **of a thing** [real] explains the nature and being of a thing & is either.
      1. **essential**, by essential and intrinsick terms [Genus & Diff:]. so man is a Rational Animal.
      2. **Accidentall** cald description by genus instead of Diff: { by property, as man is a Risible Animal ; by more common Accident as man is an Animal with 2 leggs without feathers.

[186]

This is used either when { the Def: is not known.
{ the Definite is an Individual.

{ Nominal definition notify
{ By Common words or Etymology
{ Reall, essentiall, Genus, Difference
{ Acc: property, or common Accidents.

Requisites to Definition are.
1. that it be plain; for its end is to explain, [not by more obscure terms] as a forester is the Diaphanous part of an ædiface to Intromit luminous particles into an opaque concavity &c.
2. as short as may be; tis best when only the Genus & Diff: are expressed in 2 words as Rational Animal.
3. Equall to the thing Defined.

not { too large, as man is a 2 leg'd Animal [that comprehends birds]
{ too narrow, as man is a Learned Animal, that shutts out the unlearned.

{ For Definition 'tis required you bring
{ That which is short plain equalled thing

2. Division, is the Resolution of the whole into its parts, is either
  1. Nominal, when an ambiguous [or equivocal word] is Resolved into its several significations as a dog is either

  a { star
    { fish } 'tis called distinction.
    { beast }

  2. Real, when a thing is so Resolved, 'tis either
    1. perfect, when the whole is divided into parts intrinsicall, the whole is
      1. universall into its part that are under it [substitutive]

A Logick System

as
- Genus into species, by the Diff: As Animal
  - Rational
  - Irrational
- Species; Individualls by Accidents as man into
  - John
  - Tom
  &c.

2. Essentiall into its essentiall parts [constitutive] as those are either
   1. Methaph. [Genus & Diff:] so man is divided
into
- Animal and
- Rational

   2. Physical [matter & form] so man is divided
into
- body
- souls

   3. Integral, into integrant parts so a human body
Into
- head
- members.

- Divisions Nominal Do shew thereby
- What words Equivocal do signify—
- Real & Perfect parteth Generall,
- Essential, Metaphysicks, Physicks, and Integral—

2. Imperfect, when the Division is made by terms extrinsick: & so is divided.
   1. Subject by Accident as water is
either
- hot
- cold

[188]

2. An Accident by its Subject so there is one heat
of { fire and / sun }

3. An Acci: by Accidents so colour is
either { light / dark }

{ Imperfect Subject by accident represents.
Accident by Subject & Accident by Accident. }

Requisites to Division are.
1. that the members be lowest [i.e.] only 2 if it may be with conveniency. Division by 2 is called Dichotomie, and is best for acuracy.[21]
2. opposite, as moral action is
either { virtue | grace / vice | sin }

3. Adequate, that is equal, as man is
either { wise / unwise } adequate

but man is either { wise / honest } is inadequate, for many are neither one nor the other.

{ if you will make divisions Aright
the members few, adequate, opposite }

[21] This is a favorable nod to Ramists.

A Logick System

Syn. cap. 12.

Second simple terms
- Defi:
  - Species
    - nominal, by
      - common words
      - Etymology.
    - Real
      - essential — by Generall Diff:
      - Accidental
        - made by
          - A property instead of a Diff:
          - more common Accidents
        - used when
          - Diff: is not known.
          - Definite is Individual.
  - Rules
    - plain.
    - short.
    - adequate.
- Division
  - Species
    - nominal of Equivocall words, cald Distinction.
    - Real of a thing
      - Perfect when Intrinsicals divide the whole
        - universall
          - Gen. into Species
          - Species Into Individuals.
        - Essentiall
          - Metaph.
            - Genus.
            - Diff:
          - Physical
            - matter
            - form
        - Integrall
          - head.
          - hand.
          - &c.
      - Imperfect when Extrinsecalls
        - Sub. by Accident.
        - Acci: by Substance.
        - Acci: by Accidents.
  - Rules the members
    - few.
    - opposite
    - Adequate

The Second Part of Logick

Cap 1. of complex terms or proposition; of the definition and parts of a proposition

A Proposition is a sentence declaring somthing true or false without Ambiguity [or Equivocation]
¶ If there be in it an Equivocall word it must be distinquished, & the sense wherein you take it declared; else it is no Proposition bec: it dos not signifie any thing certain, and therefore not true or false, hence you must distinquish, ere you can define of things.
In propositions are signs and parts.
1. Signs [consignificative, cald parts syncategorematicall] which signifie nothing of themselves, but only the quantity of quality of A Proposition, Such as all, none, some, this.
2. parts [significative of themselves, cald categorematicall or Predicamentall bec: they belong to some Predicament.] these proper parts are nouns and verbs.
　1. nouns signifie without time, as man, dog, horse, &c.
　2. verbs signify with time —   { past. was, were, wert.
　　　　　　　　　　　　　　　　　 present. is, am, art.
　　　　　　　　　　　　　　　　　 future. shall, will.

{ In Propositions Signs & Parts do ly
　Nouns without time, Verbs with time Signify. }

Thus the parts are expressed in grammaticall notions but in Logical they are called
1. Subject that of which something is predicated and it goes before the verb.
2. the Predicate, that which is predicated [and in sense at least] it follows the verb.
3. Copula, the verb substantive joyning the other 2 together in affirmation or disjoyning them in negation by a no or not, So Socrates, the subject; is, the copula; Learned, the predicate. The copula or verb substantive [am, is, art] is sometimes

A Logick System

{ 1. expressed, as Socrates is Loving
{ 2. Implied, as Socrates Loveth

{ Subject before, predicate the other side }
{ of Copula expressed or Implied }

Syn. cap. 1.

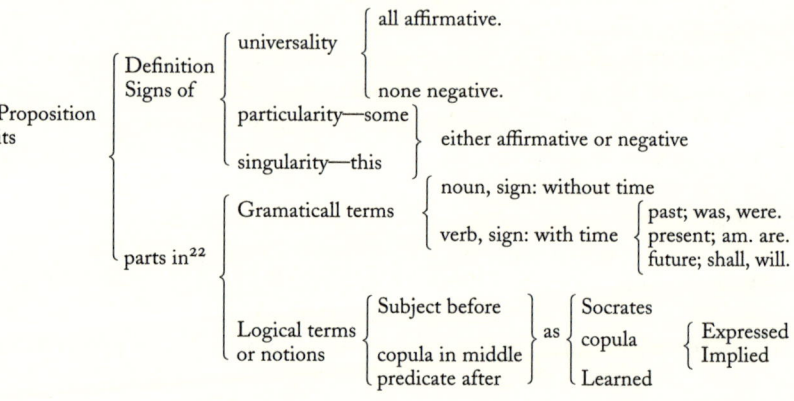

Cap 2.   of the Division of Proposition as to { Substance. Quantity. Quality. }

Prop: is divided as to substance, quantity, quality.
1. **Substance** is categoricall and hypotheticall.
¶ there is no proper substance in a prop: [for it is but a Logicall notion, and no Real thing such as substance, in the 1st Predicament, Signifies] but Analogicall or by way of resemblence, with an [as it were] and notes but the cheif constitution of it, such phrases are [the substance of a sermon or discourse; the fulness of the Godhead bodily] not that the Godhead has body, or a sermon substance, but only because [like substance] to answer the Question [What?] as what is christ? Ans: God. What did Paul

[22] Partridge mistakenly wrote "parts in" twice.

preach? or what was the substance of his Epistles? Ans: Justification by faith. here, what is the main substance of the cheif matter of a Prop:? A. something categoric or hypoth.

1. A categoricall [or simple Prop.] { Subject.
of but one as Socrates is Learned,   { predicate.
God is to be worshiped.   { copula.

2. hypotheticall [or compound] Prop: consists of most categoricalls conjoyn'd by some conjunction [as in grammar they are called] and, that, either.

    1. conditional [if] as if Socrates is Learned, he is to be honored. if there be a God, he is to be worshiped.
    ¶ this is the proper hypotheticall
    2. copulative [and] as Socrates is Learned and Brutus unlearned or Socrates wise and honest.
    3. disjunctions [either, or] as Socrates either learned or unlearned

{ A Categorick you may simple call }
{ if, and, or, either, Hypotheticall }

2. **Quality**, showing what kind of Prop: 'tis: & that in Respect of.
  1. **the thing signified**; and so tis either true or false.
    1. true, when the words agree with the thing, being represented by them as it is as man is Rational.
    2. false, when they agree not: as a Stone is Rational.
    ¶ those 2 are manifest in the 3^d part of Logick, and therefore do not so properly belong to the second part.
  2. **the words signifying**; and so it is either affirmative or negative.
    1. affirmative, when the predicate is affirmed of [or conjoyned to] the subject as Socrates is Learned, God is truth.
    2. negatives, when the predicated is denied of [or divided from] the subject as Socrates is not Learned. Man is not Justified by works.
    ¶ the particle [not] must be put before the copula, else the Prop: Remains affirmative; this is true in the Latin Tongue where [*non est*] is the phrase of negation; but the manner of speech in English is otherwise; for we say not when we would deny a thing [it not is so] but [it is not so] the {English} useth [not] Immediately after the copula, but then it must be joyned in signification with the copula, as if [is not] were but one word, and signify but one thing namely [negation] but if [not] be separated from the copula and joyned in

A Logick System

sense with the predicate, it renders the predicated an infinite [or indefinite] term and leaveth the Prop: affirmative.

so { Socrates is not—a man. negative
 Socrates is— —not a man. affirmative }

In the former Proposition—man
in the latter—not a man } is the predicate.

{ True or false Quality the thing affords.
 Affirm'd or Deny'd is of the Words— }

3. **Quantity**, showing how much or how many are contained in the Proposition. in this respect tis divided

into { universall, particular
 indefinite, singular }

1. **Universall**, whose subject is a common term [Genus or species] enlarged by an universall signe.

Such are { All—affirmatives, as all men are Rational.
 not—negative, as no man is a horse. }

¶ that the negation—not—is contained in the word [not] which includes negation and universality too.

2. **particular**, when the common term is contracted by a particular sign. [some] this signe maketh the subject an Individuall Indetermined, and the Proposition to be particular. as some man is Learned.

3. **indefinible**, when the subject has no signe.

In this if the matter be { necessary or Impossib. tis equivalent to a Universall.
 contingent & not Impossible.— — — —particular. }

as
- man is Rational [necessary] equivalent to, all men are Rational.
- man is not a stone [Impossible]—no man is a Stone.
- man is Learned ⎱ contingent not Impossible. Equivallent to ⎰ some man is Learned
- man is not Learned ⎰ ⎱ some man is not Learned

The Jansenists Logick[23] will have it universall in doctrinalls [true or false] and particularly in historicalls but I see no great Reason for it.

4. **Singular**, when the subject is determined Individuall

by
- **name**, as socrates is Learned.
- **sign**: [this or that] as this man is wise.

{ All or None, General, Some Particular
  Indefin'd, no sign, this that Singular }

¶ That those 3 distinctions of propositions manifest themselves by

answering 3 questions
{ What?
  What kind?
  how much? }

{ What Categorick or Hypothetick, of what kind true, false are
  Affirmative Negative, how much to part, Indefinite Singular. }

---

[23] A reference to Antoine Arnauld's *The Port-Royal Logic*.

Syn. cap. 2.

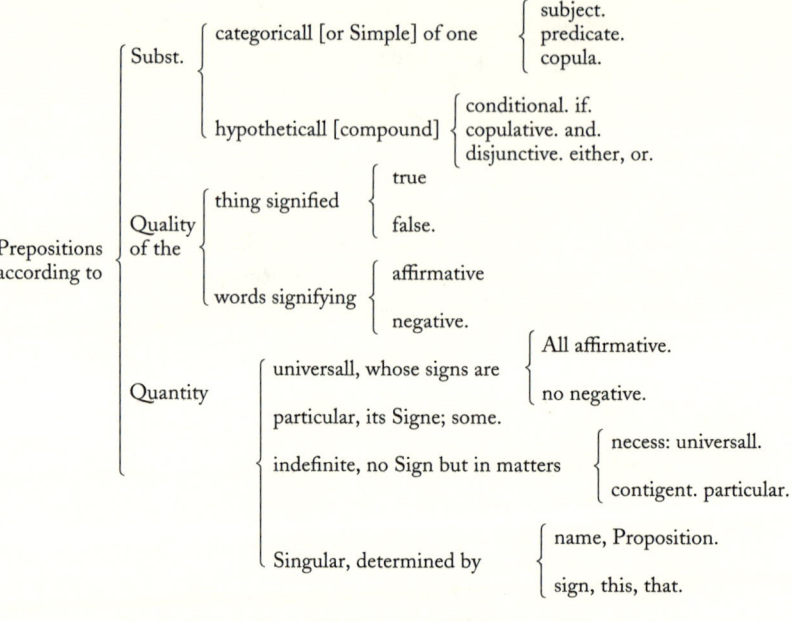

Cap. 3.   of the affections of Prop: oppos: Equiv: conversion.

Propositions as one is refer'd to another have 3 affections or Accidents
Opposition is a Repugnans of 2 Propositions

in { quantity / quality / both }   having the same   { Subject. / predicated. / copula. }

this is of 4 kinds, contraries, subcontraries, subalternates, contradictories
1. **Contraries**, are 2 universalls Repugnant in quality also.
Such may be both { false / not true }   as   { every man is Learned. / no man is Learned. }

2. **Subcontraries**, 2 particulars Repugnant in quality also.
Such may be both { true / not false } as some man is Learned, some man is not Learned
as— —is a stone.— —is not a stone.

3. **Subalternates**, differing only in quantity. Such may be
both { true / false } as { every man is Rational, some man is not Rational.
every man is a stone, some man is a stone.

4. **Contradictories**, Repugnant both in quantity & quality & this is the greatest opposition.
Such may be both { true / not false } as { Every man is Learned.
some man is not Learned.

{ False not True Contra, true not false Subcontra, you see
Both Subalterns, both Contradicts they be }

or — { Contraries may be false not true
True false not false you see
Both Subalternat true or false
Contradicts neither be— }

Equivalence, [or equipollence] is Reconciling those opposites by putting in a negative [not] & this is
either { before / after } both

1. before the sign & subject and it Reconcileth contradictories as { every man is Learned, some man is not Learned.
every man is Learned, [not] some men is not Learned.

2. after— — — — —contraries & subcontraries.
as { every man is Learned; no man is Learned.
every man is [not] Learned, no man is Learned.
some man is Learned, some man is not Learned.
some man is [not] Learned, some man is not learned. the same in words as well as sense.

3. **both** before and after and it Reconcileth subalternates

as
{ every man is Rational. Some man is Rational.
every man is Rational [not] some [or any] man is [not] Rational. }

before doth contradictories concern
after contrariants both subaltern } or

or { not set before do contradicts concern
after contraries. fore and aft subaltern }

Hitherto also referr this Translation of these 4 usuall verses.
not all, is some; but *all not*, is as none
not none, is some; but *none not*, every one
not any, one; *not some*, not all is this
not either, neither; *neither*, not both is

Conversion, is a shifting of the subject and predicate, the same quality Remaining.
1. Simple is shifting without change of quality as no man is a stone. *i.e.* no stone is man.
2. by Accident— —with change— —as every man is an Animal. *id est*, some Animal is a man.
3. by contraposition— —with changing the finite terms into infinite, as man into not man, So every man is an Animal, i.e. every not Animal is not man [or whatsoever is not an Animal is not a man.

Infinite is either
{ positive, this belongs to God only.
negative, is a negation of any Simple term; as not man, not horse &c.
It may rather be called Indefinite, bec: it has no Defined or determined signification: for, by [not a man] I can understand nothing certain, what it is; only that it is not the thing denied, namely man. }

CHARLES MORTON

¶ All kinds of Prepositions will not lawfully be turned by every end of those ways so as both shall be true; by every Preposition will turn by some so as to admit the [ergo]

- simply — universall neg: and partic: affirm:
- by Accident every universall aff: and neg:
- by contraposition — univers: — aff: & partic: neg:

A, is aff: e, neg: both univeralls are
I, is aff: o, neg: but both particular[24]

Syn. cap. 3.

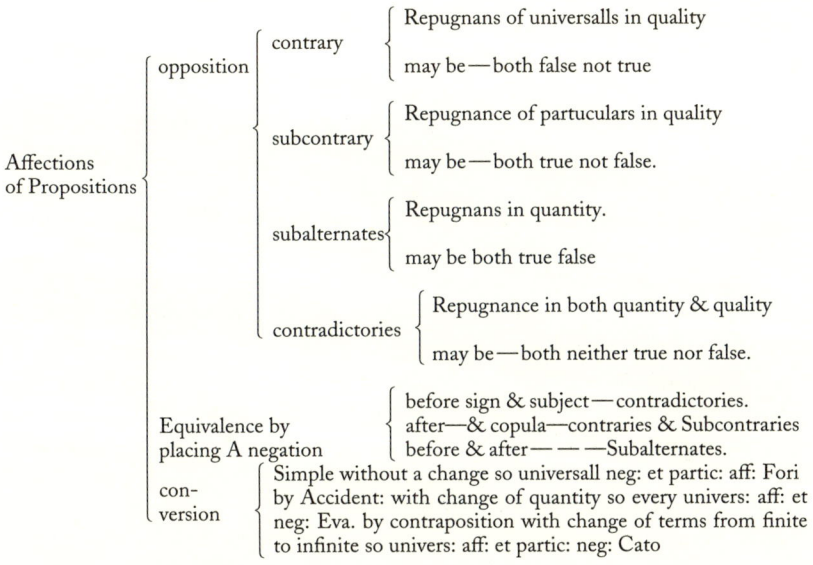

[24] AEIO was a popular designation for the four types of propositions. Since a syllogism contains three propositions and four types for each, there are 4 x 4 x 4 or sixty-four possible modes.

The Third Part of Logick
of Syllogism, or Argumentation
And Method

Cap. 1   of Syllogism

Third part of Logick containeth discourse { illative—Argumentation. / ordinative—method.

Argumentation is a speech in which from one or more Propositions another distinct Prop. is inferred by the note of Inference [therefore, Ergò]

the Species of it are { primary, syllogism. / secondary { Enthymem / Induction / Sorites— } { Example. / Dilemma.

{ Syllogism, Induction, Sortie; Enthymem / Example or similitudes Dilemma— }

Syllogism is an Argumentation in which out of 2 Propositions Rightly disposed a 3^d is inferred

as { every rational is Risible / every man is Rational E.[25] / every man is Risible.

This is 2 fold categoricall and hypothetical.
1. categoricall, if all the Props be categoricall, as in the forementioned syllog.
2. hypotheticall, if one of the Props be hypo.

as { if Soc. be Learned he is to be honored / but Socrates is Learned E. / Soc: is to be honored.

---

[25] E. is an abbreviation for Ergo.

In a Syllog. is considered the **making** & the **use**.
1. The making or fabrick, in which is considered the matter & form.
    1. the matter out of which a Syllog. is made & that is either **next** or **remote**
        1. **the next** matter out of which it is Immediately is 3 Propositions.
            1. the maj: Prop. ⎱
            2. the min: Prop. ⎰ both these together are cald the Premises.
            3. the conclusion
        2. **the Remote** matter of a syllogism is that out of which The Propositions are made. and they

are
3. Terms
⎰ 1. the maj. term, is that which is in the maj. Prop together with the means.
⎱ 2. the minor is so in the minor Proposition
   3. the means is in both the premises.

Each of which terms is twice mentioned in the Syllogism. as, in the first above mentioned Syllogism. the **mean** is Rational the **major** Risible, the minor **man**.

⎰ The[26] Prepositions do next matter same, ⎱
⎱ Of Syllogism Remote three terms the same. ⎰

¶ the mean must always be taken in the same Sense & Latitude in the minor, that it is in the major, for if the mean be equivocall or otherways taken in one of the promises then in the other 'tis called a double mean, & then the syllog. hath 4 forms which is fallacious.
¶ The minor term must always be the Subj: of the conclusion, & the middle term (or means) must never be in the conclusion. think of those 2 Rules and you will Readily & Rightly make & Judge of syllogisms.

The mean is both the Premises is one
Minor in Subject and Conclusion

---

[26] The "Memoriall Verses" has "three" instead of "the."

A Logick System

2. the form of a syllogism is the Right disposition of the matter

in { figure—of the Remote matter. terms.
mood—of this next matter. Propositions

    1. figure (or Right disposing the terms) is 3 fold According to the placing of the middle term
    { 1. Subject in the maj. & predicates in the minor.
      2. predicate in both Premises.
      3. Subject in both.
    2. Moods (or Right disposing of Propositions) are 14 usefull whereof

figures { 1–4
        2–4
        3–6

¶ There might be a 4th figure (prae: sub) and so there would be 4 more moods, but the force of their inference would be as the 1st figure & therefore as needless they may be Rejected.

    All the usefull moods are comprehended in these 3 cabbalistical verses.
1. bar-ba-ra cæ-la-rent da-ri-i for-ri-o [are Reduced]
2. cæs-a-re cam-es-tres fes-ti-no ba-ro-co
3. da-rap-ti fe-lap-ton dis-am-is da-ti-si bo-car-do fe-ri-son[27]

¶ that in the writing of these you must put the [s. and .m] to this and of the foregoing Syllables, and not to the beginning of the following.

¶ for their understanding, that in each Syllable is one of the 4 vowels [a, e, i, o] which are the signs of quantity & quality [as in part 2^d. ch. 3.] so bar-ba-ra is 3 universalls affirmative; cæ-la-rent is univers: neg: univers: aff: univers: neg:. &c. as in this Syllog: of the 4th mood of the 1st figure

{ fe—no horse is Reasonable   } e. univers: neg.
  ri—some animal is an horse   } i. partic: aff.
  o—some Animal is not Reasonable } o. partic: neg.

---

[27]. This Medieval memory device probably was not cabbalistical. The oldest known version is in William of Shyreswood's *Introductiones in Logicam* written in the first half of the thirteenth century. For a more complete discussion of moods and figures using this device, see William of Sherwood's *Introduction to Logic*, trans. Norman Kretzmann (Minneapolis: Minnisota, 1966), 60–68. Morton's trimmed down and perfunctory explanation of these important aspects of scholastic syllogistic logic is consistent with the general lack of interest and competence in humanistic logic.

Where observe
{
the quantity & qual: are according to the 4 vowels [a, e, i, o,]
the middle term (horse) is subject & pred. therefore it is of the 1ˢᵗ figure.
the minor term (Animal) is subject of the concl: & therefore concludes directly.
}

¶ the vowels in this Parenthesis (are Reduced) refer to what follows them & signifie that the moods of the 2d and 3d figure (called Imperfect moods) are Reduced to the 4 moods of the 1st figure (called perfect moods) bec: the consequence of moods in the first figure is not only certain (as it is in the rest) but more evident than it is in the rest.

Reduction is done by some consonants in the aforesaid cabalistical words these observable consonant are either

{ Initial [B. C. D. F]
{ Subsequent [S. P. M. C.]

Imperfect mood must be reduced to the perfect mood which begin with the same letter; so Baroco to Bar-ba-ra/cæs-a-re to cælarent &c. the subsequent (in the middle or latter part) of the words of art do signifie

that
{
S. (that is, the prop before which it stands) must be simply converted
P. (that is, the prop before which it stands) must be turned by Acct.
M. dos shift places (so as the min: prop: is put for Maj: & the maj: is made min:
C. is reduced to Impossible: i.e. the contradictory is manifested Impossible.
}

¶ Reduction by conversion and transposition (done by S. M. P) is called ostensive.

¶ when you have a syllog: to Reduce, first observe if you have an M. or a C. in its charactoristical word; if you have an M. then begin with the Transposition.

A Logick System

as
cam—every man is Rational	cæ—no Rational is brute	transposed & simply converted
es—no brute is Rational	la—every man is Rational	transposed & not converted
tres—no brute is a man	rent—no man is a brute	simply converted.

If you have a c: Reduce it to Impossible: this c. is found only in 2 moods (viz.) Boroco & bocardo: these must be Reduced to Barbara bec: of the B. Initiall. now in each of them you {see} an (a) that prop: being already fit for barbara must stand as it does. the other 2 props: must be thus altered. if the major be kept (as in baroco) the contradictory of the minor; must
make the conclusion (& Reciprocally) the contradictory of the conclusion must make the minor. (that is the Partic: negatives must be made univers: affirmative) if the min: be kept as (in Bocardo) then so must you do with the maj:

as
Bo—Some man is not Learned	Bar—every Rational is Learned	contradiction to conclusion
car—every man is Rational	ba—every man is Rational	kept
do—some Rational is not Learned	ra—every man is Learned	contrad: to major

Now the Reduced Syllog: in Barbara has in it manifest falshood, therefore the Syllog: in Bocardo (contrary to the other) was before certainly and is now manifestly or evidently known true; for the contradictory to it appears to be Impossible & contradictories cannot be both either true or false.

Rules of Syllog:
{ All nega: All parti: conclude not by this art
{ conclusion all ways follows weaker part

¶ the weaker part is negative and partic: therefore in Ferio the Concl. partakes of the weakness of both the premises, is neg: from (fe) & partic: from (i).
¶ Syllogism is the primary species of Argumentation, the rest are but secondary and may be Reduced to it and must be tried by it, therefore I put this in a chapt. by it self and leave the rest to the next.

Syn. Cap. 1.

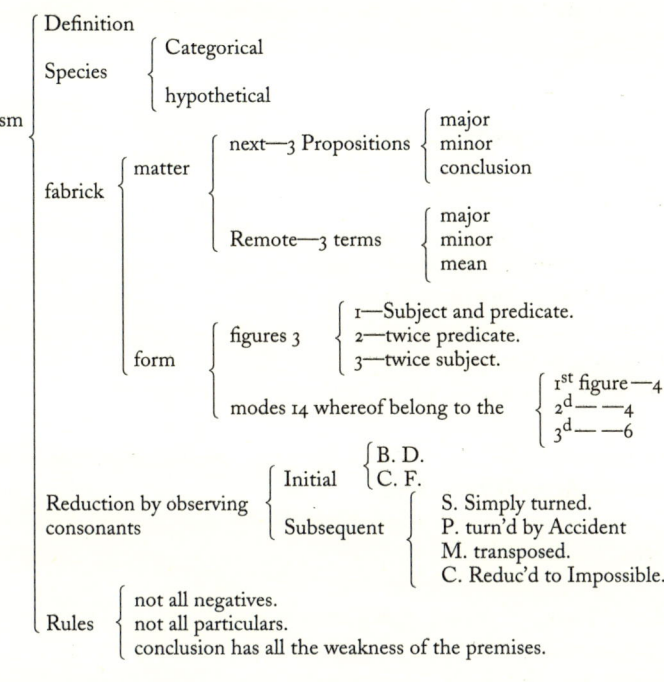

Cap. 2. Of Secondary Argumentation { Enthymem, Induction, Example, Sorites, Dilemma, violentum

1. Enthymem. [the 2^d species of Argumentation is an Incomplete Syllog: having but 2 propositions expressed; the 3^d is in the mind.

as { Socrates is Learned. E. | the 3^d which is understood is
Socrates is to be honoured | every Learned man is to be honoured.

this is { convenient for brevity, where the 3^d prop: is easily conceived.
necessary to prove the Conseq: of an hypoth: Syllog: if defined,

for a sequel must always be proved by a sequel and this Reduces the dispute again to be categoricall, which is best, thô the other be somtimes most easy and Ready to the mind.

{ Clear Brevity an Enthymem doth love }
{ Always a Sequel by a Sequel prove }

¶ if the conseq: of an hypoth: be not good (or to be denyed) the Respondent, says not [I deny the major] but (I deny the conseq:) but if the conseq. of an enthymem be to be denied, he must not say [I deny the sequel or conseq.] but [I deny the argument]

as thus { if Socrates be learned he is to be hated
but socrates is Learned. Ergò
Socrates is to be hated.

the Respondent answers [I deny the sequel] the opponent proceeds to prove his sequel by an enthymem thus:

{ Every learned man is to be hated. Ergò
if socrates be learned he is to be hated.

The respondent answers [I deny the Argument] & not sequel as before.
¶ All this is no more than one plain categoricall & therefore it is best, for it might be better thus expressed

{ Every learned man is to be hated
Socrates is a leaned man Ergò
Socrates is to be hated.

here the respondent denyes the major without more to do.
¶ In disputes, the prop: denied by the Respondent, must always be the conclusion of the opponents next syllogism.

{ In Hypotheticks, what by Sequel meant, }
{ The same is Enthymem is Argument— }

2. Induction. is an argumentation from particulars sufficiently enumerated to Infer an universall conclusion; As, John is Rational; Peter is rational; William is rational; & of the rest, Ergò Every man is Rational, this is a good Induction: whereas if one should say, John is Learned, Tom is Learned, William is Learned; & so of the rest, then the Respondent

answers [I deny the Induction] for person is not Learned, this is of use in natural Philosop: to settle general Propositions.

> { The Weakness of Induction is espied,
> If there's one that may be denied— }

3. Example is an argumentation wherein one (or more) particular Instance is brought to prove another particular from the similitude or parity of reason

as { John Let fall the glass and it brake, ergò
if you let fall the glass you'll break it. }

The Ergò is from the similitude of glass to glass in brittleness: but there are other circumstances which may alter the case; as John let fall his glass on the stones but I let mine fall on the water, therefore the Respondent answers the case is not the same or there is no parity of Reason.

¶ Examples & similitudes are very seldom of much force bec: of the great diversity which may happen in the circumstances, yet they may force in oratory to illustrate: thô in logick they prove little.

> { Examples from Similitude conclude
> In Argument they commonly delude
> Examples from them likewise do conclude
> But always fail, where'd no Similitudes. }

4. Sorites is an argumentation by many propositions so heaped together as that the subject of one is the pred: of the other, till at last the first subject and last predicate are joyned together in the conclusion. As, Peter is a man; man is Animal; Animal is a sensitive, sensitive is a liver; liver is a body; body is a subject; Ergò Peter is a subject; tis of use for brevity or Recapitulation of a foregoing dispute to show how the whole series of Syllogisms make one solid Argument.

> { By Sorites arguing is a chain
> first Subject dos the last predicate attain,
> But if one line doth hap to slip or fly
> Then all the argument is spoiled thereby. }

5. Dilemma. (or the 2 horn'd Argument) is that which smites the adversary on both sides that he cannot escape the one or the other Inconvenience:

A Logick System

As, if you marry one that is fair, others will love her; if one that is foul, you'll not love her your self; Ergò marry not at all. The weakness of it is if there be a safe mean between those 2 extreams; as if the fair be virtuous, no matter who loves her; and thô foul, if virtuous, I shall love her for her virtue; Ergò I may marry, provided she be virtuous.

$$\left\{\begin{array}{l}\text{Dilemma's horns do push on either side}\\\text{Yet Truth may safely in the main}^{28}\text{ abide.}\end{array}\right\}$$

Besides the 5 mentioned there is a sort of arguing sometimes used in disputation called Violentum [Retortion or Inversion] when an argument brought to prove one thing is restarted & turned back upon the adversary to prove the contrary to which he brings it for. As, one said to Romulus when he drank but little wine; If all men should drink as you do wine would be cheap, no, says Romulus if all men should drink as I do wine would be dear for I drink as much as I will.

This sort of arguing may be managed in any of the former kinds and therefore is not specifically distinct from them: it is an act of wit and quick fancy rather than solid Judgment, and therefore belongs rather to Rhetoric then Logic.

Syn. Cap. 2.

Secondary Argumentations are
- Emthymem
  - Def. force in the
    - truth of the Antecedent
    - strength of the consequent

    weak è contrà
  - use
    - brevity in plain matters.
    - to prove consequences.
- Induction
  - Def: force in sufficient Enumeration weak if one Exception
  - use in Natural Phylosophy to settle generall Rules.
- Example
  - Def: force in similitude; weakness in diversity of circumstances that alter the case.
  - use in oratory to Illustrate, rather than in Log: to prove.

[28] The "Memorial Verses" has "mean" instead of "main."

Sorites
- Deffinition.
- force in the exact connexion of all the parts, weakness in defect of one
- use for brevity and Recapitulation.

Dilemma
- Def:
- force in the closeness of the branches, weakness in a mean to be admitted.
- use to silence the adversary and put a stop to his motion.

violentum
- Good wit, but
- weak and fallacious Argument.

Cap. 3.   Of the use of syllogisms in { demonstration / Topical, & / Sophistical. }
And first of Demonstration.

Hitherto of the fabrick or making of Syllogisms now of the use or end which according to the matter is to

beget { Science (or certain knowl.) demonstration. / Opinion (or probable) opinion. / Deceit (or error) fallacy. }

{ A Demonstration Science compleats, / Opinion, Topic, Fallacy, deceit. }

1. Demonstration is defined from its { end. / matter }

   1. from its end, A syllog. to make to know, or to beget science, i.e. to understand the cause of a thing & cannot be otherwise; Things demonstrable are only properties; the principles (or middle term) to prove it to be in the subject is the Diff. So, Risibility (the property) is demonstrated to be in man (the subject) by Rationality. the Diff: as in this

demonstration { Every Rational is Risible / every man is Rational, Ergò / every man is Risible. }

{ By difference demonstrate property, / You'll then the thing & cause attain thereby. }

[209]

A Logick System

for demonstration are 2 propositions, ⎰ that.
or (foreknowedges) ⎱ What.
  1. That thing is,
    1. in nature, answering the question [is there such a thing?]
    2. in the subject,— — —[whether it be so?]
  2. What it is as to
    1. name [the signification of the word]
    2. thing [the definition of the thing]

⎰ To demonstrate some foreknowledge bring, ⎱
⎱ That 'tis in nature Subject, what name thing. ⎰

The things that are foreknown by those precognitions are the
⎰ Subject.
⎱ Affection.
⎩ Principle.
  1. Subject of which something is to be demonstrated
  that it is in nature
  What if is both ways?
  2. affection (or property) what as to name only.
  3. the principle (or diff:) by which the affection is to be demonstrated ⎰ that both ways
    ⎱ what as to name

2. From the matter, is a demonstration defin'd; A Syllog: made up of things true, necessary, Immediate, more knowable, Antecedant and the cause of the conclusion.
  1. **necessary** when there is a perpetual & indisoluable connexion of
⎰ Subject &
⎱ Predicate
  necessity has 3 degrees; of all, Directly, & as it self.
    1. of all, as properties of the 2^d kind (all & always) so black of an Ethiopian
    2. of it Self, (i.e. directly & not by accident) when there is an essentiall or causall connexion. This is 4 fold.

1. When the pred: is of the Def: as the Subject,

& that
- expressly, as the next
  - genus, as Animal to man.
  - Diff: as Rational to man.
- Implyed—remote
  - Genus, as body to man.
  - Diff: as mixt to man.

2. When the subject is of the Def: of the predicate, & so it is as property of the 4th sort for Risibility is defin'd [an affection in man arising from Rationality]

3. When existence is predicated of substance As, Socrates is; now what ever is, is necessary while it is: bec: nothing can be and not be at the same time. this kind of necessity is not of use in demonstration.

¶ Existence is a being of a thing actually & out of its causes; or actuated essence, as a Rose in June: Whereas essence may be in causes when it is not actuated by existence as a Rose in winter.

4. when an external cause (such are efficient & end) is predicated of its effect; as, an eclipse is the shadow of the earth.

3. as it self, when the predicate is attributed so universally, as that it is not only Reciprocated with the subject, but it is also primary in it as the Diff: So Rational in man:

{ Genus, Difference to Subject, Subject to props is direct
  Existence to Essence, External cause Effect. }

Risibility indeed is in man universally and Reciprocated with him, but it is in him, not primarily, but only secondarily & depending on Rationality.

{ Of all directly of it self these three
  are steps by & things necessary be. }

¶ In these 3 degrees of necessity the 2^{d} includes the 1st, and the 3^{d} both the other as being most perfect.

A Logick System

2. Immediate
Immediaty
is of
- the Subject when no other Subject intervenes; as man is Rational.
- the cause— — —cause—as Rational is Risible.

3 **more knowable**, so the premises must be then the conclusion, else they could not make it known.

4 **Antecedent** (in truth to the conclusion) for this is true from the premises, yet they from this.

5 **cause of the conclusion**; for the middle term must be the cause of the affection as Rationality is Risibility.

{ Of Demonstration truth 5 are the laws,
necess: Immed: is more known, preced: and Cause. }

Syn. Cap. 3.

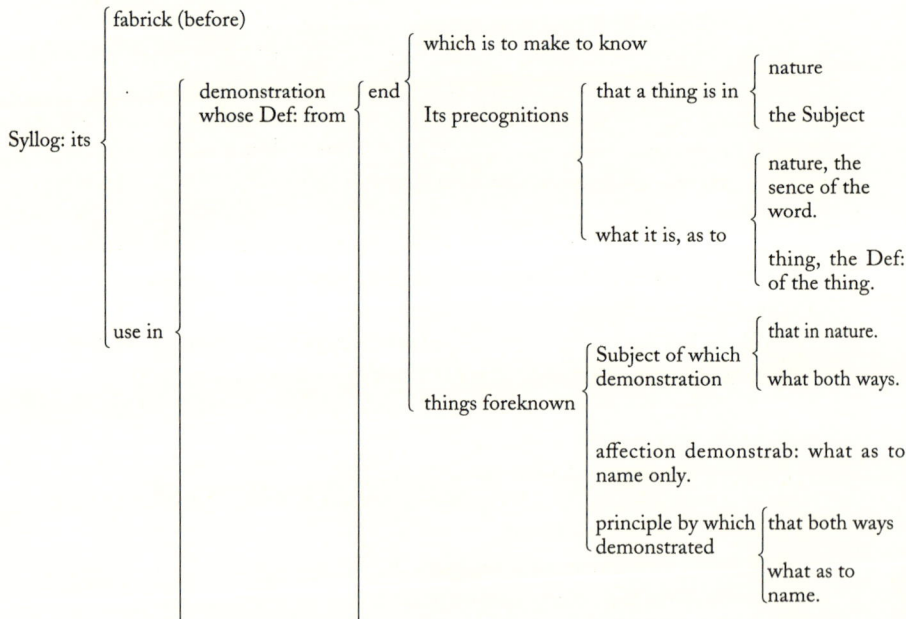

CHARLES MORTON

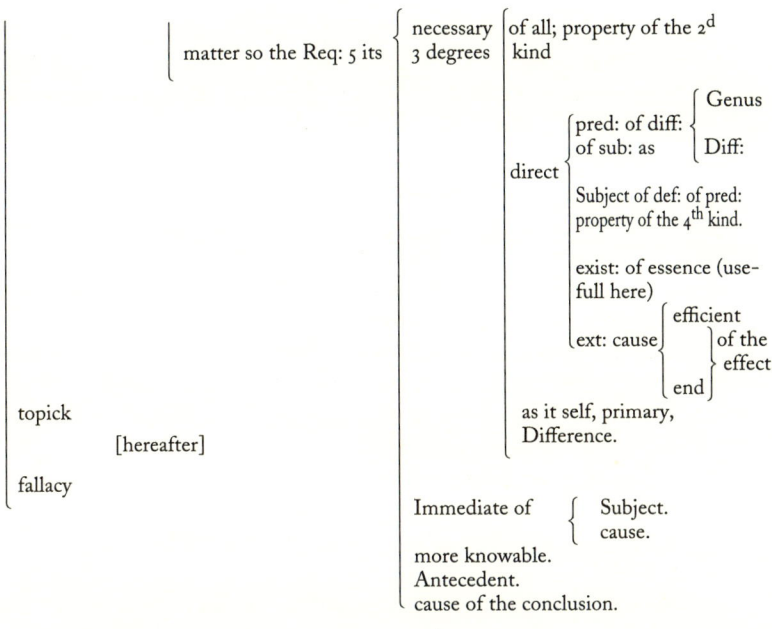

Cap. 4.　of the division of demonstration into $\begin{cases} \text{that} \\ \text{Why} \end{cases}$

That. a thing is, is demonstated when the middle term (mean or principle) is
1. Either a Remote efficient cause which is either
   1. Reciprocated (or turned) with the effect & then it makes a demonstration affirmative, in barbara, as

   as $\begin{cases} \text{Bar—every liver is nourished} \\ \text{ba—every plant is a liver.} \\ \text{ra—every plant is nourished.} \end{cases}$

   2. not Reciprocated, & then it makes only a neg: (i.e. demonstrates that the thing is not) in comestres, as

   as $\begin{cases} \text{Com—every breather is an animal.} \\ \text{es—no stone is an Animal.} \\ \text{tres—no stone is a breather.} \end{cases}$

   ¶ that living is the cause of nourishment, the remote cause, bec: the

[213]

A Logick System

nutritive power does Intervene: tis Reciprocated with liver, for every liver is nourished, and every nourished is a liver. but in the other case; breathing is the cause of the Animals remaining so to be; A remote cause, bec: the natural power to breath intervenes: is not Reciprocated, for thô every breather be an Animal, yet every Animal is not a breather, for fishes, flies, and other insects are not so.

$$\left\{\begin{array}{l}\text{In Barbara Remote Efficient lies}\\\text{If turned, if not Comestres then denies.}\end{array}\right\}$$

2. a next effect, proving its cause, that it is, or has been in being or in the same subject so Risibility proves Rationality to be in man

as $\left\{\begin{array}{l}\text{every Risible is Rational}\\\text{every man is Risible, Ergò}\\\text{every man is Rational.}\end{array}\right.$

In like manner ashes prove that there has been fire, & so we prove that being of a Deity from the creation. Rom. 1.20[29]

¶ There is an [Ergò or] therefore of
conseq: only which signifies no more than in that, or for as much as.
cause, which signifies bec: of
here in this sort of demonstration, the [Ergò] is no more than an Ergò of Conseq: As, therefore there has been fire in that (or for as much) there are ashes. not [therefore] bec: of ashes, for ashes are not the cause of fire but the effect thereof.
this sort (that) is called demonstration [from the latter) bec: the effect is later than (or after) the cause; whereas the other (why) which is from the cause is called demonstration [from the former] bec: the cause does go before the effect, & this proves not only that it is, but why it is, and is the cheife demonstration.

$$\left\{\begin{array}{l}\text{The next effect the Cause doth verify}\\\text{That so it is althô it shew not why.}\end{array}\right\}$$

Why a thing is, is showing not only the existence, but the reason or nature of the thing: tis when the middle term or principle of demonstration is the next cause moving its effect.

---

[29] "For the invisible things of him, that is his eternal power and Godhead, are seen by the creation of the world...."

CHARLES MORTON

The causes of a thing are
- Internal, i.e. such as abide in it
  - matter.
  - form.
- External, i.e. separated from its nature
  - efficient.
  - end.

So of a man
- the matter is his body; the form his soul.
- the efficient God; the end Gods glory.

1. demonstration by matter
   - Every thing of wood is combustible
   - the chair is of Wood. Ergò
   - the chair is combustible

2. by form
   - what has a Rational soul is Risible
   - a man has a Rational soul. Ergò
   - a man is Risible.

3. by effect
   - what is made by an infinitely wise being is wisely made.
   - the world is made by an infinitely wise being. Ergò
   - the world is wisely made.

4. By the end
   - that which needs cooling of the heart has lungs.
   - an horse needs cooling of the heart. Ergò
   - an horse has lungs.

{ To prove the why, the things, four causes tend,
  Matter and form, Efficient & End }

A Logick System

Syn. Cap. 4.

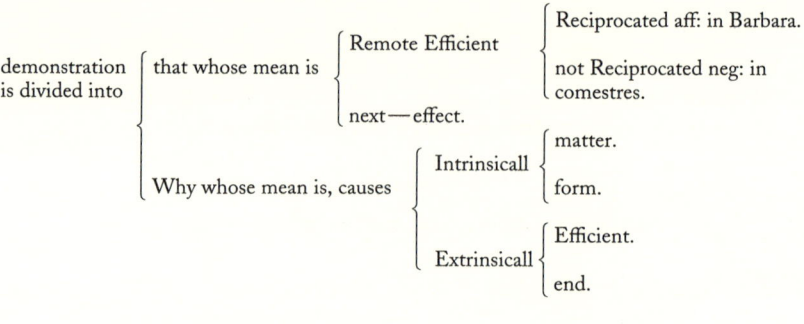

Cap. 5   of the affections of Demonstration { Analysis. Regress. conversion. }

The affections (or properties) of Demonstration are 3.

1. **Analysis**, which is the Resolving effects into their first and indemonstrable causes to get a perfect knowledge of them & quiet the mind: it is a Recapitulation of argument with a (bec:) instead of an (Ergò) beginning at the last urged & going back to the first. this is done commonly in the end of a disputation, & is but a sorites, with the latter end forwards. As

In Sorites { What is a liver is a nutritive faculty; what has a nuturitive faculty is nourished; what is nourished is encreased; E. what is a liver is encreased. }

In Analysis { Every liver is encreased, (bec) nourished. he is nourished bec: he has a nutritive faculty; he has a nutritive faculty bec: he is a liver. }

{ Analysis in Demonstration brings, Back from the last to the first proof of things. }

¶ A thing is said to be Indemonstrable
    1. for want of evidence; as a falsehood.
    2. from abundances of evidences
        an object of sense—as the sun shines.
        a first principle—as the whole is bigger than its parts.

{ A thing Indemonstratable you may call
which hath[30] proof, or what needs none at all. }

2. **Regresse** (or a lawful Reciprocall demonstration) is when by an effect Indistinctly known, we prove its cause (that it is) & then by the same cause distinctly known, we prove the effect (why it is).

{ Regress first by the Effect the cause doth shew
are then the Effect by the cause why its true. }

It differs from a vitious circle[31] which attempts to prove (a why it is) on both sides, but that is Impossible, for nothing can be the cause of that where of it is the effect: Such is the absurd popish circle about the Popes authority from the Scripture & then again the Scriptures authority from the Pope: As, why has the Scripture Authority? the Pope give it [for according to them no Scripture can be Authentick or canonical unless he allows it to be so) but how comes the Pope by this Authority? A: the Scripture gives it (thou art Peter &c)[32] but that is not the sense of the place; oh yes, it must needs be so: Why? because the Pope says so, & so on in the round till you are weary of nonsense.

{ The Circle is impossible in this
Thats judged by cause, wherefore the cause it is— }

Examples of a lawful regresse.

The cause by that effect, that it is		the effect by the cause Why it is	
	every Risib: is Rational		every Rational is Risible
	every man is Risib:		every man is Rational
	every man is Rational		every man is Risible.

---

[30] The "Memorial Verses" has "has no."
[31] Tautology or circular reasoning.
[32] Matt 16:18.

A Logick System

Examples of a vitious circle

the effects by the cause

Why it is	{ what the Script confirms has authority the Pope is confirmed by the Script E the pope has authority.	the effect by the cause Why it is again	what the P. conf: has Author: the S. is conf'd by the P. the Script. has authority

3. **Conversion**, is a turning the demonstration finished & allowed to be good into the perfect Definition of the property demonstrated

as { every Rational is Risible | tis turn'd into this Definition of
every mani is Rational | Risibility; Risibility is an
every man is Risible | affection in man arising from Rationality.

¶ that in chapt 3^d it is said that the precognition of the affection (necessary to demonstration) is only of the name, not of the thing: here the reason of it may be seen, for the thing (i.e. the Definition of the thing) cannot be known till after the demonstration be made and converted; therefore it is not necessary to be foreknown.

¶ it is said also there among the necessaries direct, the 2^d sort, that the subject is of the Definition of the predicate, this is seen here in this conversion, for man the subject is part of the Definition of Risible, the predicate or affection proved.

{ Conversion turns the proving propositions
Into Affections perfect Definitions— }

Syn. Cap. 5.

Affections of demonstration {
 Analysis —its {
  nature, Resolving effects into causes Indemonstratable { not for want of Evidence but from abundance thereof.
 }
 use { quieting the mind in perfect knowledge.
  Recapitulation of a dispute. }
}

CHARLES MORTON

Regress
—its
- nature, Reciprocall demonstration.
- use, to investigate the true cause of a thing
  - 1. cause by Effect; **that it is**
  - 2. Effect by cause; **Why it is**
- Diff: from a circle which would demonstrate both **Why it is**, which is Impossible.

conversion
—its
- nature, turning demonstration into Definition
- use, to find out a proper Def: for a property.

Cap. 6. Of Topicall Syllogism

A topical syllog: is that which consists of probable Propositions, begetting A probable assent to the conclusion

and that either in
- opinion—from an Argument.
- belief—from a Testimony.

> An Argument opinion is grounded,
> But upon testimony faith is founded.

that is probable which seems true

to
- all
- most
- wisest, & of those to
  - all
  - most
  - most noted.

As the goods of the mind[33] are better than the goods of the body, Sin is worse than sickness &c.

> Probable is by all, most, wiseest, deem'd
> & then of those all, most, or most esteem'd

The same prop: is called
- before the syllogism: is made [problem] as if cast forth to be contended for
- after the conclusion.

---

[33] Partridge mistakenly wrote "body mind" when he meant to write just "mind."

[219]

A Logick System

Problems must be { doubtfull, or they need not to be disputed.

profitable, or it is not worth the while.

{ Doubtfull & profitable must be all,
What problem first, after conclusion call }

Things thus disputed about are called topical predicates: the middle terms that prove the predicate to belong to the subject are called the Argument.

{ The Middle term doth prove an Argument.
Genus Definition property Accident. }

Arguments are found out to prove a thing probable from Logick places, called topick; hence unreasonable wicked men (2 Thess 3.2.) are (in the original) said to be without Topicks.34

In Topicks are 2 things to be considered, maxims and differences. of maxims. 1. maxims (or axioms) generall propositions on which arguments are founded. 2. Differences of maxims, certain heads or common places under which these maxims are Ranked, & from which arguments may be drawn; As, Genus, Definition, cause, &c. thus if one would prove Logick to be an art, he may take an argument from the Def: of Art which is an habit effective &c.

{ An habit effective with Right reason is an Art
Logick is an habit effective with right Reason, Ergò
Logick is an Art

This argument is grounded on this maxim [the Definite agrees to what the Definition doth] if the Def: of Art [an habit effective &c] doth agree to Logick, then doth the Definite [Art] agree with it also.

{ Maxims Differences, whence they're being let 35
Afford all Arguments that may be brought— }

---

34 Geneva Bible: "...delivered from unreasonable and evil men: for all men have not faith." The "unreasonable and evil" in Greek is atomos which can be translated as "without topic" as Morton says. "Out of place," or "improper" might make more sense as a literal translation today. Tim Vivian provided this information to me.
35 The "Memoriall Verses" has "whence they are sought."

Places (or topicks) are either
1. Artificial, such as are drawn forth by Art, those are Reduced to 7 pair, as cause & causate, Subject & adjunct, &c.
2. Inartificial, is drawn forth without art; tis onely one, Testimony.

Of the Artificial.
   1. **cause & causate** is a place or topick from whence arguments (or mediums) are drawn which are either the cause or the effect of the thing to be proved. Its maxims are:
      1. every cause is before its causate

that is $\begin{cases} \text{matter} \\ \text{form} \\ \text{efficent} \\ \text{end} \end{cases}$ go before in execution
—only in Intention.

so it must be (one way or other) bec: every effect depends on its cause.
      2. The cause being put, or granted to be, the effect is put (or necessarily follows thereon) & on the contrary; Remove the cause and you remove the effect: provided the cause be.
         1. total not partial; As, the Sun being above the Horizon, it is day.
         2. of it self, or direct, (& not by Accident) A Physitian heals directly, a musitian[36] by Accident.
         3. next, not remote; as, the heat of fire, (remote) burns when nigh[t] (next)
      3. an efficient gives not what it has not, that is

$\begin{cases} \text{If not the direct next because you have got} \\ \text{The Effect will follow otherwise it will not.} \end{cases}$

         1. formally, as an unlearned man cannot do a learned excercise. or
         2. virtually, So god gives matter that has none formally in him bec: he has it virtually (or in his power to produce) So the Sun gives fruits althô it has none formally in it.
      4. as is the cause, such is the effect, provided

$\begin{cases} \text{Formal or virtual must be with in} \\ \text{Efficient what it gives cat yeilds but skin.} \end{cases}$

---

[36] Dunbar's version has "Physician" here.

A Logick System

1. the cause be universall: as man begetts a man; a lyon a lyon.
2. the effect be like in essentialls (but not in all accidentalls) So a Learned man may have a fool to his Son, a blind father A Seeing Son.
¶ those are not all the maxims of cause that may be found in

{ As in the Cause such an Effect you see
  In Essence the universal it be. }

Logick writers, nor are they all mentioned in the other topicks that follow, but the Instances on every place are the cheif. I can at present think of, & may suffice to direct how to use maxims, & give them the due limitations.

2. **Subject & adjunct** is a topick &c (as in cause changing only what is to be changed, & so the rest that follow) Its maxims are.
   1. Subjects are demonstrated by the Accidents (or adjuncts) As, fire is called hot from the heat in it.
   2. demonstration is taken from the cheif part; As, a man may be said to be good or wise thô there be of the contrary in him; & so a wicked man thô he do some good.

{ From prevailing part denominate
  Althô the thing be in imperfect State }

3. the Subject being put, the adjunct is put, & on the contrary, i.e. if the adjunct be proper & Inseparable, not a common Acci: & separable from the subject.

3. disagreeing & compared of which
   1. disagreeing are

   either { opposites, as white and black.
            disparates, are twice opposed, as liberality to   { avarice &
            divers, as an horse and a stone   prodigality. }

   2. compared { Quantity—equal & unequal
                 Quality—like and dislike. }

{ Opposites are but two, Disparates three,
  Diverse when only not the same thing be. }

[222]

CHARLES MORTON

Its maxims are
   1. the better, the good the worse, its contrary; as if virtue be better than riches, then vice is worse than poverty.

$$\left\{\begin{array}{l}\text{The better is the good you do propound}\\ \text{Its contrasts too much the worse is found.—}\end{array}\right\}$$

   2. opposites have the same Reason both in respect of
      1. knowledge for one dos illustrate the other; so, to know what sickness is, we must know what health is; & è contrà.
      2. Subject, for they are conversant both about the same subject, so, are health and sickness in Respect of humane Body.

$$\left\{\begin{array}{l}\text{Opposites are made known by one another}\\ \text{And as for Subject they admit no other.}\end{array}\right\}$$

   3. if 2 things are equall, what is equall to one of them is equall to the other; as a line of a foot long being equal to a foot Rule another line that is a foot long is equall to either of them.

$$\left\{\begin{array}{l}\text{Two Equals in themselves a third that's just.}\\ \text{Æqual to Æqual, Æqually the other must}\end{array}\right\}$$

   4. no like is the same, for likeness is a Relation between divers things: so Alchymy (or fictitious gold) is no gold, bec: it but Resembles it, and so blanched copper does silver.

$$\left\{\begin{array}{l}\text{What ever is but like is not the same}\\ \text{An hypocrite bares but a Christian name}\end{array}\right\}$$

   5. love from a likeness; So good men love good, bad men bad company; and therefore (says fuller Ingeniously) a mans companion is a comment on the margin of his life, whereby another man may be read & understand the text of his secret Inclinations.

$$\left\{\begin{array}{l}\text{Like will to like; Bird that 'gree of a Feather}\\ \text{We usually do find will flock together.}\end{array}\right\}$$

A Logick System

4. conjugates & notations, Whereof.
  1. conjugates are words of like signification & derivation,

as { Learning / Learned. / Learnedly.

therefore if Soc: has learning, he is learned & can do Learnedly.
2. notation is the explication of a word by its Etymology; As a Prophet is one that foretells future things; for Prophet comes from a word that signifies to forspeak. Maxims are
  1. To whom one of the conjugates do agree to him dos the other also, et è contrà. Tis fallacious
    { 1. from act to habit, as he did a Just act, E. he is just man-
      2. from a power to its act, As, Ra[37] is Risible, E. he laugheth.
But the contrary: viz: from act to power is very good; as he laughs, Ergò he is Risible.

{ Conjugates hold in Concrete and Abstract / Not from one act to habit power to act—

2. if one conjugate be said of one conjugate, then the other is said of the other; As, if red be coloured, then Redness is a colour; if covetousness be a vice, then a covetous man is vitious.

{ In Conjugates if one be said of one, / The other of the other is said anon—

3. to whom the notation agrees, to him the thing noted also agrees; as he foretells future things, Ergò he is a Prophet.
¶ tis fallacious when the Etymologies are foolish & unApt: as, phantastick comes from a word that signifies light; E. he that so calls a Quaker grants him to have his pretended light within him.[38]

---

[37] Rational.

[38] Quakers, the Society of Friends, emphasized the inner light from the Holy Spirit more than Puritans. Puritans, in general, were antagonistic to Quakerism, insisting that it was a form of antinomianism and fanaticism. Puritans and Quakers shared the role of dissenters in late seventeenth-century Britain, but Puritans were especially sensitive to making a clear distinction between their form of rational religion and the Quakers' form of pietism.

CHARLES MORTON

{ Good Etymons do with the thing agree }
{ But not when foolishness unept may be. }

5. **Whole & parts**. maxims are.
1. the whole is more than the part, i.e. in the same Respect, wherein it is a whole, for otherwise it may be false: for Animal as A whole (universall) is more than man bec: it comprehends both man and beast; yet the same Animal as a part (essentiall) of the same man is less than man, for man as a whole comprehends both Animal & Rational.

{ The whole is greater than the Part be sure }
{ No part the whole's action from can endure }

2. the parts being put, the whole is put; i.e. all the parts taken together & united; else, he that Returneth all the torn peices of my book may be said to restore my borrowed book: he returns indeed all that he borrowed but not the whole that he borrowed.

{ All Parts together set }
{ And then thereby the whole you'll surely get. }

3. parts are for the whole; so, particular churches are for the universal: particular corporations for the commonwealth, for whose good somtimes they must part with their conveniences. better an hand cut of;[39] or an eye plucked out tha{n} the whole man perish.[40]

{ Parts for the whole by nature foreordain'd }
{ And in the whole is every past sustain'd— }

---

[39] Both Dunbar and Partridge transcribe "of" instead of "off." This is an indicator of the mindlessness of transcription and the way an error may spread through various branches of transcriptions.

[40] It is tempting to assign this example to the particular problem of dissenters in Britain (especially applicable to New England after its corporate charter was revoked). Puritan churches and corporations were legally repressed and forced to give up "conveniences" that would normally have been their legal right. Morton, however, takes the view of the universal church and the whole commonwealth here rather than the particular church and corporation that suffer being cut and plucked. Statements such as this in the textbook would have been excellent for inciting classroom discussion of Puritan politics and religion.

6. **Genus and Species**. maxims are.
  1. take away the genus and you take away the species; not on the contrary; as, if there be no animal, before there is no man; but if there be no man yet there may be An Animal: and by the same reason it holds as to Species and Individualls; for if there be no body in a place then {John} is not there.

$$\left\{\begin{matrix}\text{Destroy the genus \& you do deface}\\ \text{The Species that under it have place.}\end{matrix}\right\}$$

  2. of what the species is predicated, of the same is the genus; but not on the contrary: as, if Socrates be A man he is an Animal, but a horse may be an Animal yet it follows not that he is a man, for genus and Species will not convert.

$$\left\{\text{or thus}\begin{matrix}\text{From Species the Genus you infer}\\ \text{But if from Genus, Species you err}\\ \\ \text{Of Species is affirmed of that}\\ \text{The Genus may be also predicate}\end{matrix}\right\}$$

7. **Definition and division**. maxims are.
  1. Whatever is Defined is a species; i.e. perfectly defined by Genus and Diff: for highest genus and Individualls have no genus which is required to a perfect Definition therefore they are only described as they may be.

$$\left\{\begin{matrix}\text{That what's defin'd is Species gather hence}\\ \text{Because it hath Genus and Difference.}\end{matrix}\right\}$$

  2. to what the Definition dos agree to the same dos the definite; As, if Socrates be a Risible living creature (the Definition of man) then Socrates is a man: the Definite by the Definition.

$$\left\{\begin{matrix}\text{To what the Definition doth agree}\\ \text{To that the Definite apply'd may be.}\end{matrix}\right\}$$

  3. every division must be of two members only; bec: the members should be opposite, now opposition is between two: this must be

CHARLES MORTON

observed for accurateness, if it can be so conveniently without overmuch multiplication of distinctions: but in popular discourses men usually take a greater latitude.

> { Two members only doth Division crave }
> { If you it Phylosophical would have. }

These are the Artificial Topics;
The Inartificial which draws forth arguments
without Art is only one, namely Testimony: saying
it is so for he said so.

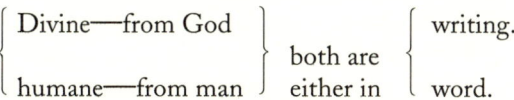

> { All Divine Testimonies from the Lord. }
> { Humane from man, both writing is writing is a Word }

Its maxims are.

1. To Divine Testimony we must give certain and universall credit, bec: God can neither deceive (from his truth) nor be deceived (from his omniscience.)

2. humane testimonies are according to the credit of their Authors: honest and wise men are most credible: knaves and fools may well be suspected.

> { As are with men that speak better or worse }
> { Such is with Humane Testimonies force. }

3. humane testimonies cannot be Infallible yet they may be indubitable; as when they are universall and uncontrol'd; when the testifier has had opportunity enough to know and no Interest to byas from the truth then it is reasonably supposed that he is neither deceived nor a deceiver, whence we see besides the Testimony at least a Reason not to disbelieve it; so that the force of this lies more in the reason than in the Testimony.

Such Indubitable Testimonies or traditions are, that there is such a city as Paris or Rome; that there were such men as Alexander, Cæsar &c. which I may undoubtedly believe thô I never saw the one or the other.

$$\left\{\begin{array}{l}\text{Men not deceiving nor deceived may tell}\\ \text{Indubitable not Infallible.}\text{—}\end{array}\right\}$$

4. skilfull men are to be believed in their art; i.e. unless contradicted by 1. men more skillfull in that art.

$$\left\{\begin{array}{l}\text{When not from sense or reason men depart}\\ \text{Or skilfuller believe this in their art—}\end{array}\right\}$$

2. a mans own sense or Reason.

5. one Scripture is worth 10 arguments, and one Argument is worth 10 humane Testimonies;[41] for in arguments our Reasons being weak and corrupted may deceive us, yet reason is to be preferred before humane Testimonies, bec: we must always use a Judgment of discretion and walk by our own light (gods candle in us) and not by others; therefore the Romanists Implicit faith is foolish & absurd, seeing our reason must Judge if the Testimony be credible.

$$\left\{\begin{array}{l}\text{Ten Arguments one Scripture proof outweighs}\\ \text{One argument ten humane witnesses.}\end{array}\right\}$$

¶ that maxims are aright and good ground of argument when rightly understood & applyed; therefore bounding of maxims by distinctions

---

[41] It is not whether clear Morton meant exact ratios here. He does, however, repeat this formula twice more. Possible applications of mathematics to testimony was an exciting area of study in the late seventeenth century. C.A.J. Coady in *Testimony: A Philosophical Study* (Oxford: Clarendon, 1992) devotes a chapter to post-Lockean mathematical calculations of the rate of diminishing credibility in testimony, leading to predictions of when a particular testimony (such as the New Testament) would have no credibility. One anonymously written study, "A Calculation of the Credibility of Human Testimony" in *Miscellanea Curiousa...being the most valuable Discourses, Read and delivered to the Royal Society*, (1708), 3, 1–8, for example computes: "If two concurrent reporters have, each of them, as 5/6ths certainty; they will both give me an assurance of 35/36ths, or 35 to one: If three: an assurance of 215/216, or 215 to one" (p. 4).

CHARLES MORTON

answers fallacious arguments pretending to be grounded in them, and therefore all disputes arise from misapplying maxims.

{ From Maxims misapplied disputes arise
Resolved by the Distinction of the Wise. }

Syn. cap. 6.

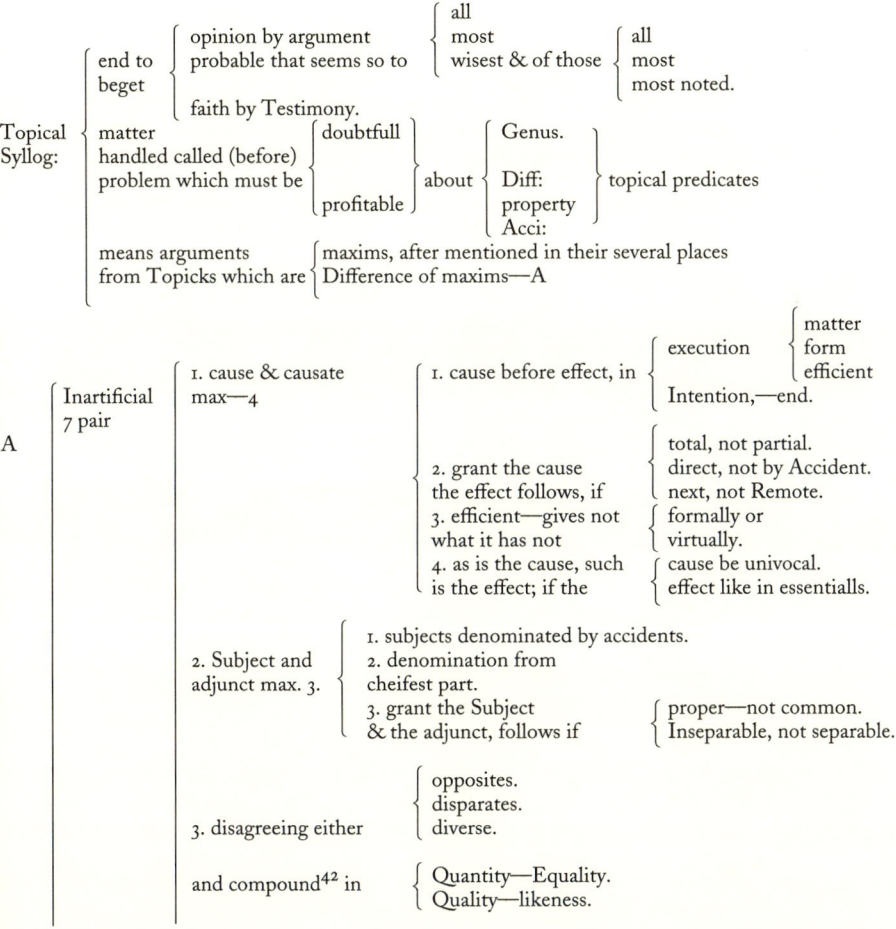

[42] Dunbar's version has "compared" which is what Partridge probably meant to write.

A Logick System

their maxims 5
- 1. better good, worse contrary.
- 2. opposites have the same reason as to { knowledge / Subject }
- 3. what—to one of—is—to the other.
- 4. no like is the same.
- 5. love is from likeness.

4. conjugates & notation max—3.
- 1. to whom conj: belongs to him the other, if { not from one act to habit / not from power to act. }
- 2. if one conj: be said of one conj: the other is of the other.
- 3. where notations agree, so do the things noted, if the Etymol: are not { foolish. / unept. }

5. whole and part max. 3
- 1. the whole is more than the part.
- 2. the parts being put, the whole is part, if the parts be { all together. / & unified. }
- 3. part are for the whole.

6. Genus and Spec: max. 2.
- 1. take away the genus you destroy the species.
- 2. of what the Spec: is predicated, of the same the genus.

7. Def: & Div: max. 3.
- 1. what ever is defined (i.e. perfectly) is species.
- 2. to what the Def: agrees, to that the Definite.
- 3. every division must be of 2 members.

Inartificial Testimony

Div: { Divine / humane } both in { word. / Writing. }

max. 5.
- 1. give credit { certain & universal } to God, as { true / omniscient. }
- 2. humane testimonies are according to the authors.
- 3. humane testimonies may be Indubitable, if { universal. / uncontrolled. / sufficient meanes / no byas. }
- 4. believe Artists in their arts, if not against { sense. / reason. }
- 5. one Scripture worth 10 arguments, and one argument worth 10 Testimonies.

CHARLES MORTON

Cap. 7.   Of Fallacies.

Fallacy (or Sophism) is a syllog: that from fallacious premises collects a false conclusion so beget deceit, handled

in Logick { not that we should deceive. / but that we should not be deceived. }

¶ some think this chapter superfluous, bec: it is forestalled by the foregoing præcepts, which if well observed we need not fear a fallacy. however the Antients thought fit, and custome has confirmed the treating of fallacies distinctly by themselves (besides what is before noted) that the learner may better discern and avoid them. there is one generall rule to discover fallacies: viz: all fallacies have 4 terms, or a double mean, i.e. when the middle term is otherwise taken in the minor proposition then it was in the major. The kinds of fallacies Reckoned by Aristotle are 13

{ Would you know fallacy how it comes to pass, / Four terms or Double mean it always has. }

whereof are { 6—in the words. / 7—out of the words. }

1. In the words are 6 Topicks or places for fallacy.
   1. Equivocation when a word is taken ambiguously that is in one sense in the major & another in the minor

as are { proper, and / metaphoricall. }

   2. Amphiboly is Equivocation

in a sentence as { He that washes a blackmore uses water (proper) / he that reprooves a scorner washes a blackm: (metaph) / he that reprooves a scorner uses water. }

{ equivocation in the words doth frame / Amphiboly in sentences the same, }

A Logick System

3. composition when taken conjoyned that should be taken
divided, as
{ 2 & 3 are even & odd (disjoyned.)
5 are 2 & 3 (conjoyned) Ergò
5 are even and odd.

4. division on the contrary,
as
{ 5 is not even and odd (disjoyned.)
2 & 3 are 5 (conjoyned) Ergò
2 & 3 are not even and odd.

5. likeness of sound in 2 distinct words
as
{ Air is a fluid body
John is an heir. Ergò
John is a fluid body.

6. figure of a word, when from likeness of the words is argued that the grammaticall notions belong to both,
as
{ Musa is of the feminine gender
therefore so is poeta.
} a silly fallacy only Imposing on Ignorance.

{ Like Sound & shape of words do trifle at
Only T'impose upon a slender wit }

¶ that all these fallacies are rather merriments, than cheats, being easily answered by distinquishing on the words; but those that follow deserve better consideration.

{ Quibbles in words are more for merriment.
Than to deceive with intent— }

2. out of the words, and in the sense of them.
   1. of an Accident adjoyn'd in the minor, not intended or thought on in the major; thence that will seem to belong to a thing of it self which is only
   by Accident
   { What you bought you eat
   you bought raw flesh. E.
   you eat raw flesh
   } i.e. what for substance raw the Accident is added.

{ From accident unto Substance join'd
Sometimes a subtle fallacy is coin'd[43] }

[43] This distich does not appear in the "Memorial Verses."

[232]

2. from a Respective saying to an absolute; when that which is only true in some respect, is taken as if absolute true.

as { A mad mans sword is his own goods
you must not give a sword to a mad man. Ergò
you must not give a man his own goods.

{ A Sophister makes the Respondent mute }
{ by respective taking absolute— }

3. Ignorance Imposed on, when one thinks through Ignorance, that he is contradicted when he is not

as { Christ is Davids lord
how then is he his son } it puzzells, but not perswades.

{ Man's ignorance often impose'd upon }
{ By false suppos'd contradiction }

¶ our saviour used this not as a fallacy, but as an enigma to supress their Insolence: he proposed to them a difficulty wherein they could not and he would not satisfie them.

4. not cause for cause, when something is offered as a cause which either is

not { a cause at all—
such a cause, as is required. } { the cause of drunkeness must be destroyed
wine is the cause of drunkeness. E.
wine must be destroyed

Ans: wine either
  1. is not the cause, but rather Inordinate Appetite, which indeed must be destroyed.
  2. not such a cause as must be destroyed: it is only Instrumentall and may be otherwise honestly used.

{ Not cause for cause deceives us very much }
{ When not at all it is, at least not such. }

A Logick System

5. bad conseq: when something seems to follow which indeed dos not,

as $\begin{cases} \text{he that says you are an Animal says true,} \\ \text{he that says you are an ass, says you are an Animal. E.} \\ \text{he that says you are an ass says true.} \end{cases}$

Answered by bringing the prop: to the rules of conversion; for thô every ass be an Animal, yet every Animal is not an ass & so the double medium dos Appear; for Animal in one Prop: is the genus, and in the other it signifies but one of the species, which it ought not, bec: (as is before noted) the medium must always be taken in the same sense and latitude in both the premises: else, thô but the same word, yet it is two mediums, there is another sort of bad conseq: here usually mention'd when things will not hang together,

as $\begin{cases} \text{the sun shines. E.} \\ \text{it rains—} \end{cases}$ Ans: by denying the sequel. this is as silly as the other is subtle, & therefore is rather nonsense than fallacy.

$\begin{cases} \text{Bad Consequence is easily descri'd,} \\ \text{When by Conversions Rules you have it tie'd} \end{cases}$

6. begging the question, when to prove a conclusion, that is taken for granted, as a principle which is œqually doubted, or denied,

as $\begin{cases} \text{things required in conformity are indifferent} \\ \text{E. every man commanded must conform} \end{cases}$

or $\begin{cases} \text{the Pope is infallible. E.} \\ \text{Popery is the best Religion.} \end{cases}$

It is answered by denying the supposed principle.

$\begin{cases} \text{Sometimes small arguments look very big,} \\ \text{When they're beg'd for which men ought to dig.} \end{cases}$

7. captious (or Implicated) Interrogations (or questions) when divers things some true, some false are packed together in one question, so that if you grant or deny it in the lump either will be against truth. As is not

[234]

the world perfect and eternal. Ans: by separating and then granting or denying each part, as it deserves, the world is perfect but not eternal.

{ All captious questions pack in the false with true }
{ Must open'd be that you its parts may view. }

¶ all fallacies are comprehended in these two memorial lines, which for memories sake are made to run like a pair of Latin verses.

Equiv: Am: comp: Div: like sound, & figure of words
Acci: Respective, Ignor: cause, con: beg: and infer:

Syn. Cap. 7.

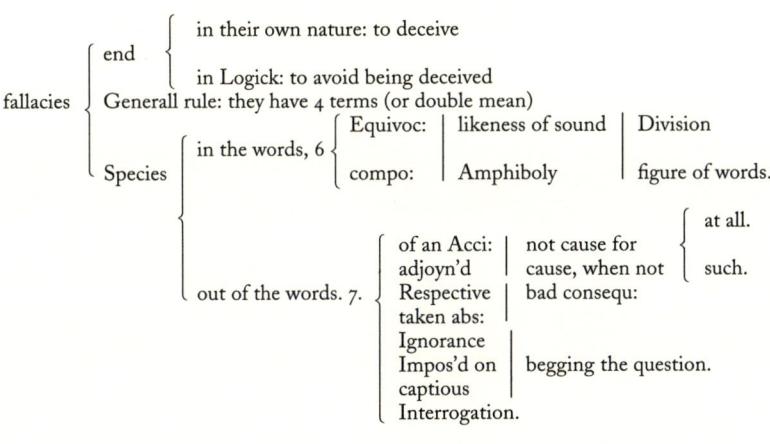

Cap. 8.   Of Method

Method is such a disposition of the parts of a discipline (or discourse) that the whole may be better Learned (i.e. understood & retained) by us.

Method is 2 fold, of Invention and of Teaching.
1. Method of Invention is, whereby by the precepts of a discipline are at first found out, and the canons and rules thereof setled.

A Logick System

Its proceeding is
- from singulars & sensibles which are more knowable to us.
- to universalls & Intelligibles which are more knowable in themselves.

¶ Universalls are more knowable in themselves (or nature) bec: they can be defin'd, whereas singulars can only be described.

The means of invention are 4
- Sense—As seeing, hearing, feeling. &c.
- Observation—i.e. considering added to sense.
- experience—is a frequent observation.
- Induction—for which by this time we are ready; as

I have seeing, observed and had experience that this heavy descends, & that that heavy descends, and that the other heavy descends, and so all the rest (for ought I know) therefore I conclude and settle this as a general rule. viz: every heavy descends. This was the method whereby learned men in former ages have found out Arts & Sciences for us, we having by their Industry gotten a shorter way to knowledge.

{ By sense observance & experience
adding Induction arts arose from hence. }

But if after experience, or better observation which say the Aintients were mistaken, tis lawfull to make new experiments, and settle new rules.

{ Change not in things divine keep what is old
In Phylosophicals you may be bold— }

2. method of Teaching & learning proceeds from Intelligibles & more universalls to less universalls & sensibles. as, from generalls to specialls to Individuals (if need be) but generally, sciences go no further down than the species & leave us to apply it to the Individuals.

This method is twofold.

1. Generally, wherein some whole discipline is handled

2. Partic:— —part of a discipline— —

both are either
- Synthetical.
- Analytical.

1. **Synthetick** (or composing) method begins with the subject of a discipline in general, than the principles of the subject, next the generall affections (or properties) & then descends to the severall species thereof.
¶ principles

are either $\begin{cases} \text{1. of being, or whence the Subject doth arise.} \\ \text{2. of knowl: (or demonstration of the affect) & they are} \\ \text{generall maxims.} \end{cases}$

In this method are handled all theoretick & speculative sciences, such as metaphysicks, pneumaticks, physick, mathematicks.

$\begin{cases} \text{In Subject, principles affections kinds,} \\ \text{Synthetick method doth instruct our minds.} \end{cases}$

2. **Analytick** (or Resolving) method begins with the end proceeds to the subject (for whose sake the end is looked after) and concludes with the means whereby that end is attainable. in this method are handled all practicall & operative disciplines. Such are prudences & arts, As, ethicks, politics, œconomics, Logick, Rhetorick, & architecture &c.
Rules of Method are

either $\begin{cases} \text{Generall & common to both} \\ \text{Special to each of them.} \end{cases}$ $\begin{cases} \text{Synthetick &} \\ \text{Analytick.} \end{cases}$

   1. Generall rules are. 5.
      1. nothing in a discipline must be wanting or Redundant.
      2. all parts must agree and not cross each other.

$\begin{cases} \text{let every part in method well agree} \\ \text{not one to other contradicting be} \end{cases}$

   3. nothing must be handled but what is homogeneal, i.e. of the same kind with subject or end.

$\begin{cases} \text{To Subject & to end be sure the all} \\ \text{and every part be Homogeneal.} \end{cases}$

   4. that must procede which may help the knowledge of what follows, and may in good part be understood without it.
   5. every part should have apt terminations that the connexion of antecedents and consequents may appear.

A Logick System

{ When Paragraphs are apt distinct & clear
Connexion of the parts will best appear. }

¶ that these rules being observed will much conduce to a clear & distinct apprehension, & thereby to a Rational memory: children & fools may retain words without connexion: but men whose dryer & more compacted brains (which are thereby better fitted for wisdom) have need of some methodicall frame, to hold things together and make A joynt Impression on their thoughts: hereby they shall better command their notions and draw forth one thing by another in the way of Ratiocination; some define Logick the Art of memory, and hence it is needfull that all people of business (in what kind soever) should be methodical therein.

2. Speciall rules of method peculiar to each kind are.
   1. to Synthetick 3

{ 1. oneness of Science depends on oneness of Subject.
2. more universalls procede less universalls.
3. the parts of it are, subject, principles, & affections. }

   2. to Analytick 3

{ 1. oneness of practical discipline depends on oneness of end.
2. less universall precede more universall.
3. the part of it are, end, subject, mean. }

Syn. cap. 8.

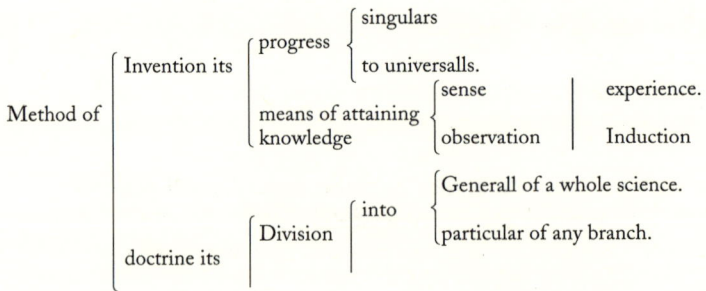

[238]

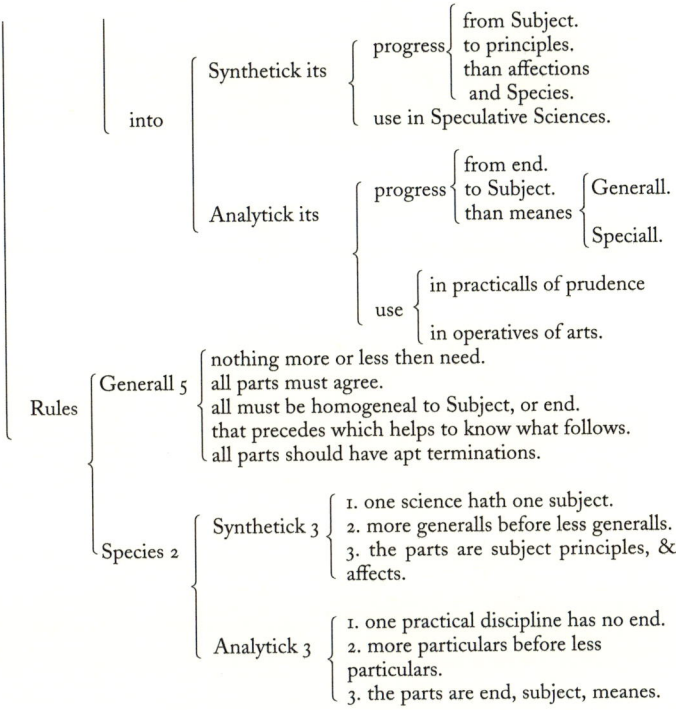

Postscript

And thus we have gone through Logick in the easiest manner I can at present Imagine. Claubergius[44] a learned man advises the reading of a book 3 times. 1st that you may have a more generall notion. 2 that you may more distinctly judge of it. 3. that you may retain it. I have endeavoured so to order this discourse that every chapter shall be (in effect) 3 times read.[45] 1. in prose. 2. in verses memorial 3. in schemes; and by that time all are read

---

[44] Johann Clauberg (1622–1655) was an influential German educational reformer and philosopher. Brattle, following *The Port-Royal Logic*, cites the model of Clauberg's *Logica Vetus et Nova* (Amsterdam, 1654).

[45] Actually 5 times read if you count the summary scheme and Memorial Verses which follow this.

A Logick System

distinctly and considerable; I hope the chapter will be fully understood. nor let any be discouraged at the hard words and many distinctions in Log: for if you can but well conquer this, all other arts and sciences will be easy.

> upon the prickly bush of logic grows
> of other sciences the fragrant rose.—

CHARLES MORTON

The Memorial Verses of the Logick System

Cap. 1   of Terms & Acts of the Intellect   [1]

Terms are as handles fitted to a thing
usefull as bones that flesh to market bring.
Logick by its 3 *parts* dos the Intellect
to *apprehend*, compound, discourse, direct.

Cap. 2   Of Predicables   [2]

A single one or Individuall is what?
Indefin'd, proper, Suppos'd, pointed at.
All universalls thus together pack
In what? *Gen: Spec:* / what *manner, diff: prop: Acc:*
Genus above *species* below are seen
and *subalternates* take their place between.
Genus and *difference* do the species make
property after difference place dos take.
not only, not all, not always possest
Are meane. All—only—always is the best.
Precisive is of what thought layes aside
negative is of what may be deny'd.
Abstraction precisive takes property
All common Accidents I can deny.

Cap. 3   of Antepredicaments   [3]

The predicaments to know 7 things forewatch,
3 *Definitions, Div's & Rules,* 2 each.
Equiv's, & *Univ's,* with their *Analogates*
Subject and form to make *denominates.*
Great Aristotle *all* created things
under 2 common heads (sub. Acci:) brings.
In not as *part,* or *place,* nor can *absent,*
that dos *inhere* and is an Accident.
Abstract, as Justice; *Concrete,* is as Just;
Simple, as man; and *complex* man is dust.

Memorial Verses

What Predicate essentially you do
of predicate, may of the Subject too.
under one Genus or a common name,
Species and Difference they are the Same.

Cap. 4   of Predicaments.   [4]

A *man, tall, wise,* that once his *friend, did greet;*
buried, in *Greece, now, lyes, in winding sheet.*
To *Predicaments,* 5 things are Requisite,
Real, univ: univers: whole, finite.

Cap. 5   of Substance   [5]

Body and spirit are it's Species [1]
But *1*st and *2*d its *Subjecting ways.*
contrary none; nor has *degrees* at all;
takes contraries; is said univocall.

Cap. 6   of Quantity   [6]

Spirits extension dos possess no *Space*
but things that are *materiall fill a place.*
Geometries *continualls, Long, broad, Thick,*[2]
discrete in number for Arithmetick.
lines common term *is point* of *surface* line,
Surface the parts *of body* dos combine.
All numbers under these distinctions fall,
numbring, numbred; cardinall, ordinall.
Contrary, or degrees, t'will not admitt,
It equalls, is potentiall infinite.

[1] In text: "Spirit & Body Substance & Species"
[2] In text: "Continual Quantity, is Long, Broad Thick"

CHARLES MORTON

Cap. 7.   of Quality   [7]

Naturall *power* and *habit* sense escape,
but sense perceives the *patible* & *Shape*.
Naturall pow'r & Impotens are *known*
by their effects, some *act* or *passion*.
Habit's Infus'd by God Immediately,
or is acquir'd by humane Industry.
firm *habits* many acts (or few strong) cost
by *force* is *disposition* and soon lost.
All *morall habits* do the will direct
but *Intellectuall* the *Intellect*.
the privative of all assent is *doubt*
Assents are some with fear & some without.
Opinion, humane faith give weak assent,
fals *error heresy* shism are confident.
Assur'd of truth is faith divine in heart
Intelligens, Sapiens, Science, prudens, Art.
Sap: Science, *Speculat:* pru: *practicall*
Art *operates*; Intelligence *is all*.
Patible quality affects one sense
Its passion is of little permanence
form is of animates; shap'd *naturall*,
figure of things shap'd *Artificiall*.
Qualities only have their *con* & deg:
by those things are alike (as egg to egg)

Cap. 8   of Relation.   [8]

To 3 In each Relation have an eye,
the subject, corrolate, and *Reason why*.
three grounds Relations are built upon
Quantity, Quality, and *action*.
*Transcendent, predicamentall, Rationall,
Real; of like*, or *divers name* (there's all)
Reciprocall by (est) and are *together*.
In *nature, knowledge*, both *made, marr'd* if either

Memorial Verses

Cap. 9   of Action and passion   [9]

Qualities *power*; Action *formality*,
Immanent in; *Transient* without doth lie.
Contraries & *degrees*, act taketh on,
by qualities; *Inferreth passion*.
Intentional to Action term doth give
Sensible change is by *Transmutative*

Cap 10.   of Respective Predicaments.   [10]

Replete, defin'd & *circumscription*
each body hath its where, no 2 have one.
Eternity, Everlastingness sublime
of God and Spirits are: of bodies time.
time has succession, none eternity
concreate; best is opportunity.
above, below, are common unto all
before, behind, Right, left, to Animal.
habits provided are; by *nature, Art.*
for *need*, or *ornament*, to *whole*, or *part.*
habits *unsuitable* become a sin
are outward signs of what is Log'd within.

Cap. 11   of Postpredicaments   [11]

Two *Simple* terms which do each other thwart
In *third*, in the Same *time, Respect* & *part*
oppos'd *Relation, contrariety,*
privative terms, and *contradictory.*
Relate's contrar's, affirm'd private's deny'd
but contradictories no *mean* abide.
before, together, after, 6 set forth,
time, nature, knowledge, order, cause, & *worth,*
Generat: & *corrupt*: *augment*: *diminish*:
altering & *placing*, motions kinds do finish.
habit for all positive Accident,
one kind of quality, last predicament.

[246]

Cap. 12.   of Definition & division.   [12]

nominall Definitions notifie,
by common words, or etymologie.
Reall, essentiall, Genus, Difference,
Acc: *property*, or common *Accidents*.
for definition tis Requir'd you bring
that which is *plain, short, equall* to the thing
Divisions *nominall* do show thereby
What words equivocall do Signify.
Reall and perfect parteth *universall*3
essentiall (meta: Phys:) and Integrall.
Imperfect *sub*: *by Acci*: Represents
Acci: *by Sub*: and *Acc*: *by Accidents*.
If you will make division aright
the members *few, adequate, opposite*.

The 2d part of Logick.

Cap. 1.   of Proposition its definite & parts   [1]

In proposition *Signes*, and *parts* do lie,
nouns without time, *verbs* with time *Signify*.
Subject before, *predicate* the other side,
of copula expressed & deny'd.

Cap. 2.   of Proposition Species   [2]

A *categorick* you may *Simple* call
if, and, or, either, hypotheticall:
true, or *false*, quality the *thing* affords,
affirmed or deny'd is of the *words*.
All, or no generall, some particular
Indefin'd no Signe; this, that, Singular.

3 In Text: "parteth Generall"

Memorial Verses

What? Cat: of Hyp: / of what kind? true, false, are
aff: neg: / how much? und: part: Ind: Singular.

Cap 3d   of Proposition & affections.   [3]

false not true *cons*: true not false *Subs*: you see
both *subalterns, contradicts* neither be. or
contraries may be false not true, true, false, not false you see
both subalternate, true & false; contradicts neither be.
not set before dos contradicts concern,
after contrar's, fore & aft, subaltern.
not all, is some; but *all not*, is as none.
not none, is some; but *none not*, every one.
not any, none; *not some*, not all is this.
not either, neither; *neither not*, both is.
envy: will simply turn. but *eva's* done,
by Acci: *Case*: contraposition.
A, is aff: E, neg: both universall are
I, is aff: O, neg: but both particular.

The 3d part of Logick

Cap. 1.   of Syllogisms.   [1]

Syllog: *Induc*: *Sorites, enthymem*
example (or Similitude) *dilemm*.
3 *propositions* do *next matter* frame
of Syllogism: *Remote*, 3 terms the same
the *mean* is both, the premises are *one*
minor is *Subject* of conclusion.
Sub præ the 1st, twice præ the 2^{d} is,
twice *sub* & 3: (mind this you will not miss.
Bar-bar-ra cæ-la-rent Da-ri-i for-ri-o (are Reduced)
cæs-a-re cam-es-tres fes-ti-no ba-ro-co / 3^{d} Da-rap-ti
fe-lap-ton Dis-a-mis Da-ti-si bo-car-do fe-ri-son
S. *Simply turn'd* & P. pt. acci: well.
M. is *transpos'd*. C. to Impossible (or

S. will be *simply turn'd.* by Acci: P.
M. is *transpose'd* Impossible is C.
All neg's, all parts, conclude not by this art
conclusion always follows *weaker part*

Cap. 2.   of Secondary Argumentation.   [2]

Clear brevity an *enthymem* doth love
always a sequel by a sequel prove.
In *hypothetick* what by Sequel's meant
the same in *enthymem* is argument.
the weakness of *Induction* is espied
If there's an *Instance* which may be deny'd[4]
example from Similitude conclude
in argument they commonly delude (or
examples from their *likeness* do conclude
but always *fail* where's *no Similitude.*
⎧ by a *Sorities* arguing in a chain
⎨ *first subject* dos, *last predicate* attayne
⎪ but if *one link* dos hap to slip or fly
⎩ then all the argument is spoil'd thereby.
Dilemma's horns do push on either side
yet truth may safely in the mean abide.

Cap. 3.   of demonstration its Definition   [3]

A *demonstration* Science doth compleate
opinion *Topick, fallacy* deceit
by *difference* demonstrate *property*
you'll then the *thing* & *cause* attain thereby.
to demonstration some *foreknowledge* bring
that tis in *nature, subject, what? name, thing*
foreknow the *subject that tis,* & both what's
affections name; principles name, both that's
Gen: Diff: to *Sub: Sub:* & *prop:* is direct
exist: to *ess: externall cause* is effect

---

[4] Partridge wrongly transcribed this line. It should end with "Implied."

Memorial Verses

of all, *directly*, *as it self*, those three,
are stepps by which things *necessary* be.
Of demonstration's truth 5 are the laws,
necess: *Immed*: *more known*, *preced*: & *cause*.

Cap. 4.   of demonstration its division.   [4]

In *barbara remote efficient* lies
if *turn'd*, *if not*, *camestres* then denyes,
the next *effect* its cause doth verify
That so it is; althô it show not *why*?
To prove the [why] of things 4 causes tend
matter & *form*, *efficient* and *end*.

Cap. 5.   of demonstration's affections   [5]

Analysis in demonstration brings
back from the *last to the first* proof of things
a thing *Indemonstrable* you may call
which has *no proof*, or what *needs none* at all.
Regress 1st by the *effect* the cause doth *show*
and then the *effect* by the cause *why tis so*.
the *circle* is Impossible in this,
that's prov'd by *cause*, whereof the *cause* it is.
Conversion turns the proving Propositions
Into *affections*, perfect *Definitions*.

Cap. 6.   of Topicks.   [6]

On *argument opinion* is grounded
but upon *Testimony faith* is founded.
Probable is by *all*, *most*, *wisest* deem'd
and then these, *all*, *most*, or *most esteem'd*,
doubtfull & *profitable* must be all,
What *problem* first, after *conclusion* call.
The middle term doth prove as *argument*
Genus, *Definition*, *property*, *Accident*.
Maxims & *differences* whence they are sought,

CHARLES MORTON

afford all arguments that can be brought.
In execution first efficient
matter & form; and only in Intent.
If *totall, direct, next* cause you have got
Th'efficient will follow; otherwise twill not.
formall & *virtuall* must be within
efficient, what it gives (cat yields but skin)
As is the *cause* such an *effect* you'l se,
in *Essence* if *univocall* it be.
under the *adjuncts* names do *subjects* fall
the man who learning hath you learned call.
from the *prevailing* part, *denominate*,
althô the thing be in Imperfect State.
Where ere you will suppose a Subject, his
proper Inseparable adjunct is.
opposites are but 2 *disparates* 3
Divers what only not the same things be.
The *better* is the *good* you do propound
Its *contrary* so much the *worse* is found.
opposite are made known by one another
and as for Subject they'l admitt no other.
two equalls in themselves a 3^d thats Just
Equall with *one*, equall the *other* must.
What ever is *but like* is not the *same*
a hypocrite bares but a christian's name
like will to *like*; birds that are of a feather
We usually do find will flock together.
conjugates hold in *concrete* & *abstract*
not from *one act, to habit*, pow'r *to act*.
In conjugates if *one* be said to *one*
the *other's* of the *other* said anon.
Good *etymons* do with the thing agree,
but not when *foolish* & *unapt* they be.
the *whole* is greater than the *part* be sure
no part the whole's extension from can endure.
All *parts together* set.
And then the whole {?} you'l surely get.
Parts for the *whole* by nature are ordayn'd
and in the whole is every part sustain'd.
destroy the *genus* & you do deface

LOGIC AT HARVARD

the *species* that under it hath place
from *species* you the genus may inferr
but if from genus, species you err.
of what the *species* is affirm'd of that
the *genus* also is the *predicate*.
that, what's *Defin'd*, is *Species*, gather hence
because it hath *Genus* & *difference*
to what the *definition* doth agree
so that the Definite apply'd may be.
Two members only do *division* crave
if you it philosophicall would have.
All *divine Testimonies* from the Lord
humane from men; both *writing* is or *word*.
certain assent, & *universall* faith,
Render to God in all what are he saith.
as are the *men* that speak *better* or *worse*
Such is a humane Testimony's force.
men not *deceiving*, nor *deceiv'd* may tell
Indubitable's not *Infallible*.
When not from *Sense* or *Reason* men depart
of *skilfuller*, believe *them in their art*.
Ten arguments one Scripture truth outweighs
one argument 10 humane witnesses.
from *maxims misapply'd* disputes arise,
Resolv'd by the *distinctions* of the wise.

    Cap. 7.   of fallicies.   [7]

Would you know *fallacy*, how't comes to pass
4 terms or *double mean* it always has.
Equivocation in the *words* do frame,
Amphyboly in *sentences* the same.
compounding and *dividing* foolish art,
parts what should *Joyne* & *Joynes* what it should *part*.
like *sound* and *shape* of words do trifle it
only to Impose upon a Slender witt.
Quibbles in words are more for *merriment*
then to *deceive* with serious Intent.
A *Sophister* makes the *respondent* mute

by a *respective* taken *absolute*.
mans *ignorance* is oft Impos'd upon
by false suppposed *contradiction*.
not *cause* for *cause* deceives us very much
When *not at all it is*; at least not such.
bad consequence is easily descry'd
when by conversion you have it tey'd.
Sometimes small arguments look very big
When that is *beg'd* for which men ought to *dig*.
all *captious questions* packing *false with true*,
must *open'd be, that* you its parts may view.
Equiv: Am: compo: Div: like Sound, & *figure of words*
Acci: Respective, Ignor: cause, con: beg: & Inferr:

Cap. 8.   of Method.   [8]

By *Sense, observance, & experience*
Adding *Induction*, Arts arose from hence.
change not in things *divine* keep what is *old*
In *philosophicalls* you may be bold.
doctrinall method *universall* Things.
begun, whence to *particulars* it brings
In *Subject, principles, affections, kinds,*
Synthetick method doth mistruct our *minds*
all *practicalls* in *Analytick* way,
first *end*, then *subject*, lastby *means* essay.
if in *good method* ought you would express,
take what is *needfull* nothing *more* or *less*.
let *every part* in method well *agree*
not one to other *contradicting* be.
To *subject* or *to end* be sure that all
and every part be homogeneall
That always must *precede* which is *most fitt*
to make you understand what follows it.
When *paragraphs* are *apt, distinct,* & *clear,*
connexions of the parts will best appear.
method doth *memory* with *reason match,*
order of things will make the *best dispatch.*
one *Subject*; *Generalls* before are sent

Memorial Verses

Synthetick parts, Subject, prin: Accident.
one end: less generall first place obtains
parts *analytick* are, *end, Subject, means.*

Upon the prickly bush of Logick grows
of other Sciences the fragrant rose.

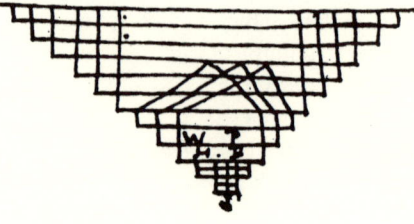

William Brattle

Compendium of Logick

A compendium of Logick, According to the modern Philosophy, extracted from Le-grand; & others their Systems.

The Prolegomenon

Chap. 1. of the nature and constitution of Logic

*M*an's mind being obnoxious to much error both in its searches for truth, and pursuits after that which is good, two arts have been sought out; the one to aid the understanding, the other to direct the will; this being called Ethicks; that Logick.

Def: Logic is an Art of thinking; or, to the same effect, An Art of using our Reason for the obtaining of knowledge; for we are not to limit this term [thinking] to an Apprehending of simple Idea's, but so to extend it as therein to Include Judgment & discourse, and this we may {doe} without Prejudice to Accurracy, Since it is a truth that to discourse, to Judge and to conceive are only different modes of thinking: some Add [rectè] & Define Logick, An Art of thinking well; which althô it makes a better sound, and at first sight may seem needful, yet on due Search is found to be needless, yea Inaccurate; the reason is because [As Aristotle observed] the mode or method is Implyed Sufficiently in the word [Art] And hence [whether we mind it or no] it is usuall with us to say [An Art of painting; An Art of numbering. &c.] not expressing the Adverb; and yet we think it Impossible that any Should misunderstand us and conceive of A painting ill, or numbering wrong when we thus barely deliver our Selves.

Objt: The object of Logick is every thing knowable; or every thing that may be proposed to the understanding of man; not as if, Logick did Instruct the mind about the nature of things, or of any one thing: [this is the Design of Philosophy] but in that it makes the way clear for knowledge in generall, and delivers such precepts as may direct (&) assist the mind, when enquiring Into the nature of any thing Whatever.

In order to mans using his Right Reason, its necessary that he perceives, that he Judges, that he discourses, & that he Methodises.

Percpt: **Perception (or Apprehension)** is the Simple contemplation of things which are in the mind: thus we consider, the Earth, the Sun, A

tree, Rotundity &c. not pronouncing any thing concerning them whether good or bad.
¶ that the form, under which we consider those things is called an Idea.
Judgmt. **Judgment** is that operation of the mind by which coupling divers Idea's we affirm or deny that this is that: thus, considering the Idea of the Earth & the Idea of Roundness we affirm or deny that the earth is round.
Disc: **Discourse** is that operation of the mind, by which out of many Judgments we draw another; thus, when we have Judged that man has Reason, & that Socrates is a man, we may Infer that Socrates has Reason.
Meth: **Method [or Disposition]** is that operation of the mind, by which we dispose, the various Idea's, Judgments & Reasonings which we have of one and the same Subject, in Such order as is most suitable for the explaining of it.

Hence [According to the 4 operations of mans mind] Logick ought to be divided Into four parts; the **first**, Respecting Idea's, or the simple Apprehensions of things: the **second**, Respecting Judgments or Propositions in which there is truth or falshood: the **third**, Respecting discourse or syllogisms: the **fourth** and last part, Respecting method, or an orderly disposing of our thoughts, by which [as by so many steps] we obtain the way of knowledge: by the first we are put upon Attention and consideration; by the second we are freed from doubts and errors. by the third, we are accustom'd to Reason; by the fourth, we Infallibly prove a truth, and demonstrate the same to others

Cap. 2. Of the use & benefit of Logick.

Logick is no less helpfull to the mind than Physick is to the body of man; & in that the mind is more noble Than the body & its diseases more latent and with greater Difficulty discovered than those of the body are: It seems but Reasonable, that Logick should have the pre-eminence; notwithstanding, our Experience teaches [what ever the Reason is] that the Physitian bares the name, and that this other Artist is of Low Repute in the world. Some (perhaps) will pretend the Reason to be, In that Althô Physick is Immediately designed only for the Body, yet the virtues thereof do greatly Influence the mind of man, It being not so with this Art; since althô it may benefitt the mind, and that in no Small degree, yet as to the body is altogether useless and uninstructive, and Indeed, were the Hypotheses undoubtedly true [which now we cannot enquire after] and the reason proposed not only pretended, but also the true and adequate Reason, it would prove the best salve Imaginable, and [for ought we know] Sufficiently Justifies the practice reflected on: Whereas should it appear, that the undervaluing this noble Art has its Root in Sensuality, and is grounded on an expectation of meeting with bliss and content in an Animal life, or [which is all one] the health & prosperity of the body, we could not but condemn this practice and censure it as highly absurd and unreasonable.

Lest we should Run Into a mistake here, It is to be noted that when we Assert Logick to be medicinal to the mind of man, we mean not, with Respect to Sin & moral defects, [for the curing of Which Theology & Ethicks take Sufficient care] but with Respect to those defects that attend the mind in perceiving of things; Such as, Ignorance & oblivion, doubting and error, confusion & obscurity and the like.

It may (perhaps) be objected, that nature [or more naturall Logick] being our guide, the forementioned operations of the mind may be performed, and consequently that it is absurd to talk of an Art for this end; And it cannot deny [Since experiences abundantly prove it] but that some who are unaquainted with the precepts of this Art may know more, and pass a better Judgment on things, than some who are acquainted therewith; but notwithstanding our concession, We answer, that the objection is weak & insignificant; and The Invalidity thereof appears even from this consideration: viz: that no man can use his reason so well naturally, but that by acquaintance with this Art he might use it much better: so that althô Reason innate with us is the foundation here [and is it not so with respect to all Arts?] yet the Art of Reason may be fairly fram'd and superstructed: And this Art is profitable unto us particularly in 3 Respects:

1. In that hereby we may come to a certain knowledge that we use our Reason. for he that follows these rules leaves no room for doubt.
2. In that hereby we may the more easily detect & explain the Defects that may be Incident to our minds: It is no unusuall thing for a man to be able to Judge that there is a fallacy in this or that argumentation, whence it will exceed the power of his nature to detect & confute the supposed fallacy; Just like the unskillfull person who viewing a draught of the Limner shall presently tax it with Imperfection and say that this is not right, that that is not accurate; and yet shall be altogether uncapable either of mending what is amiss, or of describing to another wherein the fault dos lie; Whereas the Artist [whose Reason is advanced] will readily discover all Error, and by help of his rules as readily correct and amend the same.
3. In that hereby we are brought to a more thorough acquaintance with our

Compendium of Logick

own minds: when we have considered the divers operations of the mind and acquainted our selves with it's diseases, and with it's cures, It becomes Impossible that we should be ignorant of the more noble part with us.

Cap. 3. of Some generall observables, or, Rules of truth.[1]

It is the part of a skilfull Physitian when about to eradicate any distemper or remove any illness, first to prepare the body & to leave some generall directions which may be of use to his design; in Imitation of which practice, we shall here propose some Generall rules or observables which may be no less helpfull to us in our present design of bringing the soul to it's healthfull estate.

First Rule of Truth
Nothing is to be admitted for truth which Includes any thing of doubt in it.

We are taught even by the light of nature that all doubting prevents knowledge, and that we cannot Possibly attain thereto till the thing Apprehended is without obscurity or confusion perceived by the mind, and therefore it can be no rashness to reject all doubt as adulterated images, that would lead us into error.

Corol: hence (if we would Phylosophize in earnest) we must lay aside all the prejudices of Infancy and youth. for in that they crept into our minds Antecedancously to a due search and examination by Reason, (at least as to us) it is possible that they may be false and consequently there is sufficient Reason for our doubting about and rejecting of them.

This method in obtaining knowledge is not peculiar to Descartes but was approved of by Aristotle, as may be seen in his 3 book of Metaphysicks. chapter 1.[2]

¶ that he that doubts of things only to please an humour, or to the end that he may be said to doubt of them, may properly be termed a Sceptick

---

[1] These rules are derived from LeGrand's *Institutio*.

[2] This passage is directly from LeGrand's *Institutio*, Pt. 1, chap. 2, reg. I.V. LeGrand goes on to give a title for Aristotle's chapter: "Of the Usefulness of Doubting, and what things we ought first to doubt of" (trans. Blome, 5).

and censured for folly & unreasonableness. Whereas to doubt of things and to suppose them to be all false only for the obtaining a more full and distinct knowledge is a laudable method very much preventive of error and false Judgments: and this our method seems to us to be of the like nature with that most harmless practice of the Astronomer who Imagines and Supposes an Equator a Zodiack and other Circles to be in the heavens to the end that he may the more accurately describe the course and motion of the Sun and the other Celestiall bodies.

The Second Rule of truth

Let us be Cautious how we give credit unto the Senses. Our senses both external and Internal are all Deceitfull and oftentimes lead us into error; thus: to the eye a square tower, being high appears round, and the Sun as thô not above a foot or two diameter;—to the ear, some thunder sounds like a canon, and the crowing of a boy shall not hereby be distinquished from the crowing of a Cock;—to the taste, sometimes Sweet things prove bitter, and sometimes all things are Insipid and without Relish; and in like manner the other externals do delude us, and thus likewise it is as to the Internal Sense,—to a vertiginous person all things seem to go round, and to one drunken things appear double & now in that these senses do so oft deceive, common reason does tell us that it is prudence at all times to suspect them and not hastily to give credit thereto.

¶ That this rule as also the first do concern us, when searching after truth, and not when we are about the common actions of life; for when a friend Invites me to a glass of White wine & has given me the glasse, it would be ridiculous for me to doubt about it and to doubt its being white wine, bec: that it is possible that it may prove cider.—So (as to this Rule) if a friend gives me a shilling and it appears to the eye to be Silver there is Sufficient ground for my faith without bending the Shilling or rubbing it and the like:

Note further, that this rule dos not absolutely exclude the help of the Senses in searching for truth, but dos only intend that in themselves they are unfit to discover that which is truth; for althô the senses may teach us **that** things are, or that bodies do exist, as also sometimes **what** bodies are or what their nature and qualities are, yet it is by accident and might have been otherwise; the reason of which is bec: the mediums that Intervene sense and the object are very variable and obnoxious to changes: Hence it is, that the stars which now seem red, shall at another time seem only Redish, and at another time altogether pale or of a Whitish colour.

Compendium of Logick

The Third Rule of Truth.

What ever we perceive, we perceive only by the mind. Since neither divine Revelation nor humane traditions take place in philosophy, and (according to the preceeding rule) the senses are all deceitfull, it follows that the understanding must be constituted the proper searcher for truth; hereby do we find out the natures of things, and hereby do we pass Judgment on the very things according to the very attributes which agree to them:—Which is not to be understood only concerning abstracted essences or natures (as metaphysicians term them) but also concerning every particular object which affects our Senses; for it is only the mind which (by the organs) sees, hears, feels, &c.

The Fourth Rule of Truth.

That is true which we know clearly and distinctly. The only rule which we can go by in discovering truth is a clear and distinct perception, or a perception that excludes all doubt, for it is Impossible for us to err whilst we frame such Judgments concerning things as are agreeable to our clear perceptions:—Whence, that axiome is acknowledged by us as an undoubted truth. *A nosse ad esse valet consequentia.* [from the knowledge of a thing we may argue the essence of that thing]—We Imagine not, because we do conceive the essences of a certain thing, that therefore we may conclude that that thing does exist in nature; our meaning is, that whatever is clearly known by us certainly hath such an essence or such a nature as is in our minds: if the existence of a thing is clearly known by us, then may we conclude that this thing is existing; if the nature of the thing is only perceived, we can only argue that this thing hath such a nature or essence.

Hence, Descartes proves the existence of A deity for (says he) if because I have a clear perception of this or that thing, it follows, that all those things which I have an Idea of, do belong unto that thing, then consequently because I cannot have a clear perception of a deity unless I add existence thereto, therefore existence is essentiall to God, or (which is all one) God necessarily or Infallibly does exist:—now the Reason why we cannot conceive clearly of A Deity unless we give existence thereto, is because a Deity Implies a being having all perfections, one of which must be existence.

¶ That this rule does respect Philosophy or naturall things, And not the mysteries of faith, here divine Authority must set us down, but there we must get A clear and distinct perception, before we believe.

If we would know how we may be certain that we do clearly and distinctly perceive a thing; we must follow the method which Right Reason sets us, or not precipitate our Judgment or determine any thing before the evident truth of perception shines forth, or a perception free from all manner of doubt is obtained by us.

The Fifth Rule of Truth.
To obtain a clear and distinct perception, it conduces much that we keep in mind so accurate a scheme or Genealogy of things and modes, that by one view as it were, we may pass through the whole universe of things beginning at the most general and ending at the most speciall.

The Reason is, because hereby (when we are searching into the nature of things) we shall know what tribe or series they belong unto, how they agree with these things and disagree with those things; and also because this will help us much in Defining things, in describing them, in dividing & distributing of {them.}

The Sixth Rule of Truth.
An Idea or perception of any thing is by so much the more clear and perfect, as it Represents many parts, causes and Adjuncts of that thing.

The reason is, because from the parts we have A prospect of the whole thing:—from the causes we gather what is contained in the effect;—from the adjuncts (as complements and ornaments) the nature of the subject and it's disposition is Apprehended, especially from proper and innate qualities or adjuncts.

Compendium of Logick

The Seventh Rule of Truth.
Those things may be said to agree, which do agree in some common Idea or Respect (or those things one of which is Included in the Idea of the other those things may be said to disagree which are the objects of different Ideas (or those things one of which is not Included in the Idea of the other).

For those things only do agree which do agree either in their Genus or Species or parts or causes or effects or subjects or adjuncts or some other respect; and those things which differ in them do only disagree.

Hence distinction (or disagreement) in generall is nothing else but a diversity which we observe among beings. which diversity (to speak properly) is found only among beings that do exist:—for that which actually is not cannot be said actually to be distinquished.

The Eigth Rule of Truth.
That Idea or perception of a thing is clear & distinct which represents the thing to the mind, according to the preceding rules of truth; that is obscure & confus'd which does recede from them more or less.

For since that Idea is the clearest & most distinct which Includes least of doubt and which represents more parts of adjuncts of a thing and does separate it from other things, it follows of necessity that that perception is clear & distinct which represents the very thing according to the preceding Rules.

The Ninth Rule of Truth.
Any one will excell in knowledge and understanding so much the more, as he gets his mind furnished with more & more perfect Idea's.

Since every thing is manifested by its Idea, & whatsoever is known of a thing is contained in its Idea, it follows necessarily, that the fuller our minds are of idea's, so much the larger our knowledge will be.

LOGIC AT HARVARD

The Tenth Rule of Truth.
The names of things which we use in philosophizing must be clear & determin'd as to their signification; never obscure—never ambiguous.

Since the things we Interpret with our minds are delivered by externall discourse and the cheife perfection of this discourse is plainness, hence it is necessary that we use noted words and such as are apt to express the things, and that we put distinct names upon distinct things.

The First part of Logick.

Wherein is considered the nature of perception, as also the nature of the objects of perception.
We heard in the preface (pp. 257)³ operations of the mind, ought to be divided into 4 parts, and that the first part doth respect Idea's, or the simple perception of things; our business therefore now is to take into consideration this act of perception, and likewise the objects of this Art.

Cap. 1. of perception, and it's modes.

PERCEPTION in generall the minds being conscious of, or making present unto it self, an Idea.

The MODES of species of perception are 3. pure INTELLECTION; IMAGINATION; & SENSE; for each of these ways does the mind of man perceive or think of things.

The mind is said partly to understand, when it perceives a thing whereof there was no Image or footstep in the brain:—thus the mind Apprehends or perceives Spiritual things, universalls, common notions, An Idea of Perfection and all it's own Thoughts:

The mind is said to Imagine when it Apllyes it self not to the thing itself being present to the externall sense, but to a Phantasm or footstep of the thing being Imprinted on the brain. Thus it perceives a figure, the stars. A machine &c:—These perceptions are Termed Imaginations, because the mind by Representing those things to it self does feign Images in the brain:—Hence since the mind cannot form Images of Spirituall things it follows that properly it cannot be said to Imagine them.

The mind is said to be sensible of, or, to perceive by SENCE, when the objects are present to the external sense and do affect the outward organs. Thus the mind apprehends a stone, a house, a cat, a man &c

These perceptions are called Sensations, because they require the present aid of the Senses.

That the mind perceives only those 3 ways, is thus demonstrated.

Whatever is objected to the mind is either Spiritual, or material; If it is Spiritual, It can be Apprehended only by the bare understanding: If it is materiall, it necessarily is either present or absent; If it is absent, the mind

---

³ Pages cited are to the present transcription.

ordinarily represents it to it Self only by the Imagination: If it is present, the mind perceives it by Impressions made on the organs of the senses.— hence it is manifest, that the object of the understanding is of a more large extent than the object of Imagination.

Note here, that there is no error in the understanding or Imagination whils't they do continue in the pure contemplation of things; the reason is, because if the Idea, which the mind had; does differ from the thing that is to be perceived, then it cannot be said to be a false representation of that thing; for it is no representation of it at all.

Cap. 2. of the objects of perception

Whatever is perceived by the mind is exhibited either as a THING or as an AFFECTION of a THING, or as a THING WITH IT'S AFFECTIONS:

A THING is that which subsists of it self; or, that which needs not any other Substance that so it may exist. As a Stone, a Tree, this or that man, Angells, &c, by which Definition, all affections or modes are excluded, because althô in some respect they may be said to exist, Viz: as they are found in things whereof they are modes, yet they do so depend on these things that they cannot exist separated from them, as figure, motion, and the like and therefore they cannot properly be termed Things. By a THING here we understand that which others call SUBSTANCE.

Note, that althô we Define Substance a Being subsisting of it Self, yet we cannot distinctly understand any substance unless by some Attributes which do agree to it, nay, the truth is, by how much the more Attributes are known in a Substance or Thing, so much the clearer will the knowledge of that thing be; for Attributes or properties are as it were certain forms which do actuate Things and Separate one from another: Thus we more readily know what the Rational Soul is, by conceiving it as a Thinking Substance, Then by conceiving it as existing; for in that I know that it does think I may conclude necessarily, that it does exist, since it is Impossible that any thing should Think and yet not exist.

AN AFFECTION of a thing is that which gives a certain denomination to a substance, and can by no means subsist without it. Thus, when I consider of Roundness, I have an Idea which denominates a thing round, which I cannot conceive of as existing unless at the same time I conceive of a body in which this roundness is.

Compendium of Logick

A THING WITH IT'S AFFECTIONS or a thing modyfied is a being determined by some certain mode or affection. Thus, when I Joyn a mode with a body and consider of a round body, the Idea, which I then have {exhibits to me} a thing modified.

HITHER may be Reduced the ten Predicaments of Aristotle, In that they were classes or heads to which that Philosopher did reduce all the objects of perception, for after he had divided Ens[4] into Substance & Accident, he sought out these 10 categories under which all Substances and Accidents Imaginable were said to be contained, all Substances being reduced to the first, all accidents to the other 9 categories or predicaments. We shall mention them particulary.

1. **Substance**, which is either Spiritual or corporal.
2. **Quantity**, which is either discrete when it has divided parts, as in number; or continual, when its parts are conjoyn'd; which is either successive as in Time and motion, or permanent which is called a space or extension into length wedth & profundity: Bare Longitude makes line; longitude with latitude make a superficious; all three constitute a Solid.
3. **Quality**, whereof Aristotle makes 4 species, The first whereof comprehends all the habits of the mind and dispositions of the body which are obtained by reiterated acts, As Sciences, Virtues, Vices, The art of writing, painting, Dancing, &c: The second denotes the natural powers; such are the faculties of the mind and body, as the understanding, the will, the memory, the five senses, the faculty of walking &c. the Third denotes the Sensible Qualities, such as hardness, softness, Gravity, heat, cold, colours, sounds, odours, savours, &c. the fourth species denotes that form and figure which is the extrinsick determination of Quantity; as to be Round, Quadrated, Spherical, cubical &c.
4. **Relation**, or a Respect of one thing to another; as of A father to a son, A master to a servant, a power to the object and to which we may annex all things which are notes of comparisons, as to be like, equal, greater, less, &c.
5. **Action**, either considered in it self; as to walk, leap, know, love &c; or without, as, to smite, to cut, to break &c.
6. **Passion**, as to be smitten, broken, manifested &c.
7. **Whereness**, when we answer a question concerning place; As, {he} is at Rome, in his chamber, or the like.

---

[4] *Ens* means something that has existence or being.

8. **Whenness**, when we make answers to a question concerning time, As when he lived? An hundred years since: when was this acted? Yesterday, &c.

9. **Scituation**, As, to sitt, to stand, to lye down &c.

10. **Habit**, As, to have something about one self for cloathing, ornament, defence and the like.

Thus we have a view of Aristotle's ten categories, which (according to some) are so many mysteries to be admired at and adored; but to speak plainly they are altogether unprofitable and so far from being helpfull in passing a right Judgment (which is the only scope of Logick) that they very often are prejudiciall and do great harm in this respect, & that especially on 2 accounts.

1. In that they do suppose that ens is truly divided into Substance and Accident: for this is a notion altogether destitute and void of Reason, since it is most certain that Accidents (As taken by the Aristotelians) can by no means properly be said to be beings or things; for could they be so termed we might undoubtedly conceive of them as capable of existing in themselves; the Consequence of which argument appears from the Definition which we gave of *res* in this Chapter.

2. This predicamental doctrine is faulty in that it constitutes 9 classes or heads of Accidents & numbers them thus, Quantity, Quality, Action, Passion, &c, as, before: for hereby 1. those things are made distinct heads which really do not differ: as Quantity, figure and quality; when as physical qualities are nothing but the result of quantity, figure & motion; So likewise, action & passion are species or modes of motion & consequently Improperly made distinct heads or predicaments. 2. Relation is constituted the third head, whenas it by no means belongs to the Genealogy of things, because it is not any thing absolute, but a bare affection of reason Viz. an opposition which some respect, so that althô we do approve and allow of Aristotle's design in finding out severall heads, to which he might reduce every thing that we may can perceive, yet we cannot but highly condemn & reject the method which was taken to accomplish this his design.

In the room of these 10 categories, some do propose seven heads which they express in this latin distich viz.

Compendium of Logick

Mens, Mensura, quies, motus, positura, figura
Sunt cum materia, cunctarum exordia rerum.[5]

And they are persuaded that the whole of nature is contained under these 7 classes: by *mens* they understand a thinking substance. by *materia*, an extended substance:—by *mensura*, magnitude:—by *positura*, the site or disposition of parts among themselves:—by *figura*, *motus*, et *quies*, that which is usually understood thereby.

Sr Kenelm Digby[6] is of the mind that Aristotle is highly abused, here by his followers; and that that Great philosopher never intended or Imagined (as his followers do assert of him) that these 9 predicaments which are termed Accidents, were positive entities really distinct from the thing or substance wherein they are, or to which they do belong. In his Conclusion annexed to his treatise of bodies[7] he thus expresses himself concerning the case that is before us.

> "I think not amisse to touch the late sectatours, or rather pretenders of Aristotle (for truly they have not his way) have Introduced a modell of Doctrine (or rather of Ignorance) out of his words, which he never so much as dreamed of; howbeit they alledge texts out of him to confirm what they say, as hereticks do out of Scripture to confirm their assertions; for

---

[5] The only reference I have found to Brattle's *Compendium* in philosophical literature is a footnote reference to this distich in Abraham Edel's "Aristotle's Categories and the Nature of Categorical Theory," *The Review of Metaphysics* 29 (1975): 59. Edel states that these seven heads instead of the Aristotelian ten are "particularly significant" for "the substitution of matter for the Aristotelian substance, the mathematical emphasis in measure, and the similarity of the remaining categories to Locke's primary qualities. Aristotle's category of quality is explicitly reduced to the effects of figure and motion, but mind is regarded as irreducible, a category distinct from all material ideas." Edel points out the important difference with Aristotelian logic here; however, he is wrong to see Locke's influence. The distich comes from early seventeenth-century Dutch Cartesianism. See Theo Verbeek, *Descartes and the Dutch: Early Reactions to Cartesian Philosophy, 1637–1650* (Carbondale: Southern Illinois, 1992): 14.

[6] Sir Kenelm Digby (1603–1665). See the discussion of his influence and other Roman Catholic Aristotelians on Charles Morton in Kennedy's "Humanism, Religion, and Dogmatism." Digby first had great hopes for Cartesianism before returning to an emphasis on Aristotelianism.

[7] Kenelm Digby, *A Treatise of the Nature of Bodies*, first published in Paris in 1644 with three subsequent London editions, the last in 1669.

whereas he called certain collections or positions of things by certain common names (as the art of Logick required) terming some of them **Qualities,** others **Actions** others **Places,** or **Habits** or **Relatives,** or the like; these his later followers have conceived that these names did not design A concurrence of sundry things, or a diverse disposition of the parts of any thing, out of which some effect resulted, which the understanding considering Altogether, hath expressed the notion of it by one name; but have Imagined that every one of these names had correspondent unto it some real positive entity or thing separated (in it's own nature) from the main thing or Substance in which it was, & indifferent to any other Substance, but {in all} unto which it is linked, working still the effect which is to be expected from the nature of such a quality {or} Action {&c}. And thus to the very negatives of things as to the names of points, lines, Instants, and the like; they have Imagined positive entities to correspond: likewise, to the names of actions, places & the like, they have framed other entities; as also to the names of colours, sounds, tasts, smells, Touches and the rest of the sensible qualities, they have unto every one of them allotted Special entities, and generally to all qualities whatsoever; whereas nothing is more evident than that Aristotle meaned by qualities no other thing, but that disposition of parts, which is proper to one body & is not found in all:"

Afterwards the forementioned Author adds.

"Let these so peremptory pretenders of Aristotle shew me but one text in him, where he admitteth any middle distinction (such as those modern Philosophers do, and must needs admitt who maintain the qualities we have rejected) betwixt that which he calleth numericall, and that which he calleth of reason or of notion, or of definition (the first of which we may term to be of or in things, the other to be in our heads or discourses; or the one natural, the other Logical) and I will yeild that they have reason & that I have grosly mistaken what he hath written and that I do not reach the depth of his sense: but this they never will be able to do."

Compendium of Logick

Thus the Author in the conclusion—p. 426. 427. 428. & in the treatise it self Chap^r: 1: p. 6. Sr Kenelm, having said that there are 2 sorts of words to express our notions, the one common to all men, the other proper to scholars, does deliver these words:

> "Of the first kind are those 10 Generall heads which Aristotle calleth predicaments; under which he (who was the most Judicious orderer of notions and director of mens conceptions, that ever lived) hath comprized whatsoever hath or can have a being in nature: for when any object occurreth to our thoughts, we either consider the essentiall & fundamentall being of it, or we refer it to some species of quantity; or we discover some qualitites in it; or we perceive that it doeth or that it suffereth something, or we conceive it in some determinate place or time & the like; of all which every man living that enjoyeth but the use of reason finds naturally within himself at the very first naming of them, a plain, compleat, & satisfying notion which is the same without any of the least variation, in all mankind, unless it be in such who have Industriously and by force, and with much labour, perplexed and depraved, those primary and sincere Impressions which nature had freely made in them."

From all which it's evidently Sr Kenelm's opinion that the Doctrine of the predicaments as it is now taught by the Aristotellians and rejected by the late philosophers, never was taught or thought of by Aristotle whom it is fathered on.[8]

Cap. 3. of Substance & its Divisions

We heard in the foregoing Chapt: that substance is that which stands not in need of any other substance in order to it's existing: we may here further observe how it is divided.

---

[8] These long sections from Digby are not derived from LeGrand's *Institutio* or Arnauld's *The Port-Royal Logic*. Neither of those books have this argument that the neo-Aristotelian use (i.e. Morton's use) of the ten predicaments is not to be found in Aristotle. Although the ten predicaments had been revised and standardized during the Middle Ages, Digby and Brattle make a weak argument.

SUBSTANCE is 2 fold; created & Increated.—**created** is that, which althô it stands in need of the divine concorse and cannot possibly exist without it, yet may be perceived as existing without the help of any other thing. **Increated** is that, which is simply & Absolutely independent on every other being; As the Eternal God.—

CREATED things, or substances are either intellectual or material.

AN INTELLECTUAL substance is a thinking substance; or a thing where in Immediately there is cogitation; As the mind, to which belong all cogitative arts or modes as to understand, Imagine & to perceive by sense [sentize].

A MATERIALL substance or a body is a substance extended into length, weadth & profundity. Or, it is the Immediate subject of local extension & all those modes which do presuppose extension; As magnitude, motion, figure, site and all other things which cannot be perceived without local extension as their foundation.

FROM the premises it appears that there are but 2 kinds of things or Substances to be admitted, viz. material & intellectual; all other objects of perception are referred to those things as modes or affections, of which we shall discourse in the following chapters.

Cap. 4. of the affections of things & their divisions.

We heard in the second chapter that an affection of a thing is that which gives a certain denomination to a substance or thing, and can by no means subsist with out it.

These affections may be distinguished into Attributes, modes, & qualities.

ATTRIBUTES are such affections as give denomination to a thing but do no way alter it or distinquish it from other things: As one-nesse, verity, bonity, Perfection, and the like.

ONENESSE is that whereby any thing is said to be undivided in it self. It is 2 fold, per se & per accidents. Those things are said to be one [per se] by themselves, which have an undivided nature; whether they are simple or compound; for the multitude of parts hinders not unity, or one-nesse, if so be that the connection of the parts be entire; thus man is said to be one althô he consists of parts of a differing nature and separable one from the other. those things are said to be one by Accident [per Accidens] which are so compounded of disjoyn'd parts as that there is no perfect union between them; Thus an army, is termed one body, because it consists of men, among whom there is not but an Imperfect union.

VERITY is that, whereby a name is said to agree with a thing signifyed by that name: so that to find the truth of a thing is nothing else but to find out the real nature of a thing: otherwise it is described, That whereby a thing is agreeable to it's Idea:

BONITY is that, whereby a thing is fit for use, or serves to the end for which it was made:

¶ That if a thing has such an essence as it ought to have, i.e. if it is true, it will necessarily likewise be good; hence we oftentimes confound the denominations of good & true: Thus we call a True Syllogism a good one & the like:

¶ further, that althô the 3 forementioned attributes are by most accounted the most generall or common affections of things, yet some account the notion as absurd:—As for unity, these say that it is no manner of way distinquished from the thing it self, or that it adds nothing to a being, but is only a mode of thinking whereby we do separate one thing from others which are like to it, and do agree with it in some respects.—as for *verum* and *falsum*, these Authors assert that they are only extrinsick denominations of things and are attributed to them only Rhetorically:—As for *bonum* and *malum*, according to these authors they are relative or respective terms; A being being termed good or evill as it conduces to the advantage or disadvantage of some other thing.

MODES are such affections of things as do not only denominate a thing but also do in some measure distinquish it from other things.

They are either universal or Speciall

UNIVERSAL modes are such as do agree to many things: they are termed Genus, Difference, Species, *proprium et accidens* of which we shall discourse in a distinct chapter.

SPECIAL are such modes as do agree only to particular things. Thus, Intellection & understanding &c are modes of a thinking thing:—Quality, or magnitude, figure, site, motion &c are modes of extended things:—Appetite; as hunger & thirst:

the Senses { Internall;—Phantasie or Imagination & memory.
externall;—seeing, hearing, smelling, Tasting.

and touching and their affections, as Watching and sleeping and the affections or passions, as Love, hatred, Joy, Greif, hope, fear & their species all which result from the conjunction of a thinking and extended substance, are all modes of such a substance. also to be a totum or apart; a cause or an effect, a subject or adjunct, like or dislike, equal or unequal, and the like (for which we shall reserve the 6th chapter) may all be termed modes of things, in as much as they denominate things and in a measure distinquish between them.

QUALITIES we reckon such attributes or affections, as do not only denominate things, and in a measure distinguish them, but also denote the such-ness of things: or in other words, a Quality is that whereby *Res talis denominatur*.[9] qualities as heat, and cold, moisture and dryness, rarity and density, fluidity and hardness and the rest of which Physicks treat. likewise among this number we may reckon Justice and Injustice, fortitude and cowardize and the other moral virtues and vices of which ethicks or moral Phylosophy does discourse. This mode answers the question (i.e. accidentally) what kind or sort of as, what kind or what sort of man was Solomon: Wise &c.

Cap. 5. of the 5 Universalls, [Genus, Species &c]

Among the universalls GENUS obtains the first place and that for its dignity. It being as it were the head on which the others as so many members do depend, & without which they perish & come to nothing.

GENUS is an universal which is predicated of more things specifically distinct, answering to the question **what is**? Thus substance is a Genus in respect of an extended substance, which is called a body, and of a thinking substance which is termed a mind, or Spirit, for if we ask, what is a body? What is a spirit? the answer is, A Substance, A Substance, that to be specifically distinguished is to differ essentially, so that there is an essentiall part in the one that is not in the other.[10] distinguished, bec: in man there is a mind or Rational soul which is not in a beast.

Genus is twofold; most generall is the highest; & Subalternate. The most generall genus is that which has no genus above it, whether it be *ens* or *substantia* it matters not, neither does this question belong to Logick but Metaphisick.

---

[9] A Quality is that whereby a substance is denominated such a kind.
[10] Note the separation of extended substance from thinking substance. Morton insisted that spiritual/thinking substance is also extended, but is penetrable. See Morton *A Logick System*, Pt. 1, chap. 6, (p. 163 of typescript).

Compendium of Logick

A subalternate Genus is that which is placed between the highest genus & lowest species: or, that which in respect of what is above, is a species, & in respect of what is below is called a Genus. Thus, a beast, if considered with respect to Animal, is a species, but if with respect to a dog, a bear, a lyon &c then it is a Genus. Henc Animal is the remote genus of a dog, bear &c and the next genus of a beast.

SPECIES is an univerall which is predicated of more things distinct only in number, also in the question, **What is**? thus to the question, What is peter? What is John? &c we answer, he is a man.

Species is twofold; most special or lowest, & middle or subalternate: the latter althô in respect of a Genus under which it is, is named a species; Thus (lest the multitude of examples should confound us) a beast which is a species of Animal, is termed a Genus when it respects a dog and a bear.

The most special species (which especially we here intend) is that which Immediately is predicated of Individualls: as man of Peter & John: a Circle of every particular Circle:—It is termed most special or lowest because it has no species below it, but only Individualls.

DIFFERENCE may be considered divers ways:

1. as it is constitutive of a species; and then it may be defined, that by which a species exceeds a genus: as man adds Animal to rational.

2. as it is something predicable; & thus it usually is defined, an universall which is predicated of many things in their species distinct essentially, answering to the question What sort or manner?—as what kind of animal is man? A. Rationall:—This Definition does agree only to an Intermediate difference.

3. as it divides Genus into divers species:—Thus Animal is divided into Rational & Irrational, & constitues 2 species, viz. man & beast.

4. As it is an essential part of an whole compositum, and then it enters into it's essence & belongs to it's definition; whereby it is distinquished from proprium & Accidens which do not enter the essence.

5. that in every species there is necessarily found something besides the Genus; otherwise there would be no distinction among species since they all do agree in their genus: hence there must be some difference whence this distinction may be taken. Therefore Difference as it constitutes the 3^d predicable may be thus defined, viz. that which is predicated of a species and those things which are contained under it, answering essentially to the question, What kind of &c:

WILLIAM BRATTLE

PROPRIUM, property is taken 4 ways.

1. It denotes that which agrees only to a species, but not to the whole of species; i.e. not to all the Individualls of that species, thus, to be a Physitian belongs only to the species of man, yet belongs not to every Individual man.

2. It denotes that, which agrees to an whole species, but not only to that species:—thus, to go on two feet belongs (naturally) to every Individual man, but not only to men, because birds likewise go on two feet. This is the meanest property.

3. It denotes that, which agrees only and wholly to a species but not at all times:—Thus, the hoary head agrees only to man & to all men, but not at all times, for childhood and youth are (naturally) destitute therof.

4. It denotes that, which agrees only, wholly and at all times to a species. Thus it is the property of every circle, only of a circle, and evermore of a circle, that all the lines which are drawn from the center to the circumference are equal:—This last kind of property constitues the 4th predicable or univeral, and then it may be defined, that which is predicated of many things, by it self and necessarily, yet not essentially NECESSARILY, because a property does so belong to a thing as that it cannot so much as by our mind be separated therefrom; It so follows the essence of a thing as that it is converted therewith:—thus it is an essential property of a triangle that 2 of it's sides be greater then the third; that it's 3 angles be equall to two right angles &c.

AN ACCIDENT is that which is not the substance, neither dos necessarily belong to it, but only contingently annexed to it:—otherwise; It is that which may be present or absent without the destruction of the Subject.

It is 2 fold Separable and Inseparable.

Separable is that which can easily be removed from the subject wherein it is conceived to be: as to sleep from man. Inseparable is that which by the strength of nature cannot be taken from the subject wherein it is:—As whiteness from a swan; blackness from an Æthiopian &c.: althô by our thoughts this whiteness & blackness may be removed, since we can think of a swan without whiteness, and of a man without blackness:

¶ Note: (as before) that hereby an Accident is distinquished from a property which cannot thus be separated from it's subject.

That this division of universal is adequate, containing no more, nor yet fewer members then it ought, is thus demonstrated.

The Idea which we form in our minds and use to represent many things, either exhibits many things specifically distinct, and so a GENUS is framed; or many things numerically distinct, & so a SPECIES is constituted; or represents the differences wherby many singulars differ among themselves and from other things and so DIFFERENCE is made; or a property which belongs only to these things and hence PROPRIUM; or lastly a certain contingency seperable from the essence of things and hence ACCIDENT, or the 4th universal is constituted.

Many things are wont to be objected against the notion of an Universal; but the arguments no ways reach us, who explain them after another manner then the Peripateticks do, and assert that these universalls are nothing else but diverse modes of thinking, whereby the same thing is this way and the other way conceived in our minds and considered of by us: Le. Gr. P.27.—[11]

Cap. 6th of a Totum and parts; Cause & effect &c.

We heard (cap. 4.) that to be a Totum or a part, a cause or an effect, like or dislike, equal or unequal &c, were accounted modes, and we then promised to explain the nature of these modes in pursuance of which promise we shall Improve this sixth chapter.

TOTUM is that which hath parts and may be divided thereinto, for that which is destitute of parts is Improperly termed a totum; hence the Aristotelians err when they assert that mans soul is wholly in mans body and wholly in every part of it, since the soul being an Intellectual substance, is without parts & consequently exists in the body after an indivisible manner: for an Immaterial Substance cannot be termed an WHOLE unless negatively.

A totum is 3 fold, essential, Integral & universal.

An essential Totum is that which consists of parts whereof one is in the other; As matter and form; Thus man consists of a mind and a body.

An Integral totum or an Integrum is that which has parts without parts: Thus man consists of an head, of hands, feet &c.

An Universal totum is a genus related to it's species: as animal to man & beast: man to Socrates and Plato &c.

A PART is that which helps to the constituting of a totum: It is either principal without which a totum cannot consist, as the head in a mans

---

[11] This page reference refers to LeGrand's *Institutio*, 1680 edition, Pt. 1, chap. 4.

body; or less principal, which being taken away the totum indeed is not destroyed, yet is mutilated; as the hand in a mans body.

A CAUSE (as the schooles teach us thô obscurely) is that, by the force of which anything is produced; or that from which a thing is:

Its division into material, formal, efficient & final is very famous & must be insisted on: Le-Gr: partis: 1 Cap: 9.[12]

A material cause is that out of which things are made or formed; As wax is the matter out of which torches are made:—Hence whatever agrees or disagrees to matter does likewise agree or disagree to the things which are constituted out of that matter.

A formal cause (or form) is that which constitutes a thing, and does discriminate it from other things. Thus, the rational soul is the form of man. Thô, whether the forms of other things are Physical entities (as they speak in the schooles) distinct from the matter it self, and not the bare modification of matter or disposition of parts is a Quare to be resolved in Physick. These two causes are term'd Internal because they remain in those things whose essence they constitute.

An efficient cause is that which produces another thing: It is manifold for an efficient cause is

1. TOTAL and PARTIAL

Total, or adequate when it produces an effect of it self, without the help of any other efficient. Thus God created Adam.

Partial, when two or more efficients concurr in producing an effect.—Thus man & woman in producing a child.

2. PROPER and ACCIDENTAL

Proper,—Thus the Sun is the proper cause of Light.

Accidental,—Thus the Sun is the Accidental cause of that mans destruction who is killed by too much heat; Bec: it is from an ill disposition of that mans body, that the Sun's heat Injures it.

3. NEXT and REMOTE

next,—Thus the father is the next cause of the son.

Remote,—Thus the grandfather is the remote cause of the son.

4. PRODUCING and CONSERVING

Producing or effective,—thus the mother of a son, because she effects things which did not before exist.

Conserving,—Thus the nurse because she preserves that which

---

[12] LeGrand's *Institutio*, Pt. 1, chap. 9.

Compendium of Logick

before did exist.
5. UNIVOCAL and ÆQUIVOCAL
univocal,—Thus the father with respect to his sons, because they are of the same nature with himself.

Æquivocal,—Thus God with respect to the creatures, because their natures are different from his.
6. PRINCIPAL and INSTRUMENTAL
Principal,—which acts from it's own will,—as the Artist that builds the house.

Instrumental,—which acts as it is directed by the principal cause,—as the hammer, saw, &c in the hands of the Artist.
7. UNIVERSAL and PARTICULAR
Universal,—as water coming out of a fountain and moving divers machines is the universall cause of that motion.

Particular,—Thus the figure and disposition of the pipes which determines the universal cause & restrains it to some certain effect.
8. NATURAL and VOLUNTARY
Naturall,—which acts from the propension & necessity of nature without any precedaneous knowledge. As the fire, Sun &c.

Voluntary; which acts Spontaneously and not from any force or necessity.
9. PROPER and IMPROPER
proper,—Thus when the chamber is enlightened by the Sun, the Sun is the proper cause of that light.

Improper,—(or *causa sine quâ non*) Thus the opening of the window is the *causa sine quâ non* of the chamber's being enlightened.
10. PHYSICAL and MORAL
Physical, thus fire burning the house is the Physical cause of the burning, because fire of it's own nature does properly burn.

Moral, Thus, the serpent by persuading the first parents to eat of the forbidden fruit was the moral cause of their fall.

The final cause, or end is that for which a thing is thus the end of a mans studying is that he may obtain knowledge. The end is 2 fold, Primary & Secondary.

PRIMARY is that which is principally Intended. thus the end of a knife is to cutt.

SECONDARY or less principal is that which moves the efficient less, and is considered as a motive &c. Thus cloathes being an ornament to the body is a secondary reason why we wear them.

An effect is that which exists out of the causes: from the fourfold division of cause effect must be accounted (says Le-Gr.p. 47) fourfold.[13]

A subject is that to which any thing is adjoyned, or, to which anything happens besides it's essence: Thus the body is the subject of cloathes &c. A subject is 2 fold Inhærentiæ & Adhærentiæ

of Inherence, wherein something is received. Thus, the sponge is the matter wherein water is contained.

of Adherence, which receives something to it: Thus the hand is the subject of the glove.

Subject sometimes is taken some for the Object, and then it denotes that which is proposed to another power, that it may act something in it, or about it. thus the object of hearing is sound; of sight, Colour &c.

An adjunct is that which is a thing besides it's essence: whether this Accident carry any proper reality with it; or is nothing else but a mode of substance, as in the mind, love knowledge, in the body, motion figure &c.
¶ Note that an accidental adjunct is predicated of its subjects in concrete not in abstracts: Snow is white, not whiteness &c.

Comparison is not the simple consideration of one thing, (says Le-Grand) but the collation of one thing to another, to which we assent or dissent; and therefore he treats of it in the 2^d part of Logick under Proposition or Judgment.

Comparison is either in quantity or quality. comparison in quantity constitutes *paria* or *Imparia*.

Paria [equalls] are such things, which being compared do contain an equal proportion. Thus at the equinoxe, the night is equall with the day.

Imparia [unequalls] are such things as do contain an unequal proportion; or, do disagree in their quantity: Unequals are either greater or less.

Greater are unequalls which do exceed in quantity.

Lesse are unequalls which are exceeded in quantity.

Comparison in quality constitutes similia or dissimilia.[14]

Like are such things as do agree in quality: or, which being compared, have some like affection: Thus the Sun and the fixed stars

---

[13] LeGrand's *Institutio* (1680 edition), Pt. 1, chap. 9.29.
[14] Brattle begins his logic strictly in English, following the ideal presented in Morton's preface. From here on he increasingly becomes lazy in translating Latin terms and sentences.

being compared among themselves, in respect of light which is found in each, are like.

UNLIKE are such things whose Qualities are diverse. or, such things as disagree in Qualities, actions, or passions. Thus a wise man is unlike to the moon &c.

Cap. 7th of a thing with it's affections

A MODIFYED THING or a thing with it's affections is (as we have heard) a being determined by some certain mode or affection: So that it is not the substance or being simply considered, nor yet the affection that becomes the object of perception here; but properly the being cloathed with some appendage or mode.

These Appendages or additaments are somtimes made by pronoun relatives, and somtimes without them being expressed, for it is necessary that they be always understood and Implyed—thus, the body which is white; or the white body, which Intend the same thing.

That which is principally to be observed in these complex terms is, that there are two kinds of these additaments, whereof one may be termed explicative, the other determinative.

EXPLICATIVE is that which by apt words does explain that which before lay hid; Thus, when I say man who is an animal endued with reason; or, man who naturally desires happiness; and the like, these additaments are barely explicative, because that which is added does no ways change or alter the Idea which belongs to man in generall.

If these additaments are the essentiall Attributes of a thing then it is called a perfect explication or Definition; if they are only accidental, or not fully essential, it is then called an Imperfect explication or description.

Definition is either *nominis* or *rei*; the one explains the name, the other explains the thing: This difference is carefully to be heeded, and the parts to be distinquished, otherwise we shall run into many absurdities, which some of the Aintients by reason thereof were led into. See Legrands Appendix to his 10th Chap. Log: P. 52. book 1.40: also *ARS cogitandi* Part. 1. Cap. 7. 11. 12[15]

---

[15] LeGrand's *Institutio* (1680 edition). *Ars Cogitandi* is more commonly called *The Port-Royal Logic.*

of this first kind of additaments are all such as are applyed to names distinctly signifying Individuals, as when I say that Aristotle was the prince of Philosophers; that william the conqueror was king of England; for these singular terms being thus considered do loose nothing of their extension.

DETERMINATIVE is that which restrains the signification of the generall term so that it cannot be taken in it's due extension. Thus, when I say white bodies, wise men, Rational Animals and the like, these additaments are not simply explicative but determinative because they do mutilate and cutt short the extension of the first term; for (if we mind it) the name of body, of man and of Animal here does signify not every body, man & animal but only some of them.

The nature of these additaments is such sometimes, that they will constitute a singular out of a common term; viz: when they contain in them Individuating Circumstances; thus when I say the king of England now reigning, the common name of king is determined to the particular person of James the Second.

There are also two other kinds of complex terms whereof one is complex in words, the other only in sense.

of the first kind are only those terms which have an expressed addition: here the forementioned examples are proper.

of the other kind are those terms {wherein} one is not expressed but only understood: Thus when english-men speak of the king; this term is in it's self complex. because when we thus pronounce this name, the Idea of the common name [king] is not solitarily considered in our minds but has annexed to it the Idea of James the Second who now rules us, and is the king of England: there is an infinite number of terms which being after this manner complex do most frequently occur in discourse; Thus, in every family, A Master &c.

Also how are some terms which are complex both in words & in sense, but after a different manner. Thus Princeps Philosophorum is complex in words, because the name of a prince is determined by the word Philosophers; but in respect of Aristotle whom the schoolmen do thus term it is only complex in sense, since the Idea of Aristotle is only in the mind and yet there is no speech that does expressly denote Aristotle in what is said.

The end of the first book.

The Second Part of Logick.

Wherein is considered the nature of a proposition it's kinds and affections

Cap. 1. of Judgement or Proposition its Definition &c.

In the Preceeding part we considered the simple notions of things, and discussed the natures and properties thereof, it follows that we compare them, one with the other, and explain how they agree and disagree among themselves, which is to affirm or deny, and in one generall name is termed to Judge.

This judgement is otherwise termed Proposition, and from what hath been already said, it is manifest that Proposition is a certain sentence declaring something true, or false;—which manifests 2 things.

1. That there must be two terms, The one that of which something is affirmed or denyed, which is called the subject; The other, that which is affirmed or denyed, which is called the predicate, or attribute.

2. That these 2 terms be conjoyned or separated by the mind; for otherwise this would be simple perception or apprehension, which is the first operation of the mind and consequently belongs to the first part of Logick.

These two terms are conjoyned or separated by the verb substantive [*est*] which is termed the copula or vinculum of the Proposition, because the 2 parts are connected there by: when the verb is solitary, it betokens affirmation, when it hath the particle [*non*] annexed to it, then it betokens negation.

Although it is necessary that every proposition consist of these 3 things, yet may a proposition be fully contained in 2 words, or in one.

Men for the Compendiousness of Speech have found out very many words which signifie both the affirmation, i.e. that which the verb substantive denotes and the attribute, or something which is predicated. of this number are all those verbs which are called substantives: Thus *Deus existit*, i.e. *est existins. Deus amat homines*, i.e. *est amans homines*:[16] solitary (as when I say *cogito, Ergò Sum*) ceases to be purely substantive; because

---

[16] God exists i.e. is existing. God loves humans, i.e. is loving humans.

then the most generall of Attributes [*ens*] is annexed to it, for *ergò sum* here is just as much as *ergò sum ens*, or *ergò sum aliquid*.

Among the Latines one word may constitute a Proposition, since it may Include in it besides the copula both a subject and a predicate; Thus *veni, vidi, vici*, do constitute 3 entire axioms or propositions; and the latine word (*sum*) contains as much in it as *ego sum ens*,[17] where both the subject and predicate are proposed and connected by the vinculum or copula [*sum*].

Cap. 2ᵈ: Of a Proposition it's division.

A Proposition may divers ways be distinquished, according to the different considerations which it may pass under, for if not consider it as to it's substance, it may be divided into simple & complex; if we consider it as to it's quality, it may be divided into true and false; affirmative and negative; and if it be considered as to it's quantity, we may then divide it into universal, Particular and singular, all which considerations we shall pass on Proposition and distribute it according to each respectively.

If we respect the substance of proposition, or consider it as genus, it may be divided (as we said before) into simple & compound.

A simple proposition is that which besides the copula consists only of one subject and one predicate. thus if I assert that man is an Animal, the subject is one viz. man; the predicate is likewise one viz Animal.

A simple proposition is either purely simple or complex.

A Proposition purely simple or incomplex is a proposition which contains in it besides the copula nothing but an incomplex subject and predicate: as in the forementioned instance, man is an Animal.

A complex proposition is a proposition which contains in it besides the copula a subject and predicate one of which at least is a complex term including another proposition in it which we may term an Incident proposition.

This incident proposition, when it falls on the matter of the main proposition (for sometimes it falls on the form thereof, as we shall see afterwards) is part of the subject or predicate conjoyn'd there with by the pronoun (*qui*) the nature whereof is so to knit many propositions as that

---

[17] The "sum" in the Cogito—"I think, therefore I am"—means more fully "Ego sum ens" or "therefore, I am a being."

they will all grow into one propositon: Thus when our Saviour saith, *ille, qui facit, voluntatem patris mei qui in coelis est, regnum coelorum possidebit*,[18] the subject of that proposition contains two other propositions which are conjoyn'd by the pronoun *qui*, and so made parts of one subject; otherwise then when I say, *bona et mala à deo proveniunt*,[19] for they I make truly two subjects, since I was well say, as *mala as bona*, that it does *provenires à Deo*.

And it is all one whether we deliver these propositions by noun adjectives or participles without any verb and pronoun, or by a verb and pronoun, since it is the same thing to say, *Deus invisibilis creavit mundum visibilum*, as to say *Deus qui est invisibilis creavit mundum qui est visibilis*; for in either expressions it is not primarily asserted *Deum esse Invisibilem*, or *mundum esse visibilem*,[20] but these two things supposed or taken for 2 propositions which were before asserted, we now only affirm *hunc Deum Creasse hunc mundum*.

These complex propositions are of 2 sorts since the complexion (if I may so term it) may fall either on the matter of the proposition, i.e. on that subject or predicate, or each, or on the form; i.e. the verb.

The complexion falls on the subject when the subject is the complex term; as *Deus qui est invisibilis Creavit mundum*.

> *Beatus ille qui procul negotiis,*
> *ut prisca gens mortalium,*
> *paterna rura bobus exercet suis*
> *Solutus omni Fænore.*[21]

---

[18] Brattle takes this section from Arnauld's *The Port-Royal Logic*, Bk. 2, chap. 5. It is interesting but trivial to note that the Bible does not quote Jesus making the exact phrase "He who does the will of my father who is in heaven shall enter into the kingdom of heaven." One would think that Arnauld's Jansenism and Brattle's Puritanism would have alerted them to a phrase that appears outside the border of each man's theology of salvation. Jesus's parable of the two sons (Matt. 21: 28–31) seems to be the closest source.

[19] Goods and evils come from God.

[20] The invisible God (Or God who is invisible) created the visible world (or world that is visible).

[21] (Horace, *Epodes* 2.1–4), translated by James Dickoff and Patricia James in *The Art of Thinking*, 116, as "Happy he who like the ancient mortal race / Far from commerce and from trade / Tills with beast the ancestral fields, / From all negotiations free."

In this last proposition the verb [*est*] is understood, *beatus* is predicated, all the rest is subjected.

The complexion falls on the predicate, when the predicate is the complex term; as here, *Deus creavit mundum qui est visibilis.*

Sum pius Æneas fama super æthera notus.

The complexion falls both on the subject and on the predicate, when each is a complex term: as in this proposition, *potentes qui pauperes opprimunt à Deo punientur, qui oppressorum protector est.*[22] Also in this,

> *ille ego qui quondam gracili modulatus avenâ*
> *Carmen et egressus Sylvis, vicina coegi*
> *ut quamvis avido parerent arva colono:*
> *gratum opus agricolis; at nunc horrentia martis*
> *arma virumq cano Trojæ qui primus ab oris*
> *Italiam fato profugus, lavinaq venit*
> *Littora.*[23]

Here, the 3 first verses with half of the 4th are the subject of the proposition, the remainder is the predicate, the affirmation being included in the verb *cano*.

These are 3 ways whereby propositions may be complex in respect of their matter, i.e. either of their subject or predicate.

The complexion is said to respect the form or copula, when an incident proposition or term conjoyn'd with a proposition affects it's form, i.e. the affirmation or negation noted by the verb (*est*) as, when I say, *ego assero terram esse rotundam, ego assero*, is an incident proposition and part of the main proposition; yet is it evident that it neither affects the subject nor the predicate, because it changes nothing in them, they being conceived after no other manner then they would have been had I only said, *Terra est rotunda*; so that the incident proposition here falls only on the affirmation

---

[22] Brattle introduced the example of Aeneas' fame but copied the example of God punishing the oppressors of the poor from Arnauld's *The Port-Royal Logic*, Bk. 2, chap. 5.

[23] (Virgil *Aeneid* 1.1a–d, 1–3). Dickoff and James in *The Art of Thinking*, 117, translate this: "I, who once tuned my song to a slender reed / But then left the woodland, bidding the neighboring fields / To serve the landsman, however demanding, / A servitude welcome to farmers, sing of Mars-bristling / Arms now and the man who once from the coast of Troy / Exiled by Fate to Italy and Lavinian Shores first came."

Compendium of Logick

which may be expressed two ways, viz: either by the verb (*est*) as it is ordinarily, or more expressly by the verb (*assero*).

After the same manner it is in these forms of speech, *nego; verum est, non est verum*, also when to a proposition there is conjoyned a reason propping and supporting the proposed assertion; as here, *Rationes Astronomicæ convincunt Solem esse terrâ multò majorem*: For the first part of the proposition is only the ground of the affirmation:[24]

But here we must note that of these propositions there are some which have an ambiguous sense and ought to be understood diversly according to the different intention of the speaker: for if I should say, *omnes Philosophi docent res graves spontè deor sum ferri*;[25] and my intent should be only to show, that heavy bodies naturally tend downwards, then the first part of the proposition will be only incident; but if on the contrary I should propose this as the opinion of Philosophers not approving of it, then this first part will be the principal proposition and the remainder only a part of the predicate; for so I should not affirm that heavy things naturally tend downwards, but only that all Philosophers do teach this doctrine: nor is it difficult to understand, that these two modes of this proposition to be understood do so change it, that two different propositions may be made, having 2 different significations; but it may evidently appear from what follows in which sense such a proposition ought to be understood; for if to the forementioned proposition (for example sake) I should subjoyn, *sed lapides sunt res graves ergò sponte deorsum feruntur.*[26] It would thence be evident that I gave the first signification to it, and that the first part was only incident; Whereas on the contrary, if I should thus assume, *sed hoc est falsum; ergò evenire potest ut omnes Philosophi doceant id quod est falsum*,[27] it is thence manifest that I gave the second signification to it, i.e. the first part will be the principal proposition and second will be only part of the predicate.

Among complex propositions whose copula, not subject or predicate, is affected by a complex term, Philosophers have especially noted those

---

[24] Brattle jumps from chapter five to chapter eight in *The Port-Royal Logic,* Bk. 2, for this section and Latin examples of asserting the roundness of the Earth and that Astronomers have reasons when they convince us that the Sun is much bigger than the Earth.

[25] "All philosophers teach that heavy things fall of their own accord."

[26] "Now stones are heavy things, therefore, they fall of their own accord."

[27] "But that is false; therefore it is possible that something false be taught by all philosophers."

which they have called modal, bec: the affirmation or negation in those is modyfied by one of the 4 modes: They are *Possibilis, contingens, impossibilis, necessarius*; and because every mode may be either affirmed or denied, as *est possibile, non est possibile*, and likewise joyned either with an affirmative or negative proposition, as *Terra est rotunda*; *Terra non est rotunda*, every mode may have 4 propositions, and all the modes together, sixteen.[28]

Cap. 3. Of the nature of incident Propositions, which constitute a part of complex Propositions.

Before we proceed to compound Propositions, it will not be amisse to propose some farther considerations concerning the nature of incident propositions which are parts of the subject and predicates in Propositions complex according to their matter.

1. It was said that those are termed incident Propositions, whose subject is the pronoun *Qui*; as here, *homines qui sunt creati ad cognoscendum et amandum deum*; or, *homines qui sunt pii*; the term *homines* being taken away, that which remains is the incident proposition:[29]

But here we must call to mind what we proposed in the 7th chapt of the forementioned part, (Page. 28) how that Additaments of complex terms are of 2 sorts; The first, which may be termed simply explicative, being, when the Additament does no ways change the Idea of the term, or when nothing is added which does not agree to the term in it's full extension; as in the first example, *homines qui sunt creati ad cognoscendum et amandum Deum.*

The Second, which we called determinative, being, when the Additament does not agree to the term in it's full extension but restrains and determines the signification thereof; as in the second example, *homines qui sunt pii*:—whence it follows, that the pronoun is somtimes explicative, somtimes determinative.

Now we are to note, that when the pronoun is explicative, the predicate of the incident proposition is affirmed of the subject to which the pronoun is referred (althô it happens only incidently in respect of the

---

[28] Arnauld's *The Port-Royal Logic*, Bk. 2, chap. 8, goes on to give the AEIO and explain the mnemonic words that go along with it. Brattle will give the AEIO later.

[29] Brattle backtracks to *The Port-Royal Logic*, chap 6, for this section. The Latin: "men who are created to know and love God; or men who are pious."

whole proposition) so that the subject it self may be put in the place of the pronoun, as we may see in the first example, for instead of saying *homines qui sunt creati ad cognoscendum et amandum,* we might have said *homines sunt creati ad cognoscendum et amandum Deum.*

But if the pronoun is determinative, the predicate of the incident proposition is not properly affirmed of the subject to which the pronoun is related; for if as to this proposition, *homines qui sunt pii, sunt misrecordes*,[30] I should put in the place of, *Qui, homines,* and say *homines sunt pii,* there would be a false proposition, for so men *quatenus* men[31] would be said to be pious, which is not true. but in the other proposition *homines qui sunt pii, sunt misrecordes,* neither all men in generall, nor any men in particular are said to be *pii*; but the mind from an Idea of man and an Idea of piety joyn'd together, frames a total Idea; to which it Judges that the Idea of *misrecordia* does belong: and so the mind in the incident proposition only Judges expressly that the Idea of piety may consist with the Idea of man which Idea's it may thence consider as united, and examine together what may agree to them from this union.

2. We may note that propositions are somtimes found doubly or trebly complex, since they may consist of many members; every one of which maybe complex by it self: in such propositions, the incident propositions may also be many and of a different kind since in these the pronoun may be determinative, in those it may be explicative, as in this example, *doctrina quæ collocat summum bonum in voluptate corporis, quæ fuit tradita ab Epicuro, est indigna Philosophe.*[32] *Indigna Philosophe* is the predicate of this Proposition, the rest is the subject which is a complex term including 2 incident propositions the first whereof has a determinative Pronoun, the second and explicative pronoun for it's subject.

3. And lastly we may note, that to know the nature of propositions and to find out whether the pronoun in the incident propositions be determinative or explicative, we must mind more the sense then the words of the speaker.

for complex terms occurr somtimes which seem to be incomplex or at

---

[30] Partridge uses the spelling "misrecordes" but Jeffries and Dunbar used "misericordes." The term means merciful or charitable; therefore, the Latin: "men who are pious are…"

[31] Men in general.

[32] Dickoff and James translate this in *The Art of Thinking,* 119: "The doctrine which identifies the sovereign good with the sensual pleasure of the body and which was taught by Epicurus is unworthy of a philosopher."

{least} not only complex, as really they are, because part of the signification is only in the mind of the speaker, and so is understood and not expressed as appears from what was Cap. 7. part. 1. where it was hinted that nothing is more usual in common discourse than to signifye singular things by genericall words.

Cap. 4. Of a Compound Proposition and the Species thereof.

A compound proposition is a proposition whose either subject or predicate is (at {least}) 2 fold. It has 2 sorts; one, when the composition is expressed; The other, when the composition lies hid; called *exponibilis*.

We may divide propositions of the first kind into 6 species; viz. copulative and disjunct; conditional and causal; Relative and discrete.

Of Copulative Propositions

Those are called copulative propositions which have more subjects or predicates connected by an affirmative or negative conjunction; i.e. *per et, nec:* for *non* or *nec* do act the same thing in these propositions which *et* does, if the negation be transferred from the nouns to the verb; as when I say, *Scientia et divitiæ non faciunt beatum*; here I do as fully couple *Scientiam* & *divitias* as I should, had I said *Scientia et divitiæ faciunt hominem vanum*.[33]

Copulatives may be divided into 3 sorts.

1. When more subjects do occur: as here *mors et vita sunt in manibus linguæ*.

2. when there are more predicates: as here, *homo habet vitam et rationem*.

3. When there are more both subjects and predicates: as here, *homo et angelus, existunt, et sunt creati*.[34]

---

[33] Brattle takes this chapter from Arnauld's *The Port-Royal Logic*, Bk. 2, chap. 9. The Latin: "Knowledge and riches will not make one happy.... Knowledge and riches make one vain."

[34] Example 1, that death and life are in the hands of the tongue, is from Arnauld's *The Port-Royal Logic*, Bk. 2, chap. 9; however, Brattle chooses his own examples for 2, "a person has life and reason," and 3 "humans and angels exist and are created."

Compendium of Logick

¶ Note, that the verity of these propositions does depend on the truth of both parts; for if I should say *Fides et bona opera sunt ad salutem necessaria*,[35] the proposition would not be true unless each were necessary unto salvation; according to which, if I should say, *fides et divitia sunt necessariæ ad salutem*, the proposition would be false althô faith is necessary and that reason is because riches are not necessary.

of Disjunct Propositions.

Disjunct propositions are such propositions as contain in them a disjunct conjunction: as, *Amicitia pares aut accipit, aut facit*.[36]

The verity of these propositions ariseth from a necessary opposition of the parts which admitts no tertium.

Of Conditional Propositions.

Conditional propositions are such whose parts are united by that conditional particle [*si*]. The former part wherein the condition is found, is called the Antecedent, the latter part the consequent:—*Si anima est Spiritualis*, this is the antecedent, *erit et Immortalis*, this is the consequent: This consequence is sometimes mediate and somtimes Immediate: MEDIATE when there is nothing in the terms which conjoynes the 2 parts: as here, *Si terra stataria est, sol movetur:—Si Deus est Justus, mali punientur*.[37] these consequences are good but yet not Immediate; bec: the parts having no common term are connected only by that which is in the mind and is not uttered. IMMEDIATE, when the 2 parts are conjoyn'd by a common term. as here, *Si mors est transitus ad vitam meliorem, mors est expectibilis*.[38]—Vid. page 89. 90. *cui tit Ars cogitandi*.

Here the truth of the propositions is not looked at, but only the truth

---

[35] This phrase, "Faith and good works are necessary for salvation," is used by both Arnauld and Brattle and derived from James 2: 14–26.

[36] (P. Syrus, *Sententiae* 25) translated by Dickoff and James in *The Art of Thinking*, 129: "Friendship either finds friends equal or makes them so."

[37] These examples are from Arnauld's *The Port-Royal Logic*: "If the earth is stationary, then the sun moves; If God is just, then evil is punished."

[38] "If death is the transition to the happy life, death is to be desired." I have not been able to find which edition Brattle is citing.

of the consequence; for althô each part be false, yet if the consequence be legitimate, the proposition as conditional is to be accounted true. as here, *si voluntas creata potest Impedire re voluntas Dei absoluta effectum. Sortiatur, Deus non est omnipotens.*[39]

Of causal propositions.

Causal propositions are such which contain 2 propositions connected by those causal conjunctions, *Quia,* or *ut.*

> *Væ divitibus, quia in hoc mundo reaperunt consolationem suam: Tolluntur in Altum, et lapsu graviors ruant:—Possunt, quia posse videntur. &c:*[40]

To these propositions are reduced those which are called reduplicatives: as,

> *Homines quatenus homines sunt rationales; Reges in quantum reges soli Deo subsunt.*[41]

In order to the verity of these propositions it is requisite that one part be the cause of the other; hence it behooves each part to be true, for that which is false neither is nor can be a cause. yet each part may be true and yet false as causal. Thus a man may be unhappy and born under such a sign and yet his unhappiness not be because he was born under that sign:

---

[39] Dickoff and James in *The Art of Thinking,* 131, translate this: "If the will of the creature is capable of keeping the absolute will of God from being accomplished, then god is not omnipotent." This example was a fundamental premise in the logic of Christians who insisted on predestination.

[40] Brattle mixes three examples, apparently well known to his students. Dickoff and James in *The Art of Thinking,* 132, translate them: "Woe to the rich, because they have their comfort in this world. The wicked are exalted that, falling from a greater height, their demise may be the greater. (Claudian, *In Rufinum* 1. 22–23) They are able, because they believe themselves able. (Virgil, *Aeneid* 5.231.)

[41] "Men in general are rational; kings as kings depend on God alone."

Compendium of Logick

Of Relatives.

Relative propositions are such which contain any comparison or relation.

> *ubi est Thesaurus, ibi est cor:*
> *Qualis vita, Talis mors.*
> *Tanti es, quantum habes.*[42]

The truth of these propositions depends on the accuracy and goodness of the comparison or relation.

Of discretes

Discretive propositions are such in which there are divers Judgments, and this variety is noted by the particles, (*sed, tamen,*[43] of the like nature.)

> *fortuna opes auferre, non animum potest.*
> *et mihi res, non me, rebus submittere conor.*
> *cælum non animum mutant qui trans mars currunt.*[44]

The verity of these propositions depends on {the truth} of both parts and of the discretion used. for althô {each} part be true yet the proposition would be absurd, if there should be no opposition between the parts, as if I should say *Judas erat fur et latro et tamen ægre tulit quid Maria Magdalæna unguenta pretiosa in christum dominum effuderit.*[45]

---

[42] Dickoff and James in *The Art of Thinking*, 133, translate these three: "Where one's treasure is, there is his heart. As a man lives, so he dies. You are valued in the world in proportion to your wealth" (Seneca *Epistles* 65.14).

[43] But *or* however, nevertheless *or* yet.

[44] Dunbar and Jeffries have these three examples in a different order; however, Patridge's order follows *The Port-Royal Logic*. Dickoff and James translate these three classic adages in *The Art of Thinking*, 134: "Fortune can take away one's goods, but it cannot take away one's heart. (Seneca, *Medea* 176) Rather than being a victim of my circumstances, I try always to rise above them. (Horace, *Epistles*, I.1.19) He who crosses the seas changes only his county, not his disposition" (Ibid., II.27).

[45] This example from John 12: 3–5 is translated by Dickoff and James in *The Art of Thinking*, 134: "Judas was a theif, and nevertheless he could not abide Magdalene's pouring her ointments on Christ."

The second sort of compound propositions is such whose composition is more hidden: These may be reduced to 4 species. Viz: Exclusives, Exceptives, comparatives, Inceptives and desitives, of which we may read in *Ars cogitandi*, page 92 &c cap 8. p. 2d[46]

Cap. 5. of A Proposition as to it's quality & quantity:

A Proposition with respect to it's quality may be divided:
1. Into true & false.[47]

A true proposition is that which pronounces concerning a thing, as it is: as when I say, *Terra est rotunda*, the proposition is true, because I assert that of the earth which does agree to it; Viz. a sphærical figure.

A false proposition is that which pronounces concerning a thing otherwise then it is; as when I say, *homo est animal irrationale*.

The same proposition cannot be true and false together, for thus there would be 2 contradictories which is most absurd.

If it be objected, that this copulative proposition, *Cladius et Theophilus astra contemplantur*, is both true and false, because one of them does the other does not contemplate the starrs; The answer is most ready from what we before said concerning copulative propositions, viz. that their verity does depend on the truth of each part.

2. into affirmative and negative.

An affirmative proposition is that wherein the subject and adjunct are conjoyn'd or do agree: as when we say, *homo est animal*, the proposition is affirmative bec: the predicate [*Animal*] is said to agree with the subject [*homo*]

A negative proposition is that wherein the subjt & attribute are disjoyn'd or do disagree. as in this proposition, *homo non est brutum*.

The manner of the English speech differs from the Latine way as to this point, for [*non est*] in the latine tongue is the phrase of negation; whereas when we would deny, we do not say [It not is so] but still put the adverb after the verb, saying [it is not so]. Therefore to know whether the english proposition wherein [not] is contained, be affirmative or negative, we must consider whether, the adverb [not] bejoyned in signification with

---

[46] All the manuscript logics transcribe this wrong reference. Chapter eight should be chapter ten of *The Port-Royal Logic*, Bk. 2.

[47] Although the chapter uses a title similar to *The Port-Royal Logic*, Bk. 2, chap. 4, Brattle here draws mainly from LeGrand's *Institutio*, Pt. 2, chap. 13.

Compendium of Logick

the verb or copula, or whether it be separated therefrom; if the adverb be joyn'd with the copula, then [is not] is as it were but one word and denotes only negation, if it be separated from the copula and joyned with the predicate, it then makes the predicate an indefinite term and so leaves the proposition affirmative, as thô there was no [not] in the proposition; as in this instance,

   Man is not—a stone: is neg:
   Man is—not a stone: is affirm:[48]

And thus much concerning the quality of a Proposition.

A Proposition with respect to it's quantity may be divided (according to the difference of terms) into universal, particular and singular.

An universal proposition is that whose subjt, as a common term, is prefaced with an universal sign; such as ALL—being affirmative; and NO—being negative; for the term NO includes in it negation besides universality: NO man—ALL men—&c:

A particular proposition, is when a common term, is limited by that determining sign or note [some] Whether it affirms, as here, *aliquis amans est miser*; or denies; as here, *aliquis aulicus non est justus*.

A singular proposition is that, whose subjt is an individuum determined either by name, as when I say Aristotle is the prince of philosophers; or by sign, as when I say *hic vel ille homo est justus*.[49]

As for those propositions which are called Indefinite (viz. Such which have an universal term for their subject but note either of universality or particularity prefixed to that term, as here *homo est animal*, as to these propositions, I say) they are evermore to be accounted universal in disputes, and when used in common discourse or found among authors, they are to be accounted universal or particular propositions according to what the matter will allow, so that we need not constitute them as a fourth head of propositions.

Althô a singular proposition does differ from an universal, in that whereas the subjt of an universal is a common term, of a singular, an individual term, yet it has a greater affinity with an universal then with a particular, because the subject in as much as it is singular is necessarily taken

---

[48] This example does not appear in either *The Port-Royal Logic* or the *Institutio*; however, it does appear in a similar section in Morton's *A Logick System*, Pt. 2, chap. 3.

[49] This or that man is just.

according to it's full extension which is the cheif thing that is essential to an universal proposition, for though a proposition may be universal it signifies little whether the extension does comprehend more or fewer things, so that if it comprehends all that belong to the terms hence singular propositions in disputes are accounted universals: Therefore all propositions may be reduced to 4 kinds, being noted for the memory sake by the 4 vowels. A. E. I. O.

    A universal affirmative, as—*omnis vitiosus est servus.*
    E universal negative, as—*nullus vitiosus est beatus.*
    I particular affirmative, as—*aliquis vitiosus est dives.*
    O particular negative, as—*aliquis vitiosus non est dives.*[50]
And that they may be kept the more firmly in our memories they are proposed to us in this latine distich.

    Asserit A, negat E, verum generaliter ambo
    Asserit I, negat O, Sed particulariter ambo.[51]

Cap. 6. of the Opposition of Propositions having the same subjects and predicates.

Among Propositions which have the same subject and likewise predicate, some are termed subalternates, some contraries, some subcontraries and others contradictories.

    Subalternates are such as agree in quality and differ in quantity. as, *omnis circulus est figura—Quidam circulus est figura.* These subalternates prove somtimes to be both true, and somtimes to be both false. True—as some circle is a figure, every circle is a figure. false—as some circle is a triangle; every circle is a triangle.

    Contraries are 2 universal propositions of a different quality: As, *omnis homo est opulentus—nullus homo est opulentus.*[52]
These may both be false, but cannot both be true.

---

[50] "All viscious people are slaves. No viscious people are happy. Some viscious persons are rich. Some viscious persons are not rich."
[51] The distich is given in Arnauld's *The Port-Royal Logic*, Bk. 2, chap. 3: "both are general" or "both particular."
[52] *Opulentus* means splendidly rich.

Compendium of Logick

Subcontraries are 2 particular propositions of a different quality: as, *quidam homo est medicus,—quidam homo non est medicus.*

These may be both true, as, *aliquis homo est justus,—aliquis homo non est justus.* but cannot both be false; for if it be false,—*aliquem hominem esse justum,* it will necessarily be true, *nullum hominem esse justum,* bec: this proposition is contradictory to the former.

Contradictories are 2 propositions which differ both in quantity and quality; which causes opposition in the highest degree as,—*omnis homo est animal—Quidam homo non est animal.*
These cannot be both true nor yet both false.

Some term the opposition an affection of propositions, and annex to it 2 more Viz. Equivalence and conversion. and accordingly do define

Equivalence to be a reconciling these opposites by inserting the negative particle [*non*]

Conversion is a changing of the subject & predicate the same quality remaining:—but it is enough that we have mentioned these things and therefore we here conclude this sixth and last chapter of the second part and passe hence to our Third part of Logick.

The Third Part of Logick

Wherein is considered the nature of discourse or argumentation &c.

Cap. 1. Of Reasoning, discourse or argumentation.

We now come to the third operation of the mind, or discourse which is the inferring of one axiome from another: for to reason or discourse is nothing else but to know one thing from another being known, and there reasoning is the knowledge of one thing deduced from the knowledge of another; as when a man inferrs *Cællum esse extensum* from this that everybody is extended.

Whence, as Judgment or the second operation of the mind adds assertion to the first, so Reasoning or the third operation adds, to the second, deduction or illation.

In every argumentation or discourse 2 things specially are to be attended to, viz the question or thing proposed, and the argument or reason to prove.

Hence an argumentation or reasoning consists of 2 parts, the Antecedent & the consequent, or in the words of the schooles, the part inferring and the part inferred: THAT is propos'd or promis'd, THIS follows, and is gathered from what proceeded; as when it is said, *Angelus est Immaterialis, igitur est indivisibilis*; for the former sentence has the notion of an Antecedent, and the latter of a consequent.

If the Antecedent is not more known and certain then the consequent, it will by no means attain it's end of arguing.

There are 3 propositions contained in an argumentation:

The first is called the Major, in which the major term is disposed with the medium and is put in the first place in a syllogism; whence by many (in way of eminence) it is called Propositio, in that it is proposed as the foundation of the whole argumentation.

The second is called the minor, in which the less term is disposed with the medium and placed in the second place in a syllogism. By some it is called Assumptio because it is as it were assumed for aid to infer the 3^d Proposition.

The third is called conclusio, in which the major and minor terms are disposed: some term it ILLATIO and CONSEQUATIO in that it follows upon and is inferred from what went before, by force of the illative, *ergò, igitur*, &c.

The 2 former propositions in an argumentation are called the premises, because they do preceed the conclusion which necessarily follows from them if the syllogism be perfect; for it cannot be that the premises being true, the conclusion should be false: yet there is no need that in every argumentation the premises be expressed, for somtimes one alone may suffice that the understanding may perceive (at least confusedly) two propositions: for he that from this Antecedent, *omnis lapis est corpus* dos deduce this consequent, *Adamas est corpus*, did know it in the Antecedent in which it is Implicitly contain'd; and he that from this that, *corpus est Substantia*, does inferr that *Adamas est Substantia*, by knowing it to be a body does likewise know it to be A substance.

Every perfect syllogism consists of 3 Ideas. the Idea, which is the subject of the proposition, which is called *minor terminus*, because the subject is less extended than the predicate: 2. The Idea, which is the predicate otherwise called *major Terminus*, because more extended than the subject.

Compendium of Logick

3. The medium, or Idea which is found twice in the premises and which connects the 2 Ideas, as in this argumentation.
omnis substantia intellectualis est cogitans
mens est substantia intellectualis,
igitur mens est cogitans.[53]

It's evident that *Substantia intellectualis* is the middle term, that *cogitans* is the greater term, and that *mens* is the lesse term.

ARGUMENTATION in generall is divided into perfect and Imperfect:— perfect is a syllogism consisting of 3 propositions whose form is exact and most apt to persuade: for syllogism is nothing else but an internal speech or discourse of mind whereby out of 2 propositions laid down, {a third more} unknown is deduced, for if to this Proposition *Saturnus est planeta*, you add this *omnes planetæ à sole lucem mutuantur* you may deduce a third viz. *Saturnus igitur à sole lucem mutuatur*. Imperfect is an Enthymem, Induction, example, dilemma, and sorites whose form is less accurate, and less accomodated to perswade.

Cap. 2. Of Simple Syllogisms, both complex and incomplex. Syllogisms are either Simple or conjoyn'd.

Simple syllogisms are such as consist of simple propositions, or, those in which the middle term is at once conjoyn'd only with one of the terms of the conclusion.

Conjoyn'd, are such in which the middle term is at once coupled with both the terms of the conclusion. Thus this syllogism is simple.

omnis bonus princeps à subditis diligitur
omnis rex pius est bonus princeps, Ergò
omnis rex pius à subditis diligitur.[54]

Because the middle term is only separately conected with the subject of the conclusion [*Rex pius*] and with the predicate of it [*diligitur à subditis*]
But the following Syllogism for the contrary reason is is conjunct.

---

[53] "All intellectual substance is thinking substance / mind is intellectual substance, / therefore mind is thinking substance."
[54] "All pious kings are loved by their subjects."

> *Si regnum electivum factionibus obnoxium sit, non est diuturnum*
> *Sed regnum electivum factionibus obnoxium sit, Ergò*
> *Regnum electivum non est diuturnum.*[55]

Simple syllogism are of 2 kinds, viz, Incomplex or complex.

Clear or Incomplex syllogisms are those in which each term of the conclusion is entirely {connected} with the middle term; i.e. with the whole predicate in the major and with the whole Subject in the minor.

Implicite or complex syllogisms are such, in which the subject or predicate of a complex conclusion is only in part connected with the middle term in one of the premises, the remainder being conjoyn'd with the other proposition in the premises. as in this Syllogism.

> *Lex divina jubet ut Reges honoremus.*
> *Ludovicus XIV est Rex, Ergò*
> *Lex divina jubet ut Ludovicum XIV honoremus*[56]

These are called complex, not as if all syllogisms wherein complex propositions are contained are complex syllogisms, but because none do belong to this kind in which complex propositions are not found.

These Syllogisms are more usual then Incomplex ones which are seldom or never used, but in the schooles, and althô at first sight they may seem to deviate from the rules of the figures, yet they will appear true, when they are Reduced to incomplex syllogisms: for this syllogism

> *Scriptura Imperat ut medicos honoremus.*
> *Fernelius est medicus, ergò*
> *Scriptura Imperat, ut Fernelium honoremus.*[57]

---

[55] Dickoff and James in *The Art of Thinking*, 178, translate this as "If an elective state is subject to division, the state is not of long duration. / But an elective state is subject to division. / Therefore, an elective state is not of long duration."

[56] Dickoff and James in *The Art of Thinking*, 179, translate this as "The divine law binds us to honor kings. / Louis XIV is king. / Therefore, the divine law binds us to honor Louis XIV." LeGrand, in the *Institutio*, when he takes this example from *The Port-Royal Logic*, changes the king to Charles II. LeGrand obviously believed such changes would help with the acceptance of his logic. Brattle does not seem to have been concerned with such changes.

[57] This example from LeGrand's *Institutio*, Pt. 1, chap. 16. Fernelius is the name of a physician.

Compendium of Logick

Althô it be in the Second figure seemingly, yet the term *medicus* which is the medium is not properly the Attribute or predicate in this axiome, althô it be united with the Attribute, *Imperat*, for that which is truly the attribute is affirmed and does agree; whereas *medicus* is neither affirmed of nor does agree to, *Scriptura*; the whole argument is plainly in those propositions.

> *Medici sunt honorandi*
> *Fernelius est medicus, Ergò*
> *Fernelius est honorandus.*

and therefore this proposition (*Scriptura Imperat*) which before was accounted as the principal proves to be only Incident to the argumt being proposed only as a proof thereof; Whence it is manifest that this argument belongs to the first figure and is found in barbara; the term *Fernelius* being a singular name and so to have the force of an universal, as what were taught in the doctrine of propositions.

Cap. 3. of the figures and modes of Syllogism.

Something having been said as to the matter of simple Syllogisms, it remains that the form thereof be taken into consideration.

The form of a Syllogism is the lawfull disposition of the medium with the parts of the question which consists in these 2 things, viz: 1. that the middle term be suitably disposed with the extremes, i.e. the major and minor: & 2—that the propositions be duely described according to their quantity and quality; i.e. universality and singularity; affirmation & negation.

The first disposition of the terms i.e. of the medium with the 2 terms of the conclusion, is called, the FIGURE.

The second which is the description of the 3 Propositions according to these 4 differences A. E. I. O. is called the mode or MOOD.

So that, as the figure respects the remote matter of the syllogism, viz. the 3 terms in it, i.e. the medium and the 2 extremes: so the mode respects the next matter of it, viz, the 3 Propositions—Major, minor & conclusion.

The figures of Syllogism are usually accounted 3: (*Ars cogitandi*, makes 4.)[58]

The first figure is, when the middle term is the subject in the Major Proposition, & the predicate in the minor.

The Second figure is, when the middle term is the predicate in each of

---

[58] *The Port-Royal Logic*, Bk. 3, chap. 3, names the same three that Brattle names.

the premises; i.e. in the Major and minor.

The Third figure is, when the middle term is the subject in each of the premises.

The modes of Syllogism are commonly accounted 19 but may be reduced to 14 which we may include in the following verses.

> *Barbara, Cælarent, Primæ: Darii, Ferioque.*
> *Cæsare, Camæstres, Festino, Særne, Secundæ.*
> *Tertia, Darapti Sibi vendicat, atque Felapton.*
> *Adjungens disamis, datisi, Bocardo, Ferison.*[59]

The modes of the first figure are called direct and perfect, bec: all kinds of Questions, both affirmative and negative, universal and particular may be concluded by it: whereas in the second, only negations; and in the Third only particulars can be inferred.

In all the Artificial names proposed in the 4 verses, there are 3 syllables whereof the first denotes the major, the second the minor, and the Third the conclusion: and the vowel of every syllable signifies of what kind, the Proposition is; For A argues the Proposition to be universal affirmative; E, to be universal negative; I, particular affirmative; & lastly O, denotes the Proposition to be particular negative; According to the forementioned distick.

> *Asserit A, negat E, verum generaliter ambæ*
> *Asserit I, negat O, Sed particulariter ambæ.*

And for the further elucidating the nature & meaning of these figures and modes, We shall annex examples of the several modes of every figure.

The several modes of the first figure.

Bar—omni corpus est extensum
ba—omni saxum est corpus, Ergò
ra—omne saxum est extensum.[60]

Cæ—nullus modus est substantia,
la—omnis figura est modus, Ergò
rent—nulla figura est substantia.

[59] Both *The Port-Royal Logic*, Pt. 3, chap. 5, and the *Institutio*, Pt. 1, chap. 16, teach this memory device.
[60] Saxum means rock.

Compendium of Logick

Da—omni quad movetur, ab alio movetur,
ri—quoddam corpus movetur, Ergò
i—quoddam corpus ab alio movetur.

Fe—nullus spiritus est materialis,
ri—aliqua substantia est spiritus, Ergò
o—aliqua substantia non est materialis.[61]

The several modes of the second figure.

Cæ—nullus Lapis est planta,
Sa—omnis quercus est planta, Ergò
re—nullum quercus est Lapis.[62]

Cam—omni corpus est in infinitum divisibile,
Est—nullum punctum est in infinitum divisibile, Ergò
res—nullum punctum est corpus.

Fes—nullus usurarius Salvabitur,
ti—quidam Judæus est Usurarius
no—quidam Judæa non Salvabitur[63]

Ba—omne universale est pluribus communicabile.
ro—quædam natura non est pluribus communicabilis,
co—quædam natura non est universalis.

The several modes of the Third figure.

Da—omne corpus est in infinitum divisibile,
rap—omne corpus est Substantia, Ergò
ti—aliqua Substantia est in infinitum divisibilis.[64]

[61] Here again is the assertion of spiritual substance that is not material.
[62] Lapis is a stone.
[63] Jews, being usurers, will not be saved.
[64] Infinite divisibility was a conundrum often pondered and disputed in the second half of the seventeenth century.

Fe—nullus Angelus loco circumscribitur,
lap—omnis Angelus est quid finitum, Ergò
ton—aliquid finitum nullo loco circumscribitur.

Di—aliquis numerus potest augeri,
sa—omnis numerus est rerum affectio, Ergò
mis—aliqua rerum affectio potest augeri.

Da—Quisquis deo servit, Rex est,
ti—aliquis Servit Deo, qui pauper est, Ergò
si—aliquis pauper Rex est.

Bo—aliqua Stultitia non est vituperabilis,
car—omnis Stultitia est recta rationis defectus, Ergò
do—aliquis recta rationis defectus non est vituperabilis.

Fe—nullum corpus grave sponte deorsum tendit
ri—aliquod corpus grave est materia, Ergò
son—aliqua materia non sponte deorsum tendit

Cap. 4. Of some gen: rules of Syllogisms.

Since any conclusions cannot be deduced from all premises, it is requisite that some common rules or laws be proposed which are to be observ'd in all syllogisms.

The first Rule.

The Medium ought to be distributed; or the middle term cannot be taken particularly twice, but once at least must be universal.

 Because if the medium be taken twice particularly, it may then be taken according to different parts of the same totum and so nothing (at least) necessarily be concluded; for it is sufficient to argue an argument vicious, that the conclusion drawn from the premises might have been false, since (as we have heard) the syllogism only is to be accounted good whose conclusion so necessarily flows from the premises, that it cannot but be true.

Compendium of Logick

The Second Rule

Out of mere negatives nothing can be concluded.

The reason is, because two negative propositions do separate the subjt from the medium, and the predicate from the same medium; for from this, that two things are separated from a third thing, It does not follow that these 2 are or that they are not the same thing themselves as now, from this, *quòd mens non est corpus, et corpus non est perceptionis capax* It does not follow *quòd mens est perceptionis capax*.[65]

The Third Rule

The extremes of the conclusion must not be taken more universally, then they were taken in the premises.

Hence if either of the extremes be taken universally in the conclusion, the syllogism of necessity will be false, if that it was taken particularly in the 2 former propositions:—the Reason of this rule is deduced from the first rule, viz because, to argue to an universal from a particular is unlawfull: for from this, *Quòd aliquis homo sit vino deditus*, it cannot be inferred *Quòd omnis homo sit vino deditus*.[66]

The fourth Rule

The conclusion must always follow the weaker part that is; if either of the premises be negative, the conclusion ought likewise to be negative; and if either of the premises be particular, the conclusion also must be particular.

The reason of this rule is, bec: a negative Proposition being given, the medium is removed from one of the extremes of the conclusion, and therefore can by no means connect them, which is required to conclude affirmatively: And if any proposition be particular, an universal conclusion cannot be deduced from it; bec: if the universal conclusion be affirmative, the medium since it is universal, ought also to be universal in the assump-

---

[65] "Mind is not body, and the body is not receptive to perceptions. It does not follow that the mind is receptive to perceptions."
[66] "That one man has surrendered to wine does not mean that all men have surrendered to wine."

tion or lesse proposition; and then it should be the subject of it, since an attribute or affirmative Proposition is never taken universally; therefore the medium conjoyn'd with this subject will be particular in the minor: therefore it must be universal in the major, otherwise there would be a particular twice: therefore it will be the subject, and thence that major will also be universal; and so there cannot be an affirmative particular proposition in an argumentation, whose conclusion may be universal.

Cap. 5. Of conjunct or compound Propositions.

Those syllogisms are called conjunct which have each or at least one proposition conjunct: for it is not necessary to the constituting a compound syllogism, that it should consist of 2 conjunct Propositions, but only that it's major proposition be so compounded as to include in it the whole conclusion: but now since the major proposition of such a syllogism may be four fold, viz. conditional, copulative, Disjunct, & analogical.

CONDITIONAL syllogisms are those in which the major proposition is conditional and contains in it the whole conclusion; As.

> *Si mens humana sit corporea, potest dividi in partes*
> *atqui mens humana non potest dividi in partes, Ergò*
> *mens humana non est corporea.*[67]

The major consists of 2 Propositions, the first being the Antecedent (*simens humana sit corporea*) the second being the consequent, (*potest dividi in partes*).

There is a 2 fold figure of conditional syllogisms

The first figure is.

When in the minor proposition being simple; the Antecedent of the major is so placed, as that it is made the consequent of it in the conclusion, as in this Syllogism.

---

[67] "If the human mind be corporeal, it can be divided into parts. / But in fact human minds are not able to be divided into parts; therefore / human minds are not corporeal."

Compendium of Logick

> Si omnia creata per se subsistere nequeunt, necesse est ut a Deo con-
> serventur,
> alqui omnia creata per se subsistere {nequeunt ergo}
> necess: est ut à Deo conserventur.[68]

And this argument rests on this maxime; *posito Antecedente, ponitur et consequens.*[69]

The second figure is

When the consequent of the same major Proposition is taken away, that the Antecedent may be removed. As

> Si Johannes hanc uxorem ducit, desipit,
> Sed Johannes non desipit, Ergò
> hanc uxorum non ducit.[70]

This kind of argument is founded on this maxim, *Sublato Antecedente, tollitur et Consequens. Ponere*, is to affirm the Antecedent which was affirmed, and to deny the Antecedent which was denyed: and on the contrary remove is to affirm the consequent which was denied, or to deny the conseqt which was affirmed.

Conditional arguments may be vitiated 2 ways: 1. when a false conclusion is deduced from a true Major: when to wit the Antecedent is inferred from the conseqt; as when one argues

> Si Lapis est vivens, est Substantia,[71]
> Sed Lapis est Substantia, ergò
> Lapis est vivens.

---

[68] "If every created thing cannot subsist through itself, it is necessary that they subsist through God. / Indeed, every created thing cannot subsist through itself therefore, / it is necessary that they subsist through God."

[69] Loosely: "an antecedent must be followed by a consequent."

[70] "If John is married to this wife, he acts foolishly, / But John does not act foolishly, therefore / he is not married to this wife."

[71] "If a stone is living, it is a substance."

2. when the negation of a conseqt: is inferred from the negation of the Antecedent. as in the forementioned example.

> *Si Lapis est vivens, est Substantia,*
> *Sed Lapis non est vivens, Ergò*
> *Lapis non est Substantia.*

COPULATIVE syllogisms are only of one kind viz. when a copulative negative proposition being assumed afterwards one part is placed [*ponitur*] to take away the other part. as

> *non potest unum corpus planum simul esse et rotundum*
> *sed terra est rotunda, Ergò*
> *terra non est plana.*[72]

DISJUNCT syllogisms are those whose first proposition is disjunctive: i.e. whose parts are connected by *Vel*, or *Aut*. as

> *mors homini Accidit, vel anima vitio, vel corporis,*
> *sed non accidit animæ vitio, Ergò*
> *accidit corporis vitio.*[73]

There are 2 figures of disjunct syllogisms

The first figure is,

When one part is put that the other may be removed: [*ponitur, ut tollatur* &c:] as in the formentioned example.

---

[72] "A body is not able to be a plane and round at the same time / but the earth is round, therefore / the earth is not a plane."
[73] "Human death happens either to the corrupt soul or body, / but it does not happen to the corrupt soul, therefore / it happens to the corrupt body."

Compendium of Logick

The Second Figure is

When one part is taken away, that the other may be placed as here.

> *qui primò nobis retulerunt dari Antipodes, verum dicebant, aut nobis Imponebant,*
> *sed illi verum dicebant, Ergò*
> *nobis non Imposuerunt.*[74]

A disjunct syllogism is grounded on this principle; viz: *duo contradictoria simul esse vera non posse.*[75]

ANALOGICAL (or proportional) syllogisms are when the proposition which is in the Major, is protracted or dilated which happens when the Consequents in the minor being accounted as Antecedents are further referred to other consequents; as when it is said, *Ita se habent 2 ad 4.sicut 3 ad 6. Ita se habent 4 ad 8. ut 6. ad 12. Ergo Se habent 2 ad 8.sicut 3. ad 12.*[76] and because the relates are the media with which the extremes do agree therefore hence it may be inferr'd that the extremes do agree among themselves.

Cap. 6. of Imperfect Argumentations.

Imperfect Argumentations receive their denomination not on account of the matter out of which they are compounded, but of their form which is less accurate and in comparison of a syllogism less disposed and digested: for in these argumentations, the Antecedent consists only of one proposition whether simple or complex; and such argumentations are Enthymema, Inductio, Exemptum, Sorites et dilemma.

ENTHYMEM is an argumentation in which only one of the premises is expressed, the other being undiscovered; which yet if any one should add, would constitute a perfect syllogism: as here

---

[74] "Those who first reported to us that antipodes existed either were telling the truth or were imposing upon our credulity, / but they were telling the truth, therefore / they were not imposing upon us." Jeffrey B. Russell in *Inventing the Flat Earth* (New York: Praeger, 1991), discusses the significance of knowledge of the Antipodes in history which were considered the opposite quarter of the Earth.

[75] Loosely: "It is impossible for contradictories to be both true at the same time."

[76] "2:4 = 3:6 = 4:8 = 6:12 therefore 2:8 = 3:12"

> *Te à periculo liberare valui,*
> *Ergò et perdere*:

for by adding the Major it becomes a syllogism, thus

> *Quicunq Salvare valet, valet et perdere.*
> *Sed ego te liberare valui, Ergò et perdere.*[77]

INDUCTION is an argumentation by which from the reckoning up many singulars, some universal is concluded; as

> *hic Triangulus comprehenditur tribus lineis, et iste triangulus comprehenditur tribus lineis, et ita de cæteris, Igitur omnis triangulus comprehenditur tribus lineis.*[78]

Here it is requisite that the enumeration be made of all the species or parts, for if any one is wanting, the proposition will be denied.

EXAMPLE is an Imperfect Argumentation whereby from one syllogism singular, by reason of a like respect between them, another Singular is inferred as when from this, that
Cæsar magis clementiâ quàm armis populum Romanum abstrinxit, I gather *Principem magis ad clementiam quàm ad arma debere recurrere, ut Subditos sibi devinciat.*[79]

SORITES is an argumentation consisting of many propositions so disposed, that the predicati of the Precedent Proposition becomes the subject of the following one: and thence the last predicate in the conclusion must be given to the first Subject. as here

---

[77] "He who is powerful enough to save you is powerful enough to destroy you. / Now I am powerful enough to liberate you, and therefore to destroy you."
[78] "This triangle...and that triangle..., and so do the rest; therefore, all triangles have three lines."
[79] "Caesar controlled the Roman people through clemency more than through arms....Thus a ruler ought to resort to clemency rather than to arms in order to subdue his people."

> *Avari multa concupiscunt; qui multa concupiscunt, plurimis {rebus} indigent; qui plurimus rebus indigent sunt miseri; Igitur avari sunt miseri.*[80]

N.B. This argument dos not conclude the truth, unless when what is spoken of the Attributes is also said of the subject; thus this argument is not good.

> *Caro salsa ad bibendum excitat; bibendo situs extinguitur; ergò caro salsa sitim extinguit.*[81]

because saltness in flesh does not excite to drink only by Accident, in as much as it causes a certain dryness in the throat which calls for moisture.

DILEMMA is from a disjunction of many Prepositions opposite amongst themselves whereby the Respondent is put to a stand which part so ever he looks upon & considers of as when a man argues against another for acting some wickedness.

> *Aut Scivisti te in Regem deliquisse aut non; Si Scivisti, qui ausus es majestatis Legem violare? si non, cur patrato Scelere, te in pedes conjecisti?*[82]

A Dilemma maybe vitiated 2 ways; 1. when the disjunctive proposition (on which the dilemma is founded) does not contain in it all the members of the dividend. As, if one should thus argue against marriage.

> *Aut uxor ducenda, pulchra est aut deformis, si pulchra, Zelotypiam pariet; si deformis, displicebit. Ergò uxor non est ducenda.*[83]

---

[80] "The avaricious are very greedy; those who are very greedy desire many things; those who desire many things are miserable; therefore, the avaricious are miserable."

[81] "Salty meat makes one desire to drink; drinking solves the problem; therefore, salty meat was the problem to be solved."

[82] "Either you know you have disobeyed the king's law or not. If you know you have, who are you to have dared to disobey the king's law? But if not, why, once the crime has been committed, do you throw yourself down to be trampled?"

[83] *The Port-Royal Logic*, Pt. 3, chap. 16, the *Institutio*, Pt. 1, chap. 19, and Morton's *A Logick System*, Pt. 3, chap. 2, (p. 0) all use similar examples for this type of dilemma: "Either a wife is beautiful or ugly, if beautiful then she incites jealousy; if ugly she will displease. Therefore, one should not marry a wife."

for there are some women, *quæ non adeò formosæ ut Zelotypiam in maritum inducant*; and yet no *adeò deformes ut displiceant*.⁸⁴ 2. when the particular conclusions of any part are not necessary: Thus; It is not necessary that a beautifull woman should cause jealousie in her husband since she may be so prudent and chast as to give full assurance of honesty to her husband: and likewise it is not necessary, that a deformed wife should be ungratefull to her husband, since she may be so endued with other virtues and qualifications as abundantly to compensate what she wants in that respect.

He that uses a dilemma ought to take heed lest it prove such an one as may be retorted on him to prove the quite contrary to what it was brought to prove: Thus when Romulus (who drank but little wine) was told that if all men should drink as he did wine would be cheap: to whom he answered; no, if all men should drink as I do wine would be dear, for I drink as much as I will:—this is termed by some a VOLENTUM, but properly may be reduced to a dilemma.

Cap: 7: of Syllog: Apodictical, topical & Sophistical

Having heretofore spoken of the matter & form of syllogism, it remains that we now consider it as to it's end and use: and since the design of a syllogism is to beget knowledge, opinion, or error, hence it is divided into Apodictical, (which respects knowledge) Topical, (which respects opinion) and Sophistical (which designs error and deceit.)

That what is to be said concerning these several sorts of syllogisms may the better be understood, it seems needfull first to explain the nature of science, opinion, error, and faith.

SCIENCE is that certain and evident knowledge which we have of anything: for that which is so evident to us as that we are certain of it, we are said to know; wherefore that knowledge of a conclusion is certain & evident, when the premises, on which it depends as principles, are so.

OPINION is not plainly a certain knowledge, but is attended with a certain fear of wavering of the understanding in assenting. for, opinion is indeed a true assent, but doubtfull and uncertain.

ERROR is an opinion opposite to that which is true.

FAITH is a persuasion grounded on the Testimony of another, which

---

[84] "Some women are not so beautiful so as to incite jealousy nor so ugly so as to displease."

may be true or doubtfull according to the difference of the Authority on which it relyes: Thus, the faith which we have to God is most firm, because we know that he is true and cannot lye; but humane faith hath always something of uncertainty in it, since there is no man but can deceive if he will.

This Premised,

DEMONSTRATION (or Apodictical syllog:) is a syllogism consisting of true, Immediate and more known premises which are the causes of the conclusion. those propositions are said to be true and Immediate which cause faith by themselves and not by any other thing; or those things which are known from their own terms; as, *Quod libet est, vel non est*:[85] for there is a power innate with us, whereby we do assent to first principles.

demonstration is 2 fold: first, *a Priori*, and *proptor quid*; Second *a posteriori, et quia*.

Demostration *à priori* (which only is simply demonstration) is that in which the effect is demonstrated by it's cause, as when we prove the existence of light, by the existence of the Sun.

Demonstration *a posteriori*, is when the cause is demonstrated by the effect: as when by the existence of light, the existence of the Sun is shown.

TOPICAL syllogism, (which is also termed *suasorious*[86] and probable) is that which is concluded from probable premises: or, whose premises do not carry before them a necessity of connexion between the subject and medium, or medium and predicate: for althô A conclusion which it proves has more of evidence than of obscurity in it, yet it leaves something of hesitation and doubt behind it, whereby it comes to pass that the understanding cannot assent to it without a scruple: whence it is said, that a topical syllogism does indeed persuade, but does not force to an assent as demonstration does.

Probables are such axiomes as seem to all men, or the most of men, or the wisest of men, and of those to the most or choisest, to be true: Thus it seems probable to all men, that the Summer will be hot, yet it is not certain, since it sometimes happens to be cold in the Summer season. to many it seems probable, that medicine is necessary to cure diseases, when yet it oft times happens, either thrô the ignorance of the Physitian, or the difault of the sick person, or the ill temperament of the air, that the Physick does more hurt then good: Thus, wise men think that Learning is

---

[85] "Either a thing pleases or it does not."
[86] Persuasive.

to be desired by all men; yet there are many who despise it: Lastly, it seems to the eminentest[87] of men, that the earth is moved in a circle, and that the Sun stands still in the midst of the world, and yet many there are who despise this notion, and maintain the contrary.

Wherefore all those syllogisms whose premises are contingent, and argue no necessary connexion, between the subject and medium, or between the medium and predicate, are called topical or Probable

SOPHISTICAL, or paralogistical syllogism, is a discourse consisting of Propositions of none but only apparent truth: & bec: it consists of false propositions, It begets errour & deceit, for from such a cause such an effect is produced. as here

> *Omnes lineæ à puncto ad punctum ductæ sunt æqualis,*
> *Sed linea recta et obliqua possunt ab eodem puncto duci ad idem punctum,*
> *Ergò linea recta et obliqua sunt æquales.*[88]

For althô this demonstration seems to be geometrical, and the præmises to be necessary, yet are they false.

This fallacy arises 3 ways, either from the matter; as if one should say

> *Quicquid non amisisti, habes,*
> *uxorum non amisisi, ergò, uxorum habes.*[89]

The major here seems to be probable, when yet it is false. or from the form; As

> *veritas odium parit,*
> *quoddam mendacium odium parit, Ergò*
> *quoddam mendacium est veritas.*[90]

---

[87] The *Institutio*, Pt. 1, chap. 19.13, has "Spectatissimus," meaning a precise astronomer or careful sky-gazer.
[88] "All lines between two points are equal, / Now a straight line and a slanting line run from the same point to the same point, / Therefore the straight and slanting lines are equal."
[89] "Whatever you haven't lost, you have. / If you haven't lost your wife, you have a wife."
[90] "Truth incites hatred, / A lie incites hatred, Therefore / truth is a lie."

For altho̊ at first view the consequence seems to be legitimate, yet it is false, since this syllogism consists of 2 affirmative præmises and yet is found in the 2^d figure. or from each; i.e. Matter and form; As

> *Quicquid non perdidisti, habes,*
> *Sed pileum (quem semel amissum recuperâsti) habes, Ergò*
> *hunc pileum non amisisti.*[91]

This argumentation neither consists of a probable Major, nor of a form suitable to conclude any thing, since it is contrary to the rules of the 2^d figure:

Aristotle reckons 13 sorts of those fallacies, 6 being in the words themselves, and 7 in the sense of the words, but of this we have heard sufficiently elsewhere.

To Avoid those catches of fallacies there is no safer way, then to reduce the argt: to it's due form, and to mind the medium whether it bears the same sense in the major proposition which it does in the minor: for thus the caviller will readily be discovered.

Ars Cogitandi reduces sophisms to nine heads, accounting all others so crasse and palpable, as to need noe caution against.[92]

The first sophism, is
To Prove Something That Is Aliene to the Question.

This sophism by Aristotle is termed *ignoratio elenchi*, i.e. the ignorance of that which is to be proved against the Adversary.

The second sophism, is
To Suppose That Which Is in the Question.

This by Aristotle is termed Petitio Principii.

---

[91] "Whatever you haven't lost, you have, / But your hat (which once was lost but now is found) you have, Therefore / You haven't lost that hat."
[92] *The Port-Royal Logic*, Bk. 3, chap. 19.

WILLIAM BRATTLE

The third sophism, is
TO ASSIGN SOMETHING FOR A CAUSE WHICH IS NOT A CAUSE.

This sophism is called, *non causa pro causâ*, and is very usual.

The fourth sophism, is
AN IMPERFECT ENUMERATION.

When we argue that this or that thing is not, bec: it is not this or that way, when as it may be several other wayes.

The fifth sophism, is
TO PRONOUNCE CONCERNING A THING, FROM SOMTHING THAT AGREES TO IT ONLY BY ACCIDENT.

This sophism in the schooles is termed FALLACIA ACCIDENTIS: an absolute conclusion and without all restriction is deduced from something that is true only accidentally.

The sixth sophism, is
TO ARGUE FROM A DIVIDED TO A COMPOUND SENSE, OR FROM A COMPOUND SENSE TO A DIVIDED ONE.

Of these sophisms one is termed, FALLACIA DIVISIONIS the other FALLACIA COMPOSITIONIS: *cæci vident*, i.e. *illi qui fuorunt cæci, et Iam non sunt, vident*.[93]

The seventh sophism, is
TO ARGUE FROM SOMETHING THAT IS TRUE *Secundum Quid*, SOMETHING TO BE SIMPLY TRUE.[94]

In the schooles it is termed *à dicto secundum quid, ad dictum Simplicitòr*.

---

[93] "The blind see, ie. those who were once blind and not able to see, now see."
[94] Confusing a qualified truth to a truth.

Compendium of Logick

The Eighth Sophism, is
TO ABUSE THE AMBIGUITY OF WORDS.

Hither may be reduced all those syllogisms which labour under a fourth term.

The ninth Sophism, is
FROM A VICIOUS INDUCTION TO INFERRE AN UNIVERSAL CONCLUSION.

Of all those heads *Ars cogitandi* treats at large in the nineteenth chapter of his third part.

Cap. 8. Of the places whence the medium is fetched.

The PLACES OF ARGUMENTS, as they are called by Rhetoricians and Logicians, are certain generall heads, to which may be reduced those common proofs which we may use when treating on several things.

Ramus finds fault with Aristotle and the schoolmen for treating of these places after their having proposed Rules about argumentation.

He argues that the matter ought to be gathered together, before we think of disposing it, and therefore that whereas the deduction of those places does find out and heap together this matter, therefore it ought to preceed &c.

But Ramus's argument is very weak; for althô it be necessary that the matter be found out before it be disposed, yet it is not necessary that we should learn to find out the matter, before we learn to dispose it; for here it is sufficient, if we have in readiness some general matter out of which examples may be formed; and this, the mind it self & common sense without the help of Art, may sufficiently help to: It is therefore true, that we ought to have matter before we propose the rules of syllogism; but also false, that this matter ought first to be found out by the places of arguments, or by the help of Art.

They that have treated of these *places*, have differently divided them.

The division which Cicero and Quintilian made is very Immethodical, thô accomodated to court orations which it especially looks at.

Ramus's division does unprofitably trouble us with subdivisions.

Claubergius is most accurate, and therefore we shall keep to him in this chapter.[95]

Arguments are either fetched from Grammar, from Logick, or from Metaphysicks.

Grammatical Places.

Are taken either from Etymology; or from words derived from the same root, which by Latines are called conjugata and by Graecians παϛώνυμa

Logical Places

Are taken from universalls, (Genus, Species, difference, Proprium et Accident) as also from definition and division. And here we may add some common axioms which, althô not very profitable, yet because commonly received and embraced, will not be needlessly proposed.

1. *Quod affirmatur aut negatur de genere, affirmatur aut negatur de specie*: As, *Quæ in homines cadunt, etiam in potentes cadunt.*[96]
2. *destructo genore, destruitur species*: As, *Qui nunquam Judicat, iniqß non Judicat.*[97]
3. *destructis omnible, Specieble, distruitur Genus*: Thus, *formæ, dictæ substantiales (exceptâ animâ rationali) nec corpus sunt, nec Spiritus, Ergô non sunt substantia.*[98]
4. *Si de re quâlibet affirmari vel negari possit differentia totalis, negari vel affirmari*

---

[95] These criticisms and the praise for Johann Clauberg's *Logicae, Vetus et Nova* (1654) come from *The Port-Royal Logic*, Pt. 3, chap. 18.

[96] Dickoff and James in *The Art of Thinking*, 241, translate this as "Whatever is affirmed or denied of the genus is affirmed or denied of the species. What belongs to all men belongs to great men."

[97] Dickoff and James in *The Art of Thinking*, 241, translate this as "In denying the genus, we also deny the species: He who does not judge does not judge ill."

[98] Dickoff and James in *The Art of Thinking*, 241, translate this as "In denying the species, we deny the genus: 'Substantial' forms (except the rational soul) are neither body nor spirit; therefore, these forms are not substances."

Compendium of Logick

poterit Species: As, *extensis non convenit cogitationi, Ergô illa non est corpus.*[99]
5. *Si de re quâlibet affirmari vel negari possit proprium, affirmari vel negari poterit Species*: thus *cum Impossibile sit cogitationis medietatem Imaginari, vel cogitationem Sphæricam, vel quadratam, Impossible est, utilla sit corpus.*[100]
6. *affirmatur vel negatur definitum, de quo affirmatur vel negatur definitio*: as, *Pauci mutmuntur Justi, quia pauci sunt qui firmam stabiliunq voluntatum habent suum unicuiq reddendi.*[101]

Metaphysical Places.

Are some general Attributes agreeable to all beings, unto which many arguments may be reduced, such as those that are taken *à causa, effectu, Toto, Partibile, Oppositis*,[102] therefore add nothing further to this third part of Logick. next follows the fourth part of Logick.

The Fourth Part of Logick

of Method, or an orderly disposition of our thoughts.

Cap. 1. of the general method of knowing.

Althô perhaps there may be some men of so sagacious a witt, that without difficulty they may peirce into difficult things, and know how to solve

[99] Dickoff and James in *The Art of Thinking*, 241, translate this as "If we affirm or deny a difference, then we affirm or deny the corresponding species: Extension does not belong to thought, thought is not matter."
[100] Dickoff and James in *The Art of Thinking*, 242, translate that as "If we can affirm or deny the essential attribute then we can affirm or deny the species: It is impossible to imagine half a thought, or a round thought, or a square one; so thought cannot be body."
[101] Dickoff and James in *The Art of Thinking*, 242, translate this as "We affirm or deny what is expressed by the defined word when we affirm or deny what is expressed by the defining words: Few persons are just, because few persons have the firm and abiding will to give to each what is due."
[102] "Cause, effect, whole, part, opposition."

abstruse questions, yet will none ever obtain certain knowledge, unless they first know how their mind is to be directed, and what order it ought to observe: and therefore method is necessary, or some doctrine whereby the mind may be helped in searching for truth; and may free it self from error, confusion and obscurity.

This METHOD may be defined, such a series or disposition of things to be handled as may be most accomodated to the capacity of the Learner.

That our minds may be sufficiently helped here, & so knowledge obtained 3 things are requisites

1. that the thing proposed be clearly and distincly perceived.
2. that we pass a right Judgment on the things thus rightly perceived. &c
3. that we lay up in our memories truths thus discovered, or those things which we have rightly perceived and Judged of. by the due observance of these 3 precepts we may help all the infirmities of our minds. for since the ostacles of knowledge are either, 1—Too great præcipitance of mind, A clear & distinct perception takes away that; 2—Error or doubt: they are removed by this right Judgment, or, 3—oblivion and forgetfulnesse: that likewise will be prevented by this memory or Remembrance.

A clear and distinct perception will be much furthered, if removeing all precipitance, we attend heedfully to the thing proposed, and view it as it were with internal eyes; to which it will conduce much if we consider of but one thing at once, for plenty of objects does certainly breed confusion.

That we may duely observe the 2^d precept, is requisite evermore that knowledge preceed Judg: and that simple terms be placed before such as are complex and if at any time it happens, that we are brought into doubt concerning any thing, we shall readily escape error, if we suspend Judgment, affirming or denying nothing til more light is brought, and all obscurities therefore removed.

Yet we are not to think that all things which are true do carry the same certainty with them; for some things are only contingently true, i.e. they might be false. thus, if I Judge that a man is pious because he frequents the church, lives in the practice of prayer &c which things ordinarily are sufficient for me to Judge a man pious by, and yet it is possible that this man may be void of all true piety notwithstanding these his actings. somethings are altogether certain and true; as propositions of eternal verity, *bis quatore sunt octo, Ternarius est numerus* &c:[103]

---

[103] "2 x 4 = 8, 3 is a number."

But because it availes little or nothing to know the nature of things, unless we withall Remember them, we are therefore to Learn how things understood by us may be committed to memory, and so to be Imprinted on it as to be hardly lost or removed thence: and this will readily be attained if we follow the order of our method, i.e. if we commit nothing to memory but what has been found out and rightly Judged of by us: for we dayly find that things clearly perceived are most strongly fastened on our mind, and that such things as are proposed in order are more easily retained, then such as are confused.

How ever we shall yet further promote and help memory, if we get a tranquill and even spirit, and suffer not our understanding to be distracted about too many objects: and we shall the better retain things in memory if we oft go over them in our minds, diligently reflecting on them, and attending to them as we speak them.

Cap. 2. of Special method and first of Analysis.

The word Method is here to be taken somewhat more strictly then it was in the preceeding article: for our design there was only to teach Novists what order they ought to keep in the obtaining of knowledge: Whereas here we are not only to treat of the forming conceptions, but also enquiry is to be made how we may regularly dispose our conceptions when framed. and therefore

METHOD is 2 fold; for it either finds out the truth and so is called Analysis, or method of Resolution (which likewise may be termed method of invention) or it teaches the truth when found out, and is termed Synthesis, or method of composition, which likewise may be called the method of handling a doctrine.

Of Analysis

The whole body of any science is seldom Analysed or delivered Analytically; Analysis being only in use to solve questions. Every question is either concerning a name, or a thing.

By the question of a name here we understand not that which hunts for names whereby things may by signified, but that which searches for things signfied by names. of this kind are such as tend to the solving of

(Ænigma's or) Riddles; and such as do explain the obscure sense of A criptical Reader.

The question of A thing is 4 fold.
 1. when we search for a cause from effects: Thus when we consider the Attractive power in a Load Stone and enquire into the cause of it.
 2. the 2^d kind is; when from causes we find out effects as when we consider of the wind's blowing and the water's flowing, and enquire into the benefit of the one or other; how they might prove useful and advantagious to us.
 3. the third kind is; when from parts we are lead to a knowledge of an whole: thus many numbers being given, enquiry is made what the summe of all would be, they being added together.
 4. the 4th and last kind is; when an whole being given and one part, enquiry is made what another part is. thus when a numberd is given, and part of it is taken away, we ask, what is the remainder.

Here we are to note that as in Analysis so in synthesis, we are evermore to proceed from A thing more known to a that which is less known. this rule is common to all method, neither is any method to be accounted good which at all deviates from this principle: yet in this, Analysis or method of Resolution differs from that which is called method of composition, that Analysis proceeds from lesse generalls to more generalls, whereas synthesis begins at a more general and goes to a less general: for thus if we enquire whether man's soul is Immortal its evident that we do not go from universal axioms after this manner, *nulla substantia propriè dess{...}itur, destructio nihil aliud est, quam partium dissollutio*, and thence qu*od partibus caret destrui nequit*;[104] but on the other hand we gradually arise to those general notions: so that those 2 methods [Analysis and Synthesis] do not differ among themselves any other way than the ascent & descent of the same mountain: or the way whereby we go from a valley

---

[104] Brattle and LeGrand both follow *The Port-Royal Logic*, Bk. 4, chap. 2, on the use of logic in this example. Dickoff and James in *The Art of Thinking*, 307, translate this, "Strictly speaking, we may say that no substance perishes. / What is called destruction is only a rearrangement of parts. Therefore, what has not parts cannot be destroyed."

Compendium of Logick

to the top of a mountain and that very way whereby we go from the top of the mountain to the valley which lies at the foot of it.[105]

Cap. 3. Of the Method of Composition.

Synthesis, or method of composition consists cheifly in this, that it proceeds from more general things to lesse generals and from more simple to more compounded things: and by this mode of proceeding all repetitions are avoided which ever more breed either confusion or tediousness.

That this method may be in all respects taught clearly, and first to obtain it's designed end, Viz a clear and distinct knowledge of the truth, many things are heedfully to be observed: but since generall precepts separated from all matter are very difficult to be understood; we shall consider the synthesis of Geometricians which is always thought most efficacious to demonstrate truth and persuade: we shall therefore show what is commendable in their Method, & then propose what their defects and failings were.

Since then Geometricians design'd to assert nothing but was most evident and certain, they Imagined that this their design might be attained if so be that they did heedfully observe these 3 rules.

1. that they left nothing ambiguous in the terms proposed.
2. that they deduced reasoning only from certain and evident principles; such principles as could be doubted of by no man that had his witts about him.
3. that they demonstratively proved every conclusion: demonstratively. i.e. by the help of premised definitions, evident and granted axioms, or propositions which no sooner are demonstrated but obtain the title of principles

To these 3 heads the whole of what Geometricians observe may be reduced, and so far they kept to a good rule and fam'd themselves, in that hereby they banished all disputations and controversies out of their schooles.

Nevertheless it cannot be denied, but that they have fallen into some

---

[105] Logic textbooks often used this analogy of climbing and descending a mountain which, to my knowledge, was first given in *The Port-Royal Logic*, Bk. 4, chap. 2. Arnauld gave two analogies, one geneological and the other ambulatory. The geneological never caught on. The image of climbing a mountain in pursuit of Truth was increasingly used in the late seventeenth century.

errors or defects, which althô (possibly) they have not carried them from their proposed end, have led them thrô many by-wayes and occasioned much roughness, of which their method or way might have been void, and wholly destitute.

      Their defects then were

1. That they laboured more about certainty then evidence; more about convincing the understanding then enlightning it. that is they laboured not so much to show the way how these and those truths came to be so, as to demonstrate that they are truths.

2. that they oftentimes prove those things which need no proof. i.e. althô they acknowledge that such things as are clear of themselves need no truth, yet they often attempt the proof of such truths.

3. that they demonstrate by something impossible. i.e. by some absurdity or Impossibility that would arise from that which is contrary to their Position:

4. that they demonstrate by things aliene & remote. This is an Imperfect way of demonstrating, being contrary to the ordinary course of nature which takes but one step at once.

5. that they do not observe the natural order of things i.e. by going from simples to compounds, and from generals to particulars: this fault, as also the 4th and some others are too often to be found in Euclids Elements.

6. that they do not sufficiently use divisions and partitions.

That which is censured and found fault with here as to the method of Geometricians is not, that they omitt any species of a genus which they design at any time to handle, but this viz—that they do not at first say of the genus that it has so many species and cannot have more because the general Idea of the genus cannot receive more differences and so proceed to the species: to make this more plain let us take this example.

Euclid in his first book has definitions of all the species of a triangle without premising the distribution of triangle in general; now who can but see that it would be much more clear if the matter were thus proposed.

A Triangle may be divided either according to it's sides or according to it's angles,

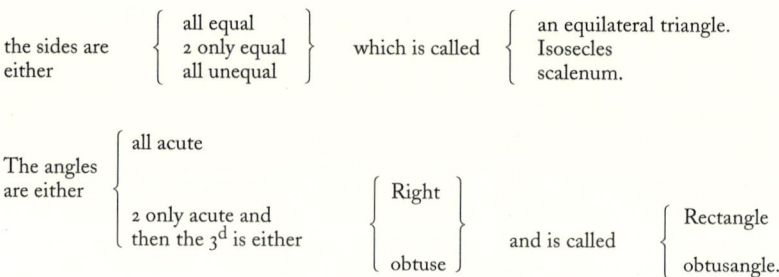

Thus have we at Large shown what is good & what is bad in the method of Geometricians and hence: we may be abundantly informed as to method in general, or in other sciences when we are called to make use of it therein.

Cap. 4. of the 8 principle Rules relating to Method.

From what has been said in the foregoing chapter it may be Justly concluded that we shall attain to a method indeed more perfect and absolute than that which is in use among Geometricians themselves, if so be that we do carefully attend unto 8 rules which we shall here propose, whereof the 2 first do belong to Idea's and so respect the first part of Logick; the next do belong to axiomes and consequently the 2^d part: the 5 and 6th do respect argumentation and are related to the 3^d part: and the 2 last rules are about order and so more Immediately belong to the fourth and last part of Logick.

The 2 Rules of definitions.

1. That we Leave nothing obscure, ambiguous or æquivocal in the terms, but define the same most plainly.
2. That in all definitions we evermore use terms either perfectly known in themselves, or such as were before sufficiently explained.

WILLIAM BRATTLE

The 2 Rules of axiomes

3. That we lay down no axiome (or nothing for an axiome) which is not amost clear and evident truth.
4. That we take that only for evident, which by a moderate attention is known to be a truth.

The 2 Rules of demonstration.

5. That we prove all obscure propositions, by the help of premised definitions being granted axiomes or demonstrated propositions.
6. That we never abuse the ambiguity of terms.

The 2 Rules of Method

7. That we handle things, as much as we can, according to natural order, by beginning at the more generals and the more simple, and by explaining whatever belongs to the nature of a genus before we descend to particular species.
8. That we divide as far as we can every genus into it's species, every totum into all it's parts and every difficulty into all it's cases.

In those 2 last rules are inserted those words (as far as we can) for it somtimes happens that they cannot be rigorously observed, whether by reason of the limits of mans mind, or those bounds which we are forced to assign every science.

And thus we have proposed these 8 rules, which if we attend heedfully to, will be of great use to us in delivering any science, as the neglect and non-observance thereof will prove prejudicial unto knowledge and with these rules doth our fourth and last part of *Logick* conclude.

> Upon the prickly bush of Logick grows
> of other Sciences the fragrant rose.[106]

---

[106] Partridge fills the bottom of the final page with a design around this distich.

Colophon

This book has been designed following, with some modifications, the Colonial Society of Massachusetts' Volume 33, as designed and printed by D.B. Updike, Merrymount Press, Boston, in 1940, and also following the handwritten manuscripts, which were individually remarkably consistent and even elegant in their lay-out. The type is Adobe Caslon family, based on the font as originally designed by William Caslon in 1725. The binding is smythe sewn. All materials are library grade.

Editing, design, and production are by Elizabeth M. Burke of Portland, Maine. The dust jacket design is by Jeannie Abboud of West Acton, Massachusetts. Typesetting is by Pine Tree Composition, Lewiston, Maine; printing by BookCrafters at Fredericksburg, Virginia.

INDEX

"academies," 63–66, 70, 72
Adams, John C., 19n40
Age of Logic, 3, 48
Age of Reason, 4
Agricola, Rudolphus, 38–39
  De Inventione Dialectica, 11, 13
Ainsworth, Henry, 30–31, 80, 83, 89
Akkerman, F., 11n18
Aldrich, Henry, 56, 58, 91
almanacs, 111–112
Alsted, Johann Heinrich, 28, 69n178
Alston, R.C., 23n51
ambiguity, 102
Ames, William, 18–19, 21, 49n126
analysis, 102
angelography, 68
Anglicans, 2, 56, 63, 92, 103, 120–124
antepredicaments, 79
arguments, 21–23, 50
Aristotelian logics, 2, 25, 29, 33, 35, 49, 78–79
Aristotelianism, 32, 59, 82
Aristotle, 10, 12, 33, 48
Arnauld, Antoine, 33, 34n78, 36n85, 39n92, 66, 91, 95, 99–101
  and Jansenism, 45, 81
  The Port-Royal Logic (Ars Cogitandi), 36, 39, 42–52, 96, 102, 131
Ashworth, E.J., 10n16, 11n19, 26n55–56, 28n64–65, 78n200, 79n202
Aston, T.H., 79n201
Augustine, 14, 15, 70, 105
Augustinian/Calvinist doctrines, 44
Augustinianism, 14–15, 20–21, 66
authority, 9, 27
axioms, 20, 49–50, 89, 102, 104
Axtell, James, 34n76, 35n82

Bailyn, Bernard, 109n260

Barnard, Howard C., 46, 47n118–119, 67n172
Barnard, John, 96n230, 130–131
belief, 104
Bellomont, Governor, 117
Beurhaus, Friedrich, 18n37
Bible, 13, 21, 51, 107–108, 131
  as divine testimony, 128
Blackloists, 58–59, 60, 66, 100
Blome, R., 53n133, 54n135
Bossuet, Bishop, 52
Brattle, Edward, 109
Brattle, Elizabeth (née Tyng), 109
Brattle, Thomas (brother of William), 75, 92, 109–110, 113, 116, 123, 33–134
Brattle, Thomas (father of William), 109, 110
Brattle, William, 2, 3, 7, 75–76, 89, 91–93
  and Augustinianism, 15n28
  Compendium of Logick, 19, 37, 93–108, 128
  and divine faith, 5, 50
  as divinity professor, 108–132
  and Morton, Charles, 61, 91
Brekle, Hervert E., 43n109, 52n132
Bretshneider, Carolus Gottlieb, 111n264
Brockliss, L.W.B., 8n14, 47n118, 52n131
Buckingham, J.J., 44n112
Bunting, Banbridge, 74n191
Bunyan, John, 6
Burgersdijck, Franco, 27–28, 29, 31–32, 80, 85
Burgesdicius, 36
Burr, George Lincoln, 94n226

Caderton, Laurence, 18n37
Calamy, Edward, 62n156, 63n159, 65n165, 68n174, 69, 70n182–183
calendars, 112

[329]

INDEX

Calvin, John, 40, 64
Calvin College, MI, 137
Calvinism, 30, 136
   and Jansenism, 44
   and Puritanism, 63, 65
Cambridge University, 16, 18, 29
   Cartesianism and, 55
   and Platonism, 4, 65
   Queen's College at, 19, 62, 63
   St. Johns College of, 54
Carmelites, 53
Cartesian logics, 2, 29, 33, 35, 49, 56, 81, 93–94, 131, 134
   as textbooks, 36, 52^860, 90
Cartesianism, 41, 54, 77, 91
   described, 94–95
   origins of, 37
Case, John, 78
Categoriae Decem ex Aristotele Decerpta, 14
categories, 12, 48–49, 59–60, 82, 99
certainty, 5, 41, 88, 100–101, 103, 104, 105, 124, 128, 132–134
   of Christianity, 27, 83
   and knowledge, 20, 23, 103
Chauncy, Charles, 119
de Chevreuse, Duc, 46
Christians, 14, 23, 36, 37, 130
Church of England, 114, 120, 122, 124, 130
Cistercians, 45
Clarendon Code, 63
Clark, Kelly James, 137n327
Clark, Stephen R.L., 42n103
Classical logic, 37
Coady, C.A.J., 9, 9n15, 22n46
Coke, Zachary, 30–31
   The Art of Logick, 30, 83, 89
Colman, Benjamin, 112n266, 116, 118–119, 122, 122n289, 124n296, 126
Colonial Society of Massachusetts, 68
communal knowledge, 22
compendia, 33
   See also encyclopedias
Condy, Jeremiah, 134

Congregationalism, 92, 120–123
conscience, 76–77
Corrigan, John, 116n274, 119, 132
Cowie, Leonard W., 121n287
critical thinking, 137
   See also humanistic logics
Cromwell, Oliver, 30–31
Curley, E.M., 40n96
Curtis, Mark, 55n140

Daniel-Rops, H., 44n112
definitions, 102
Defoe, Daniel, 67
Derrick, Christopher, 138n328
Descartes, Rene, 33, 39–42, 40, 48, 54, 58, 93–94
   Discourse on Method, 39, 54
   as father of modern philosophy, 49
   Meditations on First Philosophy, 40
   Principles of Philosophy, 42, 95
   Rules for the Direction of the Mind, 95
   See also Cartesianism; Cartesian logics
devotional manuals, 7–8
diagrams, 80–81
   See also schematic drawings.
dialectic logic, 14, 37
   See also probabilistic logic
Dialectices (Melancthon), 12
dichotomization, 82
Dickoff, James, 34n78, 43n109, 46n116, 52n131, 102n246
Dickson, Richard E., 16n32
Digby, Kenhelm, 59, 100
dissenters, 63, 73, 76
divine faith, 5, 37, 106, 128
   See also divine testimony
divine grace, 15, 44, 71, 106
divine revelation, 37, 106
divine testimony, 13, 21, 22–24, 37, 50, 88, 104, 106, 127, 133–135
   See also testimony
dogmatism, 5, 21, 37–39, 81, 84, 88, 102,

[330]

INDEX

103, 104, 124, 134
  humanist position on, 11
  See also certainty
doubt, 40, 101
Downame, George, 18n37
Downey, Edward, 41n98
Draper, Johanne, 98n234
Dudley family, 109
Dunbar, Samuel, 90
Dunn, Catherine M., 17n33
Dunn, Edward, 125

Edghill, E.M., 82n211
Edwards, Jonathan, 4, 7, 28n63, 78, 127n306, 131
Edwards, Timothy, 7
Eliot, John, 33–34
encyclopedias, 68–69, 80
ens, 100
"enthusiasm," 126–127
epistemology, 3, 20, 36, 81, 95, 104, 127
  of divine testimony, 24
  and God, 51
  modern, 9
  reformed, 137–138
epitomes, 33
Erasmus, 35, 37, 38, 107–108
Ermatinger, Charles J., 3n3
error, 104
Eucharist, 59
  See also transubstantiation
Eusden, John Dykstra, 19n38
external knowledge, 49–50
  See also testimony
Eyre, John, 109
Eyre, Katherine (née Brattle), 109
  See also Winthrop, Katherine

faculties of the soul, 13
faith, 5, 9, 13, 27, 37, 104, 106
  mysteries of, 51, 107
  versus science, 50–51
  true holy, 27

  See also divine faith; human faith; testimony
fallacies, 79
fanatics, 58
faulty reasoning, 39
Feingold, Mordechai, 63n158
Fiering, Norman, 3, 3n4, 4n5, 61, 62n157, 65–66, 68, 93, 97n232, 32n315
first principles, 106
Fitch, Jabez, 90, 96
Flint, Henry, 66n167
Flynt, Henry, 90, 96n228, 115, 125–126, 129
fortress of knowledge (*scientia mirabilis*), 41
Franciscans, 53
Franklin, Benjamin, 6–7
Fraunce, Abraham, 22

Gale, Theophilus, 64–66, 73, 81
Gascoine, John, 63n158
Gear, Allen, 31
Genevan Academy, 64
genus and species, 26, 102
geometry, 49, 81, 95, 101
Gilbert, Neal W., 26n55, 33n75
Gillispie, Charles Coulston, 26n55
Goodin, John, 31n71
grace, 85
Grafton, Anthony, 8n14, 17n34, 33n75
grammar, 49
Graves, Thomas, 113–114
Greenleaf, Daniel, 95n227
Greenleaf, Stephen, 95n227, 96
Gregory XIII, Pope, 112

habit, 82, 85
Haddan, Arthur West, 15n28–29
Hall, David D., 119n282
Hall, John, 54n137
Hall, Michael, 75n194
Hall, Roland, 43n109
Hambrick-Stowe, Charles E., 7
Hardwig, John, 9, 9n15

[331]

INDEX

Harris, Edward-Doubleday, 108n258, 117n278
Hart, Hedrik, 41n98
Harvard, John, 6, 16
Harvard College, 2, 9, 29, 33, 64, 73–74, 110–111
   library of, 16, 66, 73
   logic textbooks used at, 8, 19, 75–76, 90, 93, 95–97, 136
Hatch, Nathan O., 3n4
Hedge, Levi, 135–136
Heereboord, Adrian, 28
Hendel, Charles W., 52n131
Henry VIII, 15
heresy, 84
Heyd, Michael, 8n14
Hoitenga, Dewey, 41n98
Hollis, Thomas, 73
Holy Spirit, 13, 24–25, 51, 83, 85
Hornberger, Theodore, 1n2, 81n206
house-schools. *See* "academies"
Howe, Daniel Walker, 4, 4n5, 4n6
Howell, Samuel, 29n66, 52n131
Howell, Wilbur Samuel, 10n16, 43, 57n144, 58n148, 91n220
Hughes, Merritt Y., 35n81
human faith, 37, 106, 128
   See also human testimony
human reason, 39
human spirit, 77–78
human testimony, 24, 50, 88
   See also testimony
humanistic education, 32–33
humanistic logics, 2, 3, 10n16, 11, 20, 78, 88, 105, 137
humanistic tradition, 16, 99
humility, 103

inborn capacities, 82
individualism, 40
infused habits, 82
Inquisition, 44
intellectual certainty, 39

internal testimony, 50
   See also testimony

Jacob, A., 55n138
James, Patricia, 34n78, 43n109, 46n116, 52n131, 102n246
Jansen, Cornelius Otto, 43–44
Jansen, English. *See* Gale, Theophilus
Jansenism, 2, 36, 43–45, 53, 66, 81
Jardine, Lisa, 8n14, 10n16, 11n17–18, 12n23, 16n30, 17n34, 33n75
Jesuits, 2, 44–46, 53
Johnson, Thomas H., 34n76

Kaledin, Arthur, 123n290
Keckermann, Bartholomaeus, 14, 22–23, 25, 26–27, 27, 80
Kennedy, Rick, 46n116, 75n194, 94n226, 108n258, 113n268
Kenney, Anthony, 10n16, 78n200
Kenney, W. Henry, 35n82, 79n201
Kilcullen, John, 45n115
Klauber, Martin, 8n14, 94n225
Kneale, Martha, 10n16, 43
Kneale, William, 10n16, 43
knowledge, 17, 24, 41, 82, 88, 95, 103, 105
   sources of, 15, 21
   systemization of, 49, 68
Krailsheimer, A.J., 38n88
Kretzman, Norman, 10n16, 78n200

Lake, Peter, 63n158
Lamprecht, Sterling, 54n136–137, 55, 58n147, 59n150
Lancelot, Claude, 47n119
Lang, Robert, 47n118
Lathrop, Samuel Kirkland, 116n274
latitudinarianism, 4, 6, 103
lazy thinking, 36, 39
LeClerc, Jean, 33, 56, 97
Lee, Samuel, 64–65
LeGrand, Anthony (Antoine), 33, 52–54, 66, 68–69, 81, 93, 98–99, 101

[332]

INDEX

Leibniz, Gottfried W. von, 41, 57
Leverett, John, 3, 32–33, 36, 75–76, 89, 93, 95, 96, 111, 113, 114–115, 30
Lindall, Timothy, 90
Locke, John, 33, 35, 97
Lockean logic, 29, 3, 96–98, 134–135
logic, 3, 6, 7, 35, 36 49
   as art of right thinkng, 99, 128
   definition of, 99
logic textbooks, 2, 50, 62, 98, 137
   of Britain, 52–60
   humanistic, 11, 13, 15
   See also individual logics
   See also vernacular textbooks
Loringhoff, Bruno Baron von Freytag, 43n109, 52n132
Love, Harold, 33n75
Loyola, Ignatius, 8n13
Luther, Martin, 2, 11, 13
Lynde, Benjamin, 94

MacIlmaine, Roland, 17–18
Manschreck, Clyde Leonard, 11n19
Mary, Queen of England, 76
Massachusetts Bay Company charter, 74
mathematical demonstration, 4–5, 49, 104, 106
   See also geometry
Mather, Cotton, 34n76, 35, 36, 36n83–84, 65, 69n179, 73, 76, 110–111, 15–118
Mather, Increase, 3, 32, 34, 61, 65, 74, 75, 93, 95
   and Brattle, William, 113–118
Mather, Nathaniel, 93
Mather, Warham, 7
Maurer, Wilhelm, 12
Mayhew, Jonathan, 132
McGahagan, Thomas, 94n225
McGarry, Daniel D., 59n151
McGhee, Michael, 42n103
McLachlan, Herbert, 63n160, 65n162
Meil, Jan, 47n118

Melanchthon, Philipp, 2, 10–16, 21, 25, 60, 79
   Compendiaria Dialectices Ratio, 12
   Erotemata Dialectices, 12, 13, 36, 83, 89
memory devices, 26
metaphysics, 3
method, 102, 103, 105
Mico, John, 109
Mico, Mary (née Brattle), 109
Miller, Perry, 1, 19, 34n76, 44n111, 78
Milton, John, 20, 34, 35
missionaries, 53–54
de Montaigne, Michel, 39, 41
More, Henry, 4, 55, 94
Morgan, John, 8, 8n14
Morison, Samuel Eliot, 1n2, 28n63, 62n157, 66n168, 73, 75n194, 13n269, 116, 120n285, 136n326
Morris, William, 28n63
Morton, Charles, 1n2, 3, 5, 7, 15n28, 56, 62–78, 113, 114, 134
   and Brattle, William, 61, 91
   Compendium Physicae, 68, 90
   A Logick System, 25, 78–90, 133
   Philosophical Translations, 69
   Pneumatics, 68, 69
   The Spirit of Man, 69, 77

Nadler, Steven M., 42n104, 45n115, 47n118
natural introspection, 100
natural *versus* supernatural, 10–11
neoterics, 32–33
Newington Green, 64–66, 70, 72, 79
Newman, Henry, 120n286, 121–122
Newton, John, 81
Nicholson, Francis, 120–122
Nicholson, Margorie, 54n137
Nicole, Perre, 46
Noll, Mark A., 136n326
Norris, John, 66
North, Roger, 55–56
Norton, Arthur O., 68n173, 94n224

INDEX

Oliver, Elizabeth (née Brattle), 109
Oliver, James, 111, 113, 114
Oliver, Nathaniel, 109
Ong, Walter J., 3, 3n3, 10n16, 26n56, 48, 49n125
opinion, 104, 106
order. *See* method
Oxford University, 16
    Exeter College at, 80
    Magdalene College at, 64
    Waldham College at, 62

Parsons, Bethiah (née Brattle), 109
Parsons, Joseph, 109
Partridge, William, 7, 90
Pascal, Blaise, 38, 39, 46n116, 53, 132
    The Geometrical Mind, 48
Paul, Saint, 85
de Paul, Vincent, 53
Pauline tradition, 21
pedagogical reform, 16–17
Pemberton, Ebenezer, 6
Perkins, William, 18n37
Philippo-Ramists, 25
physics, 49
piety, 63, 119
Pinborg, Jan, 10n16, 78n200
Plato, 33
polemics, 48, 59
polity, 83–84
Popkin, Richard H., 37, 40
Porphyry, 26
Port-Royal des Champs, 45–46
    Little Schools of, 46–47, 67, 74
    See also Arnauld, Antoine: *The Port-Royal Logic*
predestination, 43, 44, 71, 82, 108, 125, 132
predicables, 79
predicaments, 79, 99–100
    See also categories
Prideaux, John, 80
Prince, Walter, 95n227
Principia Dialectica, 14

probabilistic logic, 10, 12, 89
propositions, 48
Protestants, 2, 12, 16, 27, 63
psychology, 68
Puritanism, 1, 4, 6, 16, 18–19, 22, 24, 44, 78
    and conscience, 76–77
    examples of, 61–62
    Favoritism of, 32–37
    and logic, 29, 60
    in New England, 4, 91–93, 104, 130
Puritan–Ramists, 49, 62

Quakerism, 58, 88, 120, 126
quality, 82–87, 99
Quincy, Josiah, 116n274

Ramean "recipe," 48
Ramism, 1, 18, 34
Ramist logics, 20, 33, 49, 58, 81
    See also "six-sided view of life," 49
    See also grammar; logic; mathematical demonstration; physics; rhetric; theology
Ramus, Petrus, 11, 16–25, 25, 32, 35
    Dialecticae Libri Duo, 16
    and human reason, 38–39
    as martyr, 17, 34
Rand, Benjamin, 96–97, 135n322
rationalism, 1, 13, 37, 113, 119–120, 125, 137
reason, 15, 37, 39, 43, 78, 100
Recollects, 53
Reedy, Gerhard, 24–25
Reformation, 2, 71
Reid, Thomas, 35, 134–135
Restoration, 62
resurrection, 59
rhetoric, 49
Richardson, Alexander, 16, 18–25, 26, 51, 62, 108
    The Logicians School-Master, 19, 24–25, 96

INDEX

risibility, 81
Rogers, J.G.A., 97n233
Roman Catholics, 2, 7, 12, 51, 54, 63
    calendar of, 112
Ross, U.D., 82n211
Rowe, Thomas, 65
Rubidge, Bradley, 8n13
rules of art, 20
rules of reason, 34
rules of truth, 101–102
Ryan, John K., 53n134

Salem witch trials, 92, 133
de Sales, Francis, 53
Salisbury, John of, 59n151
Sanderson, Robert, 28–29, 78, 80
Schaff, Philip, 14n27
schematic drawings, 26
    See also diagrams
schism, 84
Schmitt, Charles B., 10n16, 27n60, 28n64, 78n200, 79n202
Schneider, John R., 11n19, 12n20–21
scholastic logic, 17
scholastic philosophy, 54
Schouls, Peter, 101n241
science, 37, 69, 104, 128
    as knowledge, 50–51, 106
    and logic, 10, 12
    of reasoning, 14
scientia, 20
scientia mirabilis, 41
Scottish Common Sense logic, 134–135
Sebba, Gregor, 41n99
Sedgwick, Alexander, 44n110, 44n112, 46n116
senses, 82
Sergeant, John, 56–60
Sever, Charles W., 111n262
Sewall, Joseph, 117n278
Sewall, Samuel, 61n154–155, 117–118, 124
Shank, Michael, 8n14
Shapin, Steven, 9n15, 22n46

Shapiro, Barbara, 22n46, 63n158, 103–104
Shaw, J.F., 14n27
Shipton, Clifford K., 90n218, 132n315
Sibley, John L., 111n262, 116n274, 124n293, 124n295, 125n300, 30n312
Siegel, Thomas, 97n231, 98n234, 134
simples, 20
skepticism, 11, 36–38, 40, 8, 71, 79, 81, 83, 88, 89, 101
Sleigh, R.C., 45n115
Smith, J.W. Ashley, 56, 62n157, 67n171
Smith, Samuel, 80, 8
Society for the Promotion of Christian Knowledge, 121
Society for the Propagation of the Gospel, 121
solitaires, 44, 46–47
Southern, Richard, 38n87
Southgate, Beverley C., 59n149
Sowards, J.K., 35n80
Spencer, Thomas, 23
Spinoza, Baruch, 37
spirits, 71, 77–78
Sprunger, Keith L., 19n38, 49
Stevens, Joseph, 120n284
Stewart, Dugald, 34–35
Stiles, Ezra, 131
Stout, Harry S., 3n4, 118, 119n282
Streater, John, 31
Sulpicians, 53
Sweet, William Warren, 136n326
syllogisms, 10, 79, 86, 88–89, 95
    rules for, 48
synopses, 37
synthesis, 102
systematics. *See* Philippo-Ramists

Tappan, David, 136
Tayler, J.L., 64n161
Temple, William, 18n37
terms, 36, 79
Test Acts, 63

[335]

INDEX

testimony, 9, 13, 21, 37, 88–89, 133, 135
    See also divine testimony; external knowledge; human testimony, divine faith, human faith
textbooks, reductions of, 33, 97–98
theological apology, 15
theology, 49, 68, 130
    Calvinistic, 30
    and logic, 107, 131
    and schematics, 27
Thomas, Ivo, 78n200
Tillotson, John, 4, 5, 6
toleration, 84
topics, 48, 95
tradition, 13, 14, 51
transubstantiation, 54
Trappists, 53
Trinity, 107–108, 132
trust, 9
truth, 36, 133
Tyng, William, 109

Unitarians, 136
universal church, 36, 51–52, 54
    See also Roman Catholics
universalists, 128

Valla, Lorenzo, 11
Van der Hoeven, Johan, 41n98
Vanderjagt, A.J., 11n19
Verbeek, Theo, 94n225
vernacular textbooks, 67–68, 80–81, 95
Verstraete, Beert C., 35n80
vulgar logic, 36

Wallis, John, 112
Watson, Richard A., 41n99, 42n105, 43n109, 52n131, 53n134
Watts, Isaac, 65, 98, 134–136
Watts, Michael R., 63n160
Wesley, Charles, 66
Wesley, John, 66
Wesley, Samuel, 66–67, 68n174, 70

White, Thomas, 59
Whitefield, George, 127–128
Wigglesworth, Edward, 126–130
Wilkins, John, 62
will, 14, 43, 132
    See also human will
Willard, Samuel, 115, 118
Williams, Bernard, 41n99–100
Williams, Ebenezer, 68n175
Williams, Elisha, 7, 131
Williams, Roger, 31
Winthrop, John, 122–123
Winthrop, Katherine (née Brattle), 109
    See also Eyre, Katherine
Winthrop, Wait-Still, 109
Wolterstorff, Nicholas, 41n98
women, education of, 68
Wood, Anthony, 55
Wright, Thomas, 16n31
Wynne, John, 97

Yale College, 131
Yolton, John, 79n201

Zabarella, Jacobi, 27, 80